ALSO BY BENJAMIN CARTER HETT

The Death of Democracy:
Hitler's Rise to Power and the Downfall of the Weimar Republic

Burning the Reichstag:
An Investigation into the Third Reich's Enduring Mystery

Crossing Hitler:
The Man Who Put the Nazis on the Witness Stand

Death in the Tiergarten:
Murder and Criminal Justice in the Kaiser's Berlin

Otto John:
Patriot oder Verräter: Eine deutsche Biographie
(with Michael Wala)

THE NAZI MENACE

THE NAZI MENACE

HITLER, CHURCHILL, ROOSEVELT, STALIN, AND THE ROAD TO WAR

BENJAMIN CARTER HETT

HENRY HOLT AND COMPANY

NEW YORK

Henry Holt and Company
Publishers since 1866
120 Broadway
New York, New York 10271
www.henryholt.com

Henry Holt® and 🔲® are registered trademarks of
Macmillan Publishing Group, LLC.

Library of Congress Cataloging-in-Publication Data

Names: Hett, Benjamin Carter, author.
Title: The Nazi menace : Hitler, Churchill, Roosevelt, Stalin, and the road to war /
    Benjamin Carter Hett.
Other titles: Hitler, Churchill, Roosevelt, Stalin, and the road to war
Description: First edition. | New York : Henry Holt and Company, 2020. |
    Includes bibliographical references and index.
Identifiers: LCCN 2020002916 (print) | LCCN 2020002917 (ebook) |
    ISBN 9781250205230 (hardcover) | ISBN 9781250205247 (ebook)
Subjects: LCSH: World War, 1939–1945—Diplomatic history. | Anti-Nazi
    movement—History. | Germany—Politics and government—1933–1945. |
    Hitler, Adolf, 1889–1945. | Churchill, Winston, 1874–1965. | Roosevelt,
    Franklin D. (Franklin Delano), 1882–1945. | Stalin, Joseph, 1878–1953.
Classification: LCC D748 .H45 2020 (print) | LCC D748 (ebook) | DDC
    940.53/2—dc23
LC record available at https://lccn.loc.gov/2020002916
LC ebook record available at https://lccn.loc.gov/2020002917

Our books may be purchased in bulk for promotional, educational, or business use. Please
contact your local bookseller or the Macmillan Corporate and Premium Sales Department at
(800) 221-7945, extension 5442, or by email at MacmillanSpecialMarkets@macmillan.com.

First Edition 2020

Designed by Kelly S. Too

Printed in the United States of America

1   3   5   7   9   10   8   6   4   2

For Corinna

CONTENTS

PART THREE: WAR

CAST OF CHARACTERS

THE GERMANS

Ludwig Beck (1880–1944): Chief of the general staff of the army from 1933 to 1938, Beck gradually became disillusioned with Hitler and by 1938 had moved into full-scale opposition to the regime.

Franz Bernheim (1899–1990): A salesman who was fired from a department store job in Gleiwitz, Upper Silesia, in 1933. He brought a petition to the League of Nations in Geneva protesting Nazi discrimination in Upper Silesia that, because of the unusual treaty status of the region, succeeded.

Johannes Blaskowitz (1883–1948): A general who was briefly the military commander in occupied Poland in 1939 and 1940, he repeatedly protested SS atrocities against Jews and other groups.

Werner von Blomberg (1878–1946): Hitler's minister of war from 1933 to 1938. Although subservient to Hitler, he was dismissed from his office in 1938 amid a sensational sexual scandal.

Walther von Brauchitsch (1881–1948): Commander in chief of the army from 1938 to 1941. Brauchitsch was too weak-willed to oppose Hitler's plans, even when he knew they would be disastrous.

Wilhelm Canaris (1887–1945): An admiral and chief of Germany's main intelligence service, the Abwehr. Devious and secretive, he turned the Abwehr into a haven for the resistance.

Hans-Heinrich Dieckhoff (1884–1952): German ambassador to the United States from 1937 to 1938.

Hans von Dohnanyi (1902–1945): A brilliant jurist and supreme court judge from a young age, he became one of the core members of the anti-Nazi resistance.

Gerhard Engel (1906–1976): Hitler's army adjutant (or liaison officer to the army) from 1938 to 1943.

Werner von Fritsch (1880–1939): Commander in chief of the army from 1934 to 1938. Although not ideologically opposed to Nazism, Fritsch grew increasingly worried by Hitler's recklessness. Like Blomberg, he was driven from office by a sexual scandal.

Max and Margot Fürst (1905–1978 and 1912–2003): Left-wing activists and bohemians in Berlin before the Nazi takeover. Max was a furniture maker and Margot a legal secretary. Their Jewish background and connections to radical politics drove them to emigrate in 1935.

Hans Bernd Gisevius (1904–1974): A civil servant, intelligence officer, and major figure in the anti-Nazi resistance. As one of the few survivors of the resistance, he became one of its most important chroniclers after World War II.

Joseph Goebbels (1896–1945): A failed writer with a doctorate in literature who became a smashing success as the Nazi Party's chief propagandist and "minister of popular enlightenment and propaganda" after 1933. One of the few Nazi insiders whom Hitler respected and found interesting to talk to.

Carl Goerdeler (1884–1945): A former mayor of Leipzig and price commissioner under Hitler who became the leader of the civilian side of the anti-Nazi resistance movement.

Hermann Göring (1893–1946): A dashing First World War fighter pilot who became one of the leading Nazis and held many high offices under Hitler, including commander in chief of the Luftwaffe and head of the Four-Year Plan Authority.

Helmuth Groscurth (1898–1943): A deeply religious, highly principled intelligence officer whose moral repugnance at Nazi crimes drove him into determined resistance activity.

Eva Gruhn (1913–1978): A former prostitute and pornographic model in Berlin, she married Minister of War Blomberg in early 1938, precipitating a major scandal.

Heinz Guderian (1888–1954): A senior German army commander and one of the main advocates and tacticians of fast-moving armored formations.

Franz Halder (1884–1972): A cerebral army officer who was chief of the army general staff from 1938 to 1942. Although he was contemptuous of Hitler and close to resistance circles, his willingness to participate in a coup fluctuated wildly.

Ulrich von Hassell (1881–1944): A senior diplomat and ambassador, one of many fired in the purge of early 1938. After his dismissal he gravitated toward the resistance.

Count Wolf-Heinrich von Helldorff (1896–1944): A dissolute aristocrat and war veteran, he became the commander of the Nazi Stormtroopers in Berlin and later Berlin's police chief. Nonetheless, by 1938 he had joined the resistance.

Heinrich Himmler (1900–1945): From 1929, the head of the SS, the rapidly growing paramilitary and police organization. By the late 1930s, he was one of the most powerful and dangerous men in Germany.

Adolf Hitler (1889–1945): An obscure First World War veteran who became leader of the National Socialist German Workers' Party, then chancellor of Germany in 1933, and "chancellor and Führer" from 1934.

Friedrich Hossbach (1894–1980): Hitler's armed forces adjutant (liaison to all branches of the armed forces) from 1934 to 1938. Stubborn, fearless, and of unshakable integrity, he was one of the most important witnesses to developments around Hitler before early 1938.

Wilhelm Keitel (1882–1946): An army officer who was given the position of chief of the OKW (supreme command of the armed forces) in the shakeup of early 1938. But Keitel was a mediocre nonentity and yes-man to Hitler whom other senior officers mocked for his subservience.

Erich Kordt (1903–1969): A diplomat who in the late 1930s was working at the Foreign Office in Berlin when he became involved in the resistance movement, along with his brother Theo.

Theo Kordt (1892–1962): A diplomat who was working at the German embassy in London in the late 1930s when he became involved in the resistance movement.

Wilhelm Ritter von Leeb (1876–1956): A senior and highly respected army commander who tried to organize a coup against Hitler in late 1939.

Erich Ludendorff (1865–1937): Deputy commander of the German Army in the second half of the First World War and the main architect of Germany's total mobilization in that war. In the 1920s and '30s, he was one of the leading theorists of total war and what it meant for a totalitarian society, in which capacity he strongly influenced Adolf Hitler.

Erich von Manstein (1887–1973): Widely considered the most gifted of Hitler's generals, he was the main architect of the "sickle cut" plan for the attack on France in 1940.

Arthur Nebe (1894–1945): A senior criminal police official and originally ardent Nazi who, like Count von Helldorff, gravitated to the resistance by 1938.

Konstantin von Neurath (1873–1956): An establishment conservative and diplomat of the old school who served as Hitler's foreign minister from 1933 to 1938.

Hans Oster (1887–1945): A swashbuckling and charismatic intelligence officer whose outrage at Hitler's treatment of Werner von Fritsch in 1938 drove him to become one of the central players on the military side of the resistance movement.

Wolfgang Gans Edler Herr zu Putlitz (1899–1975): A German diplomat whose anti-Nazi views led him to become an important agent for prewar British intelligence.

Erich Raeder (1876–1960): Commander in chief of the German Navy until 1943.

Walther von Reichenau (1884–1942): One of the few truly enthusiastic Nazis among the German generals.

Joachim von Ribbentrop (1893–1946): A sparkling wine salesman who played a significant role in Hitler's coming to power and then worked his way up to be foreign minister from 1938.

Hjalmar Horace Greeley Schacht (1877–1970): A half-American banker and financial expert who helped Hitler into power and became central bank president and minister of economics, but increasingly fell out with the Führer when Hitler refused to put economic rationality ahead of his armaments drive.

Paul Schmidt (1899–1970): An interpreter at the Foreign Ministry who served as Hitler's interpreter for numerous high-level diplomatic meetings in the 1930s and during the Second World War.

Rudolf Schmundt (1896–1944): The successor to Friedrich Hossbach as Hitler's armed forces adjutant from 1938 to 1944. Died of wounds received next to Hitler in the Valkyrie assassination attempt of July 1944.

Count Lutz Schwerin von Krosigk (1887–1977): Hitler's finance minister through the entire duration of the Third Reich.

Cläre Tisch (1907–1941): A brilliant doctoral student in economics at Bonn University and protégée of Joseph Schumpeter, she found it impossible to pursue her chosen career after 1933 and dreamed of immigrating to the United States.

Jona "Klop" von Ustinov (1892–1962): A German journalist and employee of the German foreign ministry who worked as an agent for British intelligence in the Nazi era.

Ernst von Weizsäcker (1882–1951): A senior diplomat and state secretary in the Foreign Office under von Ribbentrop from 1938 to 1943, but involved with resistance circles.

Erwin von Witzleben (1881–1944): A blunt-spoken army officer, he was commander of the Berlin garrison in the late 1930s and joined the resistance in 1938.

THE BRITISH

Leo Amery (1873–1955): A Conservative MP and cabinet member whose fierce interventions in parliamentary debates had a powerful impact in 1939 and 1940.

Duchess of Atholl (Katharine Stewart-Murray) (1874–1960): A Conservative member of Parliament and one of the pioneering women MPs from

1923 to 1938. The party "deselected" her over her opposition to Neville Chamberlain's appeasement policy, and she lost her seat.

Clement Attlee (1883–1967): Labour MP and leader of the Labour Party from 1935.

Stanley Baldwin (1867–1947): Conservative leader and three-time prime minister. With his matchless gift for finding and exploiting the political center, Baldwin dominated British politics in the interwar years.

Alexander Cadogan (1884–1968): Permanent undersecretary in the Foreign Office from 1938 to 1946; in his diaries, an often-acerbic witness to the high-level politics of the time.

Ronald Cartland (1907–1940): An independent-minded young Conservative MP, first elected to the House of Commons in 1936, but heading for a collision with Prime Minister Chamberlain by the outbreak of war.

Neville Chamberlain (1869–1940): Prime minister of the United Kingdom from 1937 to 1940. Highly competent, arrogant, and caustic, with a visceral hatred of war, Chamberlain set himself the task of trying to find a permanent peaceful solution to the problem of Adolf Hitler.

Winston Churchill (1874–1965): Adventurous soldier and politician, holder of many high offices in the British government, Churchill had fallen far out of public esteem in the early 1930s when he started warning about the rising Nazi menace.

Hugh Dowding (1882–1970): Senior Royal Air Force officer in charge of research, development, and procurement through much of the 1930s, and then air officer commanding RAF Fighter Command from 1936 to 1940. One of the main architects of Britain's formidable air defense network.

Alfred Duff Cooper (1890–1954) An opponent of appeasement, he was first lord of the Admiralty in Chamberlain's cabinet, but resigned in protest over the Munich settlement.

Reginald Plunkett-Ernle-Erle-Drax (1880–1967): The admiral sent to head the British delegation conducting talks with the Soviet Union about a potential alliance in the summer of 1939.

Anthony Eden (1897–1977): A very young foreign secretary from 1935 to 1938, he fell out with Chamberlain over appeasement and became a somewhat reluctant focus of resistance to the government's policies.

King Edward VIII (1894–1972): King for only eleven months in 1936, he was pushed by Stanley Baldwin to abdicate when he insisted on marrying the divorcée Wallis Simpson.

King George VI (1895–1952): The younger brother of Edward VIII, he acceded to the British throne following the abdication crisis.

Arthur Greenwood (1880–1954): Labour MP, deputy leader to Clement Attlee, and a member of Churchill's war cabinet in 1940.

Lord Halifax (Edward Wood) (1881–1959): A prominent politician of the interwar era, viceroy of India from 1926 to 1931, and foreign secretary under Chamberlain and Churchill from 1938 to 1940.

Nevile Henderson (1882–1942): British ambassador in Berlin from 1937 to 1939 and a wholehearted supporter of Chamberlain's appeasement policy.

Leslie Hore-Belisha (1893–1957): Secretary of state for war under Chamberlain.

Thomas Inskip (1876–1947): Minister for the coordination of defense under both Baldwin and Chamberlain from 1936 to 1939.

Ivone Kirkpatrick (1897–1964): A senior diplomat, he was first secretary at the British embassy in Berlin from 1933 to 1938.

Basil Liddell Hart (1895–1970): One of the most influential writers on military and strategic affairs in the 1930s, well known for his advocacy of "the British way in warfare."

David Lloyd George (1863–1945): One of the most important British leaders of the twentieth century, he was prime minister from 1916 to 1922 and, by the late 1930s, very much a "lion in winter" who could still rouse himself for highly effective parliamentary speeches.

Ramsay MacDonald (1886–1937): Longtime leader of the Labour Party and prime minister in 1924 and from 1929 to 1935.

Harold Macmillan (1894–1986): In the 1930s, a rebellious, progressive-minded anti-appeasement Conservative member of Parliament.

David Margesson (1890–1965): Neville Chamberlain's dreaded chief whip, he was so mercilessly effective at his job that Churchill kept him in it after May 1940.

R. J. Mitchell (1895–1937): Chief designer at Supermarine Aviation, where he created Schneider Trophy–winning seaplanes and the Spitfire fighter.

Harold Nicolson (1886–1968): National Labour MP from 1935 to 1945 and a well-connected commentator on the British political scene.

Eleanor Rathbone (1872–1946): Independent MP for the Combined Universities from 1929 to 1946. Early in her life a suffrage activist, as the 1930s went on she increasingly turned to issues of international affairs and support for refugees. She was a strong and influential backer of Churchill's becoming prime minister.

Hugh Trenchard (1873–1956): Chief of air staff, in effect commander of the Royal Air Force, in the 1920s. He was a determined advocate of strategic bombing as the way to win a future war.

Robert Vansittart (1881–1957): Permanent undersecretary at the Foreign Office from 1930 to 1938. He was a firm opponent of appeasement who essentially ran his own personal intelligence system and quietly backed politicians such as Churchill, with whose views he agreed.

Horace Wilson (1882–1972): One of Chamberlain's most influential advisors, whom Chamberlain used for critical missions, such as communicating with Hitler.

THE AMERICANS

Leone Baxter (1906–2001): One-half of the husband-and-wife team Whitaker and Baxter, pioneers of political consulting who began devising simple, repetitive, often misleading campaigns in the 1930s.

Hadley Cantril (1906–1969): A professor of psychology at Princeton and pioneering researcher into public opinion, who studied the effects of Orson Welles's "War of the Worlds" broadcast of 1938.

Charles Coughlin (1891–1979): A Canadian-born Catholic priest who settled in Michigan and became a huge success on the radio, promoting antisemitism and support for the regimes of Hitler and Mussolini.

Cordell Hull (1871–1955): Tennessee politician and secretary of state under Franklin Delano Roosevelt from 1933 to 1944, the longest-serving of all secretaries of state.

Harold Ickes (1874–1952): Secretary of the interior for all of Franklin Delano Roosevelt's administration (and some of Harry Truman's). A bull in every china shop, he was unapologetically progressive and fiercely anti-Nazi.

Joseph P. Kennedy (1888–1969): A self-made millionaire whom Roosevelt named to be ambassador to Great Britain. He grew close to Chamberlain and the appeasers and strongly supported their policies.

Harold D. Lasswell (1902–1978): A diversely talented communications theorist, political scientist, and lawyer, and a professor of law at Yale, he formulated the idea of the "garrison state" as a serious danger of the mid-twentieth century, an idea that had influential effects on Roosevelt's policies.

Ivy Lee (1877–1934): A journalist who became one of the founders of the field of "public relations," representing large companies, including Germany's IG Farben, and the governments of Germany and the Soviet Union.

Charles Lindbergh (1902–1974): Famous aviator who became the most prominent spokesperson for the isolationist, antisemitic America First Committee.

Walter Lippmann (1889–1974): A highly influential syndicated columnist who was an advocate of "Atlanticism" and American engagement in world affairs, as well as a critic of the effects of modern mass media.

Breckinridge Long (1881–1958): A diplomat who was assistant secretary of state under Roosevelt, with special responsibility for refugee affairs, where his ingrained antisemitism became another obstacle for Jews trying to flee Hitler's Europe.

Ernest Lundeen (1878–1940): A U.S. senator from Minnesota who worked covertly with agents of the German government, making use of the congressional franking privilege to distribute pro-German, pro-isolationist propaganda.

Gerald P. Nye (1892–1971): A progressive Republican U.S. senator from North Dakota who, between 1934 and 1936, chaired a Senate committee investigating the arms industry and its links to American entry into the First World War. The work of his committee led directly to the passage of the Neutrality Acts.

Franklin Delano Roosevelt (1882–1945): The thirty-second president of the United States, he was elected in 1932 to combat the Great Depression but soon found himself facing the rising threat of dictatorships.

William Shirer (1904–1993): A reporter for CBS Radio based in Berlin in the 1930s and one of the most influential witnesses to and chroniclers of the Nazis' drive toward war.

Dorothy Thompson (1893–1961): A pioneering reporter, columnist, and radio commentator who was expelled from Nazi Germany and thereafter commented on the rise of right-wing extremism in the United States.

George Sylvester Viereck (1884–1962): A German American activist who became the leader of an extensive covert influence operation by the German government using isolationist members of Congress to try to keep the United States out of the Second World War.

Orson Welles (1915–1985): An actor and director who created the notorious "War of the Worlds" broadcast in October 1938.

Sumner Welles (1892–1961): Undersecretary of state from 1937 to 1943. He had a stronger connection to Roosevelt than did Cordell Hull and worked closely with the president on all foreign policy matters.

Clem Whitaker (1899–1961): The other half of the Whitaker and Baxter political consulting partnership.

THE SOVIETS

Georgii Astakhov (1897–1942): Chargé d'affaires at the Soviet embassy in Berlin from 1937 to 1939, after which he became a late victim of Stalin's purges.

Lavrentiy Beria (1899–1953): Stalin's longest-serving secret police chief, whom the Soviet leader proudly introduced as "our Himmler." He became head of the NKVD in late 1938 as Stalin began to realize the purges were directly threatening Soviet security.

Maxim Litvinov (1876–1951): People's commissar for foreign affairs under Stalin from 1930 to 1939. He was comparatively Western-oriented and favored Soviet involvement in efforts to contain Nazi Germany.

Ivan Maisky (1884–1975): Soviet ambassador in London from 1932 to 1943 who enjoyed good back-channel connections to anti-appeasement politicians such as Winston Churchill.

Vyacheslav Molotov (1890–1986): People's commissar for foreign affairs who replaced Litvinov and reversed his Western orientation, leading to the Molotov-Ribbentrop Pact of 1939.

Konstantin Rokossovsky (1896–1968): Nearly a victim of Stalin's purge of the officer corps, he survived to become one of the most effective Soviet commanders of the Second World War.

Joseph Stalin (1878–1953): One of the group of Bolsheviks around Vladimir Lenin who led the second Russian Revolution of 1917 and later became general secretary of the Central Committee of the Communist Party. After Lenin's death he maneuvered himself into a position of absolute power and from 1927 was the all-but-unchallenged, and extraordinarily brutal, dictator of the Soviet Union.

Mikhail Tukhachevsky (1893–1937): A brilliant general, strategist, and theorist of modern war, and one of the first and most costly victims of Stalin's purge of the officer corps.

Kliment Voroshilov (1881–1969): People's commissar for defense from 1934 to 1940, an eager instrument of Stalin's will in the purge of the army, personally denouncing many officers and signing many death warrants. His incompetence as a commander was made clear in Finland and, later, at the defense of Leningrad.

Nikolai Yezhov (1895–1940): Head of the NKVD from 1936 to 1938 at the height of Stalin's Terror. He was made a scapegoat for the Terror in late 1938, when Stalin changed course.

THE FRENCH

Léon Blum (1872–1950): Leader of the French Socialist Party and prime minister of the Popular Front government in 1936 and 1937 and very briefly again in 1938.

Georges Bonnet (1889–1973): Foreign minister under Daladier in 1938 and 1939 and an advocate of appeasement.

Édouard Daladier (1884–1970): Defense minister from 1936 to 1940 and prime minister from 1938 to 1940. He pursued appeasement but always seemed to regret it.

Joseph-Édouard-Aimé Doumenc (1880–1948): A very able and forward-thinking general who led the French delegation that went to Moscow to negotiate an alliance with the Soviets in 1939.

André François-Poncet (1887–1978): The very well-connected and well-informed French ambassador in Berlin from 1931 to 1938.

François de La Rocque (1885–1946): A right-wing, arguably fascist activist in interwar France who founded the veterans' group the Croix de Feu and later, when the Croix de Feu was banned, the Parti Social Français, probably the most popular French party in the late 1930s.

Alexis Léger (1887–1975): Secretary-general of the Foreign Ministry from 1932 to 1940, he advocated a stronger line against Germany than did Daladier. Under the pseudonym Saint-John Perse, he won the Nobel Prize in Literature in 1960.

THE POLES

Józef Beck (1894–1944): Foreign minister from 1932 to 1939, he tried to fulfill the nationalist vision of Poland standing as a great power between the Germans and the Soviets.

Józef Lipski (1894–1958): Polish ambassador in Berlin from 1934 to 1939 who played a key role in resisting German efforts to strike an alliance in 1939.

Józef Pilsudski (1867–1935): The strongman of interwar Poland and effectively dictator from 1926 to 1935, who enjoyed great respect from the Nazis.

THE ITALIANS

Bernardo Attolico (1880–1942): Italian ambassador in Berlin at the time of the Munich crisis, who enjoyed good relations with anti-Nazi Germans such as Weizsäcker and the Kordt brothers.

Count Galeazzo Ciano (1903–1944): Mussolini's son-in-law and foreign minister. Though he was vain and incompetent as a diplomat, his diaries nonetheless reveal him to have been a sharp and often critical observer of world affairs.

Benito Mussolini (1883–1945): Leader of the Italian Fascist Party and dictator of Italy from 1922 to 1943.

THE CZECHOSLOVAKS

Edvard Beneš (1884–1948): President of Czechoslovakia from 1935 to 1938 and again from 1945 to 1948. He suffered the unique fate of twice being driven from office by totalitarian takeovers.

Emil Hacha (1872–1945): Beneš's successor as president, he was forced to turn the rest of his country over to Hitler in March 1939.

Konrad Henlein (1898–1945): The leader of the Sudeten German Party in Czechoslovakia, he played a key role in stirring up agitation in favor of a German takeover of the Sudetenland.

Jozef Tiso (1887–1947): A Catholic priest who became the ruler of a Slovak puppet state under Nazi influence from 1939.

THE AUSTRIANS

Kurt Schuschnigg (1897–1977): Chancellor of Austria from 1934 to 1938. He tried unsuccessfully to maintain Austrian independence in the face of Hitler's threats.

Arthur Seyss-Inquart (1892–1946): An Austrian Nazi who played a key role in the Anschluss of 1938.

THE NAZI MENACE

PREFACE

The Crisis of Democracy

There had been a democratic revolution across much of the world just a few years before. Old authoritarian regimes collapsed; hopeful new democracies took their place. The democratic wave originated in central and eastern Europe, and it touched places as far away as East Asia. But now that wave had crested and was receding.

Once again, the trend started in central and eastern Europe, and once again, it had implications around the world. A desperate financial crisis had shaken the foundations of the global economy. Even in the long-established heartlands of democracy, in western Europe and the United States, alarming portents appeared. Many people there, too, seemed drawn to the vigor and confidence of the new dictatorships, even as these regimes vented their hostility and aggression on the democracies. Democratic leaders had to figure out how to confront these threats, with one nervous eye fixed on their own people. And in the dictatorships themselves, there were some who feared where their erratic leaders might be taking them and who tried their best to restrain the wilder bouts of aggression.

This may sound like the world today. In fact, it is a description of the 1930s.

So many of us have accepted an easy-to-understand narrative of the

1930s and the Second World War. Of course, we think, Franklin Delano Roosevelt and Winston Churchill were the wise and eloquent champions of democracy. Of course Adolf Hitler was always bent on precisely the war into which he led the world. And of course Joseph Stalin was an inscrutable offstage presence before he became an inscrutable partner in the Grand Alliance.

We often fail to realize how contingent and unpredictable these developments were. Hitler was probably always bent on a war of some kind, but the kind of war he expected and the time line he foresaw fluctuated wildly. As late as the spring of 1939, when he was in a fearful hurry to get a war going, he was still not sure exactly whom he would be fighting.

Roosevelt and Churchill also started the 1930s a long way from where they ended up. In the early 1930s, Churchill's commitment to democracy seemed halfhearted at best. His concerns were geostrategic, and he sometimes voiced them in language not so different from Hitler's. The case he made evolved under the pressure of events in the second half of the decade until, by late 1938, there was no more eloquent spokesman for the crucial role of British democracy in opposing the Nazi menace. Similarly, Roosevelt had little to say about foreign policy until 1937. After that, he was, as he openly admitted, looking for a policy and was not sure what he would find. He recognized with rare foresight the dangers that lay on the horizon, but he was a cautious political strategist who hardly ever revealed his thoughts and was reluctant to move any distance ahead of public opinion or congressional support. The pressure of events eventually pushed Roosevelt into supporting democracy through supporting Britain, buttressed by a tactically shrewd (but possibly also heartfelt) argument that Christianity was the true opposite of totalitarianism. Stalin, for his part, pursued a consistent goal—security for the Soviet Union, coupled with a wildly paranoid pursuit of his own security in power. He foresaw the shape of events less accurately than the others, and by late 1938, he had been driven into an ever-more-panicked quest for that elusive safety.

The other thing we often forget is just how new were the problems that confronted these leaders.

The end of the First World War had seen a democratic revolution not only as old empires collapsed but also in many of the established democracies, where old property or tax qualifications were abolished and women were enfranchised. Britain and America saw their electorates triple in size between the early 1900s and the 1930s, which created a new and entirely unpredictable kind of democracy. This political fact was compounded by the surge of new media technology—radio, film, and phonograph records, on which politicians' speeches were also disseminated. Propaganda, or "public relations," was moving in to exploit the new voters and the new technology.

The First World War had also revealed the deadliness of industrialized total war, and the new military technologies it introduced, particularly air bombing and poison gas, opened up the prospect of a still-more-destructive war in the future. People in the 1930s lived under the dreadful fear that the next war would begin with swarms of bombers leveling their cities and killing most of the residents. As it turned out, this was an absurdly exaggerated view of what a bomber of that era could do. But few could know this at the time, and the fear was a reality that politicians had to consider.

The antidemocratic regimes that developed in Italy, Germany, and the Soviet Union were as new as the fear of air bombing—and just as much a product of the First World War. It was the Italian dictator Benito Mussolini who first proudly called his Fascist regime "totalitarian," and there was a close link, linguistically and practically, between "totalitarianism" and "total war." A totalitarian regime was above all one permanently organized to fight a total war. The totalitarian regimes were born out of the mobilization efforts of 1914 to 1918—the ways in which governments had been forced to reach into economic organization, the conscription of people for production and fighting, the endless spread of propaganda to keep their populations loyal and motivated, and the crushing of dissent from those on whom the propaganda failed. The new regimes devoted themselves to all these operations with a thoroughness, a brutality, and a set of technological tools that were without historical precedent.

This book tells the story of how the Second World War emerged out of this shocking new world and its crisis of democracy, and of how, little by little, democratic leaders learned to respond to these challenges. It does not pretend to be a comprehensive narrative of the 1930s, something that many fine scholars have done before. It does not try to explain what happened in every country—there is little, for instance, on Italy or Japan. Instead, it traces its themes through a narrative of exemplary events in a few representative countries, above all in Germany, Britain, the United States, and the Soviet Union.

The problems the leaders of the 1930s had to confront were new, but they will seem especially familiar to us—more familiar, perhaps, than would have been the case a few decades ago, when Western democracy seemed not only secure but triumphant, and the threats to it were minimal. What should national security officials do if they think their leader is reckless, dangerous, or incompetent? This was the problem that some German officers and diplomats faced. How should democracies respond to a security threat posed by a vicious regime? How should they think about strategy? What role should technology play in their strategic thinking? For what goals should a democracy go to war, and how should it fight? What do you do when your own democratically elected politicians serve as mouthpieces for the propaganda of a hostile foreign state? All the democracies faced these problems. For the United States, the crisis grew particularly severe as the presidential election of 1940 approached. And how should governments communicate to their people what must be done and what must not be done? These were the questions that the Nazi menace posed for the leaders of the world's democracies.

Above all, the world of the 1930s was wracked by a fundamental conflict: Should the world system be open and international, based on democracy, free trade, and rights for all, anchored in law? Or should the world be organized along racial and national lines, with dominant groups owing nothing to minorities and closing off their economic space as much as possible to the outer world? Today we face this very conflict once again.

The Nazi regime and the democracies alike learned to define themselves and their purposes as they fell into ever more severe conflict with one another. Opposition to and eventually war with Nazi Germany pushed the British and Americans into a more ambitious program of democratization and human rights for themselves and the world, even if the lofty ideals were shadowed at every turn by hypocrisy and narrowly defined national self-interest. And at several key turning points, the opposition of the Western democracies drove Hitler to pursue an ever more extreme campaign of hatred and murder.

The same process was at work for those within Germany who opposed Hitler's regime, particularly the soldiers, diplomats, intelligence officers, and other high officials who were in the best position to remove him from power. Most of these people did not oppose the Nazis in 1933, when Hitler came to power. But years of watching a reckless demagogue drive their country toward ruin forced many of them into active resistance, and forced them as well to think about *why* they were doing so.

This book, then, tells the story of how the world's leaders of the 1930s and early 1940s, in Germany and beyond, worked out solutions to these problems step by unanticipated step, "looking for a program," as Roosevelt put it. Maybe their experiences will help us think about how to tackle our own problems.

PART ONE

CRISIS

— 1 —

Reich Chancellery, Early Evening

He is nervous and awkward. These are precisely the kinds of people who make him uncomfortable. Most of them are aristocrats, confident of their status, their prestige, the resonance of their ancient family names. All of them are powerful and accomplished senior commanders who need not, and do not, feel in any way inferior to the new arrival. He, on the other hand, is a man who has risen from nothing. In the army that these confident men command, he never made it past the rank of private first class. His formal clothes do not fit him well. He makes repeated, nervous bows in all directions to the assembled officers. The company sits down to dinner, but he has no gift for small talk, either. The awkwardness continues.

It is February 3, 1933.

Adolf Hitler has been chancellor of the German Reich for all of four days. His new war minister, Field Marshal Werner von Blomberg, has invited him to celebrate the sixtieth birthday of Foreign Minister Konstantin von Neurath and to meet the armed forces High Command. More than a dozen officers are present, among them many who will play critical roles in the years to come, such as the future army commanders in chief Werner von Fritsch and Walther von Brauchitsch, the future army chief of staff Ludwig Beck, and the future field marshals Wilhelm Ritter von Leeb and Gerd von Rundstedt. The scene is the official residence of the army's present commander in chief, General Kurt von Hammerstein-Equord, in the Bendlerstrasse in central Berlin. Hammerstein is strongly anti-Nazi and anti-Hitler. One guest thinks his greeting to Hitler is no better than "benevolently condescending," betraying the contempt Hammerstein bears for the new arrival.

With dinner over, Hitler has the chance to do what he does best: speak. And as always, he warms to the task, even with this audience. He begins to get excited, stretching out across the table to his listeners, often repeating himself for emphasis.

He starts with a message he has been driving home for more than a decade, since the beginning of his political career in Munich, just after the last war. Europe faces a crisis, he says. The "strong, European race" built up culture and created empires, exchanging industrial goods for colonial products from African and Asian territories. But now the capacity of European production exceeds anything the colonies can absorb, and regions such as East Asia are industrializing and using low wages to outcompete the Europeans. Germany's exports to advanced countries only trigger higher levels of imports and the automation of industry, driving unemployment yet higher. In short, the global economy is nothing but a trap for Germany. And since the Russian Revolution of 1917, there has also been "the poisoning of the world through Bolshevism," the ever-present threat of Communist revolution.

"How can Germany be saved?" he asks his listeners. Only, he concludes, through a "large-scale settlement policy, which assumes the expansion of the Lebensraum*"—living space—"of the German people." In other words, by conquering other people's territory. Germany will have to get ready for this task. This means "the consolidation of the state . . . We can no longer be citizens of the world. Democracy and pacifism are impossible . . . What use is an army made up of soldiers infected with Marxism? What use is compulsory military service when before and after serving the soldier is exposed to every kind of propaganda? First Marxism must be exterminated." Hitler promises that the educational work of his Nazi Party will ensure that the officers eventually receive "first class recruit material."*

With this, Hitler moves to the heart of his message. After six to eight years of Nazi rule, the German Army will be ready to expand "the living space of the German people," most likely in the east. He grows even blunter. "A Germanization of the population of the annexed or conquered land is not possible. We can only Germanize the soil." What will happen to the people who can't be Germanized? When the war is over, Hitler says, the Germans will "ruthlessly expel a few million people."

He concludes by asking the generals "to fight along with me for the great goal." But he promises that he will never call on them to use force in domestic politics. For that he has his own people, the brown-shirted Stormtroopers. The army, he insists, is only for fighting foreign enemies.

This last is the part the officers like best, and the part they will most clearly remember afterward. Being drawn into domestic conflicts has been the army's biggest nightmare in the preceding years of political turmoil. By contrast, the officers don't seem to notice the part about "living space." Maybe they don't take it very seriously. Maybe they don't think this chancellor will last long enough for his ideas to matter much—after all, he is the fourteenth person to hold this office since 1919. Maybe they hear something different in what he is saying, nothing more than a plan to recover the territory Germany lost after the First World War. They are all in favor of that. A few years later, General Beck will claim that he had had no idea at all what Hitler was trying to say, and in any case, he wasn't very interested.

Remarkably, there is a spy present at the gathering. General von Hammerstein's teenage daughter Helga is in love with a prominent Communist activist. This relationship has led her to act as an agent for Soviet intelligence. Through her, an account of Hitler's speech makes its way to Moscow. The Soviet intelligence services and Foreign Minister Maxim Litvinov, therefore, have a good idea from the beginning what plans Hitler has for their country. Litvinov starts talking to the French about an alliance to contain German aggression.

By contrast, the German officers' response to Hitler's speech is cool and skeptical. Their applause is no more than polite. Hitler is accustomed to speaking at mass rallies, where people greet his words with ecstasy, women fainting, men jumping on tables and shouting. He doesn't know that the officers have an unwritten rule against showing much enthusiasm for a speaker, any speaker. But he knows he doesn't like it. "The whole time," he complains later, "it was like talking to the wall."

The evening is a foretaste of how the relationship between the Führer *and his generals will unfold. They will never like each other, they will never trust each other. But the officers want at least some of the things Hitler can deliver: rearmament, the expansion of German power in Europe, the restoration of their own prestige. As the years go by, the officers sink deeper into complicity with Hitler's regime, though a few hold out and try to stem the tide.*

But for now, most of them simply underestimate the new chancellor. After he has left the gathering, the officers linger for a while, chatting. "He'll get a few surprises in his life," says General von Brauchitsch drily.

But years later, another of the officers will admit, "The surprises were all on our side."

BERLIN IS A northern city, at 52.5 degrees, lying at a higher latitude than most Canadian towns and such Soviet cities as Kiev and Kursk. On Friday, November 5, 1937, by four thirty in the afternoon, the twilight shadows were already beginning to spread. At six degrees centigrade, it was seasonably cool. There had been no rain, but it was cloudy. The weather forecast called for fog in the evening.

It was in this gray, deepening November twilight that three senior military officers and two cabinet ministers made their way to the Reich Chancellery at 77 Wilhelmstrasse.

The Führer and chancellor of the German Reich, Adolf Hitler, had called the meeting to resolve conflicts among his military commanders over the allocation of resources for Germany's massive rearmament drive. Hitler was trying to do many things: build up his army to be ready for a European ground war, with all the necessary tanks and artillery pieces; expand Germany's tiny navy so that its fleet of battleships and cruisers could at least deter the great naval powers of Britain and the United States; and develop an air force that could support the army in its ground operations. Germany could not produce enough steel to do all this at once. A few days earlier, the commander in chief of the navy, Admiral Erich Raeder, had complained about cuts to his construction program. He asked for a meeting to resolve priorities among the three services. Hitler granted his wish, and the war minister, Field Marshal Werner von Blomberg, formally invited Raeder, army commander in chief Colonel-General Werner von Fritsch, Luftwaffe commander in chief Colonel-General Hermann Göring, and Foreign Minister Konstantin von Neurath to see Hitler at the Chancellery on this gloomy November afternoon.

When the meeting convened, one more officer was present as well, sitting directly across the table from Hitler. This was Hitler's military adjutant, Colonel Friedrich Hossbach.

Hossbach was forty-two years old, but his smooth, boyish face made him look younger. He had been serving as Hitler's adjutant for just over three years, since the death of Reich president Field Marshal Paul von Hindenburg in August 1934. One of Hindenburg's roles as president had been the supreme command of the armed forces. When Hindenburg died, Hitler had quickly taken this job for himself. He needed an officer to serve as liaison to his new command. This was Hossbach's role.

Anyone inclined to see only Hossbach's relative youth or inexperience might not have noticed the stubborn line of his mouth, suggesting a man who would not be bullied. Hossbach revered the Prussian tradition and the stern code of values that went with it: discipline, obedience, frugality, service, sacrifice. He was punctilious about rules and could be humorless. A fellow officer referred to him as a *Komisskopf*, a martinet, a drill sergeant type. Like most army officers, Hossbach was no opponent of Hitler's new regime. Long after the Second World War, he wrote with his characteristic blunt honesty that he had hoped Hitler would bring "recovery and strengthening" after the political and economic chaos of the last years of the Weimar Republic. "I do not," he said, "count myself among those who already in 1933 or even before that foresaw the developments up to 1945."

But Hossbach was equally blunt with Hitler, even when it meant telling the Führer things he didn't want to hear. Hossbach tried to convince Hitler to emulate the great Prussian king Frederick William I, who had ruled from 1713 to 1740. Frederick William is known to history as the "Soldier King," but he had preached that a king did his greatest work for his country in peace and not in war. Hossbach went so far as to put a copy of Frederick William's famous testament in front of Hitler. Here, among other things, the Soldier King had warned his successor against conducting an "unjust war," and admonished him "not to be an aggressor." Hossbach had thought that this advice "could also be of value to Hitler." Of course, Hitler paid no more attention to it than had the Soldier King's successor, his son Frederick II ("the Great"), who had no sooner gained the Prussian throne than he launched his first war, an attack on the Austrian Empire.

Nonetheless, Hossbach thought Hitler would listen to advice and could be persuaded to change his mind, if only with difficulty. He remembered one occasion when Hitler was agitated over a dispute with his economics minister and Reichsbank (Central Bank) chief Hjalmar Schacht. Hitler paced up and down, pouring out his grievances. Hossbach sympathized with Schacht, who sometimes tried to temper Hitler's radical impulses by emphasizing financial stability over limitless expenditure on armaments. When Hossbach tried to intervene in Hitler's monologue, the Führer curtly cut him off. Irritated, Hossbach told Hitler, "There is obviously no point in speaking openly today." At this, Hitler stopped his restless pacing, looked at Hossbach with wide eyes, and said, "On the contrary, tell me the truth, like always."

But Hossbach was coming to realize that "in the long term, there was no place for upright men in Hitler's inner circle." Hitler demanded unquestioning loyalty but gave none himself, except to those "who praised and acknowledged his infallibility and unconditionally devoted themselves to it." For such devotees, Hitler would overlook "weaknesses, dark sides and misdeeds."

Hossbach, like other military men, could get away with bluntness because Hitler respected soldiers, and enjoyed having them around him. But on no account did he want to live like them. Hossbach found that his biggest challenge as Hitler's adjutant was negotiating the gulf between the military High Command's "punctuality and order" and Hitler's "disorderly way of living and working." Hitler almost always spent his Sundays at the Berghof, his mountain retreat high above the town of Berchtesgaden, in the Bavarian Alps. This meant that his staff could usually not reach him for business on Saturdays or Mondays, when the Führer was in transit. In any case, Hitler was restless and seldom stayed in one place for very long. So it was always difficult to get to him at an appointed hour and for a definite length of time to give reports and receive orders. Hitler spoke with anger and sarcasm about his staff's efforts to turn him into a regular, orderly bureaucrat. He was never the kind of ruler who sat late at his desk reading reports. "For him, desks were mere pieces of decoration," one subordinate recalled. Fritz Wiedemann, Hitler's personal adjutant, remembered that Hitler "disliked reading files." "Sometimes I got decisions out of him, even on very important things, without his ever having asked me for the file. He was of the view that many things took care of themselves if they were left alone." Hitler imposed his own rhythms on the state. Occasions such as army maneuvers, when he was forced to follow a military routine—rising early, spending long hours outside in all kinds of weather—exhausted him completely. Afterward, he would fall asleep in his car or, as Hossbach once found him, on a table in his train.

By November 1937, Adolf Hitler had been Germany's leader for nearly five years. His time at the helm had already lasted far longer and proven more politically successful than experienced observers had imagined possible when he came to office in January 1933. The elites of the military and big business who had brought Hitler to the chancellorship had seen him as nothing more than a useful tool. They intended to exploit the political following the Nazi leader had been able to gather— few executives or officers could understand *why* Hitler had such a following—to reach their most important goals: putting an end to parliamentary rule, rolling back social and economic reforms, destroying the power of organized labor, restoring capitalism on corporate-friendly terms, and rebuilding Germany's armed forces. After that, they would dispense with Hitler himself. This lower-class demagogue, so they thought, could never be a match for the aristocratic gentlemen and shrewd managers who ruled over the economy and the armed forces.

Yet, with stunning speed and skill, Hitler had wriggled out of their grasp. Any independent organization that might have served as a base for opposition—the press, political parties, labor unions, Germany's federal states, professional organizations—was abolished or brought under Nazi control. At the end of June 1934, Hitler had even murdered the leaders of his own paramilitary force, the SA (Sturmabteilungen, or Stormtroopers), who had been growing angry at what they felt was the conformist drift of their own revolution. At the same time, Hitler struck at a more dangerous threat: a group of political and military insiders who had been plotting to remove him from power. A member of Vice Chancellor Franz von Papen's staff, along with a prominent conservative intellectual and two senior army officers (one of them, Kurt von Schleicher, also a former chancellor), fell victim to this murderous purge. But the result was that the army, believing the SA's threat to its own power was now gone, lined up more contentedly than ever behind Hitler's leadership. Just over a month later, the venerable President von Hindenburg died. Hitler abolished the position and took over the powers of the presidency. At the suggestion of war minister von Blomberg, all members of the armed forces swore an oath of loyalty to Hitler personally. Earlier, they had sworn an oath of loyalty to the constitution.

In the years that followed, Hitler's personal power grew stronger and the regime more settled. Unemployment, the scourge of the late 1920s and early 1930s, disappeared: while the official rate had stood at 40 percent in 1932, Germany faced a labor shortage by 1938. In 1935, Hitler gambled that he could get away with a major breach of the Treaty of Versailles, the post–First World War settlement that had severely limited Germany's armed forces. That March, he announced the reimposition of conscription and the creation of an air force (the Luftwaffe), two things the treaty forbade Germany to do. Britain, France, and Italy (the wartime Allies) accepted Hitler's move with little more than a murmur. Italy, in any case, under its Fascist "Duce," Benito Mussolini, was moving toward Hitler's side. In 1936, Hitler took another gamble and sent a small military force across the Rhine to the territory between the river and the French, Belgian, and Dutch borders—the Rhineland, as it was known. The Treaty of Versailles had forbidden Germany to station troops there. Again, the Allies bowed to Hitler's daring, although the most limited military resistance would have sent the German formations scurrying back across the bridges. Hitler himself had found this risky move so terrifying that he confessed to his staff he did not want to go through such an experience again for at least ten years.

The pace of the German arms buildup quickened dramatically. In 1936, some steel and arms manufacturers began to balk at meeting the orders Hitler demanded. What would happen, they wondered, when the rearmament was completed and they would be left with excess capacity?

Wouldn't the German economy be deformed by too much concentration in defense industries? The dictator responded by establishing a new state authority to govern heavy industrial and armaments production. Hitler, the burning anticommunist, chose an unlikely model for this venture: the five-year plans by which Joseph Stalin was transforming the economy of the Soviet Union. So as not to sound *exactly* like the Communist dictator, Hitler called his version the "Four-Year Plan" and placed it under the authority of the Luftwaffe commander in chief Hermann Göring. Some of the more thoughtful business leaders continued to worry about shortages of resources, balance of payments problems, and the serious risk of inflation.

The nub of the crisis was the supply of steel. Before 1933, Germany's steel barons had been among the most politically right-wing of industrialists and had been disproportionately well represented among Hitler's backers. Now, in order to build the huge and ever-increasing numbers of tanks, guns, ships, and planes that Hitler demanded, German arms factories needed ever-larger quantities of steel. This would normally have been good news for the steel barons. But German steel mills could not make as much as the regime demanded. And there was a further problem. The manufacture of steel requires good-quality iron ore. The German steel firms liked to import their ores from Sweden, but this meant Germany needed to use its scarce foreign exchange resources to pay for them—and, ironically, to earn this foreign exchange, it had to export its finished steel, thus defeating the purpose. One possible solution was to use iron ores that could be mined in Germany. The problem was that these ores were of much lower quality, and the steel barons found it more economical to use the Swedish imports.

Hitler did not want to import ores or export steel. He did not want Germany depending on the global economy. He wanted economic self-sufficiency. So, when the steel makers balked, the regime used all the powers at its disposal to create a huge conglomerate, the Hermann Göring Works, to make steel from lower-quality domestic ores. But this took time to develop, and the conflicts between the branches of the armed forces over steel allocation continued as bitterly as ever.

Military leaders were also beginning to worry about where Hitler was taking the country. They wanted to return to the power and prestige they had enjoyed before 1914, before they had lost the First World War. What they absolutely did not want was another war with Britain and France—which they prudently figured Germany would lose again. The experience of the First World War had sobered them on Germany's prospects in a war against these wealthy, world-spanning empires, especially as the European democracies would likely be backed once again by the immense resources of the United States.

But Hitler was in a hurry. In 1939 he would turn fifty years old. His mother had died of cancer at the age of forty-seven, and he was obsessed with the fear of dying young himself. If he were to die, who would lead Germany on the campaign of expansion he believed it desperately needed? In his earlier years in power, Hitler had assumed that the job of expanding Germany's territory would probably fall to someone else. But now he was beginning to believe it might be up to him after all. People in Hitler's inner circle saw him begin to change his habits: he was socializing less with his old cronies and taking more and more strange pills, as he became frightened that he would not live long enough to carry out his mission. Now everything had to speed up.

Hitler believed he had to instill this sense of urgency in his military and foreign policy advisors. This, for him, was the point of meeting his military commanders on that gray November afternoon.

From the moment Hitler entered the room, the meeting took a course the men present had not expected. Hitler had come prepared with notes, which he used to deliver a lecture. He spoke, Hossbach remembered, calmly and "without passion," but his words were sensational nonetheless—not least because he began by telling the gathering that in the event of his death, what he was about to say should be taken as his "last will and testament."

"The German racial community," Hitler explained, comprised eighty-five million people, many of whom lived beyond the borders of Germany. Nine million were in Austria, and another three million in Czechoslovakia—an accidental result of "historical development" constituting "the greatest danger to the preservation of the German race at its present peak." The eighty-five million Germans were a "tightly packed racial core" living on an inadequate amount of land, implying "the right to a greater living space than in the case of other peoples." Germany's overriding goal, he said, had to be "to preserve the racial community and enlarge it." In other words, "it was a question of space."

No one had been assigned to take minutes of the meeting. But startled by the importance Hitler seemed to attach to his words, Hossbach decided he had better make a record of them. He began furiously scribbling notes.

THE MOST IMPORTANT of Hitler's listeners on this day were the war minister, Werner von Blomberg, and the commander in chief of the army, Werner von Fritsch.

Blomberg, fifty-nine years old, had served in the First World War with enough distinction that he was awarded the coveted Pour le Mérite, or "Blue Max," the Prussian Army's highest decoration. By 1927, he had risen to be chief of the "Office of the Troops," a coded designation for what really was the position of chief of the army general staff, except that the Allies had forbidden the German Army to have any such thing. But then political intrigues caused Blomberg to be sacked and sent to a field command in East Prussia. His comeback began when he was named the chief German negotiator for international disarmament talks in Geneva in 1932, and from there was suddenly elevated to war minister when Hitler came to power in 1933.

Blomberg was an outgoing and sociable man, a stately officer who looked like everyone's idea of a senior general. He was also politically adaptable. Under the Weimar Republic, he had been considered one of the more democratically minded of German generals. When he was in East Prussia, Blomberg supported his chief of staff, Erich von Bonin, whose views were so far to the left of those of most officers that he was known as "Eric the Red." But then Blomberg seems to have fallen under the influence of Walther von Reichenau, one of the few openly Nazi army officers, and his sympathies shifted all the way over to Hitler—so much so that other senior officers mockingly dubbed him "Hitler Youth Quex," after the hero of a Nazi propaganda film.

Werner von Fritsch was as different from Blomberg as a senior officer could be. Fritsch was a shy, taciturn man who hated talking about himself and had only contempt for wasted words in any form. From childhood he was very short-sighted in his left eye. As an adult, he wore a monocle, which contributed to his severe, ultra-Prussian image. He, too, had served as a staff officer during the First World War and was able to hold on to his commission after Germany's defeat. Like most officers, he was a conservative monarchist who disliked the democracy of the Weimar Republic, but unlike some, he disapproved of demagoguery and coup attempts, favoring peaceful political evolution instead. Early in 1934, at the insistence of President von Hindenburg, Fritsch rose to become commander in chief of the army, beating out Reichenau, who had been Hitler's preference. Fritsch proved to be a cautious innovator and enjoyed the heartfelt loyalty of the officer corps. But from the beginning, he was locked in conflict with the specifically Nazi elements of the regime, above all the rapidly growing police and paramilitary force the SS (short for Schutzstaffel, or "protection squad"), under its commander Heinrich Himmler. The SS wanted a piece of military responsibility, which Fritsch on no account wanted to grant.

For nearly four years, Blomberg and Fritsch navigated the difficult path of army leaders in Hitler's dictatorship, presiding over a dramatic rearmament but also contending with Nazi Party claims on their traditional authority. Now, on this November evening in the Reich Chancellery, the taciturn Fritsch and the extroverted Blomberg listened as Hitler expounded on the needs of the "German racial core." Then the Führer turned to economic issues. Colonel Hossbach kept writing furiously.

Was a solution to Germany's problems possible through "increased participation in the world economy" or through a policy of "autarky"? Hitler asked. His listeners could not have been in much suspense about the Führer's views on this point. Autarky is an extreme form of economic nationalism in which a country tries to cut itself off from world markets for capital, food supplies, raw materials, and finished industrial goods, relying instead on its own resources. From their beginnings in the 1920s, the Nazis had been primarily a protest movement against the effects of economic globalization.

As he had often done before, Hitler expressed grave doubts about how well the world economy could ever function for Germany. Price fluctuations in the global market made Germany vulnerable, and

"commercial treaties afforded no guarantee for their actual obser-
vance." The 1930s was an age of economic empires, Hitler insisted, and
for countries outside the great empires, "opportunities for economic
expansion were severely obstructed." The critical point for Hitler was
that "there was a pronounced military weakness in those states which
depended for their existence on foreign trade." Furthermore, German
trade had to be carried on "over the sea routes dominated by Britain."
Like most Germans, Hitler vividly remembered the hunger of the First
World War, when the British naval blockade had stopped all German
seaborne supply routes.

But there were problems with autarky as well, Hitler continued.
Within its present borders, Germany could not be self-sufficient in
some key metals such as copper and tin, and of course iron ore, and
certainly not in food supplies.

"The only remedy," he concluded, "and one which might seem to
us visionary, lay in the acquisition of greater living space." And if "the
security of our food supply [is] the principal point at issue"—as in Hitler's mind it certainly was—"the space needed to assure it can be sought
only in Europe, not, as in the liberal capitalist view, in the exploitation
of colonies." Let the British raise their banner over far-flung territories
in Africa or Asia. Though Hitler did not say so explicitly at this meeting,
there was no doubt what he meant: for Germany, the solution lay above
all in the grain-growing areas of the Soviet Union.

But Germany, Hitler warned, "had to reckon with two hate-filled
antagonists": Britain and France. In contrast to his cranky grasp of
economics, the Führer demonstrated a shrewd appreciation of these
countries' strategic problems. The British faced pressure from the
"Dominions" (the self-governing territories of Canada, Australia, New
Zealand, and South Africa) not to make colonial concessions to Germany. Britain's empire also confronted the problem of overextension.
The imperial territories were surrounded by states that were stronger
than Britain. How, Hitler asked, could Britain defend Canada against
attack by the United States, or its East Asian possessions against attack
by Japan? Furthermore, the struggles for Irish and Indian independence
demonstrated that the empire could not maintain itself through "power
politics" alone. France's empire was better situated for defense, Hitler

thought, but France's challenge in the near future would be internal political division, perhaps leading to civil war.

Germany's problems, he concluded, could be solved only by "force." He laid out three possible scenarios. The first one was a war to "solve Germany's problem of space" no later than 1943 to 1945. Hitler did not want or need to specify that this meant aggression against eastern Europe. The second scenario was more specific. If domestic conflict in France distracted the French Army, then "the time for action against the Czechs would have come." The third scenario went a step further. If France were to get involved in a war with "another state"—he meant Italy—Germany should take the opportunity to "overthrow Czechoslovakia and Austria simultaneously." Knocking out these countries would in turn keep Poland neutral in any war between Germany and France.

Hitler thought the British had already written off Czechoslovakia, and he surmised that the French would follow the British. Italy would not object to a German annexation of Czechoslovakia, although its attitude to Austria was not predictable. Poland would not want to take on a victorious Germany so long as events unfolded quickly. The Soviet Union would likely be held back by fear of Japan.

The optimism of Hitler's scenarios did not rub off on the generals. Blomberg and Fritsch protested that Germany could never face a war with Britain and France. Even a war between France and Italy, they said, would tie down only a small portion of the French Army and would leave a force on the Franco-German border that would still be superior to the available German units. Germany had not yet had time to fortify its western border, while France could rapidly mobilize its motorized divisions and strike at Germany's industrial heartland in the Ruhr Valley. Blomberg added that Czechoslovakia was no soft target, either—its border fortifications had "taken on the character of a Maginot Line [the supposedly impregnable French border fortifications] and would add the utmost difficulty to our attack."

Foreign Minister Neurath protested that the likelihood of a war involving Britain, France, and Italy was not as great as Hitler had suggested. Hitler explained that he was referring to the coming summer of 1938, as if this should calm Neurath's worries. He tried to soothe Blomberg and Fritsch's anxieties by insisting that Britain would stay out of any continental war, which meant that Germany did not have to fear an attack from France, either—the French would not dare act without the British.

In later years, Hossbach regretted that his dry and factual notes from the meeting had not conveyed the intensity with which Blomberg, Fritsch, and Neurath argued these points with Hitler—"a sin of omission on my part," he said. Hossbach also remembered that Blomberg and Fritsch had sparred with Göring about "technical armament issues," although he could not remember the details. The generals, probably frustrated that Hitler had left them little time to discuss the bottlenecks in steel supplies, vented on Göring the anger they had to contain with Hitler. They criticized Göring's incompetence as manager of the Four-Year Plan with such ferocity that Göring was finally reduced to whining that he deserved a chance to state his views, too. Hitler did not intervene in this confrontation. As a skilled craftsman in the art of power, he probably enjoyed watching his chief lieutenant's humiliation.

But Hossbach remembered the expression on Hitler's face as Blomberg and Fritsch voiced a "decisive rejection of Hitler's plans for war." Hitler would not forget their opposition. At the same time, the two generals had made an enemy out of the powerful Göring. Hossbach thought that Fritsch was the opponent Hitler had to take more seriously. There was no chance that Hitler could win the army commander over to his view on the need for war for Czechoslovakia and Austria, and so he must then and there have started to think about getting rid of Fritsch. Hitler, said Hossbach, could count on Göring to agree with him about this. Yet it was Blomberg who stood in the way of Göring's hopes to gain control over the whole armed forces. Göring knew that it would be much more difficult to persuade Hitler to part with Blomberg. "A reason would have to be found," Hossbach thought, that would "force" Hitler to let Blomberg go.

Unlike the scene in February 1933, there were no generals pouring another glass of wine this time and swapping self-satisfied jokes about the surprises in store for the Führer. Everything was different now. Within days, what Hitler had said on that November evening at the Chancellery became the subject of a growing round of furtive, anxious conversations among Germany's senior military, diplomatic, and intelligence officials.

An alliance sprang up between Neurath and Fritsch, each recognizing that the other would be tougher than Blomberg in opposing Hitler's schemes. On November 9, Fritsch met privately with Hitler before going on leave. A hint of his concerns appears in a letter to his friend the Baroness von Schutzbar: "Again and again new and difficult things are brought to me which must be attended to before I leave." Fritsch repeated to Hitler his worries about French and British intervention following any German attack on Austria or Czechoslovakia. As he had done at the meeting, Hitler assured Fritsch that he did not plan to do any such thing "in the immediate future." Neurath also requested a private audience, but the Führer kept putting him off, and the meeting did not take place until January. When they finally spoke, Hitler responded coldly to Neurath's plea that he seek his goals peacefully. He told Neurath that he had "no more time."

In the days after November 5, Colonel Hossbach wrote up his notes from the conference into a memorandum, which circulated around the military and intelligence offices. The Hossbach Memorandum, as it is known, became one of the most famous historical documents of the era. The meeting it recorded is even remembered as the Hossbach Conference.

ONE OF THE most revealing reactions to Hossbach's memorandum came from the chief of staff of the army, Lieutenant General Ludwig Beck.

Beck was the kind of highly intelligent, highly competent soldier that Germany seemed to produce in numbers unmatched by other countries. A tall man with a habitually grave expression, he had, in the words of the senior diplomat Ernst von Weizsäcker, a "fine, clever countenance, laden with responsibility and almost melancholy." One sign of Beck's intellect and the wide respect in which he was held was that he was invited to join the Wednesday Society, an eclectic group of distinguished scholars and professionals who met regularly to hear one another's lectures. Here Beck's peers included the renowned surgeon Ferdinand Sauerbruch and the equally renowned physicist Werner Heisenberg. Like most senior army officers, Beck had welcomed Hitler's arrival in the Chancellery, even gushing that it was "the first ray of hope since 1918." But after becoming chief of staff in 1933, effectively second in command of the army, Beck grew steadily more disillusioned with Germany's political masters.

Beck was no pacifist, and he had no moral objection to war—such a person would hardly have made a career as an army officer—but he did think war was a last resort and that its frequency could be minimized. Like most professional soldiers, Beck did not want to enter into a war his country would lose. In his judgment, a conflict against Britain and France, to say nothing of one against the United States, would be just such a war.

It was for these reasons that Hossbach's memorandum had a "devastating" effect on Beck, as Hossbach remembered long after. Hitler's claim that Germany needed to expand its territory left Beck cold. Major changes to Europe's human geography could not, the general wrote, be made without "the most severe convulsions, whose duration could not be foreseen." Ideas about autarky, such as those that lay behind the Four-Year Plan, were only "emergency solutions for a limited period." Beck conceded that it was "only too true" that participation in the global economy limited Germany's independence. But, scorn coloring his words, he concluded, "To deduce from this fact the winning of a greater living space as the only solution seems to me to want to master the difficulty without thinking it through adequately." With even more contempt, he added that purely military questions were not a politician's business and had to be reviewed by military experts.

Ironically, Beck approached Hitler's claims about the hostility of France and Britain with the same idea of "appeasement" that would drive British and French policy toward Germany in this era. Politics was, as Beck wrote (quoting Bismarck), the art of the possible. The French, British, and Germans were "together in the world, and in Europe," and so "all possibilities of coming to terms must be exhausted." This was, in any case, "cleverer in case of a later break": if you have tried everything to avoid a war and war comes anyway, at least you have put your enemy morally in the wrong.

German officers such as Beck were not the only ones to worry about Hitler's ambitions. The French intelligence service had an agent in the German High Command, who revealed the gist of what had been said at the Hossbach Conference. On November 6, the French ambassador in Berlin, André François-Poncet, reported home that "a large conference" had taken place there the day before, with Blomberg, Raeder, Neurath, and Göring attending. It had concerned "the problem of raw materials and the difficulties that the lack of iron and steel are causing for rearmament." He dropped a hint of what he probably knew from the agent's report: if the meeting had been only about raw materials, the ambassador wrote, surely so many generals would not have been summoned. One French embassy official who heard the news was blunter. "My God, it's not possible!" he exclaimed. "This is war."

Hitler's response to Hossbach's memorandum was revealing. Blomberg read and initialed the memorandum. But Hitler, who had called his words on that November evening his "testament," twice refused even to look at the document. He claimed he had no time.

Hitler then left Berlin and retreated to his Bavarian mountaintop to sulk—for weeks. Soon enough, it would become clear where that sulking would lead.

— 2 —

The Meaning of Gleiwitz

Franz Bernheim lives in the town of Gleiwitz in Upper Silesia, a border region where southeastern Germany meets Poland. Bernheim was born in Salzburg, Austria, but he has moved around a lot. From September 1931 until the end of March 1933, he worked at the Gleiwitz branch of the Deutsches Familien-Kaufhaus (German Family Department Store). Then he was summarily fired. He was fired because he is Jewish.

Bernheim is not politically active. But his brother-in-law is a man named Wieland Herzfelde, a prominent Communist publisher whom the Nazis hate. Herzfelde's brother is the brilliant collage artist John Heart-field, who for years has been savagely lampooning the Nazis on the covers of the Workers' Illustrated News. *A typical Heartfield piece: Hitler stands with his right hand raised and turned slightly backward in his usual "Heil" salute as a beefy suited figure behind him slips banknotes into his raised palm. "Millions are behind me," the Führer declares. Fearing that connections like Herzfelde and Heartfield could land him in trouble, Bernheim moves to Prague and from there—with the help of activists from Paris, who have been looking eagerly for someone just like him—he launches one of the most extraordinary legal actions of his time.*

Bernheim is making use of a new form of international law. He brings a petition to the League of Nations in Geneva, asking the League to compel the German government to cancel its laws discriminating against Jews, at least in Upper Silesia.

International treaties protecting minority rights have become an important feature of Europe in the 1920s and '30s, but only in certain places— that is, in countries that are either newly created or have been significantly reshaped since the end of the First World War.

The end of the war brings a democratic wave to central and eastern Europe. Entirely new countries appear, such as Czechoslovakia, and the Kingdom of the Serbs, Croats, and Slovenes, which will later rename itself Yugoslavia. An independent Poland arises for the first time since the 1790s. Finland recovers its autonomy from Russia. Austria and Hungary, shorn of their ancient empire, are reborn as independent and much smaller nation-states. Bulgaria, an ally of Germany in the war, loses territory; Romania, an ally of France and Britain, gains, mostly at the expense of Hungary. Germany loses about 10 percent of its prewar territory, some in the east to Poland, some in the west and north to Denmark, Belgium, and France.

The Western democracies, above all Britain, France, and the United States, have committed themselves to an idea put forward by U.S. president Woodrow Wilson: the principle of national self-determination. This means designing a new Europe in which every national group has its state and every state has its national group. The problem is that this can never actually work. Central and eastern Europe is a jumble of national groups, languages, and religions, and no line on a map can ever make a neat separation that everyone will welcome. The peace settlement puts approximately twenty-five million people in states that are not "theirs." The biggest minority group is the Germans. About seven million Germans live in new states outside Germany and Austria, most of them in Poland and Czechoslovakia.

The Western Allies preach self-determination, but they do not actually believe that Poles and Romanians stand on the same civilizational level as they do. The Westerners suspect that the new countries will treat their minorities badly. So, in return for international diplomatic recognition, the Westerners compel the new states to guarantee a mixture of individual and collective rights to their minority groups.

The Polish Minority Treaty, signed the same day as the Treaty of Versailles, is the first of these treaties and forms the template for the *others. It specifies that all citizens of Poland "shall be equal before the law and shall enjoy the same civil and political rights without distinction as to race, language or religion." And just to show that business is never far from the ideals of liberal internationalism, the treaty also requires Poland to extend "most favored nation" status to the Allies and protect their intellectual property. The new international body, the League of Nations, will ensure that the new states comply with the treaties.*

The victors have no intention of creating a general system of inalienable rights for all the people of the world: this would be as big a problem for French and British imperialism as for American segregation. At the Paris Peace Conference, the Western powers stop cold a Japanese bid for League recognition of racial equality.

There is also a strong dose of hard-nosed political realism in the system. The Allies are well aware of the future security threats in central and eastern Europe. Germany and Hungary have lost a lot of territory. Many Germans and Hungarians harbor fantasies of a war of revenge and reconquest. The new Soviet Union might at any time try to carry its revolutionary Communist creed westward into central Europe. What the Allies want is a belt of states surrounding and blocking these potential threats: what the French elegantly call a cordon sanitaire to contain the Soviets, coupled with alliances to check the Germans. If this system is going to work, the new states need to be politically stable. Angry minorities might upset this stability. Furthermore, angry minorities, especially if they are German or Hungarian, are a standing temptation to their "mother" countries to launch the very war of expansion the Allies are trying to contain. So the real longer-term goal of the minority treaties is that minorities will eventually assimilate and cease to be minorities.

Remarkably, there is no minority treaty for Germany: the Western powers extend respect to their former enemy that they do not grant to the new nations. But there is one small exception. In 1922, Germany and Poland negotiate a convention to regulate life in Upper Silesia, territory that was once German but is now divided between Germany and Poland. The convention incorporates most of the minority treaties' protections for the German and Polish minorities on either side of the border, and in language that can apply to other groups as well.

This is Bernheim's opening. Germany has made a legal commitment not to discriminate against minorities in Upper Silesia, including in the exercise of any "commercial or industrial calling." In June 1933, the Council of the League of Nations accepts Bernheim's petition protesting his treatment. Among the delegates to the Council who make this decision are two men who will play central roles in the international politics of the 1930s: Anthony Eden of Great Britain and Edvard Beneš of Czechoslovakia. The Germans are in a difficult position. Since 1926, they have made aggressive use of the minority treaties on behalf of "their" diasporas in central and eastern Europe. At the League Council, the German delegate argues limply that Bernheim did not have real ties to Upper Silesia and thus could not bring his petition, but that if Germany has violated its legal obligations in Upper Silesia, this was simply a mistake by local authorities, and the abuses "will be corrected."

And they are, at least for a time. From 1933 to 1937, when the original German-Polish convention expires, Jews in Bernheim's small corner of Germany live a charmed life. None of the Nazis' acts of repression, none of their discriminatory laws—dismissal from civil service jobs, loss of citizenship, prohibition of marriage, the criminalization of sex between Jews and "Aryans," and much more—can be enforced in Upper Silesia.

A world order based on international law, human rights, and democracy has met an alternative order based on nationalism, authoritarianism, and force. For a brief time, in Gleiwitz, this little corner of Silesia, the first scores a victory over the second.

A little over six years later, in this same Gleiwitz, the Nazis will dress concentration camp prisoners in Polish army uniforms, shoot them, and leave the bodies lying around a radio transmitter. They will claim this as evidence of a Polish military assault on Germany. In response, they will launch their invasion of Poland. And so, the Second World War will begin in Gleiwitz, as the world order of force opens its all-out assault on the world order of law.

WHEN HITLER TALKED about Germany moving east to claim "living space," he was talking about the world where Franz Bernheim lived. He was talking about the Europe of fragile new states, the Europe of the minority treaties, the Europe of bitterly resentful minority groups. Here the victors of the First World War had imposed their vision of democratic capitalism and international law, the key elements of what today we call globalization. Hitler arose as the most dangerous challenger to that system. The plan he laid out at the Hossbach Conference was nothing less than one to overturn the Western system and replace it with his own notion of racial empire.

The issue in Bernheim's case was really the fundamental problem of world politics in the 1930s. Was the world to be organized along liberal internationalist lines, with democratic systems everywhere, free trade, and rights for all, anchored in law? Or was the international system to be one of race and nation, with dominant groups owing nothing to minorities and closing off their economic space to the outer world as much as possible?

In the world of the 1930s, people used the word *race* all the time, and they used it differently from how we do today. The word could mean a lot of things, including nationality and ethnicity. It could describe differences in religion or language as much as, or more than, skin color. Winston Churchill often called the British an "island race." In Canada, it was common practice to refer to French and English Canadians as different races. But race, whatever it might mean, fundamentally structured politics and international affairs. This was obvious in the case of the European overseas empires, where the British, French, Dutch, Portuguese, and Belgians routinely denied full citizenship and other rights to Asian or African subjects. It was obvious, too, in the segregated American South, in U.S. immigration policy, and in Nazi antisemitism.

It was a bit less obvious, but no less important, in that belt of new nations running from Finland to Yugoslavia. In many ways, racialized ideas about the people of the region shaped how other states acted toward them. Joseph Stalin, who would emerge as the dictator of the Soviet Union in the later 1920s, had a particular racially charged hatred of Poles. So did many Germans. Adolf Hitler did not entirely share this hatred, but he made up for it with his contempt for other peoples of eastern Europe, particularly Czechs and Serbs, to say nothing of Russians and Jews. British condescension toward the people of the region was only a milder version of the same attitude. Above all, ethnic and racial hatreds within the region itself would shape what happened there. And what happened there would be crucially important for the world.

The democratic wave that followed the First World War had been concentrated in central and eastern Europe. By the 1930s, that wave had turned into a crisis of democracy, centered in the same region but reaching across much of the globe. The crisis of democracy was fundamentally a crisis of nationalism—which made it fundamentally a crisis of race.

THE NEW NATIONS of central and eastern Europe were all wracked by bitter internal divisions. Benito Mussolini sarcastically called Czechoslovakia "Czecho-Germano-Polono-Magyaro-Rutheno-Romano-Slovakia." He wasn't wrong. Ironically, for a country that had won its freedom against the multinational Austro-Hungarian Empire, Czechoslovakia replicated the old empire's diversity and divisiveness in miniature. The 1921 census showed that only 50.8 percent of its people were Czechs, and 14.7 percent Slovaks. Nearly a quarter, 23.4 percent, were Germans, most of whom lived in a horseshoe-shaped area along the border with Germany, known as the Sudetenland. Czechoslovakia also had significant communities of Magyars, Ruthenians, Jews, and Poles.

It was the same story across the region. A quarter of Latvia's population and nearly a third of Poland's consisted of minorities. Politics in these new democracies was almost always fought out as a battle between ethnic groups. In Czechoslovakia, each of the various national groups replicated the whole political spectrum within itself. There was a Social Democratic Party for the Czech lands and another for the Germans, and a Hungarian-German Social Democratic Party in Slovakia. There was a Czechoslovak Traders' Party for small business and also a German Traders' Party. There was the German National Party, banned in 1933 and then replaced by the Sudeten German Party, with no agenda other than the representation of Sudeten German interests. There was a bewildering profusion of other ethnically identified parties: the Slovak People's Party, the Zionist Jewish Party, the Polish People's Party, the right-wing Russian National Autonomous Party, and many more.

Many political thinkers in the interwar years believed that a liberal democratic state required homogeneity, and that democracy could not work amid difference. The British philosopher John Stuart Mill had made this case in the Victorian era, but now rougher thinkers, such as the right-wing German law professor Carl Schmitt, argued that modern mass democracy required not only homogeneity but "if the need arises—elimination or eradication" of diversity.

The postwar democratic system had been a product of the power vacuum in central and eastern Europe following the collapse of the German, Russian, Austrian, and Turkish Empires. The coming of Hitler's regime in Germany in 1933 stimulated a rise in racial nationalism across the region, accompanied by a new level of violence and persecution directed toward minorities, and a steadily mounting refugee crisis.

Ethnic hatreds often gain strength and direction from economic grievances, and the Great Depression contributed its share to the democratic crisis of the 1930s. At the same time, the politics of ethnic division in central and eastern Europe made it all but impossible for politicians to take effective political action against the Depression. The sharp decline in world food prices in the 1920s hit the region particularly hard, as most countries, including even industrialized states like Czechoslovakia and Germany, depended heavily on agriculture. Then came the onset of near-global depression in 1929, made dramatically worse by the financial crisis of 1931. The economic problems sparked a turn to authoritarian rule. There were two main reasons for this. Orthodox economics taught that a government's proper response to an economic downturn was "deflation"—today we call it "austerity"—which meant cutting government expenditures to match depressed tax revenues, until the magic of the market brought recovery by itself. The problem is that a democratic political system can tolerate only short periods of deflation. If deflation goes on for a long time—for years—the misery in the population will eventually force a different political response. This means that only an authoritarian state can impose a long-term deflation. Or, to put it another way, in a long-term crisis, classical liberal economics can be maintained only by antiliberal politics. However, economic policies that move *away* from the classical free-enterprise model also tend to be anti-global and antidemocratic in outlook. This is because a state-planned economy, whether fascist or Communist, has to be insulated from world financial markets.

The weakness of the Western democracies after the financial crisis of 1931 accelerated the trend toward authoritarian politics. It seemed to millions that global trade and global finance were at the root of all the misery. The bitter ethnic divisions in so many European countries meant that politics were deadlocked and democratic governments were unable to take effective action—which further discredited democracy. Hungary and Italy had shown the way to authoritarian rule soon after the First World War, in 1919 and 1922, respectively. They were followed by Bulgaria, Austria, Poland, Yugoslavia, and Romania in the late 1920s and early 1930s. After that, as the political and economic crisis deepened, regimes responded by concentrating ever more power in the hands of authoritarian rulers. Yugoslavia's king Alexander rewrote the constitution to heighten his own power in 1931. Bulgaria's king Boris III took a similar step in 1934. Romania's king Carol would make himself dictator in 1938. By that year, Czechoslovakia would be the only central European state still functioning as a parliamentary democracy. But its deep internal divisions gave it something of the quality of a wounded antelope to the German lion. Hitler would know how to prey on it.

The condescending imperialism with which the Western powers treated central and eastern Europe emerged again: as these democracies failed, Western leaders decided that democracy had never been an appropriate system for them anyway, an attitude that reflected the Westerners' own racialized ideas about eastern Europeans. Westerners could operate with a lofty disdain for the domestic politics of the new nations—as long as what happened was consistent with their own strategic interests. The French had alliances with Poland and Yugoslavia, so they did not much care if Yugoslav police treated minority Macedonians badly, or if the Polish government carried out a brutal "pacification" campaign against its Ukrainian population. The main thing was that the ally was politically stable and could put up an effective military effort if needed. The British believed that the League of Nations' efforts to enforce minority rights simply kept the minorities from assimilating. "So long as these people imagine that their grievances can be aired before the League of Nations," a British Foreign Office official wrote in 1922, "they will refuse to settle down." *The Times* of London expressed a characteristic British attitude when it argued against British involvement in the Spanish Civil War. "Their quarrel is not a British quarrel," the paper

wrote of the contending sides. "It may be that the system of parliamentary Government which suits Great Britain suits few other countries
besides."

Colonel Hossbach would observe years later that Hitler thought
like an Austrian, not a German—meaning his gaze was turned toward
the eastern European lands that had been a part of the old Austro-
Hungarian Empire, whereas the senior military men he had to deal
with thought only about reclaiming the territory Germany had lost
after the First World War. Hossbach had a point, but the point went
farther than he took it. Hitler was driven by the most extreme possible
version of the social Darwinism common in Europe and America at the
start of the twentieth century. The only reality for Hitler, and the only
value, was the group—the nation or the race. It should expand if it were
strong enough, claiming territory and resources from other groups, and
contract and fail if it were too weak. Hitler was not even a conventional
nationalist: so violent was his social Darwinism that he was, in the historian Timothy Snyder's clever phrase, really a "zoological anarchist."

There was no place in Hitler's world for international law or international institutions. At best, Hitler preferred bilateral, never multilateral
relations. At worst, he sought war, conquest, and ultimately enslavement
or extermination. Germany's international lawyers and representatives
soon started taking his tone. Each race had its own law, they argued.
There was no point in trying to create an international law that would fit
everyone. These men did not even want to spread German legal concep-
tions abroad: "It should never, and shall never, be our function," wrote
one Nazi legal scholar, "to convert by example to German legal notions
the negro republic of Liberia, or Abyssinia, or Red Russia, in order to
construct a genuine society of nations of universal character."

There were direct connections between the multi-ethnic composition
of most of the new states, the failure of democracy in almost all of them,
the spread of fascism, and the older democracies' response of a policy
of "appeasement." All these phenomena were aspects of the broad crisis
facing global democracy.

The British, with their disdain for eastern Europe, might have stood
by and let Hitler expand in that direction. Perhaps Hitler's Germany
might then never have turned on Britain. Hitler spoke endlessly of how

he admired the British Empire and wanted to share the world with it, not fight it. This idea had been a major theme of his *Second Book*, written in 1928 but set aside and not published until the 1950s. According to one report, as late as August 1939, Hitler told a visitor, "Everything that I undertake is directed against Russia. If those in the West are too stupid and too blind to understand this, then I shall be forced to come to an understanding with the Russians to beat the West, and then, after its defeat, turn with all my concerted force against the Soviet Union."

But France, with much more to fear from Germany, needed its alliances in central Europe. And the British in turn needed France and its large army, which formed a central pillar of British defense thinking.

Here, then, in the lands between Germany and Russia and between the Baltic and the Aegean, several fatal trends intersected. Here the crisis of European democracy was at its most intense, largely because here the racism and extreme nationalism of the era were at fever pitch. Here the ambitions of Hitler the Austrian zoological anarchist were concentrated, here the Soviet dictator Joseph Stalin also cast a covetous eye, and here Western statesmen looked on with an uneasy mixture of condescending disinterest and strategic calculation.

These intersecting trends produced the perfect formula for war.

"In the Circle of Guilt"

Mikhail Nikolayevich Tukhachevsky is an unlikely army officer and an even more unlikely Communist. Born in 1893 on an estate near Smolensk, he comes from an aristocratic and cultured Russian family: his father and younger brother play the piano, while he and one older brother play the violin and another the cello. But when his family falls on hard times, he abandons his dreams of a university education and enrolls at Moscow's Alexandrovsky Military College. Here he discovers a love of military strategy. He can read German, French, and English, and he graduates in June 1914 as one of the best students the college has ever seen. Two months later, the First World War breaks out. Young Lieutenant Tukhachevsky goes to the front dreaming of military glory.

Those dreams remain unfulfilled. Tukhachevsky is captured by the Germans in early 1915 and sent to a POW camp at Ingolstadt, from which he tries repeatedly to escape. One of his fellow prisoners is a young French officer named Charles de Gaulle. In 1917, Tukhachevsky succeeds in breaking out and makes it back to Russia just in time for the October Revolution. He volunteers his services for the Red Army.

In the nearly three years of a brutal civil war, Tukhachevsky establishes himself as the most daring and brilliant of Red Army commanders. He wins some crucial victories, but his advance on Warsaw (in the

Polish-Soviet War, which develops alongside the Civil War) is checked by a successful Polish counterattack, and the war ends in the spring of 1921 on terms favorable to Poland. This outcome leads to long-lasting, and fateful, recriminations between Tukhachevsky and his rival Red Army commanders Kliment Voroshilov, Semyon Budyonny—and Joseph Stalin.

But for now, Tukhachevsky's rise continues. In May 1924, he is named deputy chief of the general staff, and when the chief of staff dies unexpectedly in 1925, Tukhachevsky is promoted to his position. In 1928 comes the first setback. Tukhachevsky is demoted to command of the Leningrad military district. The reason for this demotion is murky. It probably has to do with Tukhachevsky's efforts to create a general staff on the German model, which irritates the Soviet leaders because they fear it could become a rival power center.

One of Tukhachevsky's good connections is with the Stalin crony Sergo Ordzhonikidze, however, and in 1931, Ordzhonikidze brings Tukhachevsky back to Moscow to become head of the army's Technology and Armament Department. For a few years, all seems to go well again. In 1935, Tukhachevsky is promoted to the army's highest rank, marshal of the Soviet Union. Early in 1936, he accompanies Foreign Minister Maxim Litvinov to Britain for the funeral of King George V, a particular honor. While abroad, he meets a number of British and French politicians and military officers, impressing all of them with his grasp of languages, powerful intellect, and original mind.

Tukhachevsky lives well. He maintains a huge apartment in Moscow's House on the Embankment, the building for the Soviet elite, which features unheard-of luxuries such as central heating, a tennis court, and a library. Here he hosts musical evenings, sometimes featuring his friend Dmitri Shostakovich, sometimes the state military orchestra. He is a man with a powerful presence, and Joseph Stalin nicknames him "Napoleonchik" (Little Napoléon). Tukhachevsky's good looks and his dashing manner make him attractive to women. Among men, however, he has a lot of enemies.

There is no doubt that Tukhachevsky is ruthless and can be cruel. He has a reputation from the Civil War for crushing uprisings by taking hostages and shooting rebels and bystanders alike at random. He does not suffer fools. And some of Stalin's senior military officials, notably Budyonny and Voro-

shilov, are clearly fools. They come in for a good share of Tukhachevsky's wrath. On one occasion, Tukhachevsky delivers a report in front of Voroshilov, who is the defense commissar—his superior. Voroshilov offers some criticisms, which Tukhachevsky calmly rejects. When Voroshilov asks why, Tukhachevsky explains: "Your amendments are incompetent, Comrade People's Commissar." This will hurt him later, but not as much as the hatred of Stalin, which is also a legacy of rivalries from the Polish war.

His original mind causes trouble, too. Tukhachevsky is a military innovator focused on the possibilities of new technology, particularly tanks. But in Stalin's world, innovation is usually a threat to those in power. On one occasion, after reading a Tukhachevsky memorandum advocating military mechanization, Stalin complains that the general's ideas are "nonsense" and do not "suit a Marxist." At the 17th Communist Party Congress in 1934, the dim-witted cavalry general Budyonny fiercely criticizes Tukhachevsky's campaign for mechanization. A Pravda article of May 1936 attacks those who prefer mechanization to horses. The article does not name Tukhachevsky, but there is no doubt about its target.

Stalin is an avid reader of Machiavelli. He understands that a charismatic and successful soldier can be a threat. Machiavelli recommends that a prince should have such an officer killed, or at least discredited. And so, in early 1937, one of Stalin's spectacular "show trials" produces scripted evidence, clearly the product of torture, that casts doubt on Tukhachevsky's loyalty to the regime. The fact is that by early 1937, Stalin has concluded that disloyalty is widespread among his senior army officers. At the same time, targeting the army for terror is not the same thing as targeting peasants in Ukraine. If it wants to, the army can fight back. It can possibly win. To avoid this danger Stalin needs persuasive evidence of military treason. Evidence from abroad would be particularly effective.

Stalin and his spy agency, the Foreign Department of the NKVD (People's Commissariat for Internal Affairs), gather damning evidence against Tukhachevsky, most of it false and some of it fabricated by top Nazis, such as Himmler's deputy Reinhard Heydrich, and slipped to the Soviets. Some is planted by the NKVD on the French intelligence service and played back to Moscow. Stalin's paranoia will do the rest, and the Soviet Union will be rid of its most capable soldier.

Rumors have been going around Moscow diplomatic circles that

Tukhachevsky's arrest is imminent. In April, an official announcement still has it that he will be traveling to Britain for the coronation of King George VI, but in May the story changes: Tukhachevsky, it is said, is now too ill to make the trip.

On May 10, 1937, the Politburo orders Tukhachevsky's demotion from deputy defense commissar to commander of the remote Volga military district. He is arrested when he arrives at his new headquarters. His wife and daughter return to Moscow, where his wife is arrested soon after, along with his mother and surviving siblings. His wife and his brothers are later shot on Stalin's orders. Three of his sisters are sent to the Gulag. His daughter, Svetlana, is sent to a home for the children of "enemies of the people."

"WHAT WENT ON in Number One's brain?"

This was Nikolai Rubashov's question. Rubashov is the main character of the novel *Darkness at Noon*, by the disillusioned Communist Arthur Koestler, one of the classic narratives of the Terror that wracked the Soviet Union in the late 1930s. "Number One," of course, was Iosif Vissarionovich Dzhugashvili, better known to the world as Joseph Stalin. Since the late 1920s, Stalin had been the increasingly unquestioned dictator of the Soviet Union.

No one has ever been able to give Rubashov a very clear answer. We know what Stalin did. *Why* he did it remains an enigma. The German journalist Emil Ludwig, who interviewed Stalin in 1932, wrote, "Among the rulers of our time—and I have seen most of them—he is the most impenetrable." Stalin's former secretary remembered, "He possessed in a high degree the gift for silence, and in this respect he was unique in a country where everybody talks far too much."

Stalin kept no diaries and wrote no memoirs. Unlike Adolf Hitler, he did not force his entourage to sit through endless monologues. Often, he kept quiet and simply watched and listened to what went on around him, his striking eyes alert and ominous. When he spoke, his voice was soft and low. Listeners had to strain to hear him. He liked to foster a crude atmosphere of drunken revelry with his cronies, but he never stopped watching everyone. A woman who was a guest on his Black Sea yacht remembered Stalin drinking and dancing, oafishly "staggering and stamping" around the cabin, and yet the dictator "still seemed sober enough to observe my reactions to his conduct." His alertness was usually chilling. "Why are your eyes so shifty today?" he would say to an associate, or "Why are you turning so much today and avoiding looking me directly in the eyes?"

Stalin read voraciously and possessed a remarkable memory. His reading ran from Marx and Lenin to the German military strategist Clausewitz to the classics of Russian literature, such as Tolstoy and Chekhov. Interviewing the dictator in January 1937, the exiled German writer Lion Feuchtwanger observed, "He feels himself quite free in many areas [of knowledge] and cites by memory without preparation names, dates, facts always exactly." An aviation official remembered a meeting at which "Stalin went through the main military aircraft of the air forces of Germany, England, France, and the United States," speaking about "their weaponry, carrying capacities, rate of climb, maximum altitude. He did all this from memory, without any notes, which surprised the specialists and aviators present."

But this low-key dictator gave orders of a murderousness without parallel. In the early 1930s, when he ordered the forced collectivization of Soviet farms, expropriating family farms and amalgamating them into huge, state-run operations, the result was a famine that killed approximately 5.5 million people. In December 1934, a lone gunman assassinated Stalin's friend, the Leningrad party boss Sergei Kirov. Stalin used Kirov's murder exactly as Hitler had used the Reichstag fire nearly two years before. He pushed through a law providing for speedy executions of "terrorists." He began speaking darkly of plots within and against the Soviet leadership. In time, he launched a series of purges, arrests, show trials, and executions known simply as the Terror. His bloodletting was so wildly disproportionate to any possible political threat that it seems to elude rational explanation. But it always came back to paranoia—and on a broader scale, so did the foreign policy of his regime.

Paranoia and isolationism were all but inevitable functions of the Soviets' political culture. The very formula of "socialism in one country"—the Bolshevik answer to the problem that their revolution had not spread to other capitalist countries, as they had expected it would—easily lent itself to paranoia about the capitalist world. "We are a hundred years behind the advanced countries," Stalin told a conference in 1931. "We must make good this gap in ten years. Either we do it, or they will crush us." Soviet leaders saw themselves as inevitably, and permanently, at war, and not only with the capitalists abroad. There were also the "enemies within," social classes or nationalities the regime considered a threat—usually because they might be linked to foreign powers. This fear could easily slide into the racial hatreds so common elsewhere in eastern Europe. Before 1939, Stalin killed a thousand times more people because of their ethnicity than did Hitler. In 1937, as the NKVD was systematically targeting Soviet Poles in a campaign of mass murder, he expressed his satisfaction in a memo to NKVD chief Nikolai Yezhov: "Very good! Keep on digging up and cleaning out this Polish filth."

Like Nazi Germany, the Soviet Union rested on a conscious rejection of Western, liberal, capitalist democracy. And although it claimed to base its actions on a rational, scientific doctrine, it in fact operated on a tribalism not much different from that of the Nazis. Perhaps this was why Nazis and Communists often enjoyed one another's company. A Nazi diplomat meeting with Soviet counterparts in Moscow found that the experience was like being in "a circle of old [Nazi] party comrades."

Stalin's notorious chief prosecutor Andrey Vyshinsky instructed his subordinates that evidence was less important than "political flair." "Class instinct" for right and wrong, he thought, was superior to evidence. This approach was not very far from the Nazi notion of "thinking with the blood." The individual human being disappeared along with evidenced-based judgments. This was the essence of totalitarianism.

There were also some remarkable parallels between the early lives of Joseph Stalin and Adolf Hitler. Both men came from regions peripheral to the powerful countries they ultimately ruled: Hitler from Upper Austria, Stalin from Georgia. Both men came from peasant families that had moved up a few rungs on the social ladder: Hitler's father had become a minor civil servant; Stalin's father was a shoemaker. And in both cases, there is some uncertainty about the exact line of descent. Hitler's father was born out of wedlock, and speculation continues about who might have been the dictator's grandfather. In Stalin's case, it is his own parentage that is obscure: apart from Vissarion Dzhugashvili, the husband of Stalin's mother, Yekatarina "Keke" Geladze, several exotic candidates (princes and explorers) have been proposed as Stalin's real father. More plausibly, Stalin's father may have been a wealthy local merchant in whose home Keke worked as a domestic servant. This man is sometimes said to have paid for the good education that young Joseph Dzhugashvili received, schooling that was rare for children as poor as he was.

Opponents often dismissed Hitler as looking like a hairdresser or a waiter in a railway station restaurant. Even when he became chancellor of Germany in 1933, his conservative cabinet colleagues assumed they could control and use him for their own purposes. It was the same with Stalin. A Socialist rival wrote that during the Bolshevik revolution of 1917, Stalin had been nothing more than "a grey blur, emitting a dim light every now and then and not leaving any trace." The dashing Leon Trotsky thought that Stalin was "the most outstanding mediocrity in our party," and most of the other leading Bolsheviks thought the same, well into the 1920s. This is why they made Stalin the party secretary. They thought he was good enough to do the boring administrative work while they applied their theoretical genius to building a new society.

Like Nazi Germany, the Soviet Union had been born out of a highly democratic predecessor: the Russia of the Provisional Government of 1917. And so, like Nazi Germany, the Soviet Union was another expression of the crisis of democracy in the 1930s. But what kind of role could or would the Soviet Union play in world affairs? What went on in Number One's brain was just as mysterious here as elsewhere. Winston Churchill called Soviet policy "a riddle wrapped in a mystery inside an enigma." Like Hitler's Germany, the Soviet Union appeared to be a grievous threat to the Western democracies. Its agents, like Nazi agents, carried out acts of terrorism and murder against their political opponents around the world. The NKVD's murder of Stalin's most high-profile opponent, Leon Trotsky, in Mexico in 1940 was only the most notorious of these acts of terror. Soviet espionage activities against the West were far more extensive than those of the Nazis, and far more skillful and successful.

But for years the Nazis had preached nothing but hatred of Soviet communism. Everyone saw the two major totalitarian regimes as mortal enemies. Might the enemy of democracy's enemy be democracy's friend? Some in the West thought so—including Churchill, who worked steadily for an anti-Nazi alliance with the Soviet Union. There was an internal debate within the Soviet regime about how to approach the world, which made it still harder to gauge Soviet intentions. Foreign Minister Maxim Litvinov was oriented toward the West, the League of Nations, and collective security, while Litvinov's eventual successor Vyacheslav Molotov—and probably Stalin—were more isolationist. Which way would things go? From the middle of 1937, it seemed the tide was running toward isolationism.

STALIN USED THE threat of war with Germany to justify his Terror. The purges took in Communist Party members, Soviet officials, and army officers. Mikhail Tukhachevsky was among the half dozen officers who were the first victims. One shot himself when the NKVD came for him. The rest had to face NKVD interrogation.

This meant torture, threats, and broken promises. Tukhachevsky, like the others, confessed to the charges of conspiracy when he was promised that the lives of his family would be spared if he did. The official statement reported that "all measures were taken to break down his resistance." His written confession was stained with his blood, in patterns showing that he was being beaten even as he signed. The interrogation transcripts went directly to Stalin, who met daily with NKVD chief Nikolai Yezhov to manage the cases.

On June 2, 1937, armed with this material, Stalin addressed the military council of the Defense Commissariat. The irrationality of arresting his most capable commander in an increasingly dangerous time was so glaring that even Stalin seemed to struggle to explain it. "Comrades," he told the gathering, "I hope no one doubts now that a military-political plot against Soviet power existed," inspired and financed by "German fascists." Stalin's speeches were usually well organized, but here he rambled. He denied but then seemed to confirm that the officers had been arrested for being "Trotskyists." Stalin asked if the delegates had read Tukhachevsky's testimony, and insisted, "He passed on our operational plans—our operational plans, the holy of holies—to the German army. He had dealings with representatives of the German army. A spy? A

spy." Some of the officers present seemed uneasy at this palpable madness. But none spoke out.

Tukhachevsky and the other officers were tried in secret by judges
chosen by Stalin. Some of the judges, such as Budyonny, already
hated Tukhachevsky. The trial lasted one day, with the interrogators and torturers present, in case anyone was tempted to retract his
confession—a typical Stalinist touch. There were no witnesses, no
defense attorneys, and no appeal. The officers stuck to their confessions,
although they were more evasive or noncommittal when the military
men on the panel asked them questions. One judge, for instance, asked
Tukhachevsky if he had engaged in espionage before 1932. Referring
to his contacts with the German Army in the 1920s, when this conduct had been Soviet state policy, he replied, "I don't know whether that
could be considered espionage." Later he said, "I feel as if I'm dreaming."

Tukhachevsky's last words to the tribunal were as brave as they
were subject to different interpretations. "And so, citizen judges," he
said, "I want you to know that both you and we here on the prisoners' bench are involved in the circle of guilt. To look on all this and
remain silent is a crime. And for all these years we have looked on and
remained silent. And for this both you and all of us deserve to be shot."

Predictably, the court sentenced Tukhachevsky and his comrades to
death. They were taken immediately to the cellar and shot. When Stalin
asked how the judges of the military court had conducted themselves,
he was told that only Budyonny had shown enthusiasm for convicting
the officers. Stalin was enraged.

In early 1937, there were about 144,000 officers in the Soviet armed
forces. Over the next year and a half, 33,000 were purged, of whom
9,500 were arrested and about 7,000 executed. The carnage was worst
at the highest levels of command. Between 500 and 600 of the top 767
officers were executed or imprisoned; 154 of 186 division commanders;
8 of 9 admirals; and 3 of 5 marshals of the Soviet Union.

In this dark time, the Soviet Union affected European politics rather
like an offstage magnet, pulling here and repelling there. The purge of
army officers raised serious doubts in Britain and France about the value
of a Soviet alliance to contain the Nazi menace. Hitler followed the fate of
Tukhachevsky and other senior Russian officers with astonishment and

disbelief. He, too, wondered what went on in Number One's brain. "Stalin is probably mentally ill," he told Goebbels soon after Tukhachevksy's execution. "Otherwise the bloodletting can't be explained." But that, he said, meaning Stalin's madness, was "the danger that we must someday crush."

The Soviet bloodletting was just one of the developments that made Hitler feel the world was in motion and that it was high time for German expansion. A Soviet Union that was so weakening itself was not only a tempting target but also seemed to open up space for interim moves against Austria or Czechoslovakia. There was a straight line from the death of Tukhachevsky to Hitler's words at the Hossbach Conference.

In June 1937, the Leningrad Communist Party boss (soon to be chairman of the Supreme Soviet) Andrei Zhdanov gave a speech arguing that the decline of Western democracy was the key feature of the international situation. Britain and France, he said could "do nothing useful for the cause of peace. Because their maneuvers have been so halfhearted the fascists have become less and less interested in peace and more and more inclined to aggression." Stalin called the plot he imagined to have been brewing among his officers "not so much internal as external."

Of course, this argument deflected the responsibility away from him and his own consolidation of power. But it also showed a Soviet Union that seemed to be pulling further away from any alliance to contain Nazi Germany, just as the purge of the army drastically weakened the military means the Soviets could contribute. Stalin would soon come to realize what catastrophic errors he had made.

—— 4 ——

"We Are Looking for a Program"

He is in his study one evening, painting. He has been a passionate and strikingly talented amateur painter since the First World War. He doesn't usually paint portraits, but on this occasion, he is trying to copy a portrait of his father, who has been dead for many years. As he works, he feels a strange sensation. He turns around and sees his father, sitting in a red leather armchair. The old man appears as he did in his prime, when he was chancellor of the exchequer in the administration of Lord Salisbury. Father and son begin to converse, mostly about what has happened in the years since the older man's death in 1895.

It is not clear how fancifully Winston Churchill means us to take this story. He writes it at his children's urging and then leaves it in a locked box. But in any case, it is deeply revealing. The conversation he describes is mostly about the horrors of modern war.

The conversation begins when Winston makes a passing reference to the intelligence service MI5, "formed in the war."

Lord Randolph Churchill is startled. "War, do you say? Has there been a war?"

Winston replies, making a connection that would surprise many people: "We have had nothing else but wars since democracy took charge."

Lord Randolph struggles to grasp the scale of the wars his son is describing. "You mean real wars, not just frontier expeditions? Wars where tens of thousands of men lose their lives?"

"Yes, indeed, Papa," Winston replies, "that's what has happened all the time. Wars and rumors of war ever since you died."

Winston describes the sequence. First there was the Boer War of 1899 to 1902, in which the British Empire subdued the Dutch-African farmers, or Boers, only with great and often cruel effort. Then came "the wars of nations, caused by demagogues and tyrants."

As he processes this information, Lord Randolph realizes that "wars like these must have cost a million lives."

His son assures him that they took the lives of many millions. "Far gone are the days of Queen Victoria and a settled world order," Winston observes. "But, having gone through so much, we do not despair."

Lord Randolph confesses to being "stupefied" by the news. "I would never have believed that such things could happen," he tells his son in wonder. "I am glad I did not live to see them."

Then another thought strikes him. "As I listened to you unfolding these fearful facts, you seemed to know a great deal about them."

ON MAY 31, 1937, the British Conservative Party's parliamentary caucuses from the House of Commons and the House of Lords filed into London's Caxton Hall to officially elect the newly minted prime minister, Neville Chamberlain, as the leader of their party. Amid what one observer called "all the wealth and grandeur of England," Lord Derby proposed the nomination. But by tradition it fell to the senior privy councilor in the House of Commons caucus, who happened to be the member of Parliament for Epping, to speak in its favor. The member for Epping was Winston Spencer Churchill.

Churchill gave a nomination speech that *The Times* dubbed proof, "not for the first time, that personal generosity is a prominent feature of his character." And so it was. But there was a complex undercurrent in Churchill's speech, which the more careful listeners detected.

Through two coalition governments since 1931, led by the Labour Party's Ramsay MacDonald and then the Conservatives' Stanley Baldwin, Neville Chamberlain had been the prince in waiting, clearly the most competent and energetic member of both governments. He had served through these years as chancellor of the exchequer, the medieval-sounding designation for Britain's finance minister. When Baldwin decided to step down after the coronation of the new king, George VI, Chamberlain was the obvious successor.

Churchill paid full tribute to this fact in his speech. He spoke of Chamberlain's "memorable achievement" when, after the world financial crisis of 1931, he had restored Britain's financial standing and stimulated its foreign trade. But Churchill went on to remind the gathering that the office of party leader had never been interpreted "in a dictatorial or despotic sense." The House of Commons remained "the arena of free debate," and Churchill was sure that "the leader we are about to choose will . . . not resent honest differences of opinion arising between those who mean the same thing, and that party opinion will not be denied its subordinate but still rightful place in his mind." The Conservative MP Henry "Chips" Channon described this as "an able, fiery speech not untouched by bitterness."

Churchill expanded on the point in an article for the American magazine *Collier's*, in which his defense of Chamberlain's character seemed more ambivalent than enthusiastic. "There has grown up a conception of Neville Chamberlain as a cold, aloof, rather inhuman figure," he began. Conceding that Chamberlain "dislikes and mistrusts facile enthusiasms," even that "he has few friends and that he shuns society," Churchill nonetheless insisted that "this certainly does not imply that he is cold and unfeeling." He cited Chamberlain's work as health minister in the 1920s as proof of his "passion for social justice," noting as well that his successful campaign against maternal mortality was rooted in the fact that his own mother had died in childbirth. And if his favorite pastimes of fishing and bird watching were those "best pursued alone," it was not "any lack of normal human feeling" that limited his social life, but rather "the happy comradeship of his home life" and the fact that "throughout his career, [Chamberlain] has been too busy doing things to bother about meeting people."

No character sketch could have portrayed a man more different from the gregarious and talkative Churchill. Chamberlain knew this, too. He had once said of Churchill, "There is too deep a difference between our natures for me to feel at home with him or to regard him with affection." Their ideas on how to cope with the steadily worsening challenges that Britain faced in the late 1930s were also starkly different. But Churchill strove to handle Chamberlain with careful respect and deference, a natural stance for a back-bench member of Parliament to take toward a party leader and prime minister. And yet Winston Churchill was no ordinary backbencher; Chamberlain returned the careful treatment.

Chamberlain was under no illusions about the motives behind Churchill's friendliness. Churchill was five years younger than Chamberlain but had reached cabinet rank nearly two decades sooner. Now Churchill had fallen on hard times. Since 1931, he had been in the "wilderness," made untouchable by what were seen as his extreme views and his reputation for erratic irresponsibility. He desperately wanted a way back to the power that only a cabinet minister could exercise, not just out of personal ambition, but because he considered British policy toward Hitler's Germany to be disastrously mistaken, while the danger grew ever greater.

But Churchill remained an outcast within his own party. Since 1931, under both MacDonald and Baldwin, Britain had been governed by a coalition known as the "National Government," with participation of the three main parties: the center-right Conservatives, the center-left Liberals, and the left-wing Labour Party. The Conservatives overwhelmingly dominated the House of Commons (winning 522 of 615 seats in 1931, and 429 in 1935), which meant they also dominated the administration. The parliamentary opposition was made up largely of disgruntled Labour and Liberal MPs. Although a Conservative, Churchill opposed his party's administration and prime ministers as strenuously as did any Labour or Liberal member. But to get back into the cabinet and be in a position to change anything, he had first to win the favor of the new prime minister. So Churchill treated Chamberlain graciously and often stifled his criticisms.

In private, neither man was very kind about the other. In 1935, Chamberlain scoffed that Churchill "makes a good many speeches, considerably fortified by cocktails and old brandies," but "his following tends to shrink rather than to increase." A year later he was thankful that "we have not got Winston as a colleague." (Although they would use only the last name for anyone else, everyone in British politics always referred to Churchill simply as "Winston," as if he were a beloved soccer player or musician—a sign of his unique status even in bad times.) "He is in the usual excited condition that comes on him when he smells war, and if he were in the cabinet we should be spending all our time in holding him down instead of getting on with our business." Churchill was even more scathing about his rival. Even after Chamberlain's death, he would describe him privately as "the narrowest, most ignorant, most ungenerous of men."

Yet, in 1937, neither man could afford to avoid or ignore the other. They circled each other as they had for over a decade, wary and respectful. And more and more, British policy toward Germany took on the quality of a duel between them.

WINSTON SPENCER CHURCHILL was sixty-two years old in May 1937. In his veins ran the very bluest of blood. He was a grandson of the Duke of Marlborough, born at the family's ancestral seat of Blenheim Palace. But his own father, Lord Randolph Churchill, had been a younger son of the duke, and thus inherited neither title nor wealth. Partly for this reason he made an advantageous marriage to a well-heeled young woman from Brooklyn, New York, Jennie Jerome, who became Winston Churchill's wayward and inattentive mother.

After a disastrous time at the prestigious public school Harrow (like all British "public" schools, actually a pricey private boarding school) ruled out a university education, Winston was sent to the military academy Sandhurst to train for a career as a cavalry officer. But garrison duty in a remote imperial outpost did not suit his lust for adventure, and he repeatedly managed to get himself assigned to places where he could actually fight. In 1898, he found himself in what would prove to be the British Army's last significant cavalry charge, at the Battle of Omdurman, near Khartoum in what is now Sudan. The next year, he was posted to South Africa, where he served as a correspondent during the Boer War. He was captured by the Boers and then made a daring escape. His dramatic flight made headlines around the world and gave him the boost he needed to enter politics. He was elected as a Conservative member of Britain's House of Commons in 1900. With one brief interruption, he would remain a member until 1964.

In 1900, Britain's Conservatives were solidly in power under the last titled aristocrat to hold the office of prime minister, Robert Gascoyne-Cecil, the third Marquess of Salisbury. But under the influence of Joseph Chamberlain, father of Neville, the Conservatives were starting to favor the imposition of tariffs. Churchill strongly supported Britain's traditional policy of free trade. He also detected a coming shift in political fortunes. So he crossed the floor to join the Liberal Party in 1904, in time for the Liberals' landslide victory in the elections of early 1906. Thereafter, Churchill's rise was rapid. He became a cabinet minister at the age of thirty-three, holding in quick succession the portfolios of secretary of the Board of Trade, home secretary, and first lord of the Admiralty. He was at the Admiralty when war broke out in 1914, and this led to his first career disaster. When the Ottoman Empire entered the war on Germany's side, Churchill formulated a daring plan to seize the Dardanelles strait as a first step to knocking Turkey and then Germany out of the war. This was a typically Churchillian scheme to use Britain's great resources of sea power to win with mobility and imagination. But the operation proved a catastrophic failure, and Churchill had to take the blame. He was dismissed from the Admiralty and did a spell as a battalion commander on the Western Front, though he managed to work his way back into public life with a successful stint as minister of munitions in the last two years of the war.

In the 1920s, as the rising Labour Party eclipsed the Liberals on Britain's center-left, Churchill drew the consequences and found his way back to the Conservative Party. He served five years as chancellor of the exchequer under Prime Minister Stanley Baldwin. The most important event of his time at the Treasury was his 1925 decision to put the British pound back on the gold standard—symbolizing a return to the free-market global capitalism that the Great War had upended. But postwar Britain was unable to live with the old system. Even worse, Churchill returned the pound to gold at its 1914 value in U.S. dollars, $4.86, which meant the pound was seriously overvalued. It took a few years for the disastrous consequences of this policy for export competitiveness and employment to become apparent, by which time the Great Depression had arrived.

The Conservatives lost the election of 1929 and were replaced by a Labour government under Ramsay MacDonald. British parties typically maintain a "shadow cabinet" when they are in opposition, and so Churchill became the "shadow" chancellor of the exchequer. Then the issue of Indian autonomy arose. While the British political mainstream agreed on granting India at least some form of self-rule, Churchill exiled himself to the extreme right with his full-throated defense of British control of the subcontinent, resigning from the shadow cabinet. When the Conservatives returned to power in the National Government of 1931, Churchill took his place on the opposition benches while Neville Chamberlain became chancellor of the exchequer.

For almost all of the 1930s, Churchill would remain a backbencher, well known but not always respected and certainly not always listened to by other parliamentarians. Even a year before Hitler came to power, Churchill had warned the House of Commons of the danger of Germany's rising military clout, and from 1933 he sensed, as did few others, the threat that Hitler posed. But most British politicians and voters considered his warnings only more of his far-right madness, much like his dismissal of Mahatma Gandhi as a "seditious Middle Temple barrister." In the mid-1930s, Stanley Baldwin expressed what had become a common view of Churchill: When Churchill was born, said Baldwin, "fairies swooped down on his cradle" bringing great gifts—"imagination, eloquence, industry, ability." But "then came a fairy who said, 'No one person has a right to so many gifts,' picked him up and gave him such a shake and twist that with all these gifts he was denied judgment and wisdom. And that is why while we delight to listen to him in this House, we do not take his advice."

Still, with his acute political instincts, Baldwin understood something else important about Churchill. "If there is going to be war—and no one can say that there is not—," Baldwin wrote late in 1935, explaining why he didn't want Churchill in his cabinet, "we must keep him fresh to be our war prime minister."

It would take Churchill a very long time to return to the political position he had held in the late 1920s. Most, probably including himself, thought he never would.

ONE IRONY OF history is that in the first years of the twentieth century, Winston Churchill and Neville Chamberlain took very different positions on armaments and the German threat than they would later. When, in 1909, Britain was involved in a battleship-building arms race with the Kaiser's Germany, Churchill had been one of the "economists" in the British cabinet—meaning one who favored the least amount of money being spent on Dreadnought battleships. As he remembered later, "The Admiralty had demanded six ships; the economists offered four; and we finally compromised on eight." Neville Chamberlain was not yet in formal politics, but he was active in the Navy League and the National Service League, groups that lobbied for increased armaments. He worried that the Liberal government of Prime Minister H. H. Asquith would not do enough to maintain British naval strength and would give in to "the fanatics and demagogues who clamor for economy at any price." The "real enemy is Germany," Chamberlain insisted. "Treaties are not to be depended on for keeping the peace." He feared that "our military weakness is a temptation to our enemies."

What a difference three decades made. By the 1930s, Neville Chamberlain's views on defense, economy, and national security had changed. He and Churchill had traded places. But they were also involved in trying to solve the same problem. How should democratic, peaceful Britain respond to the Nazi menace? For both men, finding an answer would take time, and the kind of answers they came up with would change as they responded to Hitler—and to each other.

At the heart of Chamberlain's thinking about national security was a cool-eyed, unemotional assessment of Britain's global position—an outlook that today we call foreign policy realism. He knew that Britain was a nation of forty-seven million people struggling to manage a global empire from an economic base weakened by obsolescence, foreign competition, and the Great Depression, and facing three critical national security challenges: Japan in the Far East, Italy in the Mediterranean, and Germany at home. The armed forces' chiefs of staff warned the cabinet in 1937 that "we could not hope to confront satisfactorily Germany, Italy and Japan simultaneously," and so it was vitally necessary to "reduce the number of our potential enemies." Above all, if the German threat could be reduced, the others would probably follow, as neither Italy nor Japan would be likely to attack the British Empire without German aid. Having served as chancellor of the exchequer for six years, Chamberlain thought very carefully about the essential strategic goal of preserving the health of the British economy. He believed that British leaders ought to work out their defense priorities with the economic mechanism in mind.

This was where the policy of "appeasement" came in. There was nothing new about it. Since at least the middle of the nineteenth century, British leaders had been trying to come to terms with adversaries they could not afford to fight. Before the First World War, the British had neutralized threats from France and Russia by making deals over control of colonial territory. This, as historian Susan Pedersen writes, "is how empires think." In 1937 and early 1938, Chamberlain had ambitious plans for trying the same approach with Nazi Germany. But this illustrates a crucial point about Chamberlain: he had not grasped how Hitler was different from Czar Nicholas or even Kaiser Wilhelm. Hitler's Germany posed an existential threat to the whole global order, not a marginal threat to this or that colony. It was an open question whether British traditions of appeasement would work on a menace of this scale.

Of course, pursuing appeasement meant that British leaders could not afford to be morally choosy about the regimes they dealt with. Characteristically, Chamberlain thought that those who believed otherwise needed to grow up and face reality. "In the absence of any powerful ally," he said, "and until our armaments are completed, we must adjust our foreign policy to our circumstances, and even bear with patience and good humor actions which we should like to treat in a very different fashion." He was well aware of how he differed with Churchill on these points. "If we were now to follow Winston's advice and sacrifice our commerce to the manufacture of arms," he thought, "we should inflict a certain injury upon our trade from which it would take generations to recover, we should destroy the confidence which now happily exists and we should cripple our revenue."

But he was optimistic. "By careful diplomacy," he wrote to his sister Hilda, "I believe we can stave [war] off, perhaps indefinitely." When he became prime minister, this is exactly what he set out to do.

CHAMBERLAIN'S DESIRE FOR "careful diplomacy" meant reaching out to Germany and trying to resolve all the problems and conflicts in one big and final settlement. Chamberlain decided that the main instrument of his policy would be one of his most respected cabinet ministers, Edward Wood, the third Viscount and later the first Earl of Halifax.

Halifax was the consummate aristocratic Englishman. It is said that when his sons married, he asked his daughters-in-law to address him as "Lord Halifax." He stood six feet five inches in height and was cool and aloof in demeanor, though always correct, courteous, and unflappable. He spent his life as a politician and diplomat, but his passions were hunting, the Church of England, and his estate at Garrowby, in East Yorkshire. Halifax deeply loved rural England with its social hierarchy, its ordered liberty, and its—as a viscount would see it—freedom from vulgarity. He dedicated his career to the defense of it all.

Born in 1881, Halifax had been elected to the House of Commons in 1910 and served with distinction on the Western Front in the First World War. In 1925, he was named viceroy of India, an office he held until 1931. It was a sign of an approach he would take later that he favored conciliation of Mahatma Gandhi and the Indian independence movement. Halifax saw that the coming of Indian self-government was inevitable, and he thought the British should steer India to this end in such a way that the huge country remained in the British Commonwealth. To Halifax this was simple realism.

Shortly before leaving India, Halifax held a series of meetings with Gandhi. He later told his father, "It was rather like talking to someone who had stepped off another planet on to this for a short visit of a fortnight and whose whole mental outlook was quite other to that which was regulating most of the affairs on the planet to which he had descended." After a slow start, the two men made progress and developed mutual respect. Partly this was because each man recognized the strength of the other's religious faith. The fruit of their discussions was the Gandhi-Irwin Pact of March 1931, in which Gandhi agreed to curb civil disobedience and participate in round-table talks on constitutional reform. It was the negotiations leading up to this agreement that Churchill had so vehemently opposed, driving himself into the political wilderness. When Halifax and Gandhi held their first meeting in February 1931, Churchill vented his chagrin that a "half naked fakir" should stride "up the steps of the Vice-regal palace" to "parley on equal terms with the representative of the King-Emperor."

On his return to London, Halifax held a series of cabinet positions, including lord privy seal and lord president of the council—positions alike in that they do not come with departmental responsibilities, leaving the cabinet member free to take on issues that he or she prefers, or that the prime minister directs. Halifax chose to devote himself to foreign affairs.

Halifax applied several lessons from his experiences with Gandhi to relations with Germany. He had concluded that personal contact was the best way to solve problems. Successful negotiations, he thought, resulted from being careful to respect the other party's dignity and not being too thin-skinned oneself. This attitude was even more important if the trend of history seemed to be working for the other side, as Halifax thought was the case in India. Halifax agreed when one British official suggested that there was "a certain similarity" between Hitler and Gandhi. Did each man not have "the same strong inferiority complex, the same idealism, the same belief in the divine mission to lead his people and the same difficulty with unruly lieutenants"? The Conservative politician Rab Butler, who also saw strong similarities between the Indian and German situations, wrote in 1935 that Halifax was "interested in the human side of getting people together and would be very interested in getting together with Hitler and squaring him."

Hermann Göring, who in addition to his many roles in the Nazi hierarchy was a keen huntsman, planned for Germany to host an international hunting exhibition in Berlin in November 1937. When Britain's new ambassador, Sir Nevile Henderson, urged British participation in the exhibition, Chamberlain remembered Halifax's desire to "square" Hitler. Halifax was master of the Middleton Hounds, and thus a logical visitor to an international hunting exhibition. The British government presented Halifax's visit as a purely private matter. But it was Göring who formally invited Halifax to Germany, and Chamberlain and his foreign secretary, Anthony Eden, approved the visit. While on this private mission, Halifax would just happen to meet all the leaders of the Third Reich.

Halifax duly arrived in Berlin on Thursday, November 18, less than two weeks after the Hossbach Conference, where he met with Foreign Minister von Neurath and toured the hunting exhibition. Berliners, known for their wit and skill with nicknames, immediately deemed the visitor Lord *Halalifax*—"Halali!" being the German equivalent of the hunter's cry "tallyho!" Hitler was at the Berghof and could not be bothered to return to Berlin, so he asked that Halifax visit him at his mountain retreat. He provided a comfortable train for the journey.

The train arrived at Berchtesgaden station at 9 a.m. on Friday, November 19, and was met by several sleek Mercedes to drive the visitors up the mountain to Hitler's chalet. There was snow on the ground, but a path had been cleared up the steep steps to the house. At this moment, disaster almost upended whatever diplomatic good the mission might achieve. "As I looked out of the car window, on eye level," Halifax wrote later, "I saw in the middle of this swept path a pair of black-trousered legs, finishing up in silk socks and pumps. I assumed this was a footman who had come down to help me out of the car." The aristocratic Halifax was, in fact, about to hand his coat to this "footman" when Neurath alertly recognized the looming calamity. He whispered urgently in Halifax's ear: "Der Führer! Der Führer!" Halifax then realized that "higher up, the trousers passed into a khaki tunic with swastika armlet." As on most occasions in the late 1930s, Hitler was wearing a brown Nazi uniform jacket, its only decoration the swastika armband and the Iron Cross he had won on the Western Front in the First World War. Hitler "greeted me politely," Halifax recalled, "and led me up to the house and to his study, which was very overheated, but with a magnificent mountain view from immense windows."

After this awkward start, perhaps it was not surprising that Halifax's conversation with Hitler did not go smoothly. Not everyone in Britain had been happy that it was taking place at all. "I must candidly confess that I was personally anxious about Lord Halifax's visit to Germany,"

Winston Churchill told the House of Commons a few weeks later. He thought the British were trying too hard to win Germany's favor and making themselves seem too weak. Many countries were looking to Britain "to keep the flag flying in the interests of peace, freedom, democracy and parliamentary government." If these countries thought that Britain was going to abandon them and make a deal in its own interests, "I think that a knell of despair would resound through many parts of Europe." This was why, said Churchill, "Lord Halifax's journey caused widespread commotion."

"I HAVE BROUGHT no new proposals from London" was Halifax's way of opening his conversation with Hitler. He explained that he had come merely to "ascertain the German Government's views on the existing political situation, and to see what possibilities of a solution there may be." To Hitler this sounded like the same old thing he always heard from British leaders. As Hitler's interpreter Paul Schmidt translated Halifax's words, he saw Hitler begin to frown. He thought the Führer might "sulk and refuse to speak," but then he remembered that "Hitler found it hard to remain silent for long."

Schmidt was right. Hitler began by taking up a favorite complaint: the "irresponsible criticisms" of Germany dished up by the British press. It was too difficult to do business with a democracy, Hitler griped: "All his offers—disarmament, political—had been wrecked" on the rocks of "parliament and press." Halifax's response was blunt, as he explained later: "I replied by saying that if he really thought this, it was plain that I had wasted my time and, what was more important, made him waste his, by asking to see him, for I hoped Great Britain would never be the least likely to change her pattern of life or system of government." Halifax went a step further, and lectured Hitler about diplomatic conduct. Hitler's "disarmament and other offers" had not failed because of false reports in the press, but because "for good reasons or bad other nations did not feel satisfied as to the measures of security that they in fact afforded." Hitler had "ignored many treaty obligations, and it was not at all surprising that people remembered it when he offered new undertakings."

Hitler seemed taken aback for a moment, and muttered that his criticisms had been of France, not Britain. But the bad mood continued. Hitler talked about Germany's desire to regain the colonies it had lost at the end of the First World War, and he asked Halifax "what other problems there were between us." Halifax replied that people in Britain would like to know what Hitler thought about the League of Nations and disarmament. Then Halifax turned to questions of borders in central Europe.

"There were, no doubt, other questions arising out of the Versailles settlement," Halifax told Hitler, "which were capable of causing trouble if they were unwisely handled: Danzig, Austria, Czechoslovakia." What Halifax meant was that he understood that in all these places—the new states carved out of the Austro-Hungarian Empire, and the city of Danzig, formerly part of German West Prussia, now under the protection of the League of Nations—there lived millions of German-speaking people whom Hitler wanted to unite into a greater German Reich. "On all these matters," Halifax continued, "we were not necessarily concerned to stand for the status quo as of today, but we were very much concerned to secure the avoidance of such treatment of them as would be likely to cause trouble." This, of course, was careful diplomatic language: "trouble" here meant "war." "If reasonable settlements could be reached with the free assent of those primarily concerned," said Halifax, "we certainly had no desire to block them."

This was the core of the message Chamberlain had sent Halifax to deliver: the British government wanted to reach a general settlement in Europe that would prevent another major war. To get to this settlement the British were willing to see significant changes to the political map drawn up at the Paris Peace Conference in 1919. Of course, no one in the British government could have known anything about the "testament" Hitler had delivered at the Hossbach Conference, or the plans he had laid out for annexing Austria and Czechoslovakia. But here was Lord Halifax offering Hitler a path to achieve exactly this goal.

Hitler did not hear the message the way Halifax had meant it. Halifax saw himself applying a traditional British approach, which he had also used with Gandhi. The desire to seek conciliation was based on self-confident strength and a sense of justice, not on decadence and weakness. But, as Ambassador Henderson reflected, Hitler thought the timid British had just confessed to him their abject willingness to countenance German expansion in eastern Europe. This was certainly a message he was glad to hear. But it did not visibly improve his mood.

Halifax's thoughts on meeting Hitler closely resembled his comments about Gandhi of a few years before. "One had the feeling all the time," he recorded in his diary, "that we had a totally different sense of values and were speaking in a different language." Hitler told Halifax that he had risen to power "only after a hard struggle with present-day realities." By contrast, "the British Government was still living comfortably in a world of its own making, a fairy-land of strange, if respectable illusions . . . 'collective security,' 'general settlement,' 'disarmament,' 'non-aggression pacts.'"

The meeting adjourned for a lunch that was even more awkward than the conversation preceding it. Hitler, who ate no meat and neither smoked nor drank, dined on vegetable soup, mixed vegetables, and a plate of walnuts and chocolate. The guests were given "a rather indifferent meat lunch," recalled Ivone Kirkpatrick, the first secretary at the embassy in Berlin, who had accompanied Halifax to Berchtesgaden. They were served by Hitler's butler and three tall SS men in white jackets. Halifax spoke no German, but Kirkpatrick spoke German fluently and tried gamely to get a conversation going, starting with that English standby, the weather. But Hitler was not English, and he only snapped, "The weather. The weather forecasters are idiots; when they say it is going to be fine it always rains and when they foretell bad weather, it's fine." Kirkpatrick moved on to flying, to which Hitler responded, "Only a fool will fly if he can go by train or road." Comments on the hunting exhibition fared no better. To the master of the Middleton Hounds, Hitler complained, "I can't see what there is in shooting; you go out armed with a highly perfected modern weapon and without risk to yourself kill a defenseless animal." Hitler behaved throughout, Kirkpatrick thought, like a "spoilt, sulky child."

Matters did not improve when the party moved downstairs to the sitting room for coffee. This room was equipped with an enormous window that could be raised and lowered by a hand crank, affording a spectacular mountain view. There was also a movie projector and a screen, concealed during the day behind two tapestries. Hitler loved movies, and would often watch two in an evening, including American and British films—at Christmas that year he would be thrilled when Propaganda Minister Joseph Goebbels gave him a gift of eighteen Mickey Mouse cartoons. On this day, Hitler waxed enthusiastic about the 1935 film *The Lives of a Bengal Lancer*. Starring Gary Cooper, the film depicts stoic and skillful British soldiers defending the Indian northwest frontier against Muslim insurgents.

It immediately became clear that the Führer had drawn very different lessons from the British experience in India than had Lord Halifax. Hitler told Halifax he could not understand why the British "tolerated disorder" or wasted time trying to negotiate with Gandhi and the leaders of the Indian National Congress movement. Hitler thought there was a simpler way to handle matters. "Shoot Gandhi," he said, "and if that does not suffice to reduce them to submission, shoot a dozen leading members of Congress; and if that does not suffice, shoot 200 and so on until order is established. You will see how quickly they will collapse as soon as you make it clear that you mean business." Kirkpatrick recalled that as Hitler delivered this tirade, "Lord Halifax gazed at [him] with a mixture of astonishment, repugnance and compassion." Halifax thought it would only have been a waste of time to try to argue with the Führer.

Hitler was a bit more civil when, around 4 p.m., he saw the party off on its way back to Berchtesgaden, Munich, and Berlin. Halifax, Schmidt remembered, "gave no sign of emotion or disappointment," remaining "the whole time the typical, quiet, phlegmatic Englishman, and said good-bye to Hitler apparently without annoyance." Neurath, who must have been turning over in his mind the alarmingly parallel themes of the Hossbach Conference and this one, was painfully aware of how Hitler had appeared to his British visitors. On the train back to Berlin, he tried to put the best face on things. It was a pity, he told the British, that "the Führer had been tired and out of sorts," but he insisted the visit had been useful. It was at least a good thing to "bring Hitler in contact with the outside world." Kirkpatrick thought that Hitler had already made his decisions about what he wanted to do and resented having to waste his time talking to a peacemaker like Halifax.

And yet the report that Halifax delivered to the British cabinet was decidedly optimistic. On his last two days in Berlin he met with many leading Nazi officials, including Blomberg, Göring, and Goebbels. Schmidt suspected that either Hitler or Neurath had primed these officials to sound more conciliatory, and that the positive impression that Halifax took home was really the product of his meeting with his fellow huntsman Göring. In any case, when the British cabinet met on November 24, Halifax told his colleagues that he had encountered "friendliness and a desire for good relations . . . Of Czechoslovakia [Hitler] had said 'she need only to treat the Germans living within her borders well and they would be entirely happy' . . . Herr Hitler had strongly criticized widespread talk of an imminent catastrophe and did not consider that the world was in a dangerous state." Although Halifax expected the Germans to continue to press their claims in central Europe with a "beaver-like persistence," he entertained the hope that they had "no policy of immediate adventure." He thought it might be possible to reach agreement with Germany on the limitation of bomber aircraft and the return of Germany's overseas colonies, although the British could only accept the latter if it were "in return for a general settlement"—in other words, as bait to lure the Germans into other projects, like disarmament and a return to the League of Nations. Nonetheless, these were initiatives that the Chamberlain government would soon eagerly take up.

But it was clear enough how the Germans had taken Halifax's message. On November 22, as Halifax was returning to Britain, Neurath reported to the German embassies in Italy, Britain, France, and the United States that Hitler "did not spare his visitor some bitter truths about British and French policy." Nonetheless, Halifax had made clear that "certain changes in the European system could probably not be avoided in the long run." The places where changes could occur included "Danzig, Austria, and Czechoslovakia." Halifax, Neurath claimed, had also referred to Germany as "the bulwark of the West against Bolshevism."

Hitler soon after saw Joseph Goebbels at a performance of *Die Fledermaus* at the Gärtnerplatz Theater in Munich. Halifax was as "cold as ice," Hitler reported, and as "tough as leather." Their conversation had "yielded little" despite lasting four hours. Hitler's version of the talk was that Halifax had tried to "lure" the Führer into "delaying" discussion of the colonial question in return for a "free hand in central Europe." Hitler had replied that everything in central Europe was fine. Then Halifax had tried to divide Germany from Italy, which had also failed. In short, the conversation had come to nothing. Goebbels thought that this was a "pity," but "the time [for better relations with Britain] is not yet ripe."

Hitler was certainly not as indifferent to gains in central Europe as he pretended. German war plans changed dramatically after the Hossbach Conference and the meeting with Halifax. Back in 1935, the army's main deployment plan, "Case Red," had been a scheme for defense against a French attack. In mid-1937, planners had added another element: "Case Green," which called for a preemptive strike on France's ally Czechoslovakia, but only in the event of a war with France. The orientation remained defensive and still gave the decisive importance to Case Red. But in December 1937, the chief of the armed forces' operations staff, General Alfred Jodl, gave Case Green a decisive new twist. Now the attack on Czechoslovakia took precedence over defense against France. The language of the plan was clear. "When Germany has achieved complete preparedness for war in all spheres, then the military conditions will have been created for carrying out an offensive war against Czechoslovakia, so that the solution of the German problem of living space can be carried to a victorious conclusion even if one or another of the Great Powers intervene against us." The plan revealed the lesson Hitler and his soldiers had drawn from Halifax's visit. Case Green might even be launched before Germany was fully ready for war if "a situation [arose] which, owing to Britain's aversion to a general European War, [and] through her lack of interest in the Central European problem" created "the probability that Germany will face no other opponent than Russia on Czechoslovakia's side."

WHEN THE NAZI menace first appeared on the horizon of British foreign policy makers, Winston Churchill's response was shaped by two important elements of this thinking. The first was his deep understanding of the essence of modern total war. The second was his uncanny prescience in seeing it coming.

Already in 1901, as a freshman member of Parliament, he made a highly perceptive and prophetic point about the nature of modern war: "In former days, when wars arose . . . from the policy of a Minister or the passion of a King, when they were fought by small regular armies of professional soldiers . . . it was possible to limit the liabilities of the combatants." But now, "when mighty populations are impelled on each other . . . a European war can only end in the ruin of the vanquished and the scarcely less fatal commercial dislocation and exhaustion of the conquerors." Democracies, he said, were more vindictive than the monarchies of old. "The wars of peoples," said Churchill, "will be more terrible than those of kings." Few people in 1901 sensed so acutely the atrocities that would come with modern mass warfare.

In 1911, when he was first lord of the Admiralty, Churchill penned a remarkable memorandum forecasting the course of a future European war. Britain and France, he foresaw, allied with Russia, would face the coalition of Germany and the Austro-Hungarian Empire. To deal with the dilemma of a war on two fronts, the Germans would begin by attacking France through Belgium. With a large and well-trained army, the Germans would advance quickly and push the French back close to Paris. But the arrival of British reinforcements would contribute to a decisive battle that, on about the fortieth day, would halt the German advance. In the event, in August 1914 the Germans invaded France through Belgium and advanced rapidly until, between the thirty-seventh and forty-first days of French mobilization, British and French forces stopped the Germans at the Battle of the Marne, fought in part only a few dozen miles from Paris. The result was years of stalemate—and the kind of slaughter and economic ruin Churchill had foreseen in 1901.

Churchill's prescience could extend to technology as well. In 1931, probably due to his friendship with the physicist Frederick Lindemann, he foresaw the application of nuclear energy both for peace and war. He also anticipated that "wireless telephones and television" would soon "enable their owner to connect up with any room similarly installed, and hear and take part in the conversation as well as if he put his head in through the window." There would "be no more object in living in the same city with one's neighbor than there is to-day in living with him in the same house."

The second strand of Churchill's thinking came from his awareness of the scale of crisis facing the world's democracies in the 1930s. "The grand and victorious summits" won in the First World War had "largely been lost in the years which followed the peace," he wrote in 1930. "We see our race doubtful of its mission and no longer confident about its principles . . . drifting to and fro with the tides and currents of a deeply-disturbed ocean. The compass has been damaged. The charts are out of date."

Churchill always claimed to be a passionate democrat, but his commitment seemed less than enthusiastic as he watched new democracies fail across Europe, while democracy seemed unable to cope with modern challenges even in places like Britain and France.

Churchill had been mildly worried about the effects of the British electoral reform of 1918, the Representation of the People Act, which swept away the last tax qualifications for men and enfranchised women over the age of thirty. Ten years later, women won the vote on equal terms to men. The eventual result of these changes was a tripling of the electorate. Churchill wrote that "this enormous electorate composed of so many of the poorest people in the country" was an "uncertain element," and his mood only grew darker with the times. In 1930, he complained that parliamentary government "seems to lose much of its authority when based upon universal suffrage." And after the onset of the 1931 financial crisis, and his own banishment to the political wilderness, his mood grew darker still. "Democracy," he wrote bluntly at the end of the year, "as a guide or motive to progress has long been known to be incompetent." Democratic governments "drift along the line of least resistance, taking short views, paying their way with sops and doles and smoothing their path with pleasant-sounding platitudes."

It wasn't just that democracies made bad economic policy. In Churchill's view, there were serious national security implications to the new politics as well. Even before the Nazi takeover of power in Germany, he worried that "democracy has shown itself careless about those very institutions by which its own political status has been achieved." Democracies were all too ready "to yield up the tangible rights hard won in rugged centuries to party organizations, to leagues and societies, to military chiefs or to dictatorships in various forms."

Like many of his countrymen, Churchill thought that the British model of democracy was not a successful export. "The British oak," he wrote in 1931, "it appears, will not grow in Latin or Slavonic soil." He was willing to praise Benito Mussolini's Italian Fascist regime—"a service to the whole world," he said in 1927—and to say that Spain's "best years" had come under the dictatorship of Miguel Primo de Rivera.

When the Nazis came to power in Germany, Churchill worried that the obviously greater competence of a dictatorship would have a demoralizing effect on Europe's remaining democracies. "We have to consider," he told the House of Commons, "whether the Parliamentary Governments of Western Europe . . . are going to be able to afford to their subjects the same measure of physical security, to say nothing of national satisfaction, as is being afforded to the people of Germany by the dictatorship which has been established there."

Churchill's approach to Indian self-government and the Nazi menace, as different as these issues seem to us today, really sprang from the same source. He worried primarily about maintaining the power of the British empire, and he grasped the threats to that power more effectively than did most democratic politicians because he so well understood the dark essence of twentieth-century war and politics. This was the difference between Churchill and Chamberlain. Chamberlain was the cool realist who thought that economic rationality made war unthinkable. Churchill's vision was more pessimistic, more tragic, and more comfortable with violence. In fact, in the early 1930s he could sound remarkably like Hitler.

In a 1932 letter to the Marquess of Linlithgow, a future viceroy of India, Churchill grumbled that "the mild and vague Liberalism of the early years of the twentieth century" had "already been superseded by a violent reaction against Parliamentary and electioneering procedure and by the establishment of dictatorships real or veiled in almost every country." Furthermore, Churchill thought that "the loss of our external connections" and "the shrinkage in foreign trade and shipping" had brought "the surplus population of Britain within measurable distance of utter ruin." He thought that "We are entering a period when the struggle for self-preservation is going to present itself with great intenseness to thickly populated industrial countries." It was therefore "unsound reasoning" to suggest that Britain alone should give up "control over a great dependency like India," when other imperial powers such as the Netherlands or France, to say nothing of Japan and Italy, would never follow suit. "You and your friends," Churchill fumed—Linlithgow was a supporter of concessions to the Indian independence movement— "go on mouthing the bland platitudes of an easy safe triumphant age which has passed away . . . In my view England is now beginning a new period of struggle and fighting for its life," in which the retention of India would be "the crux."

Here, like Hitler, Churchill thought that national security depended on empire and autarky, not on successful integration into a capitalist world economy. This was the core of his difference with the more conventional and pragmatic Chamberlain. Language like this shows why some politicians on the British left feared that Churchill might become the head of a British fascist government. Such worries proved to be overwrought. But sometimes Churchill's own public utterances did not burnish his antifascist credentials. In the mid-1930s, he did not speak out against aggression by Japan, Italy, or the Spanish insurgents the way he did against Germany. He had, in other words, not yet moved from a purely nationalist vision to a principled and general view of the world's conflicts. When Hitler was a rising force in German politics but not yet in power, Churchill had taken the attitude that "I admire men who stand up for their country in defeat, even though I am on the other side." As he saw it, Hitler "had a perfect right to be a patriotic German if he chose." As late as November 1938, Churchill could say in a speech, "I have always said that if Great Britain were defeated in war I hoped we should find a Hitler to lead us back to our rightful position among the nations."

Which outlook—Churchill's or Chamberlain's—seemed more likely to produce the better policy for a democracy facing a threat like Hitler's Germany? Churchill's thinking in particular would change as the years went by, as he confronted the full horror of Hitler's regime and his belief in democracy rebounded. Chamberlain, on the other hand, would gradually find his faith in pragmatic accommodation eroding. In the meantime, there was another important world leader wrestling with the same problems.

By the late 1930s, editorial cartoonists had begun to draw Franklin Delano Roosevelt, the thirty-second president of the United States, as a sphinx, the mythological creature with a human head and a lion's body, famous for its opaque questions.

Really the Oracle of Delphi would have been a more accurate classical analogy. The president commonly gave vague answers or no answers at all to precise questions, rather than posing the questions himself in the riddling manner of the sphinx. But the sphinx image stuck. Roosevelt's thoughts and intentions on all issues, large and small, were usually inscrutable even to the people closest to him. Partly this was a matter of personality, the self-contained nature of an only child perhaps. But it was also about political calculation. There were many situations in which delay could enable him to gather more information before he had to commit himself to one course of action or another. It was also possible that difficult problems would go away on their own. Waiting on events, and holding his cards close while he waited, allowed the president to stay in control.

This had long been his manner, on issues large and small. The Louisiana governor (and demagogue) Huey Long once complained that whenever he spoke to Roosevelt, "He says 'Fine! Fine! Fine!'" But then Joe Robinson, the Senate majority leader and Long's nemesis, would see Roosevelt the next day, and the president would say, "Fine! Fine! Fine!" "Maybe," Long concluded, "he says 'Fine!' to everybody." Roosevelt hated written records of things he had said or orders he had given, and many of his most important decisions were not formally recorded. As president, he forbade the publication of the minutes of Big Four meetings from the 1919 Paris Peace Conference—in which, of course, he had not been involved—on the grounds that such records should never have been created at all.

Nor was it just on questions of politics that Roosevelt stayed cool and unreadable. In February 1933, a month before his inauguration, he arrived in Miami after an eleven-day cruise. There he gave a short speech to a crowd at Bayfront Park. As he was leaving, Chicago mayor Anton J. Cermak (who was also in town) stepped up to Roosevelt's car to talk to the president-elect. At this moment a would-be assassin fired and hit Cermak by mistake. Roosevelt's bodyguards wanted to speed him away, but Roosevelt made them stop and place Cermak carefully on the backseat next to him. "Tony, keep quiet—don't move. It won't hurt if you keep quiet," he told the mortally wounded mayor. After taking Cermak to the hospital, Roosevelt returned to his yacht. Although he had narrowly escaped death and comforted a dying man, that evening the president-elect seemed unfazed. His advisor Raymond Moley remembered that Roosevelt showed "not so much as the twitching of a muscle, the mopping of a brow." He was entirely his usual self, "easy, confident, poised, to all appearances unmoved."

One thing Roosevelt would never do was the thing that Winston Churchill did repeatedly: risk a devastating loss of popularity and political strength from defending a deeply held principle. On one occasion, Roosevelt warned a group of rebellious students that he could solve the nation's problems only "as fast as the people of the country as a whole will let us." Another time, he responded to arguments about racial integration from the civil rights and labor leader A. Philip Randolph with the remark "Fine, you've convinced me, now make me do it"—meaning that he would respond only to organized public pressure. Conviction was not enough. For this reason, too—along with his sphinxlike nature— there was always mystery and always suspense about what the president would do on all issues, from the economy to the Supreme Court to the Nazi menace.

FRANKLIN ROOSEVELT CAME into office knowing that democracy needed saving, both at home and in the world. Others knew it, too. The British economist John Maynard Keynes thought that Roosevelt had "made [himself] the trustee for those in every country who seek to mend the evils of our condition by reasoned experiment within the framework of the existing social system."

Keynes was on to something when he used the word *experiment*.

Roosevelt had an acute sense of the problems he faced, but he had very little idea of how to solve them. Historians' evaluations of his policies have ranged from guarded praise of his flexible, open-minded, nondogmatic approach, to criticism of his tendency to "muddle through" and ignore problems in the hope they would go away. His biographer James MacGregor Burns is scathing on Roosevelt's first-term foreign policy: "He seemed to float almost helplessly on the flood tide of isolationism," Burns wrote, waiting for the day when "people would be educated by events." Roosevelt himself admitted in 1934, "Frankly, I do not know how to effect a permanency in American foreign policy." With his unquestionably sharp intellect, Roosevelt accurately identified all the problems America faced. But as a consummate politician, he knew that his course would have to be indirect, his moves improvised, his tactics secretive and inscrutable. The question was always: Would world events bring a change in American public opinion? And what could the president do to lead, or at least nudge, Americans toward more active engagement in world affairs? As Germany rearmed, as the Italians embarked on imperial expansion in Africa, as Japan's war in China escalated, this was the drama that played out in American politics.

The fight between those favoring international engagement and those preferring isolation was extraordinarily bitter, the bitterness later obscured only by the mood of national unity that followed the Japanese attack on Pearl Harbor in December 1941.

On the one side were those surviving supporters of the internationalism of President Woodrow Wilson, who had led America into the First World War and had brought the League of Nations into being. Such people were usually liberal. In the 1930s they were motivated by a deep hatred of fascism and a desire to see the United States use its clout to defend democracy around the world. Having served as assistant secretary of the navy in Wilson's administration, Roosevelt himself was clearly in this camp, however covertly.

On the other side were the passionate advocates of isolation and neutrality, one of whom was Senator Gerald P. Nye of North Dakota. Nye was a progressive Republican with an ingrained suspicion of big business. He had never ventured east of Chicago before being elected to the Senate and had never visited Europe. In 1934, Nye became the chair of a Senate Special Committee on Investigation of the Munitions Industry, whose members shared his deep suspicion of eastern business and finance and of Great Britain. The committee issued a final report in February 1936 that succeeded in spreading the idea that "the United States went into the World War in part to save from ruin the bankers who had strained themselves to the utmost to supply Great Britain with munitions and credits."

There is a cliché that generals usually prepare to fight the last war. It is equally true that politicians usually try to prevent the last war. The Neutrality Acts that grew out of the work of Nye's committee are a fine example of the second tendency.

The first Neutrality Act, of 1935, was passed in an international context that was growing steadily more alarming, with Hitler's announcement of the creation of the Luftwaffe and imposition of a draft for an expanded army, followed by Mussolini's invasion of Ethiopia. The act not only made it illegal for the United States to export arms to a belligerent country, but also sought to deter Americans from traveling on ships belonging to a country at war. Congress was keen, in the spirit of the Nye Committee, to keep "merchants of death" from leading America to war, and it wanted no second *Lusitania* incident—a risk of war created by American passengers on a foreign ship being drowned in an attack. Roosevelt was not happy about the limitations the law placed on presidential authority, but he signed it nonetheless and flattered isolationists by explaining that "despite what happens in continents overseas, the United States of America shall and must remain, as long ago the Father of our country prayed that it might remain—unentangled and free."

The main concession that proponents of the legislation had made to skeptics was to limit the term of the law to six months. Early in 1936, therefore, the Neutrality Act was extended with an important addition: it prohibited financial as well as material assistance to belligerent powers. If it was true, as the Nye Committee supposed, that America had entered the Great War only to protect banks that had made huge loans to Britain and France, then this possible road to war would be closed as well.

No sooner had this extension passed than the outbreak of civil war in Spain in July 1936 made Congress realize it had forgotten something.

The Neutrality Act assumed the paradigm of wars between sovereign states. Its provisions did not cover the war between the left-leaning Spanish Republic and the Nationalist insurgency led by General Francisco Franco. Nazi Germany and Fascist Italy supported Franco. The Soviet Union supported the Republic. The major democracies chose not to intervene, while trying unsuccessfully to keep other powers out as well. In January 1937, Congress convened to extend American neutrality to the Spanish Civil War. A resolution in these terms was proposed by Senator Key Pittman, the chair of the Foreign Relations Committee. "Two forms of government are fighting in Spain in what is called a 'civil war,'" Pittman explained, "but it is a fight of foreign theories of government, not involving democracy, in which the opposing forces are aided and sympathized with by great, powerful governments who espouse one cause or another." The resolution passed unanimously in the Senate and by a vote of 411–1 in the House.

In the wake of Pittman's resolution came the even more stringent Neutrality Act of 1937. It contained no sunset clause, and expressly extended the provisions on arms shipments to civil wars as well as wars between sovereign states. It prohibited the arming of American merchant ships, again in an effort to limit pretexts for bringing America into another conflict. This legislation, too, was passed with overwhelming House and Senate majorities. But it did contain one significant loophole, known as "cash and carry." If a belligerent power sent its own ships to a U.S. port and paid cash, it could take away American manufactured weapons. This provision was the necessary bridge between two congressional constituencies whose support was crucial: those who wanted to protect the United States from "foreign entanglements" and those who were concerned about international trade and aid to foreign victims of aggression. Everyone understood that in the event of renewed war in Europe, British sea power would ensure Britain's ability to make use of cash and carry, just as it would freeze the Germans out.

Roosevelt signed this Neutrality Act on May 1. By late July, a full-scale war between Japan and China had begun, and by the end of the year, Japan had gained control of the whole Chinese coast, and the cities of Beijing, Shanghai, and Nanjing—in a campaign marked by horrific atrocities against Chinese civilians. But then the Japanese advance bogged down. The Chinese regime under General Chiang Kai-shek refused to surrender or to make concessions. The Japanese sought an exit and kept hoping just one more victory would compel a Chinese surrender. For Japan the war became what we now call a quagmire.

Roosevelt came under increasing pressure to invoke the Neutrality Act with respect to the war in Asia. But he knew that this would only benefit Japan, the country better prepared economically for modern war. The Neutrality Act had been premised on the world of the Versailles settlement, a world in which most countries were democracies, and those democracies would naturally band together to suppress any aggression by a rogue state. If there was to be war, it would be decently declared before there was any violence. By 1937, that world was gone. Democracy was failing everywhere, the aggression of dictatorships made every war an ideological one, collective security had proven to be an illusion, and wars began with surprise attacks, not gentlemanly declarations brought by ambassadors in morning coats. The Neutrality Act was too abstract and detached to fit this world. Roosevelt knew it. But paradoxically in 1937, he felt the limits on his power more strongly than ever before, despite his landslide reelection in 1936. The year 1937 was a terrible one for Roosevelt. He failed completely in an effort to "pack" a Supreme Court that kept striking down New Deal legislation. Even many Democrats thought that his plan to add justices to the Court amounted to overreaching. And then, after four years of slow and painful growth, the economy turned down again in the "Roosevelt recession"—like the court-packing fiasco, a partially self-inflicted wound. By the autumn of 1937, it was a weakened president who faced a dramatically more dangerous world.

IT WAS IN this context that, on October 5, 1937—as competition over scarce steel was crippling Hitler's rearmament drive and setting the scene for the Hossbach Conference, Neville Chamberlain was pondering how to deal with Hitler's regime, Stalin's purges and shootings were moving to their climax, and the Japanese were taking hold of China's coast—Roosevelt made his most important intervention yet in foreign affairs. He was in Chicago to speak at the dedication of the new Outer

Drive Bridge, funded by the Public Works Administration. A crowd numbering in the hundreds of thousands came to see the president.

Roosevelt told his audience that "because the people of the United States (under modern conditions) must, for the sake of their own future, give thought to the rest of the world," he had chosen "this great inland city" to talk about an important subject. He conveniently omitted the real reason: he had chosen Chicago precisely because it was an isolationist stronghold.

The high hopes of the years just after the First World War, Roosevelt explained, had given way to an age of war, civil war, and terror. When such things happened, Americans should not imagine that "this Western Hemisphere will not be attacked and that it will continue tranquilly and peacefully to carry on the ethics and the arts of civilization." The only alternative was for "peace-loving nations" to make a "concerted effort to uphold laws and principles on which alone peace can rest secure."

"It seems to be unfortunately true," Roosevelt concluded, "that the epidemic of world lawlessness is spreading. And mark this well: when an epidemic of physical disease starts to spread, the community approves and joins in a quarantine of the patients in order to protect the health of the community against the spread of the disease." His administration was "adopting such measures as will minimize our risk of involvement, but we cannot have complete protection in a world of disorder in which confidence and security have broken down."

This was an unusually forthright statement from a politician who had worked hard since becoming president to hide his internationalism. But reaction to the "quarantine speech" was negative where it counted. Secretary of State Cordell Hull was coldly, if quietly, disapproving. The American Federation of Labor passed a resolution against involvement in foreign wars. A poll showed that a large majority of members of Congress opposed joint action with the League of Nations to resolve the war in East Asia. Press reaction was generally favorable, but a Gallup poll taken soon after the speech found 60 percent of respondents saying that they favored *stricter* neutrality laws.

In the wake of these criticisms, Roosevelt retreated back into sphinx-like opacity. At a press conference he claimed the speech was an expansion, not a rejection, of neutrality. Challenged by the reporter Ernest

K. Lindley on the seeming contradiction between "quarantine" and the Neutrality Acts, Roosevelt responded, "There are a lot of methods in the world that have never been tried yet," but when pressed further, he admitted, "I can't give you any clue to it. You will have to invent one." He told his advisor and speechwriter Samuel Rosenman, "It's a terrible thing to look over your shoulder when you are trying to lead—and to find no one there." Soon after, he told his cabinet he was trying to arrive at a way to restrain Hitler without having to lead the United States into another war. "We don't call them economic sanctions," he said. "We call them quarantines. We want to *develop a technique* which will not lead to war . . . We want to do it in a modern way" [emphasis added]. He conveyed the same idea when he explained that what he had said about "quarantine" was "an attitude and it does not define a program; but it says we are looking for a program."

This was precisely the point. There was no blueprint for what Roosevelt was trying to do: to figure out how a democracy could contain a totalitarian aggressor in the age of total war, while remaining a democracy and preferably at peace. All these problems were new. All of them raised the gravest imaginable consequences. To be wrong could mean mass death, economic ruin, occupation by a hostile state. Chamberlain, Churchill, and Roosevelt had different ideas and motivations. But they were all trying to *develop a technique*, a modern way.

5

"He Feels It *Here*"

A disgruntled socialist parliamentarian makes a remarkable prophecy upon the birth of Queen Victoria's great-grandson in 1894: "He will be sent on a tour round the world, and probably rumors of a morganatic alliance will follow, and the end of it all will be the country will be called upon to pay the bill."

As it turns out, the prospective wife is foreign, but he meets her at home, at the Mowbray hunt in 1931. He is immediately taken by her directness, her self-assurance, her hard-edged glamour. She is on her second marriage, and he is romantically linked to another married woman. But they begin to spend a lot of time together. By 1934, they have become lovers. By 1936, he desperately wants to marry her.

But this is not just any affair, not even any routine fling among the privileged Bright Young Things, fodder for nothing more than prurient tabloid gossip. He is Edward, Prince of Wales, the heir to the British throne. She is the American social climber Wallis Simpson. His love affairs have state consequences. The British monarch is head of the Church of England. The Church does not condone divorce, and in the world of the 1930s, no voice of "respectable" opinion does, either. Most experts believe it would be unconstitutional for the king to marry a divorcée.

Many Britons believe the Crown is more essential than ever in a nation shaken by the First World War and challenged by a greatly expanded democracy, the ideological threats of fascism and communism, and the crisis of the Great Depression. The press builds up the monarch into an icon of glamour and wisdom, all the better to preserve that stabilizing role. But the trick depends on the monarch's being willing and able to go along with the image.

In January 1936, Edward's ailing father, King George V, dies, and the prince is now King Edward VIII. But he is too distracted by his infatuation with Wallis Simpson to focus on his royal duties. Sometimes his conduct is embarrassing. When he meets Soviet Foreign Minister Litvinov, he asks, "Why did you kill my cousin?" and wonders why Trotsky was deported, before going on to chatter about big-game hunting in Russia. Sometimes he is more worrying than embarrassing. He seems to approve of Hitler's militarization of the Rhineland and Benito Mussolini's conquest of Abyssinia. He is careless with official papers containing military and diplomatic secrets. He lets Wallis read them. Wallis is thought to be a Nazi sympathizer.

In August 1936, Wallis and Edward take a Mediterranean cruise in a blaze of publicity. The world now knows all about the king's affair. Only the British, or at least those British who live beyond the charmed circle of London politics, do not. The British press loyally stifles all news of what the king is getting up to. In October, the Ipswich Assizes grants Wallis the divorce decree she is seeking, which will take effect in a few months. Puzzled locals wonder why so many international reporters fill the courtroom. In November, the king tells Prime Minister Baldwin that he intends to marry Wallis, even if it means abdication.

In early December, the news finally breaks in Britain and opens up a political crisis. Baldwin is determined that if the king marries Wallis Simpson, then he must go. On the other side, a "King's Party" forms. It includes the transplanted Canadian newspaper publisher Lord Beaverbrook and Winston Churchill, whose wife, Clementine, calls him "the last believer in the divine right of Kings."

The frivolous and self-involved king has a knack for wreaking havoc wherever he goes. Winston Churchill now becomes one of his victims.

Churchill explains to the labor leader Walter Citrine that it is his duty to defend the king. When Citrine objects, "Irrespective of what he has done?" Churchill puts his hands on his chest and says, "He feels it here." That one sentence reveals everything about Churchill, in all areas of life and politics. It is what makes him so different from Neville Chamberlain and Chamberlain's cool, detached logic.

Baldwin wants the king's affair resolved quickly, one way or another—at the latest by Christmas. Churchill decides that the best way to serve his king is to slow things down. On December 7, he rises in the House of Commons to ask that "no irrevocable step will be taken before the House had received a full statement" from Baldwin. But then a strange thing happens. Feelings in the House have turned against the king, and Churchill is out of step. Listening to Churchill's speech, the members react with growing rage. They call "Drop it!" and "Twister!" The maverick Conservative member Leo Amery finds that Churchill is "completely staggered by the unanimous hostility of the House." And then the speaker rules Churchill out of order, since he is making a speech during question time. In rage and frustration, Churchill loses his self-control. He yells at Baldwin, "You won't be satisfied until you've broken him, will you?" And he storms out of the chamber.

The hostile reaction to Churchill's speech continues. One senior member of the House finds it is "one of the angriest manifestations I have ever heard directed against any man in the House of Commons." Even Churchill's protégé Bob Boothby writes to his mentor in exasperation, "What happened this afternoon makes me feel that it is almost impossible for those who are most devoted to you personally, to follow you blindly (as they wd like to do) in politics. Because they cannot be sure where the hell they are going to be landed next."

Boothby has touched on the critical point. The parliamentarian and diarist Harold Nicolson thinks that Churchill "has undone in five minutes the patient reconstruction work of two years." The Spectator editorializes that "the reputation which he was beginning to shake off of a wayward genius unserviceable in council has settled firmly on his shoulders again." This is the real consequence and the real damage. In 1933 and 1934, informed political circles generally dismissed Churchill's warnings about the Nazi menace as the ravings of an extremist. But as the warnings continue and

Hitler's threat to the world becomes starker, people are beginning to listen to Churchill again. Now, in an instant, he has put himself back where he started.

On December 10, the king formally abdicates. The next day, he speaks to his people in a radio broadcast. "I have found it impossible," he says, "to carry the heavy burden of responsibility and to discharge my duties as King as I would wish to do without the help and support of the woman I love."

The consequences of this royal affair will be dramatic in the long as well as the short term, and not just in Britain. Adolf Hitler's immediate response is telling. He treats his entourage to the speech he thinks Edward should have given: "You reactionaries, plutocrats and Marxists will not keep me from marrying a girl from the people!" But these words will turn out to be ironic. Soon, Germany will have its own affair in which a high official marries a "girl from the people," and its consequences, too, will be momentous.

For now, Churchill understands all too well what has happened. He sums up his own predicament, and the world's: "I greatly fear the dangers of 1937."

WHILE MILITARY MEN in Berlin held their worried, whispered meetings about the Hossbach Conference and what Hitler's new plans meant for them and their country, Hitler himself stayed at Berchtesgaden and brooded. He believed himself to be infallible, a man who walked with destiny "with the certainty of a sleepwalker," all the more as his string of unexpected political successes grew ever longer. By this time, as the historian Harold C. Deutsch wrote, "For Adolf Hitler men tended to fall more and more into two categories: unconditional adherents and opponents." In Hitler's mind, the skepticism that Werner von Blomberg, Werner von Fritsch, and Konstantin von Neurath had voiced at the Hossbach Conference amounted to nothing less than rank insubordination.

But if Hitler was brooding and wondering what to do next about his skeptical national security officials, Göring was, if anything, angrier, and hell-bent on revenge for the humiliation he had suffered at the Hossbach Conference. Blomberg himself now handed Göring the means of obtaining that revenge.

The abdication of King Edward VIII had amazed and fascinated much of the world, including the German High Command. Blomberg believed that men in important public positions had a special responsibility to lead chaste lives. Leo Geyr von Schweppenburg, the military attaché at the German embassy in London, had briefed Blomberg in detail on the king's affair. After hearing the report, Blomberg had sighed and said, "You see, Geyr, sex!" As war minister, Blomberg had directed a sharpening of the armed forces' rules governing the marriage of officers. Ironically, his fate would soon come to resemble the British king's.

Blomberg had been a widower since 1929. Eight years later, at age fifty-nine, he was still a handsome and distinguished-looking man. His children were grown, and he was lonely, and tired of his celibate life. Sometime that autumn he began an affair with a young Berlin woman named Eva Gruhn, who was thirty-four years his junior. Gruhn's father had been killed in the First World War, while her mother had worked as a servant at the Royal Palace in Berlin. When the revolution of 1918 drove Kaiser Wilhelm II into permanent exile, Frau Gruhn took up work as a masseuse. Eva at first worked with her mother, but they did not get along well, and soon Eva went out on her own. In 1931, when she was eighteen, she posed for a series of pornographic pictures. In some of these she was shown having sex with her then boyfriend, a failed engineer from Czechoslovakia—who was also Jewish, a double outrage for the Nazis. Later, Eva had registered as a prostitute with the Berlin police and was once arrested for robbing a client, though the charge was dropped.

There are conflicting stories about how Eva Gruhn and Werner von Blomberg met. The Blomberg family's version was that Blomberg had gone to see Eva's mother for massage therapy for a broken leg. The well-informed but often malicious resistance fighter and memoirist Hans Bernd Gisevius wrote that the meeting occurred in one of the Berlin dive bars that the lonely field marshal had started visiting. But the most plausible account comes from Blomberg's adjutant Karl Boehm-Tettelbach. Boehm-Tettelbach explained later that Blomberg was in the habit of taking a horse for a morning ride in the Tiergarten, the large park in the center of Berlin. But one morning in September, Blomberg's usual horse was injured, and the replacement the stable offered was too small for the tall field marshal. Irritated at having to do without his morning ride, Blomberg told Boehm-Tettelbach that he would leave early that day for a late-afternoon walk in the Tiergarten. "All later reconstructions," Böhm-Tettelbach wrote, "speak for the fact that on one of these days," while walking in the Tiergarten, "Blomberg met the woman who became a disaster for him." He summed the point up bluntly: "The damned nag was to blame for everything!"

By the time of the Hossbach Conference, Blomberg was deeply infatuated with Eva Gruhn and wanted to marry her. There was one complication. He had a rival—Gruhn was also seeing a young man closer to her own age. Remarkably, just after the Hossbach Conference, Blomberg decided to seek help from Hermann Göring. This was not a wise decision. Göring was not only nursing a grievance against Blomberg from the conference; he also wanted Blomberg's job.

According to Karl Bodenschatz, Göring's longtime adjutant, Blomberg told the Luftwaffe commander that he intended to marry a woman who was a "child of the people" but who had "a certain past." He was worried that the class-conscious German officer corps might put obstacles in his way. Göring expansively assured the field marshal that National Socialist Germany had moved beyond outdated ideas and that Blomberg's marriage would be a welcome example of social progress.

It is possible that Göring already knew about Blomberg's affair and Gruhn's past. One of the elements of Göring's empire, a legacy of his brief time in control of the Prussian secret police in 1933–34, was an organization called the "Office of Research," responsible for the tapping of phones. Most senior military officers suspected that this office kept regular tabs on them. Werner von Fritsch was careful to put a pillow over the telephone even when he visited his mother. If a wiretap had not already brought the affair to Göring's attention, Blomberg's mention of Gruhn's "past" must have made Göring's ears perk up. There was more to come. Blomberg came back a few days later with another request: could Göring use his ample powers to move the romantic rival out of the way? Here again, Göring proved to be a friend in deed. Bodenschatz reported after the war that Göring had given a senior economic official the task of "finding a position abroad for a young man who was very close to Fräulein Gruhn." The official found the young man a "well paid position in Argentina."

The young man returned Göring's favor with a parting gift. Before leaving for Argentina, he went to see Göring and told him that Fräulein Gruhn's past was more lurid than Blomberg had been letting on.

Within a few weeks of the Hossbach Conference, therefore, Göring knew he had embarrassing information that he could use against Blomberg. Göring understood perfectly, even if Blomberg did not, that Eva Gruhn's past meant any marriage would be fatal to Blomberg's position as war minister. Göring now had to think carefully about strategy. He wanted revenge, but he also wanted Blomberg's job. If Blomberg fell, then Fritsch, the army commander in chief, was the obvious candidate to replace him. Göring would need to get Fritsch out of the way as well. He did not have the resources he needed to go after both targets, but he knew who did. He turned to two allies of convenience, Heinrich Himmler, who controlled the SS and the Gestapo, and his deputy, Reinhard Heydrich.

Himmler, the chief of an upstart but rapidly growing police and paramilitary empire, had his own personal and political reasons for wanting to damage the army and its haughty, aristocratic officers. He had been locked in a battle with Fritsch over the responsibilities of the army and the SS since 1934. The more the officer corps was humiliated and weakened, the more the way would be clear for the SS to expand its military role. Soon the Gestapo had staked out Eva Gruhn's apartment, and two agents shadowed Fritsch on his leave in Egypt. From the Gestapo's extensive files, old and discredited allegations that Fritsch had engaged in homosexual affairs were revived.

The strict rules governing German officers' conduct required them to ask their superior's permission before marrying. Blomberg's only superior was Hitler, so in December, at the funeral of First World War commander Erich Ludendorff, Blomberg informed Hitler that he wished to marry Eva Gruhn. He also hinted delicately that Fräulein Gruhn had a "past," but he gave no further details. Hitler in any case seemed to pay little attention. Like Göring, he told Blomberg it was in the National Socialist spirit that the war minister should marry a "girl from the people."

The peculiar wedding arrangements suggested that Blomberg knew all about his bride's résumé and was worried that the information might leak. The ceremony took place in mid-January at the War Ministry, in haste and near secrecy. Hitler and Göring were present as witnesses, but this had not been the original plan. Initially, Admiral Raeder and General Fritsch were to be the witnesses. This suited Heydrich and the SS, as the officers' presence would force them to share the taint of the marriage later on. Heydrich, who had been dismissed from the navy in 1931 after an affair with another officer's wife, held a particular grudge against Raeder, the navy commander in chief. But just before the wedding, Heydrich gloated about his impending triumph to a friend who knew and liked Fritsch. The friend warned Fritsch what was happening. Fritsch conferred with Raeder, and they agreed to tell Blomberg that Hitler would be offended if he were not invited to stand as witness.

At the last minute, then, Hitler and Göring were brought in as witnesses. Blomberg's children, Göring observed, were not happy about the marriage and looked embarrassed. He also said the mood at the ceremony had been "strange." The announcement in the papers did not give the bride's full name, a reticence that was, as Hans Bernd Gisevius recalled, "something noteworthy, for in the Third Reich festive occasions were always celebrated with a vengeance." At the wedding and at the funeral of Blomberg's mother a few days later—the only two occasions on which Eva Gruhn met other members of the Nazi elite—she remained heavily veiled.

But the leak Blomberg feared happened anyway, probably with the eager assistance of Göring and Heydrich. A photograph of the couple on their brief honeymoon appeared in the papers in mid-January, and it seems that the Berlin vice squad recognized the new Frau von Blomberg as the former Eva Gruhn.

Gisevius, who had good connections with the Berlin police, witnessed something of the developing investigation. One morning, he went to see his friend Arthur Nebe, head of the Reich Criminal Police, at Nebe's office in the huge police headquarters building at Alexanderplatz. "As soon as I entered Nebe's office, he looked at me in that significant manner of his," Gisevius remembered. Nebe grabbed a small file and led Gisevius out to the hall. "We went up the stairs and around corners and paused in one of the remote hallways of the complicated building." Only there could Gisevius see the file, including "five piquant photographs," which were "anything but decent." Nebe had added something else. He had checked the register of arrest warrants. Here he found that Gruhn had been arrested for theft and her fingerprints taken. "Out of malice or great foresight," he wrote, "the police had never troubled to remove the record after she was cleared of the charge." Gisevius stared in fascination at the fingerprints. "The fingerprints of a real field marshal's wife were something I had never dreamed I should see if I lived the full thousand years of Hitler's Reich."

Eva Gruhn's file started working its way up the ranks. By Friday, January 21, the Berlin police president, Count Wolf-Heinrich von Hell-dorff, had brought it to Göring. The following Monday, Göring took the file to Hitler.

The Blomberg story grew more complicated when it intersected with the Göring/SS conspiracy to discredit General von Fritsch as a suspected homosexual. Strange things were clearly happening. Fritsch wrote to a friend that he had gotten back from his vacation in early January "just in time." He remembered later that on January 15, Hitler had complained to him about monarchist propaganda that was being spread in the ranks of the army. When Fritsch offered to investigate, Hitler refused, saying he might trust Blomberg with such a matter but not his army commander—"an open vote of no confidence against me," Fritsch wrote. And that evening, Fritsch remembered later, he was warned "from someone who had to be taken seriously" that "Himmler and the Party had decided I must now finally be gotten rid of."

On this same day—nine days before Hitler officially knew anything about Frau von Blomberg's record—the Gestapo was investigating allegations that Fritsch, in 1933, had been blackmailed over encounters with a gay prostitute. Or, rather, the Gestapo was busy fabricating such a case, because its officers already knew that the allegations against Fritsch were false and rested on a mistaken identity. They actually concerned a Captain von Frisch, not General von Fritsch. The case had arisen, by various accounts, either in 1936 or 1937, driven on by Himmler and Heydrich. At that time, Hitler had shown no interest in it and had ordered Himmler and Heydrich to destroy the file. But now, probably sometime after January 15, and certainly before January 24, Hitler suddenly ordered that the file be reconstructed and brought to him.

When Göring reported the Blomberg case to Hitler on January 24, witnesses thought that the Führer's shock and distress at the news were genuine. But acting was one of Hitler's outstanding skills. He had had at least an idea of Eva Gruhn's record in late December, after his conversation with Blomberg and, probably, Göring. He could not have been as shocked as he appeared.

It is likely that Göring also gave Hitler the fabricated file on Fritsch that evening, and that Hitler spent some time brooding over what to do. He had conspicuously avoided speaking with Hossbach after seeing Göring. Eventually, Hossbach went home, only to be awakened by a phone call at 2:15 a.m. summoning him immediately to the Chancellery. With his usual independence, Hossbach refused to return to report at such a late hour and said he would be available in the morning. It was typical of Hitler to delay a difficult decision for a long time but then act immediately when his mind was made up. This phone call in the small hours is a strong sign that at that moment, Hitler had suddenly seen what he wanted to do. He knew he wanted to get rid of Blomberg and Fritsch. Blomberg had clumsily handed him grounds for dismissal. Now Hitler had decided to use the fake case against Fritsch as well.

Hossbach arrived at the Chancellery at ten o'clock the next morning. First, Hitler told Hossbach about Blomberg. "Rage, fury and shame overcame me," Hossbach remembered, as he heard about the "dishonor" that Germany's first soldier had brought on himself and the army. But Hossbach's view changed dramatically when Hitler turned the conversation to Fritsch. Pacing up and down in the spacious study, the way he usually held such meetings, Hitler continued: Fritsch had to go, too, as he was implicated in homosexual acts. Hitler had the evidence, had had it for years in fact. "First Blomberg and now Fritsch!" Hossbach thought. "That was too much. Instinctively I recognized right away that it was a matter of a vile coup against the head of the army." The allegations against Blomberg and his wife might be true, Hossbach acknowledged. But not those against Fritsch: "No, here it could only be a matter of a pretext for Hitler to dismiss the Colonel General, who had long since become uncomfortable."

Hitler ordered Hossbach not to reveal anything of the matter to Fritsch. Hossbach disobeyed the order that very night, visiting Fritsch to fill him in. Hossbach was typically direct with Hitler, telling him beforehand that he would disobey and confirming afterward that he had done so.

Hossbach warned Fritsch because he chose loyalty to his commander and to the army over loyalty to Hitler. But as things turned out, he had hurt Fritsch rather than helped him. Fritsch vented his outrage in front of Hossbach—"A pack of lies!" he insisted—and then desperately tried to reason out why such allegations had been directed at him. After all, if Hitler wanted to get rid of him, "one word would be enough and I would offer my resignation." In his distress, he failed to grasp the scale of the plot. He thought, as did Hossbach, that Göring and Himmler were probably behind it. But he assumed Hitler was acting in good faith and would be swayed by facts and rational argument. Where had the allegations come from? Maybe, Fritsch told Hossbach, it was about a poor boy from the Hitler Youth whom he had befriended a few years before. Fritsch had had the boy over to his apartment for lunch on several occasions. Hossbach immediately recognized that this fact did not look good for Fritsch's case. But he neglected to warn the general of this.

On January 26, Hossbach returned to the Chancellery and, in his forthright way, told Hitler that he had disobeyed the Führer's order and that Fritsch had firmly denied the allegations. At first, Hitler seemed to accept Fritsch's denial, but he soon changed his tone. "Homosexuals, whether in high or low positions, lie as a rule," Hitler said. Even Fritsch's willingness to give his word of honor did not clear him in Hitler's eyes. Hossbach urged Hitler to convene a military court of honor to investigate the charges, which Hitler refused to do. Hitler then called in the justice minister, Franz Gürtner, who promptly chose political self-interest over honesty: he said that the allegations in the Fritsch file were enough to support an indictment, a conclusion that no lawyer considering the case rationally could possibly reach. Tirelessly, Hossbach pressed Hitler to talk to Fritsch. Hitler eventually agreed. But he conducted the meeting in a way that amounted to more an ambush of Fritsch than an opportunity for the general to defend himself.

Someone—Hossbach again suspected Himmler—summoned the

main "witness" to confront Fritsch. This was a con man, blackmailer, and police informer named Otto Schmidt, who claimed to have seen Fritsch engaging in homosexual acts with a rent boy nicknamed "Bavaria Joey" and then later extracted blackmail payments from the general. That evening, Schmidt claimed to recognize in Fritsch the man he had blackmailed. Fritsch steeled himself to appear as the calm, self-contained Prussian officer he was. His apparent lack of emotion only gave his accusers the feeling that he accepted his guilt—or allowed them to claim this. Outrage, they said, would have been more persuasive. But Fritsch had used up his outrage on Hossbach the night before. Fritsch also mentioned the Hitler Youth who had come to his apartment for lunch. Hossbach insisted that the witness's identification of Fritsch was neither surprising nor credible. But Hitler chose to believe it.

As Blomberg said later, Werner von Fritsch was clearly not "a man for women." He had never married and had never been known to have any affairs with women. Following the mores of the time, his defenders could not imagine Fritsch was gay only because they could not conceive of a gay man being the man of integrity and honor whom they saw in their commander. But whatever the nature of Fritsch's personal life, the specific allegations he faced in January 1938 were certainly fabricated. The reason they were fabricated is the crucial part of the story.

The next morning, January 27, Blomberg came to the Chancellery, in civilian clothes, for his last audience with Hitler. Hossbach saw Blomberg in and out but was not present for the conversation. Blomberg told British interrogators after the war that "our meeting began with an extremely stormy scene, during which I gave free rein to my anger over the manner in which I had been gotten rid of." Hitler responded "in a sharp form," but then the discussion became "calmer." Hitler asked Blomberg whom he would recommend as his successor. Blomberg suggested Göring, but to his surprise, Hitler rejected that idea with a few contemptuous remarks about Göring's idleness and incapacity. Blomberg claimed later that he had not thought much of any of the other generals who might have taken over—Beck was too hesitant, Fritsch an "oddball." Instead, Blomberg suggested that Hitler himself take on the job. In a skillful bit of informal cross-examination after the war, the lawyer Rüdiger von der Goltz got Blomberg to admit his real motive for this suggestion: revenge against the officer corps whose conception of morality had cost him his job.

The crisis was now effectively resolved. On January 27, Hitler dismissed both Blomberg and Fritsch. Their firings took effect the following Friday, February 4. Hitler followed his war minister's parting advice and took over Blomberg's role himself. But he also abolished the Ministry of War and in its place created a new entity, the Supreme Command of the Armed Forces (OKW). After dealing with strong-minded personalities like Fritsch and Hossbach, Hitler wanted a nonentity to head the OKW. In his last conversation with Blomberg, Hitler asked "What's the name of that general who's been in your office up to now?" The man Hitler meant was General Wilhelm Keitel. "There's no question of him at all," said Blomberg; "he's nothing but my office manager." Hitler replied, "That's exactly the man I am looking for."

The parallels between the cases of Blomberg and Edward VIII occurred to many people. General Keitel's daughter Lisa wrote to her mother, "These old men with their youthful feelings: Look at what it all brings on. Just think of the King of England." On January 26, General Alfred Jodl wrote in his diary, "What an influence a woman can exert, without suspecting it, on the history of a people and thus of the world. The parallels arise to the English King and his wife."

But as with Edward VIII, the consequences of Blomberg's marriage went far beyond the personal. The accession of George VI to the British throne instead of Edward VIII meant that a very different king with very different priorities would decide whom to summon as prime minister in a crucial hour in 1940. With Blomberg gone, Hitler was now not just the nominal, but in a very real sense the actual commander of Germany's armed forces.

And this was just the beginning. Hitler seized the opportunity to clear out a wide range of military commanders and diplomats whom he feared stood in the way of his expansionist plans. He dismissed Neurath (another opponent at the Hossbach Conference) and consoled him with the presidency of a new privy council that never actually met. Not long before, Hitler had assured Neurath that he looked upon him as a father figure and never wanted to separate from him. Many German ambassadors in the most important world capitals suddenly found themselves dismissed or transferred. One of them, the ambassador in Rome, Ulrich von Hassell, learned of his dismissal only from the newspapers. Hitler named General Walther von Brauchitsch, up until then commander of an army group in East Prussia, to succeed Fritsch.

Hitler did not confine his shake-up of the armed forces High Command to the top two positions. Twelve other generals were also sent into retirement (six of them from the Luftwaffe), along with fifty-one other senior officers. The real motive for this purge emerges clearly from Hitler's explanation of why the navy was untouched: Admiral Raeder had "conducted himself fabulously during the whole crisis, and *in the Navy everything is in order*," Hitler told Goebbels [emphasis added]. Obviously Hitler did not think everything was in order in the army. One of the generals sent into retirement was Wilhelm Ritter von Leeb, a widely respected officer of tough and independent mind. Leeb was a friend of Fritsch's, and the two men exchanged bitter letters after the purge. Fritsch wrote to Leeb that "after everything that I have gone through, it is impossible that I would ever carry out an official function in this state again."

The "whole affair" had to be "covered up," Goebbels wrote. Knowledge of the actual or alleged scandals around Fritsch and Blomberg remained confined within a small circle of senior officers and officials. As Gisevius added, "What cynicism to dismiss Fritsch for homosexual misdemeanors that were entirely unproved, on the same day that [Hitler] appointed a notorious homosexual, [Walther] Funk, to the office of a cabinet minister!" Funk had replaced Hjalmar Schacht as minister of economics, though for now Schacht retained his position as president of the Reichsbank. Funk's appointment demonstrated that Hitler had never had any interest in whether or not Fritsch was gay. He cared only that Fritsch was standing in the way of his plans.

On February 5, Hitler summoned his cabinet to ratify the changes. Where once records of German cabinet meetings had been lengthy and detailed documents of discussion and debate, this one was extremely brief: "The Führer and Reich Chancellor," it read, "gave a report on the political situation." Then the assembled ministers, Neurath among them, "expressed their deep satisfaction with the concentration and strengthening of the political, economic and military forces of the Reich," which

Hitler's "most recent decisions" had brought about. That was it. And this was the last time Hitler's cabinet ever met.

The Blomberg-Fritsch affair marked the third of Hitler's major bids to consolidate power in his own hands. The first of these had followed the Reichstag fire of February 1933, only four weeks into Hitler's time as chancellor. Hitler had used this occasion—a damaging fire in Germany's parliament building that the Nazis falsely claimed was the opening signal for a Communist uprising—to wipe out the individual rights and freedoms, along with the autonomy of the governments of the federal states, that Germany's 1919 democratic constitution had guaranteed. Sixteen months later, in June 1934, had come the "Night of the Long Knives," in which Hitler ordered the murder of opponents from within the Nazis' own ranks and from among a group of a conservative officials who were planning to remove him from power. A little more than a month after this bloody purge came the death of President von Hindenburg, after which Hitler abolished the office of the presidency, took over its powers, and received sworn personal oaths of loyalty from all civil servants and members of the armed forces.

The Blomberg-Fritsch affair completed the series. Having grown out of the Hossbach Conference, it pointed forward to the dramatic events that would bring on the Second World War. The scandals around Blomberg and Fritsch unfolded as they did because Hitler wanted it that way. As titular supreme commander of the armed forces since 1934, Hitler could have dismissed Blomberg and Fritsch at any time for any reason. The sexual scandals not only undid these officers professionally, but also threw them into disgrace—and military men felt them to be a stain on the honor of the officer corps. This put the whole German officer corps on the back foot and strengthened Hitler's hand against it. Hitler finally and grudgingly allowed a military court to rule on the allegations against Fritsch. Unsurprisingly, the court found that the evidence proved Fritsch innocent of the charges. But by then it was too late: too late for Fritsch and too late for the drastically altered power structure of the Third Reich.

The bluntly honest Friedrich Hossbach was another victim of the purge. As with the dismissals of Blomberg and Fritsch, Hitler found a pretext for Hossbach's sacking to cover its deeper motivation. Hitler had appeared to accept Hossbach's violation of his order not to warn Fritsch about the accusations. But on January 28, while at lunch with Hitler, Hossbach was called away to the phone. On the line was Major von Ziehlberg, one of Hossbach's subordinates on the general staff. Hossbach immediately guessed that Ziehlberg was calling to announce Hossbach's own dismissal. Before Ziehlberg could say anything, Hossbach put down the phone and calmly returned to lunch. Back in the dining room, Hitler seemed nervous and uncomfortable. After lunch, bringing Hitler's personal adjutant Fritz Wiedemann with him as a witness, Hossbach telephoned Ziehlberg and learned he was to be replaced immediately as Hitler's military adjutant by Major Rudolf Schmundt.

Enraged by this treatment, Hossbach returned to Hitler, and as he remembered, a dramatic scene followed "in the course of which tears of rage came over me." "You don't chase an officer from your door like a dog!" he yelled at Hitler. Hitler pointed out that he could have had Hossbach shot for disobedience. "I was prepared for that!" was Hossbach's reply. The real point, as Fritsch wrote later, was that Hitler no longer wanted an officer with the knowledge and integrity to argue with him. Hitler wanted submissive tools.

None of the direct participants in the Fritsch-Blomberg scandal were in any doubt that Hitler had conspired against the officers because of the attitude Fritsch and Blomberg had revealed at the Hossbach Conference. "Since I couldn't be gotten around politically," Fritsch commented in early February, "it is being done now in this most common and base manner." His lawyer said later that Fritsch thought the allegations of his homosexual behavior had been "kept on ice" until they could be used against him when "a change was wanted for other reasons." Soon after Fritsch's dismissal, Göring told the British ambassador, Sir Nevile Henderson, that Fritsch had been sacked because he opposed Hitler's foreign policy, adding that any British prime minister would have done the same to an argumentative chief of the imperial general staff. A few months later even Hitler admitted privately that he had always considered Fritsch an "obstructionist."

Predictably, it was Hossbach who made the most systematic case. "I am convinced," he said years later, "that Hitler made an inner break with the armed forces leadership, in any case definitely with Fritsch, but possibly also with Blomberg, as an effect of the meeting of November 5, 1937." In his orderly way, Hossbach listed the facts that supported his view. Hitler's expressions of distrust against the army leadership increased strikingly in frequency in November and December. Hossbach had been telling Hitler for a long time that he wanted to be transferred to another position, but Hitler had always refused the request. In the wake of the Fritsch-Blomberg scandal, he changed his mind. Hitler had previously been in the habit of talking over all matters with Hossbach, but Hitler never discussed the November conference with his adjutant and in fact began freezing Hossbach out of all other matters as well. The SS intelligence service, the SD, began investigating Fritsch in November and December, and Gestapo officers shadowed him when he was on leave in Egypt—a fact confirmed later by Karl Wolff, who among other things was the SS liaison officer to Hitler. "The dragon-seed for the change of course in the army," Hossbach concluded, "was planted in the last two months of the year 1937 and the first of the year 1938 and sprouted with the self-inflicted resignation of Blomberg and the perfidious overthrow of Fritsch by Hitler, Göring and Himmler on February 4, 1938."

The consequences were also clear. The sword, said Hossbach, had been placed in the hands of a "military dilettante, who ruled dictatorially over the entire apparatus of the state and the party, who influenced public opinion exclusively in his own way, and who was himself worshiped as a god by large sections of the people." This meant that "the future of the nation" had been turned over "to the will of one single man."

Senior officers soon learned that the allegations against Fritsch had been fabricated. Gisevius heard from Arthur Nebe that "the 'case' of Fritsch was a matter of confused identities." Himmler and Heydrich had covered this fact up. Gisevius got in touch with Hans Oster of the military intelligence service, the Abwehr, and told him what Nebe had found out. Oster in turn informed the Abwehr's commander, Admiral Wilhelm Canaris. Canaris told Beck. A small stone had started to roll. It was at this moment that some officers began thinking about resisting Hitler's rule. In the course of the year, the consequences would become more dramatic.

Fritsch and Blomberg were certainly not pacifists, nor were they opponents of Hitler or his regime. A few years later, still struggling to make sense of his dismissal, Blomberg noted, "I would have gone the Führer's way to Austria." But, he added, "then I would have set a time period of ten years to build up the new Greater Germany and a total rearmament." Even during the Second World War, Blomberg wrote that he never forgot the defeat of the First World War, he recognized the strength of Germany's potential enemies, and he had thought that getting into a war before Germany was ready would be "a catastrophe." Blomberg never seemed to understand that even this was enough opposition to drive Hitler to drastic measures. In late 1937, Hitler was operating under a new sense of urgency about his drive to war. He could not tolerate generals who wanted to slow him down.

Fritsch, too, was no opponent of the Nazis' program. He held highly antisemitic views. But like Blomberg, and for the same reasons, he opposed a rapid drive to war. Hitler had compared Fritsch to "an 'Englishman' who could not be influenced," Hossbach remembered, and for Hitler, Fritsch was "not a suitable instrument." Fritsch appeared before his supreme commander "as a master and not as an apprentice; in his confident manner he had an inhibiting effect on Hitler."

Nearly a year later, in December 1938, Fritsch would tell the former ambassador Ulrich von Hassell that if Hitler "went into the abyss," which Fritsch thought he would, "he will drag us all down with him. There is nothing we can do." Around the same time, Fritsch wrote to a friend, "I cannot shake the feeling that things are yet driving toward a great war." By that time, he was far from the only person who thought so.

6

"Rather Concerned re: Future"

R. J. Mitchell, chief designer at the Supermarine Aviation Works (Vickers) Ltd., spends the greater part of his working life "leaning over a drawing, chin in hand, thinking hard," as his colleague Joe Smith will remember years later. Mitchell's intense power of concentration helps to explain the extraordinary string of airplanes he has designed: twenty-four in twenty years, from flying boats to racing planes to a bomber. His brilliant imagination is always turning over new solutions to design problems. Naturally, he hates interruptions. His colleagues soon learn that when they enter Mitchell's office and see him bent over his drawing board, they must take a careful look at the back of his neck. If it looks normal, they wait for him to speak. But if his neck quickly turns red, "You beat a hasty retreat!"

Mitchell's temper can be terrifying. He can be "a damned difficult man to live with sometimes," as his son Gordon puts it. But most of the time, Mitchell is a man of great charm, with an engaging smile that can suddenly transform his usual expression of fierce concentration.

R. J. Mitchell was born eight years before the Wright brothers' first flight, but by the age of thirteen he is designing and flying his own model airplanes. When he is sixteen, he leaves school to begin an apprenticeship at the locomotive engineering firm of Kerr, Stuart and Co. A story from that time shows Mitchell's fondness for practical jokes but also a stubborn sense of his own dignity and importance. He does not get along well with his foreman, who has given Mitchell the job of making tea for him and the other apprentices. One day, the foreman tells Mitchell that his tea "tastes like piss." The next day, Mitchell fills the kettle with urine rather than water, and warns his fellow apprentices not to drink the results. The foreman drinks his cup gratefully and tells Mitchell "bloody good cup of tea, Mitchell, why can't you make it like this every day?"

Mitchell finishes his apprenticeship in 1916 with the First World War in full murderous swing. He tries twice to join the armed forces, but is turned down both times on the grounds that his engineering skills make him too valuable at home. In 1917 he finds a job at the small Supermarine Aviation Works of Southampton, a company dedicated, as the name suggests, to the design and manufacture of seaplanes. Mitchell's rise there is rapid: in 1919, aged all of twenty-four, he becomes Supermarine's chief designer, and in 1927 he is named a company director. The following year, Supermarine is taken over by the giant Vickers conglomerate, mainly to acquire Mitchell, whose continued work with the company is a term of the deal.

Accounts of Mitchell's career sound very different depending on when they are written. In 1940 the real importance of his life's work will become abundantly clear. Before that, narratives of his life focus on the brilliant success of the seaplanes he designs for the international Schneider Trophy competitions. The Schneider Trophy was first given in 1913 by a French industrialist to encourage the development of seaplanes. The rules specify that if a country's entry wins three years in a row, that country will hold the trophy in perpetuity. After the First World War, the Schneider Trophy becomes an obvious project for Supermarine, and in 1922, Mitchell's Sea Lion II wins, keeping Italy from its third consecutive victory. Then the Sea Lion's increasingly innovative successors win three consecutive Schneider Trophies between 1927 and 1931, giving Britain the cup in perpetuity. Mitchell's last Schneider entrant, the S.6B, reaches a top speed of 400 miles per hour, extraordinary by the standards of the time or, indeed, for years to come.

In 1930, with an eye on the threat from bombers in a future war, the British Air Ministry issues specification F.7/30 calling for an air defense fighter with a maximum speed of at least 250 miles per hour, a low landing speed, high rate of climb, and good maneuverability. Mitchell begins working on turning what he has learned from his triumphant seaplanes into the design of an effective fighter.

His first effort turns out to be a bit of a lemon. Known as the Type 224, it has fixed, not retractable, landing gear and an open cockpit. It can manage only 230 mph. Even before its first test flight, Mitchell is unhappy with it, and in the summer of 1933, he goes back to work on a more innovative design. Just as he begins this new project, doctors discover that he has rectal cancer. Surgery leaves him in near-constant pain and obliged to use a colostomy bag. The doctors tell him his cancer could return at any time, and if it does, they will be able to do nothing for him. Mitchell is only thirty-eight years old and obsessive about his projects. From this time on, he works frantically, in fear of running out of time.

Mitchell gives no outward sign of the gravity of his health. His coworkers do not know of the colostomy bag, and Mitchell stifles the pain he often feels. The only thing they notice is that the driven man's temper has grown even shorter.

Mitchell bites back the pain and, through 1934 and 1935, he dedicates himself to his new fighter. And a wonder of beauty and advanced technology begins to take shape. The new plane has retractable landing gear and a closed cockpit—two changes that make it much faster. Mitchell and his aeronauticist Beverley Shenstone decide to change the new fighter's wing. They make it very thin in cross section and give it a distinctive elliptical shape, wide at the root with the trailing edge tapering to a point at the tip. The result gives the plane much of its beauty and grace, but this is not the point. It is really about better aerodynamics and accommodating essential equipment. "I don't give a bugger whether it's elliptical or not," is Mitchell's comment to Shenstone about the beautiful wing, "so long as it covers the guns!" Just as important is that the new plane is designed around a powerful new engine, the Rolls-Royce PV 12, soon to be renamed the Merlin.

By late 1935, the prototype of Mitchell's fighter is nearly ready to fly. The Air Ministry has accepted Vickers's proposed name, the Spitfire—"Just the kind of bloody silly name they would think of," is Mitchell's irreverent comment. But on the last day of the year, Mitchell writes in his diary that he has been unwell. He adds laconically, "Rather concerned re: future."

On March 5, 1936, Vickers's chief experimental test pilot, Captain

"Mutt" Summers, takes the prototype Spitfire for its maiden flight. Jeffrey Quill, Summers's assistant test pilot, is watching. He remembers later, "The new fighter fairly leapt off and climbed away." After an eight-minute flight, Summers brings the plane down for a perfect landing. His comment: "I don't want anything touched."

After three more flights, Summers writes in a report, "The handling qualities of this machine are remarkably good." Air Vice-Marshal Sir Hugh Dowding, at that time the officer in charge of procurement for the Royal Air Force, gets as excited as this dour man possibly can, telling the secretary of state for air that the flights have been "highly satisfactory."

The men who fly the Spitfire later are less restrained. The plane's beauty and grace always lead them to sexual metaphors. Lord Balfour of Inchyre is the undersecretary of state for air in 1938 when he first sees a Spitfire. "I know I fell in love with her," he says later. "I was captivated by her sheer beauty; she was slimly built with a beautifully proportioned body and graceful curves just where they should be . . . Mind you, some of her admirers warned me that she was what mother called a 'fast girl.'" Along the same lines, H. R. "Dizzy" Allen, a fighter pilot in the Battle of Britain, remembers that the Spitfire "turned me on . . . [she] came close to perfection," even if "in certain of her mannerisms she was nearly as awful a bitch as the loveliest woman I ever met."

But as 1936 turns to 1937, R. J. Mitchell's pain grows steadily worse. By early 1937, it is clear that his cancer has returned. In February, doctors tell him he has perhaps four or five months to live. "Until June," Mitchell says to a visitor. "I—who have so much to do—have only until June." He can no longer go to his office at Supermarine, but his staff still come to him to discuss problems. In the spring, he makes a difficult journey to Vienna to see a renowned cancer specialist, but here, too, the verdict is that there is no further remedy. In late May, he returns to his home in Southampton, where he sits in his garden and worries only about other people: the health of his neighbor's daughter, his son's career, the professional future of his loyal staff. On June 8, Mitchell slips into unconsciousness, and three days later he dies. He has just turned forty-two.

"Mr. R.J. Mitchell—Designer of Racing Seaplanes," reads the headline of his lengthy obituary in The Times. The article focuses in well-informed detail on the engineering innovations of Mitchell's Schneider Trophy *winners. Reporters cannot yet know much about the Spitfire, including its name. Near the end of the obituary,*The Times *notes that Mitchell's last project had been a fighter, a land-based development of his seaplanes. "Its performance is still kept secret, but it is believed to be the fastest military airplane in the world."*

The Spitfire is a typically British product. British industry in the 1930s is beginning to acquire an image as a decaying backwater, stuck in declining, low-technology industries such as coal mining and cotton textiles. But this image is at best a half truth. Britain's aviation industry leads the world, both in quantity and quality. The great majority of British aircraft are meant for the armed forces, and aviation fits smoothly into a traditional British idea of how the nation's military defenses should be organized. It says something significant about British culture that the origins of both the Spitfire and the Rolls-Royce Merlin engine lay in partnerships between private and governmental initiative. In the late 1930s, the Spitfire takes its place both as a component of an extraordinary system of air defense and in a much broader concept of how the British should fight any future war. This concept is the decisive fact behind the policies that Neville Chamberlain's administration applies to Germany—the decisive fact, in other words, behind Chamberlain's approach to the Nazi menace.

OVER TWO MEETINGS on December 22, 1937, Neville Chamberlain's cabinet reached one of its most important and characteristic decisions. If war with Germany came again, the British government would make *no* plans to send a force of ground troops to France. The British Army would operate mainly in Britain's far-flung colonies. War with Germany would be a matter for the Royal Navy and the Royal Air Force.

The context for this decision lay partly in finance and partly in public opinion. In October, Chancellor of the Exchequer Sir John Simon had convinced the cabinet that Britain's defense commitments had to be brought into line with what the country could afford. Minister for the Coordination of Defence Sir Thomas Inskip presented a report at the late-December meetings on how to do this. His most important recommendation was that "cooperation in the defense of the territories of any allies"—in other words, sending ground troops to France—should be the least of Britain's defense priorities. As Secretary of State for War Leslie Hore-Belisha put it, the situation in 1937 was very different from what it had been a generation ago, in 1914. "Public opinion in this country [does] not favor the idea of sending an army to the continent," he said.

The cabinet's acceptance of Inskip's recommendations had crucial implications for British diplomacy. "In the long run," said Inskip, "the provision of adequate defenses within the means at our disposal will only be achieved when our long-term foreign policy has succeeded in changing the present assumptions as to our present enemies." The cabinet, therefore, decided that it was "desirable as soon as may be to follow up on the conversations between [Lord Halifax] and Herr Hitler," perhaps along the lines of a limitation of bomber aircraft.

Chamberlain summed up the discussion by stressing that "our economic stability" was "an essential element in our defensive strength." This also meant that Britain needed "staying power," or the ability to endure a long war. For "staying power" Britain had to think above all about the defense of its Home Islands.

The cabinet's debate and decision had a great deal to do with R. J. Mitchell's Spitfire. Inskip's defensive and cost-conscious focus led him to place particular importance on the construction of fighters, much more than on bombers. This was one of the ways in which Britain's defense policy, and therefore its foreign policy, was pointing toward the future.

Until 1935, Britain had the world's only fully independent air force (elsewhere, as in the United States, air forces were branches of the army). In the years just after the First World War, the upstart Royal Air Force (RAF) had struggled to survive. Those years were hard ones for the armed services of democracies, marked by drastic budget cuts and fierce interservice rivalries. The RAF needed a strong argument to defend its continued existence. Sir Hugh Trenchard, who held the position of "chief of air staff," effectively commander of the RAF, found this argument in the idea of "strategic bombing." His concept became known as the "Trenchard Doctrine."

The Trenchard Doctrine held that future wars would be decided by fleets of bombers bringing destruction to enemy cities. At the time, most people imagined a bombing war much as later generations would imagine a nuclear holocaust, with many of the same implications. Trenchard believed there could be no defense against a bomber attack. The only defense was to maintain a more powerful force than one's adversary, at best as a deterrent, at worst as a means of providing an overwhelming retaliation to any attack. Such visions were spread by military thinkers in many countries, such as the Italian officer Giulio Douhet, and accepted by politicians such as Stanley Baldwin, who told the House of Commons in 1932, "I think it is well also for the man in the street to realize that there is no power on earth that can protect him from being bombed . . . The bomber will always get through."

The Trenchard Doctrine was the dominant view within the RAF in the interwar years, but there were dissidents who believed in the possibility of defense. The most important was the dour, shy, and eccentric Hugh Dowding. Dowding had in fact been feuding with Trenchard over the correct role for an air force since they had both served in the Royal Flying Corps, predecessor to the RAF, in the First World War. Their respective nicknames said a lot about them. Trenchard was known as "Boom." Dowding was called "Stuffy."

Dowding never accepted that "the bomber would always get through." He believed that Britain needed fast fighters that could intercept the incoming bombers and stop them. It needed an effective warning system so that the fighters did not have to be on constant patrol, wearing out engines and pilots alike. The warning system and the fighter stations would have to be connected, with the fighters guided by a smoothly working control network. In 1930, Dowding was given the position of air member for research and supply, which meant he was responsible for developing new aircraft and other technology. His belief in the possibility of defense against the bomber opened up a fundamental and potentially bitterly divisive issue within the RAF. If there was a defense against the bomber, couldn't the Germans figure it out as well, and then what was the point of an independent air force? But despite fierce opposition from the Trenchardists, Dowding was able to create the kind of air defense system he imagined.

It started with the fighter. Dowding had stood very much as godfather to Mitchell's work on the Spitfire, as well as to its sister fighter the Hawker Hurricane, which was developed at the same time. Then there was the question of a warning system. For a long time, the British experimented with the idea of a "sound mirror," a large bowl rather like a modern satellite dish mounted at a slight angle with a microphone positioned in front of it. The ingenious, if implausible, idea was that the dish would pick up the sound of an incoming bomber and then the monitor could notify the fighter stations. But perhaps not surprisingly, the sound mirror never worked very well.

Early in 1935, the distinguished scientist Robert Watson-Watt told a British government committee that it should be possible to use radio waves to detect incoming aircraft. Receptive to new ideas but coolly rational as always, Dowding said he would approve development funding if scientists convinced him the idea might work. A test put on for Dowding's benefit showed that a bomber could be detected eight miles away. This was enough. A research station was set up at Orford Ness, on the Suffolk coast. Further experiments continued in 1936, at the Biggin Hill fighter station, near London. The new technology was called radio detection and ranging, or RADAR.

Soon, the radar transmitters could detect aircraft at a range of forty miles. If the beams of two different stations picked up an intruder, it was possible to fix its position and bearing. Work began on a chain of radar stations along Britain's east and south coasts that came to be known as Chain Home. Because Chain Home could not detect planes flying at lower than three thousand feet—literally, under the radar—a second chain, "Chain Home Low" was established in an effort to close this gap.

Once attackers were inland, the coastal radar could no longer "see" them, so the defenses relied instead on the volunteers of the Royal Observer Corps. These hardy souls perched on roofs or hilltops equipped with a telephone, binoculars, and a device for estimating the height and direction of passing aircraft. It was their job to notify the fighter control stations of the movement of enemy formations once they had crossed the British coast.

In July 1936, just as the Biggin Hill radar tests were getting under way, Dowding's career took another turn. The RAF was reorganized into functional commands, of which the two most important were Fighter Command and Bomber Command. With Trenchardist influence still dominant, Bomber Command was the one with the prestige. The unpopular Dowding was named the air officer commanding (AOC) of Fighter Command.

Dowding had the same effect on Fighter Command that he had had on research and development. A major building boom followed his appointment: the first operational radar stations were built and Observer Corps posts established. Then came all of Fighter Command's sophisticated infrastructure, notably the operations rooms to receive the reports from radar stations and the Observer Corps, pass them on to the fighter squadrons, and then direct the resulting interceptions and battles. Fighter Command developed a system of major sector airfields, surrounded by satellite fields to which fighters could be dispersed. Dowding pushed for all-weather, paved runways. Remarkably, he faced resistance on this point from the Air Ministry, on the grounds that a paved runway was too obvious a target.

If the followers of Dowding and Trenchard considered themselves bitter rivals, on another level they together represented a common British culture that valued science and technology coupled with individualism; a culture that had always—or almost always—held itself aloof from the massed armies and massed ground warfare of the European continent. Fighter Command, with its Spitfires and its radar, and Bomber Command, with its Trenchard Doctrine, were just the latest expressions of what came to be known as the "British way in warfare." This British way in warfare had a decisive impact on how Neville Chamberlain's government conducted international relations.

IN THE 1930S, the most influential theorist of the British way in warfare was Captain Basil Liddell Hart.

Liddell Hart was in many ways an unusual officer, military historian, and student of strategy. He had served as an infantry officer in the First World War and emerged sharing the rage of many of the war's harshest critics at its cost in blood and treasure and the lack of any meaningful victory. He was determined that such a war should never be repeated, and he channeled his rage into history and strategic theory. As the military correspondent for the *Daily Telegraph* and then *The Times*, Liddell Hart felt that the British had forgotten "our essentially businesslike tradition in the conduct of war," which "was based on economic pressure exercised through sea power." This was "the British way in warfare," a phrase he coined in 1931.

What did it mean?

Liddell Hart's "British way" started with the basic but profoundly important fact that Great Britain was an island, insulated over centuries from the ceaseless warfare on the European continent. Until the arrival of air power in the early twentieth century, all Britain really needed for its national defense was a strong navy—and from the days when Sir Francis Drake turned aside the Spanish Armada, it had had one. Britain was also blessed with a rich store of natural resources, including coal and iron. With its homeland safe and made rich by control of the world's maritime trade, Britain had been the first country to go through an industrial revolution. Its wealth and its strength at sea enabled it to assemble a global empire on a scale never before seen—by the early twentieth century, amounting to a quarter of the earth's surface and people. To defend themselves and their empire, the British maintained the Royal Navy at what they called a "two-power standard," keeping it larger than the next two world navies combined. They fought only limited and small ground wars. These were either matters of subduing rebellious indigenous peoples in the empire or intervening in minor ways in major conflicts. Even against major adversaries such as the French Bourbon kings or Napoléon, the British—so Liddell Hart claimed—had relied on their financial power, the Royal Navy, and, for the most part, other people's ground troops. The British fleet might land a force of soldiers here or there, but victory in continental struggles depended much more on the blood of allies such as Russia, Prussia, or Austria.

After 1870, however, Britain's strategic balance became more difficult to maintain. Germany and the United States rose to be front-rank industrial powers. They built navies and began competing with Great Britain for world markets. Other European countries followed. Britain could not be strong enough everywhere. It had to make strategic choices. Here a dilemma arose. The more the British government spent on defense, the more such spending would threaten the fiscal stability that made Britain an attractive borrower. This ability to borrow in turn was one of the reasons Britain was able to hold out in long wars against more short-winded adversaries. Military spending also took resources out of the civilian economy. Building up military forces, especially ground forces, for a continental European war might not only destroy the prosperity that British armed forces were meant to defend, but also directly harm Britain's ability to sustain a long war by crippling its ability to borrow and purchase military resources when it really needed them.

The First World War confirmed these characteristic British ways of thinking about strategy, partly because between 1914 and 1918, Britain abandoned its usual practice in one crucial respect: it mobilized six million men and deployed a huge ground army on the battlefields of France and Belgium. It paid for this army, and the staggering quantity of ammunition and other supplies it consumed, by harnessing its creditworthiness to borrow from American banks. When the war was over, every bit of this strategy looked to have been a disaster. The British government was now massively in debt to its American creditors, with New York eclipsing London as the world's financial center. And Britain had lost three-quarters of a million of her sons on the continental battlefields, with millions more bearing lifelong physical and mental wounds.

Liddell Hart thought that Britain should have fought a limited war, sending no more than its initial contingent of one hundred thousand soldiers to France. It should then have relied on its naval blockade to strangle the German economy—he thought the blockade had decided the outcome anyway—and pursued peripheral operations such as Churchill's 1915 landings on the Gallipoli peninsula. If the stalemate persisted, "fidelity to our tradition . . . would have led us to negotiate for peace— the usual ending of the wars from which we have benefitted most." The British could have relied on their "usual bargaining counters" of financial and naval might, and emerged from the negotiations "with strength less impaired than to-day." He concluded that "Victory, in the true sense, surely implies that one is better off after the war than if one had not made war. Victory, in this sense, is only possible if the result is quickly gained or the effort economically proportioned to the national resources."

There was one other key element of Liddell Hart's ideas. In the First World War, he had witnessed how massive forces of attacking infantry could be cut to pieces by machine gun and artillery fire. Like many, he concluded that in modern warfare the defense held all the advantages. A wise strategy would therefore focus on defense.

At the root of Liddell Hart's cool-eyed strategy was the fact that he was a fully engaged liberal democrat. He believed that liberal democracies needed a new political and military strategy to deal with the kind of aggressive, totalitarian threat that Nazi Germany represented. He set himself the project of devising this strategy.

Here is a vitally important point about the atmosphere of the 1930s: the ideological differences between the regimes of the time had to affect how they thought about strategy. And these ideological differences were much greater than they had been twenty years before. In 1914, Britain and France had been, in general, more democratic places than Germany or Austria, but not by a lot. In Austria and Germany in 1914, all adult men could vote in national elections. The two countries were states under the rule of law. Most aspects of European culture, from attitudes to war, to social and class relations, to the arts, were common to all. But by the 1930s, the democracies had become much more democratic and much more antiwar. The regimes of Germany and Italy, and the Soviet Union, brought systematic repression and brutality, to say nothing of militarization of society, to levels never before seen in modern history.

Liddell Hart understood that in this environment, the democracies needed to rethink how they approached the totalitarian threat. Many influential Britons, including many politicians who were against appeasing Nazi Germany, did not see this. Cabinet discussions were full of references to Britain's struggles against Louis XIV or Napoléon, as if the problems of national security were exactly the same as a century or two before. Liddell Hart understood the new ideological dimension of world politics. This was a world in which German citizens who volunteered to fight with the Communist-backed International Brigades in the Spanish Civil War could be convicted of attempted treason on their return home because, as a court found in one case, "The Spanish war was not a purely internal Spanish matter," but rather "the first great conflict between Communism on one side and Fascism and Nazism on the other," and so fighting for the International Brigades amounted to an attempt to overthrow the *German* government.

Liddell Hart understood that the First World War had led to a crisis of democracy on the European continent from which many nations had "emerged with a form of government and with an attitude to the rights of the individual that is essentially alien to the Anglo-Saxon tradition." If air power had rendered Britain "less than an island strategically," it was "more than ever an island politically." Would "England stand rocklike amid the totalitarian tide until that tide ebbs?" he wondered, observing that for communism and fascism, "uniformity is an ideal, and nonconformity a crime," whereas in Britain "toleration has never been so widespread, nor violence so widely disfavored" as in the postwar era.

The difficulty lay in getting this peaceful and liberal country to think about defense. Pacifists and "instinctive patriots" did not understand each other, but they would have to learn to do so. Young people could not be motivated to "patriotic defense" merely for the "preservation of a geographic area, its inhabitants and their material interests." There was a "need for a new vision . . . To gain this we must grasp the elements that matter in the Anglo-Saxon tradition—above all, the spirit of freedom." If fascism and communism could "raise enthusiasm among the young, how much better sources have we from which to generate it."

It wasn't just that the ideological differences between the democracies and the dictatorships were greater than in past conflicts, Liddell Hart noted. A democracy could not place the same demands on its citizens that a dictatorship could. This was why his strategy aimed at preventing war or, in the worst case, minimizing its impact. He opposed a draft for the army because he did not believe that the fight against totalitarianism could or should involve "totalitarian" methods. Although he had first made his reputation as a theorist of tank warfare, he opposed any British "continental commitment" of ground forces, advocating instead a series of tools running from containment and deterrence, the use of economic sanctions (including naval blockade, long a British specialty), and, if war came, the most limited means of fighting it: peripheral operations, war by proxy, standing on the defense. He was a strong advocate of strategic bombing, because he thought it could end a war quickly with lower casualties, even for the bombed. But he also believed that an all-out war against Nazi Germany would be pointless. He doubted Britain could win it, and even if it could, the victory would look even more like a defeat than had the last war. The best approach was to convince the other side that it could not win and so war was not worth trying.

Later writers have criticized Liddell Hart for inconsistencies, for weaknesses in his historical understanding, and for relentless self-aggrandizement. Few of his ideas were actually original. He drew heavily on the work of the earlier naval strategist Julian Stafford Corbett. But in the 1930s, Liddell Hart spoke for wide segments of the British public to whom a replay of the First World War was the greatest conceivable nightmare. His message was very welcome to the Chamberlain administration, and there are many signs of his influence on British government policy.

Shortly before he became prime minister, Chamberlain wrote to Liddell Hart to say, "I found your articles in *The Times* on the role of the army extremely useful and suggestive. I am quite sure we shall never again send to the Continent an Army on the scale of that which we put into the field in the Great War." Chamberlain was referring to Liddell Hart's idea of "limited liability" warfare, his term for the minimalist approach to defense. Chamberlain came into office determined to put limited liability into effect. The most important fruit of this determination was the cabinet's decision of December 22, 1937, that Britain would *not* send an army to France in the event of war.

Much of Chamberlain's thinking had to do with economics and finance, and here, too, there was a link to Liddell Hart. "Impressive as the marching columns may look to the awed civilian spectator," Liddell Hart wrote, the soldiers were "but giant marionettes dependent . . . upon a conveyer belt or pipe-line," which the civilian economy and its resources supplied. This meant, he said, that unless one side could find a way to win the war quickly—increasingly a mirage in modern warfare—conflicts would be decided by the economic resources that allowed a country to sustain a long war. Chamberlain had taken this point to heart, recognizing that Britain was in a much weaker financial position than it had been in 1914, having liquidated foreign assets and borrowed heavily from the United States to pay for the First World War. Then it had defaulted on American loans, which meant that under the terms of America's 1934 Johnson Act, Britain was barred from any further American borrowing.

Sir Thomas Inskip reported to the cabinet in December 1937 that "the maintenance of our economic stability would more accurately be described as an essential element in our defense system: one which can properly be regarded as a fourth arm in defense," alongside the army, the navy, and the RAF. Inskip thought that Britain's reputation for financial stability not only was essential should war come, but also played a crucial part in deterring war in the first place.

Most ministers in Chamberlain's cabinet agreed that if war came, there would have to be increases in defense spending and government borrowing. But how should they know when that moment was near? As Sir John Simon, chancellor of the exchequer, told the cabinet in March 1938, "We are in the position of a runner in a race who wants to reserve his sprint for the right time, but does not know where the finishing tape is. The danger is that we might knock our finances to pieces prematurely." The opposite danger, of course, was that planning for victory in a long war would be no use if Britain suffered a catastrophic defeat in a short one. As Foreign Secretary Anthony Eden argued, a "good financial position would be small consolation to us if London were laid flat because our Air Force had been insufficient."

This meant that there was an important connection between the ideas of Liddell Hart and Chamberlain on the one hand and those of Hugh Dowding on the other. In his December 1937 report, Inskip argued that the RAF's role should be fundamentally defensive, not offensive—heresy to the Trenchardists but in line with Dowding's ideas. Inskip did not believe the Trenchardists had made their case that bombing alone could win a war, and he thought that the RAF needed to be able to defend the British Isles through a long war much more than it needed to strike at Germany to win a short one.

Neville Chamberlain agreed fully with Inskip. Since 1934, Chamberlain had pushed for the development of fighters rather than bombers. As chancellor of the exchequer, he had even imposed a spending increase on the air ministry which the ministry didn't want because it called for fighters rather than bombers. Chamberlain also thought that the importance of home defense meant the British might have to cut back on the navy.

Ultimately, "the British way" was rooted in British culture. Much of its foundation was moral. It was based on a hatred of war and on the notion that a democracy should be a leader for peace. This outlook was based in turn on the British tradition of evangelical Christianity, sometimes in a secularized version, sometimes undiluted, as in the case of the "Holy Fox," Lord Halifax. A few days after the Second World War broke out in September 1939, Liddell Hart wrote that the Allies should make a declaration "that we were renouncing military attack as a means of combatting aggression," which would strengthen "our moral position" and "throw on the Germans the responsibility of taking the offensive."

Of course, there was one area where British strategy was fully prepared to "take the offensive," and that was in strategic bombing—the Trenchard Doctrine. Admittedly, there was a kind of democratic logic at work there, too: because a democracy is under pressure to keep its wartime casualties low, winning by bombing the other side's cities is a way of exporting the casualty count. But this bloodthirsty and aggressive doctrine sat awkwardly, both morally and strategically, with the defensive posture of the Chamberlain government. If Britain were to prepare for a long war in which its economic resources would eventually give it victory over Germany, then in the short term it had to defend its homeland against a German effort to knock it out by bombing. It is therefore entirely logical that it was some of the leading appeasement politicians—Chamberlain, Inskip, and the secretaries for air, Lord Londonderry and Lord Swinton, in alliance with the crusty Hugh Dowding—who developed Britain's sophisticated air defense network and shifted the RAF's emphasis from bombers to fighters. Here again, the Spitfire was the classic British weapon.

With hindsight, this defensive and moralizing stance may seem naïve. But Britain would have had to be a different country to come up with a different strategy. As much as Chamberlain and Churchill disagreed about policy, even they did not disagree about all aspects of "limited liability" strategy. Through two world wars, particularly as first lord of the Admiralty in the first and prime minister in the second, Churchill demonstrated his allegiance to the British way of warfare, always looking for a "peripheral strategy" that would save lives and resources and emphasize sea and air power. Here he and Chamberlain agreed, because this was the way a modern democracy could best face the kind of threat that Hitler posed.

IN THE CABINET debate of December 22, 1937, Hore-Belisha had argued that one reason that Britain could not send an army to France was that public opinion did not favor it. The hugely expanded importance of public opinion in the 1930s was one of the most important considerations for politicians trying to figure out a democratic response to the Nazi menace.

In the years after the First World War, there were many signs of a profoundly changing culture in the Western democracies—turning toward a greater degree of individualism, a lack of deference to authority, and a focus on private life. F. Scott Fitzgerald's 1934 novel *Tender Is the Night* contains a remarkable passage in which the main character explains that the First World War could never be fought again. It had required "religion and years of plenty and tremendous sureties and the exact relation that existed between the classes," all of which were now gone. After losing her fiancé, brother, and several friends in the First World War, the British memoirist Vera Brittain found she no longer had any patience for lectures on her duty to "God, King and Country" as "that voracious trio had already deprived me of all that I valued most in life."

Contemporaries were also alert to the consumerist revolution sweeping the wealthier countries. "Something new has come to American democracy," the journalist Samuel Strauss wrote in the *Atlantic Monthly* in 1924. Strauss gave the new thing an awkward name: *consumptionism*. Consumptionism, he said, was "bringing it about that the American citizen's first importance to his country is no longer that of citizen but that of consumer." The consequences were serious indeed. "No statesman, no pacifist, no League-of-Nations enthusiast, would entertain his pet scheme for a moment longer if he believed it would mean that ten years later people would buy half of what they buy today." He was right.

The new individualism, lack of deference, and even consumptionism appeared most fatefully in the revulsion against war that was widespread in the 1920s and '30s. This revulsion appeared partly in literature and film—with Vera Brittain's *Testament of Youth* among the classic examples, alongside Ernest Hemingway's *A Farewell to Arms*, Robert Graves's *Goodbye to All That*, and Erich Maria Remarque's *All Quiet on the Western Front*. There were more directly political developments as well. In February 1933, students at the Oxford Union, the great university's debating society, voted by 275 to 153 that "This House will in no circumstances fight for its King and Country." It had been well-placed young men like these who, two decades before, had died in droves as eager infantry officers, and the Oxford Union vote sent a chill through Britain's political establishment. It also inspired other students to pass similar motions at the universities of Cambridge, Manchester, and Glasgow.

Later that year, a Labour candidate won a by-election (the British term for a special election) for the once safely Conservative House of Commons seat of Fulham East by campaigning on a platform of peace and disarmament. This by-election was a political earthquake. Prime Minister Stanley Baldwin still seemed to be traumatized by it three years later. In a debate in the House of Commons in November 1936, he offered his thoughts on how a democratic politician should conduct foreign policy with what he himself called "appalling frankness." He said that he had always been an advocate of the "democratic principle" and noted that in 1933 and 1934, "there was probably a stronger pacifist feeling running through this country than at any time since the War . . . You will remember the election at Fulham in the autumn of 1933, when a seat which the National Government held was lost by about 7,000 votes on no issue but the pacifist." This meant that "my position as the leader of a great party was not altogether a comfortable one." If he had tried to fight the election campaign of 1935 by arguing for rearmament to meet the German threat, he went on, "does anybody think that this pacific democracy would have rallied to that cry at that moment? I cannot think of anything that would have made the loss of the election from my point of view more certain."

This was the clearest possible statement of the politician's predicament in the new era. Baldwin believed he had acted in a legitimate, democratic manner. "I shall always trust the instincts of our democratic people," he told the House. "They come with a unity not imposed from the top, not imposed by force, but a unity that nothing can break." After admitting that he had consciously risked national security to win an election, he concluded with a plea for trust. "It is common knowledge," he said, "that the rulers of the totalitarian states are in the happy position of not being criticized for what they may do or fail to do. They are under no obligation to make their plans known or to disclose their progress or lack of it." Even though he and his minister for the coordination of defense could not discuss publicly the details of their armament program, "there should be extended to us . . . a certain measure of trust and confidence."

It was because of the new individualism and the revulsion against war that Liddell Hart struggled to devise a low-casualty strategy for democratic war-fighting, and why British and American planners were particularly keen on using strategic bombers instead of ground troops to win a war. And it was why the Spitfire and other weapons of defense assumed paramount importance in British thinking about war.

ANTHONY EDEN WAS the bright young hope of British politics. Handsome, charismatic, and brave, he was born in 1897 into an aristocratic family. His eccentric father and wayward mother led fellow Tory politician Rab Butler to quip that Eden was "half mad baronet, half beautiful woman." Eden earned a Military Cross in the First World War for bringing his wounded platoon sergeant to safety while under fire after a nighttime raid on the German trenches. By the end of the war, at age twenty-one, he was the youngest brigade major in the British Army. Elected to the House of Commons in 1923, he rose as rapidly in politics as he had in the army. By 1935, Eden was foreign secretary, first under Baldwin and then under Chamberlain. But by early 1938, his upward progress had hit an obstacle.

A dispute between Chamberlain and Eden had been brewing for some time over policy toward Italy. Chamberlain, always eager to reduce the number of Britain's potential enemies, wanted to pull Mussolini away from Hitler's orbit by offering formal recognition of Italy's conquest of Abyssinia. Eden opposed this, arguing that Mussolini was "the complete gangster and his pledged word means nothing."

The dispute acquired another dimension in January 1938, while

Eden was on vacation in the South of France. Chamberlain grabbed the opportunity to dismiss the permanent undersecretary at the Foreign Office, the opponent of appeasement Sir Robert Vansittart, replacing him with the more compliant Sir Alexander Cadogan. Shortly thereafter, President Franklin Delano Roosevelt sent a confidential message to Chamberlain offering to launch a campaign for international disarmament. At the time, the prime minister resented the American intrusion into European affairs, fearing that Roosevelt would spoil Chamberlain's own plans for better relations with the dictators. Without consulting Eden, Chamberlain sent what was by diplomatic standards a rude reply, declining Roosevelt's offer because it risked "cutting across our efforts here," and adding that "there are certain phrases in the President's draft circular that cause me grave misgivings." Chamberlain was even blunter in private. "It is always best & safest to count on *nothing* from the Americans except words," he wrote to his sister Hilda.

Eden was outraged at Chamberlain's response, and upon returning from his holiday he sent his own telegram to the British ambassador in Washington contradicting what the prime minister had said. Eden feared, he wrote, that "the President may be registering disappointment" at Britain's negative attitude, which "was not the impression" that Chamberlain had wanted to convey. Undersecretary of State Sumner Welles, with whom Roosevelt worked far more closely than he did with Secretary of State Cordell Hull, recorded that Chamberlain's response had been like a "douche of cold water" for the president. A few days later, Roosevelt's personal response stressed his concern that Britain might recognize the Italian conquest of Abyssinia.

The prime minister and the foreign secretary could not long keep going with such fundamental disagreements. Chamberlain's response effectively stifled Roosevelt's initiative, although Roosevelt used the power shifts in Germany following the Blomberg-Fritsch crisis as an excuse for dropping it. The tensions between Eden and Chamberlain mounted, not least because of intelligence warnings that Germany was going to move against Austria and would count on Mussolini's support when it did so. Chamberlain thought this made a deal with Italy still more urgent. The climax came in a cabinet meeting on February 19 at which Chamberlain and Eden debated—to the puzzlement of the rest of the ministers, who had not known the dispute over Italy was brewing, and who knew still less about Roosevelt's initiative—the question of opening talks with Italy. The next day, Eden resigned. His replacement as foreign secretary was Lord Halifax.

Chamberlain's sacking of Vansittart and his replacement of Eden with Halifax formed an ironic counterpart to Hitler's makeover of his foreign policy and defense establishment in the wake of the Blomberg-Fritsch affair. Like Hitler, Chamberlain now had officials in place who would carry out his policy instead of criticizing or even trying to subvert it. This exercise of power to curtail opposition reflects the true nature of Neville Chamberlain's government.

After one year in office, Chamberlain had made the Conservative Party his own and had strong control of his cabinet, Parliament, and press. Now, in the wake of the Blomberg-Fritsch crisis, he faced the new German foreign minister, Joachim von Ribbentrop, who for the past two years had been the German ambassador to Britain.

When Hitler insisted to a skeptical Hermann Göring that Ribbentrop knew all the most important people in London, Göring responded, "Yes—the trouble is, they know Ribbentrop." Chamberlain felt that Ribbentrop's promotion was a setback for the project of better Anglo-German relations. "He is so stupid, so shallow, so self-centered and self-satisfied," he wrote to his sister Hilda, "so totally devoid of intellectual capacity that he never seems to take in what is said to him."

This was not an unusual opinion. Among the many exasperated notations about Ribbentrop that filled Joseph Goebbels's diary were that "Ribbentrop is altogether short on brains," "You have to explain everything to him ten times," that he was "unbearable," "arrogant," and "the Führer has wildly overestimated him." Ribbentrop had assured his fortune by marrying the daughter of a wealthy maker of sparkling wine, and he had convinced a distant aristocratic relative to adopt him so that he could add the prestigious "von" to his name. Goebbels complained cattily but accurately, "His name he bought, his money he married, and his job he got by intrigue." Even Benito Mussolini thought that Ribbentrop "belongs to that category of Germans that cause disasters for Germany."

On Friday, March 11, 1938, Chamberlain hosted a farewell lunch for Ribbentrop as the ambassador prepared to take up his new post in Berlin. In the course of this already awkward occasion came news that the German government had delivered a series of ultimatums to Austria. German invasion troops stood ready on the border.

Austria was a small and bitterly divided country struggling to cope with the loss of the grand imperial status it had enjoyed before 1918. Since the late 1920s, it had been wracked by a virtual civil war, pitting Social Democratic "Red Vienna" against the rest of the country under the quasi-fascist Christian Social Party. After Hitler came to power in Germany, the Austrian Nazis, whose primary goal was Anschluss, or annexation by Germany, developed into a third major player in Austrian politics. In 1934, Austrian Nazis assassinated Chancellor Engelbert Dolfuss, who was succeeded by his protégé, Kurt Schuschnigg. Schuschnigg tried to maintain the balance between Austrian national unity and tolerable relations with Germany. But that balance grew ever more difficult.

In mid-February, needing a distraction from the army's simmering anger over Werner von Fritsch's dismissal, Hitler summoned Schuschnigg to Berchtesgaden and forced him to accept a set of demands that all but put an end to Austrian independence. The most crucial demand was that an Austrian Nazi, Arthur Seyss-Inquart, become interior minister with full control of the police. Hitler remembered that in his own consolidation of power in Germany, having Hermann Göring as Prussian interior minister had been vital. Other ministerial appointments would consolidate the Austrian and German economies and armed forces.

Subjected to the full range of Nazi threats and bullying, Schuschnigg signed the agreement as Hitler wanted, but upon his return to Vienna, he recovered his nerve. On March 9, he came up with a desperate plan to preserve Austria's crumbling independence by calling a snap plebiscite, to ask the Austrian people if they wanted a "free and German, independent and social, Christian and united Austria," marked by "freedom and work," and "the equality of all who declare for people and fatherland." Few Austrians were likely to vote no to such a question, which of course was the point. The plebiscite was to be held on Sunday, March 13.

The likely outcome of the plebiscite would be a blow to Hitler's rising prestige and might close the door for a long time on union between

Germany and Austria. "At first," Hitler told the British reporter Ward Price a few days later, "I could scarcely believe the news" of the plebiscite. Once it was confirmed, rage was the inevitable next step. Schuschnigg's plebiscite was a "betrayal" of the Berchtesgaden agreement, "and betrayal is something that I cannot tolerate . . . I decided to act immediately." What he meant was that he decided to launch an invasion of Austria.

This hasty decision raised a problem: the German army had no plan for such an operation. There was an outline, dubbed "Case Otto," for an invasion to prevent a restoration of the Austrian monarchy. (Otto von Habsburg was the claimant to the ancient Austrian throne.) But Ludwig Beck thought invading Austria was a ridiculous thing to do, as he was sure that it would lead to a war with Britain and France. He had refused to draft any orders to turn this outline into a real plan of operations.

General Wilhelm Keitel, the new head of the OKW, was therefore astonished when Hitler summoned him to the Reich Chancellery on March 10 and ordered him to prepare an invasion of Austria. Keitel wanted Beck and Walther von Brauchitsch, the new army commander in chief, brought in to hear the orders directly. "It was quite clear to me," Keitel wrote after the war, "that Beck would otherwise simply dismiss the whole thing as quite impossible." Beck did in fact object to Hitler's ideas, but "his objections were summarily brushed aside by Hitler, so he had no alternative but to comply and report back some hours later what troop formations would be ready to enter Austria early on the 12th." The night of March 11–12 was "sheer purgatory" for Keitel: "One telephone call followed another" from various senior officers, begging to call the operation off. Keitel simply told them all that Hitler insisted on going ahead: he never actually put the officers' objections to Hitler, he said, in order to save all concerned from "disillusionment."

After another round of Hitler's threats, Schuschnigg backed down again. On March 11, he agreed to cancel his plebiscite and gave up the office of chancellor. Seyss-Inquart took his place. Now Hitler wanted Seyss-Inquart to issue a formal request for German military intervention to restore "order" in Austria. On no account was the invasion to look like what it really was: a hostile military action against a sovereign state. But Seyss-Inquart, though a Nazi, was also an Austrian patriot and refused to take this step. Wilhelm Keppler, a businessman and German Nazi representing Hitler in Austria, issued the request himself in Seyss-Inquart's name. German troops crossed the border the next morning, unopposed.

It was as well that there was no resistance, because the German Army was still a long way from the super-competence it would demonstrate on later occasions. The Second Panzer Division did not have maps of Austria or even enough fuel: once across the border, its crews had to stop at Austrian filling stations to gas up their tanks. For navigation, they made do with a Baedeker guide. Many tanks broke down along the road to Vienna, causing traffic jams. But it was enough. Hitler drove on after his troops, visiting his birthplace at Braunau and his childhood home of Linz before entering Vienna. He had not originally planned the full annexation of Austria, but the rapturous crowds in Linz and foreign reports already referring to an "Anschluss" changed his thinking. By March 13, Austria had ceased to exist. In its place was the German province of the Ostmark.

That Germany and Austria could not unite had been a key provision of the Treaty of Versailles and of the equivalent Treaty of Saint-Germain with Austria. But the Western powers accepted the Anschluss with hardly a murmur. Something else died with the Anschluss, too. Especially since Halifax's visit to Hitler the previous November, the British government had been trying to use the return of Germany's overseas colonies as bait to lure Germany back to an international order of peace and world trade. The Anschluss was Hitler's answer. The liberal international system could provide no solution to the Nazi menace.

"Tears in the eyes" in Vienna, Goebbels wrote in his diary, and with a revealing comparison of these events to the Nazi takeover in Germany, he added "The 30th of January 1933 for Austria."

And even more revealingly: "They are extremely worried in Prague."

— 7 —

Scraping at the Bars

Even as an old man, Max Fürst cannot forget a sentence from a Latin exercise book he had as a schoolboy: "The city was conquered, and whoever was not cut down was sold into slavery." The schoolboy Max cannot translate the sentence properly because, in his mind, he sees only "the terrified eyes of the people" who are being killed or enslaved. This is during the First World War. Max knows that in the world beyond his schoolroom these things are really happening. The young boy has glimpsed the full misery of war and tyranny for the first time.

But certainly not for the last. When the Nazis come to power, Max's friend Hans Litten, a courageous young lawyer who before 1933 had tried to use the criminal law to stop Hitler, is arrested. Max and his wife, Margot, hatch a plan to free Litten from his concentration camp. The plan fails, and Max and Margot find themselves in Nazi prisons as well. They are fortunate to be released, but they know they cannot stay in Germany. Max worries about his friends and family because he knows that for Nazi Germany "the end can only come with horror."

In late 1935, the Fürsts receive an anonymous phone call—Max suspects a well-meaning Gestapo officer—warning them that they will soon be rearrested, and they leave Berlin for Rotterdam with their two small children. From there they will sail to Palestine. They want their departure from

Berlin to be inconspicuous, and they arrange for small groups of friends and family to wait on the platform at every station of the S-Bahn, the mostly aboveground commuter rail line, to say goodbye. Crossing the border to the Netherlands goes more smoothly than they expect. They make it to Rotterdam, and to their ship. They breathe "a great sigh of relief" when they are on board, Max remembers.

After years of unrelenting stress—the Nazi takeover, Hans Litten's arrest, their own arrest and imprisonment, the race to get out of Germany in time—the voyage to Palestine is the first vacation they have had in a long time. Max comes to the conclusion that nirvana must actually be a sea voyage. But the first night they sail into the Mediterranean, "the giant, shadowy warships" of the Royal Navy appear, a reminder of the looming war.

Cläre Tisch is a very different person from the activist Fürsts, but she gets caught up in the same horror. A brilliant young economist, she studies for a PhD at Bonn University under the star professor Joseph Schumpeter. She writes learned treatises on the law of cartels in Germany, and on the problems a socialist economy would have with setting prices. Her fellow graduate students think highly of her, and such famous economists as Friedrich Hayek and Schumpeter cite her work with respect.

For a young woman, particularly a young Jewish woman, trying to make a career as an economist is not easy even before 1933. After the Nazis come to power, it is impossible. For a few years, Cläre works as a stenotypist and as a clerk in a shoe store. In 1936, she gets a job running an organization for the care of Jewish orphans. She devotes herself to this work and passes up several chances to emigrate because she does not want to leave the children.

After Schumpeter moves to the United States to take up a job at Harvard, Cläre writes him a steady stream of letters. Her letters form a powerful chronicle of what life is like for a young Jewish woman in Hitler's Germany.

At first, Schumpeter suspects she is not telling him the whole story, and he urges her to be franker about how things are really going. Cläre replies, "You will not much enjoy the spirits that you have summoned!" A few months later, she notes, "You know how things are here"—the pools closed to Jews, the villages that Jews cannot enter, "the newspapers that publish *the names of German girls who go with Jews," being regarded "as a second, no, bottom-class citizen," all of it a source of "unbroken pain." She is start-ing to think of emigrating. "Can you understand that I would rather work abroad in a lowly position but as a human being with equal rights, than just to be tolerated here?" And yet she fears she lacks the courage "to go to some kind of foreign country and look for a position."*

By 1939, however, Cläre knows she has to go. Schumpeter gladly sup-plies the affidavit of financial support she needs to meet American visa requirements. But there is still the quota for immigrants from Germany established by the Immigration Act of 1924. "Do you know the system of waiting-numbers in [the consulate at] Stuttgart?" she asks Schumpeter in February 1939, in a letter that now bears her legally required middle name "Sara," to mark her as Jewish. "It is a terrible thing. Everyone who wants to can be registered there, even without any prospect of an affidavit of support. Anyway, I did that too, even though very late. If I had regis-tered just now, I would have had about the number 50,000, whereas I now have 38,033." She calculates that the Stuttgart consulate might get through about 6,000 names per year. Some names on the list will fall away, so she guesses she has a five-and-a-half-year wait ahead of her—and might therefore be able to leave for the United States sometime in 1944.

"This is terrible," she concludes, "but at least now I know that the wait-ing is not in vain."

NAZI OPPRESSION OF German Jews grew steadily worse in the second half of the 1930s. In 1935, the infamous Nuremberg Laws deprived Jews of German citizenship, forbade intermarriage between Jews and non-Jews, and made sexual intercourse between Jews and non-Jews a crimi-nal offense. The destruction of the Austrian state in March 1938 opened a zone of lawlessness that the Nazis could fill with savage violence, bringing in weeks a level of misery for Austrian Jews that had taken years to achieve in Germany.

The annexation of Austria also set in motion a dynamic of violence and further flows of desperate refugees. Poland, like Germany, had been trying to pressure Jews into emigrating. But the Nazi abuses of Austrian Jews caused a rush of refugees *into* Poland. Many Jews living in Austria and Germany held Polish passports. Recognizing what was coming, the Polish Parliament hurried to pass legislation blocking the return of Polish Jews who had lived abroad for more than five years. This in turn worried the Nazis, who recognized that they might soon be unable to deport Jews with Polish passports. To get in ahead of the Polish laws, at the end of October, Germany hurriedly deported 17,000 Jews to Poland.

One of the deported families was the Grynszpans, who had been living for years in Hannover, in northwestern Germany. Their son Herschel had gone to live in Paris with an aunt and uncle. When he heard what had happened to his parents and his sister, he bought a gun, went to the German embassy, and shot a diplomat named Ernst vom Rath. This event gave the Nazis a pretext for another wave of violence, this time at home: on the night of Wednesday, November 9, Nazi Stormtroopers burned down synagogues, vandalized Jewish-owned homes and businesses, murdered perhaps one hundred German Jews—others were driven to suicide—and sent between 25,000 and 30,000 to concentration camps. The shards of broken glass in German streets the next day gave the event its name, at first meant to be sarcastic: *Reichskristallnacht*, the Reich's Night of Broken Glass.

In the wake of Kristallnacht, the Nazi regime tightened the screws further. It forced German Jews to pay collectively for the costs of repairing all the damage. Jewish children were expelled from schools. Jews could not drive cars or visit libraries. The "Aryanization" of the economy (the expropriation of Jewish-owned businesses in favor of non-Jews) accelerated. The last Jews still able to work for the civil service or as lawyers or doctors were driven from their professions. The increasing persecution of Jews was also a function of the rush toward war. The regime wanted to confiscate Jewish assets to help fund the increasingly frantic, and unsustainable, drive for armaments. And Hitler considered the Jews enemies within, agents of his likely adversaries.

In 1933, in response to the Nazi takeover, roughly 37,000 Jews had left Germany. But then, for a few years, the numbers declined. After Kristallnacht, the rate of emigration shot up as Germany's Jews seized what looked like the last chance to race for the exits: 40,000 Jews left the country in 1938 and 78,000 in 1939.

■ ■ ■

OF COURSE, THEY needed somewhere to go. France, Britain, America, and Palestine were desirable destinations. None was easily reachable. European Jews wryly observed that there were two kinds of countries in the world: those where they could not live and those they could not enter.

By the standards of his class, generation, and background, Franklin Delano Roosevelt was remarkably unprejudiced toward Jews. Admittedly, he counted himself among "the Aryan races" from which came all human progress and freedom—a widely held view among privileged American Protestants of his time, and one he had absorbed at the elite bastions of Groton and Harvard. But Roosevelt worked gladly with Jews and earned their strong support at the ballot box, as governor of New York and as president. He often showed deep sympathy for the sufferings of Jews under the Nazis. But he was as sphinxlike on Jewish policy as he was on everything else, and for the same reasons: he would seldom take a political risk. Just as with the problem of how to oppose the dictators, the question became: what would Roosevelt be willing to do, and what risks would he be willing to run, to help European Jews?

Early in his administration, Roosevelt typically preferred informal talks and back-channel communications with the German government to any open effort at advocacy for German Jews. He wanted the Nazis to understand that persecution of the Jews, like rearmament, would harm relations with the United States. But he wanted to send this message discreetly. He met with Hjalmar Schacht in 1933, after which he wrote to his friend Judge Irving Lehman: "At last the German Government now knows how I feel about things . . . It is probably better to do it this way rather than to send formal notes of protest, because, frankly, I fear that the latter might result in reprisals in Germany." When Roosevelt made a conciliatory speech on parity of armaments that seemed to draw an encouraging response from Hitler, the president congratulated himself: "I think I have averted a war," he told Henry Morgenthau Jr., his future treasury secretary. "I think that sending that message to Hitler had a good effect."

But apart from these mild hints, in his first term Roosevelt made virtually no effort to improve conditions for German Jews. There were many reasons for this. American presidents had established a principle of not intervening in the internal affairs of foreign states. When Roosevelt appointed the Chicago history professor William Dodd to be his ambassador in Berlin, he told Dodd that the Nazis' abuse of Jews was "not a governmental matter" and that the United States would have to stay out of it officially, although it was fine if Dodd took private actions. The State Department felt that getting Germany to pay its debts to American banks was Dodd's top priority. That, it seems, *was* a "governmental matter." Roosevelt knew that his domestic political opponents were often antisemitic and would never be very attractive to Jewish American voters, so he had little electoral incentive to help European Jews. And he did not want to jeopardize his main priority, finding a way out of the Great Depression, by antagonizing that opposition with what seemed to be a peripheral issue.

When it came to loosening immigration restrictions, there were other political concerns. Organized labor was much more politically important to a Democratic president than the votes of Jews, and labor stood squarely against letting in more refugees. Economists understood in the 1930s that immigrants created more jobs than they took, so that admitting refugees could only be good for the economy. But facts and evidence did not much interest those who were against immigration. An official of the anti-immigrant group Sons of the American Revolution simply suggested, "They say he [the immigrant] is a consumer. I do not see the logic of that." It didn't help that the worsening of the refugee crisis in 1937 and 1938 coincided with the "Roosevelt recession."

Then there was the tide of nativism. This reached deep into educated and well-placed corners of American life. At a hearing in 1939, Senator Rufus Holman of Oregon insisted that a union official must be speaking as an "internationalist" and not as an "American." The same year, Harry H. Laughlin, a former advisor to the House Immigration Committee and one of the most influential of American advocates of eugenics, argued that peaceful immigration would reproduce the effects of military defeat and occupation. Immigrants, he said, brought mental illness and crime, and burdened public welfare systems. Laughlin thought the immigration quotas should be reduced by 60 percent, and deportation

made easier. He argued for a complete ban on "alien races or organizations" whose past record showed that they "tend to resist assimilation in
the United States." This was racist code for Jews. "No living nation," he
concluded, "need permit its own conquest by unselected immigrants."
His book *Conquest by Immigration* was published by the New York State
Chamber of Commerce.

In fact, nativism had been rising in the United States since the First
World War, and it had an influence on obvious and not-so-obvious areas
of policy. Elite universities discriminated against Catholics and Jews.
The introduction of Prohibition had been intended as a rejection of
reprehensible foreign ways and support for "100 percent Americanism"
in the face of the massive immigration of the late nineteenth and early
twentieth centuries, with powerful support from the Ku Klux Klan. The
hugely popular radio priest Father Charles Coughlin of Detroit dished
up a steady diet of antisemitism to what was probably the largest radio
audience in the world.

But nativism's most direct expression had come in the Emergency
Quota Act of 1921 and the National Origins Act of 1924, the latter
known as the Johnson-Reed Act. These laws established a new framework for immigration to the United States, based on maintaining the
ethnic proportions recorded in the census of 1890 (a year carefully chosen because it preceded much of the wave of immigration from southern and eastern Europe). The laws permitted 150,000 immigrants per
year to enter the United States (earlier in the century, there had been
years in which the total number of immigrants exceeded one million),
with each country of origin receiving a quota based on what the 1890
census showed to be that country's share of the existing population. If
a country was unrepresented in the census figures, it was assigned a
quota of 100 persons, and the law barred migrants from most African
and Asian countries altogether. The system was to be phased in over five
years, and so it did not come fully into force until 1929. But its effects
on immigration were nonetheless immediate and drastic. The numbers
of new arrivals dropped from 1.2 million in 1914 to 360,000 in 1923–24
to 165,000 in 1924–25. The numbers from southern and eastern Europe
dropped particularly drastically, as the law intended. In the late 1930s,
when German and Austrian Jews desperately needed to find somewhere

else to go, the Johnson-Reed Act would prove disastrous—and eventually lethal.

Another critical feature of U.S. immigration law lurked unsuspected in an older statute and in a presidential executive order. The Immigration Act of 1917 contained a provision excluding persons "likely to become public charges." This became known as "the LPC clause." At the time, lawmakers assumed that the LPC clause would never apply to healthy persons who actually reached the United States. But in 1930, under the impact of the Depression, President Herbert Hoover asked the State Department to find administrative methods of limiting immigration to levels even below the quotas. The LPC clause offered the perfect means. Now, by executive order and not legislation, a prospective immigrant had to possess sufficient financial resources to provide for him or herself, even without a job, or else secure an affidavit from a U.S. resident promising financial support. After 1933, the effects of this interpretation would turn ominous indeed.

There was one loophole in the Johnson-Reed Act: the southern border remained largely open, and there was no restriction on Mexican migration into the United States. This was in part because there was still a demand for cheap labor in the South and West. Mexicans could replace the African Americans who had moved north in the Great Migration or the Europeans who, if they could have entered the country, would have taken low-wage jobs in northern cities. The U.S. Border Patrol was founded in 1924 with all of forty members, but its job was to stop Europeans and Asians from crossing the borders, not Mexicans or Canadians. The number of deportations, however, increased sharply. The average number of migrants deported annually had been in the range of 2,000 to 3,000 in the first decades of the twentieth century. By 1930, it had reached 39,000.

These laws formed the basic framework of the American response to the crisis of German and European Jews after 1933. Remarkably, for most of the 1930s, the United States did not even come close to filling its quotas for German immigrants, largely because consuls used the LPC clause to exclude applicants. For the year ending June 30, 1934, only 17 percent of the German quota was filled. The next year, it was 20 percent, and it was still under a quarter the year after that. In 1937, as the situation for European Jews grew ever grimmer, the quota was still only half-filled.

Roosevelt responded with real concern to the plight of German and Austrian Jews after the Anschluss. At a cabinet meeting on March 18, 1938, he asked what the United States could do for what he delicately called Austria's "political" refugees—this, too, was a code. He suggested combining the German and Austrian immigration quotas and also proposed raising the German quota. Vice President John Nance Garner responded by telling Roosevelt that if Congress could vote in secret, it would completely cut off all immigration. Faced with this inconvenient fact, Roosevelt bypassed Congress and combined the German and Austrian quotas by executive order. In 1939, this new quota was filled for the first time. But by then, the waiting list for American visas was long enough to last eleven years.

There were conflicts within the Roosevelt administration as well, particularly between the committed New Dealers and the much more conservative State Department. The New Dealers put their emphasis on social reform and, as the 1930s progressed, on resisting the Nazis and aiding refugees. The State Department cared mainly about resisting communism and worried that letting in too many refugees would pose a security threat.

As a bastion of the East Coast establishment, the State Department also tended to be imbued with the racial ideas that lay behind the Johnson-Reed Act. An article in *Harper's Magazine* in February 1938 concluded that Foreign Service officers had "scant regard for democratic movements and little respect for members of those races customarily dismissed by Anglo-Saxons as inferiors"—particularly Jews. At times, the New Dealers and the diplomats denounced each other angrily as "Fascists" or "Communists."

They weren't always wrong. Roosevelt's administration was heavily penetrated by Soviet agents, including even one of the president's top economic advisors, Lauchlin Currie. On the other side, Assistant Secretary of State Breckinridge Long became particularly notorious as an embittered opponent of all Jewish immigration. Long came from a prominent Southern family and was a longtime friend of Roosevelt's. But as the historian Blanche Wiesen Cook writes, Long was, in his own mind, "dedicated to keeping America uncontaminated by un-Americans." It was this man whom Roosevelt promoted early in 1940 to oversee visa and refugee issues. Driven both by antisemitism and concerns for national security, Long blocked as many refugees as he could from reaching the United States. "They were all Jewish. They all had money," was one of his typically dismissive comments about desperate people. Eleanor Roosevelt, who argued more with her husband about refugees than any other issue, once told the president bluntly, "Franklin, you know [Long] is a fascist." Roosevelt replied with irritation, "I've told you, Eleanor, you must not say that." But she was undeterred: "Well, maybe I shouldn't say it, but he is."

Nonetheless, in March 1938, Roosevelt also started to talk about organizing an international conference to bring together a large number of countries, particularly in Latin America, to find solutions to the problems of "political refugees" from Germany "and presumably Austria." What Roosevelt put forward was carefully limited: he did not expect any country "to receive greater numbers of emigrants than is permitted by its existing legislation." Private organizations would pay all the costs.

Roosevelt's proposal found widespread approval in the United States, including from the American Federation of Labor, as long as it would not result in an increase to the immigration quotas. Sumner Welles told a private meeting of newspaper editors that he thought the conference might be able to alleviate a cause of European war. But support was far from universal. Congressman Martin Dies of Texas complained that "our first duty is to our own people." Immigrants would either "take jobs that Americans are now holding, or taxpayers of America will be compelled to support them."

The nations Roosevelt invited to the conference—there were thirty-one national delegations and thirty-nine private charitable organizations (Italy did not send a delegation and Germany was not invited)—attended a week of meetings at the French resort town of Évian, on Lake Geneva, that July. Roosevelt sent Myron C. Taylor, a Republican and a former president of U.S. Steel, to represent the United States.

The French delegation set the tone for the conference by firmly defending its new restrictions on refugees. This position shocked many of the other countries, who had been hoping that France would take on more of the refugee burden. What the conference made clear—around the time that some wag discovered that Évian spelled backward formed "naïve"—was that no government was enthusiastic about receiving Jewish refugees. Their representatives cited economic troubles, lack of space, and the racial problems they already had or the ones they wanted to avoid in the future. Only the Dominican Republic distinguished itself by agreeing to take a hundred thousand refugees, and even here the dictator Rafael Trujillo's motive was not humanitarian concern but a desire to have more white people in his country. The conference's other achievement was that the governments agreed to set up a new international organization, the Intergovernmental Committee on Refugees, to sidestep the League of Nations refugee organization. An American lawyer, George Rublee, was named as its director. It was not clear what this new committee could do that the League could not.

"What a demonstration these nations might have provided for the world," the *New Republic* editorialized, "if they could have gone on wholeheartedly to act in the spirit of the cause that brought them together! If they had proclaimed at once that the unfortunate victims of persecution would be welcomed elsewhere . . . the humane superiority of democracy over its enemies would have been strikingly demonstrated."

Rublee quickly discovered that the Nazis would allow Jews to emigrate with their assets unconfiscated only if other countries agreed to accept more German exports. Germany was therefore using its Jews as hostages to force the world to support its overstrained military economy and war machine. Western governments could not and did not accept such a bargain, not least because they worried about the incentives it would create for other countries with substantial Jewish communities. For a while, the Nazis would not even let Rublee travel to Berlin to negotiate. Finally, in mid-December 1938, Rublee was able to meet with Hjalmar Schacht in London, who told him that Germany would allow Jews to emigrate if "international Jewry" funded increased purchases of German exports. Rublee came up with a counterproposal that shed the most overtly extortionate elements of the German plan. Negotiations dragged on through 1939, but finally failed when war broke out in September.

By 1938, it was clear that the path to saving German Jews ran through appeasement, because saving Jews would have to mean negotiating with the Nazis. If, on the other hand, the democracies put up firm diplomatic or military resistance to Nazi aggression, German Jews would pay the price. The American consul general in Berlin, Raymond Geist, made this point firmly in 1938. Geist thought that the Nazis had "embarked on a program of annihilation of the Jews," which made it urgent to find a solution to the refugee problem. But Geist also recognized that the United States would have to abandon the project of saving European Jews if it decided to "attack the oppressor and bring about his destruction" in order to uphold the principles of justice and human dignity. Geist understood that any Jews remaining in Germany when war came were doomed.

Under these difficult circumstances, Roosevelt took some creditable steps. After Kristallnacht, he recalled the American ambassador from Berlin, and he discreetly ordered the indefinite extension of visitors' visas for German Jews already in the United States. But Roosevelt always had to consider one grim fact: the more he pushed for help for European Jews, the more he would likely spark a backlash that would result in Congress cutting back the quotas even more. And by 1939, in the face of the mounting crisis, whatever he could do for Europe's Jews was never going to be enough.

GERMANY WAS FAR from the only country generating refugees in the late 1930s. Central and eastern Europe was ground zero for the refugee crisis just as it was for the crisis of democracy—and for the same reasons. The philosopher Hannah Arendt wrote that the "general disintegration of political life . . . though characteristic of the whole of Europe between the two wars . . . developed fully in the states newly established after the liquidation of the Dual Monarchy and the Czarist Empire." Arendt understood that minorities who did not have a state to represent them were the main victims of totalitarianism. In central and eastern Europe in the late 1930s, that meant Jews.

There were many more Jews in Poland, Romania, and Hungary than in Germany or Austria. Poland had more than three million Jews, about 10 percent of its total population. Romania had more than 750,000, Hungary nearly 450,000. By the late 1930s, these governments were increasingly copying Nazi Jewish policy. Earlier in the decade, the world had focused its limited interest in refugees on the German case. By the late 1930s, many observers feared a much larger crisis was brewing farther to the east. "I am sure that elemental floods will soon break out all over Eastern European Jewry," predicted Revisionist Zionist leader Vladimir Jabotinsky, so terrible that "the German catastrophe will soon be eclipsed." "What if Poland, Hungary, Rumania also expel their Jewish citizens?" the London *Daily Express* wondered in March 1938. The governments of these countries fed these concerns by repeatedly asking that their "Jewish problems" be dealt with and proposing that their Jewish populations be deported to other continents. Polish foreign minister Józef Beck said that he wanted 80,000 to 100,000 Jews per year to leave Poland, with all their assets remaining behind. King Carol of Romania suggested to the British that 200,000 Jews should leave his country.

The antisemitism behind the calls for Jewish emigration was a part of the same crisis that had brought authoritarianism surging back into central Europe. In Poland, for example, after the death of Marshal Józef Pilsudski in 1935, the government moved further to the right and its antisemitism became more open, with many of the hallmarks of Nazi policy: boycotts of Jewish businesses, exclusion of Jews from some professions, and periodic violence. Hungary's authoritarian governments of the 1930s moved closer to Germany and, in 1938, began passing laws expelling Jews from business and the professions.

When western European democratic governments confronted this looming problem, they had to consider that any arrangements they made for German and Austrian Jews might only encourage the other central European governments in their demands. As with the United States, their responses were also shaped by the economic problems of the 1930s and by the patterns of racial thinking common around the world at the time.

France was the home of the great revolution of 1789, the land of liberty, equality, and fraternity. It had a long tradition as a place of refuge for Europe's victims of political persecution. As a continental European country, it was physically closer and culturally more congenial to the victims of Europe's new authoritarianism than Britain or America. France stood at the center of the refugee crisis of the 1930s.

In the 1920s, France had held true to its liberal heritage, welcoming white (meaning anticommunist) Russians fleeing the Bolsheviks and antifascists fleeing Mussolini. But the Great Depression began to shift French thinking, even before the arrival of Hitler. The political right began to argue that diversity weakened rather than strengthened France.

Here again was the broader significance of the refugee crisis. There was a widespread feeling in France in the 1930s that the democratic republic that had survived the First World War was now in a terminal crisis. An invigorated political right poured scorn on France's liberal, humane, and democratic heritage. Hostility to migrants merged easily with this hostility to democracy. In the mid-1930s, the French government tried to contain the refugee problem by using abandoned army barracks in regions along the border with Germany to house refugees. Border-area politicians protested. One local politician complained about refugees being dumped in his area, and insisted that eastern France had the right to "remain French." The racist writer Georges Vacher de Lapouge complained that because of Hitler's "splendid" policy, in France it was "raining German Jews."

French refugee policy sharpened considerably when Édouard Daladier came to power as prime minister in 1938. Daladier worried that the many refugees from Nazi Germany—there were probably 40,000 in France by 1939—amounted to a serious security threat. He was sure that among the genuine refugees were many who were simply Nazi agents, the seeds of a future fifth column. One of his first actions as prime minister was to issue an executive order guaranteeing rights of residence for the Russian and Armenian refugees who had arrived in the 1920s, but not for the more recent German and Spanish refugees. His order also made it easier for border officials to turn refugees back.

Britain's island geography and cultural differences made it less accessible as well as less attractive than France for continental refugees. On top of this came policy: the British did not pretend they had a tradition as a home for the oppressed. A Home Office official explained in 1933, "We do not . . . admit that there is a 'right of asylum.'" Decisions about refugees were made purely on the basis of "whether it is in the public interest that [they] be admitted." By 1938, perhaps 8,000 refugees from Germany had arrived in Britain, of whom approximately 80 percent were Jewish. But the real concern for the British was Palestine.

The British had taken over Palestine, a former province of the Ottoman Empire, under a League of Nations mandate after the First World War. This meant that British policy would decide whether, and how many, Jews would be admitted to the Holy Land. Despite the Great Depression, Palestine actually had a booming economy. Under the impact of Hitler and eastern European antisemitism, the Jewish population of Palestine grew dramatically, from 175,000 in 1931 to 370,000 in 1937, a little under one-third of the total. The number of official Jewish immigrants rose from 11,289 in 1932 to 64,147 in 1935, and the official figures naturally did not count illegal immigrants, whose numbers were significant.

The increased Jewish migration sparked a revolt by Palestinian Arabs in 1936, and not just by them—the problem of Palestine became "internationalized" on both sides, with Muslims in places like India and in British client states like Iraq or Egypt protesting Jewish migration to the Mandate. In response, the British began to cut down on the numbers of migrants granted entry: in 1937, the number admitted fell to 10,600. Eventually, in a 1939 White Paper, the British government decided on an annual quota of 10,000 Jewish immigrants for five years, with a further 25,000 refugees to be admitted if "adequate provision for their maintenance is assured." After that, they would admit Jews to Palestine only to the extent that the Arabs agreed.

Neville Chamberlain was coldly unsympathetic to the plight of German Jews. "No doubt Jews aren't a lovable people," he wrote to Hilda in July 1939. "I don't care about them myself," although he allowed that "that is not sufficient to explain the [Nazi] Pogrom." Chamberlain felt that Jews and Jewish refugees were nothing but an unwanted complication in his efforts to reach better relations with Germany. The U.S. ambassador Joseph Kennedy spoke often with Chamberlain, and in December 1938, he wrote that the prime minister blamed Jews for the "serious setback and possible destruction" of his appeasement policies. The same attitude permeated the pro-appeasement media. The newspaper baron Lord Beaverbrook complained in late 1938 that "the

Jews have got a big position in the press here . . . The *Daily Mirror* may be owned by Jews. The *Daily Herald* is owned by Jews. And the *News Chronicle* should really be the *Jews Chronicle*." Beaverbrook feared that Jewish "political influence" would "drive us into war."

Those Britons who were sympathetic to the plight of European Jews, however, were also likely to be opponents of Chamberlain's appeasement policies. Among the most remarkable was the independent member of Parliament Eleanor Rathbone.

Rathbone came from a family prominent in politics, social work, and social reform. The actor Basil Rathbone, famous for playing Sherlock Holmes, was her cousin. In the late 1890s, she became deeply involved in the fight for women's suffrage. The success of that movement opened up the prospect of a national political career, and she was elected to the House of Commons in 1929.

Rathbone possessed a powerful combination of idealism and political shrewdness. Like Churchill, she had seen the danger of Hitler's Germany from the beginning. In 1936, she predicted that a European crisis would begin with Hitler stirring up a revolt in Czechoslovakia's German community. She could not fathom why the democracies did not back the Spanish Republic against Franco's insurgency, and this issue drew her in turn into trying to save European refugees and bring them to Britain.

Utterly indifferent to both flattery and criticism, and tireless in badgering officials, she tried to open Britain's doors a little wider to those whose lives were threatened by fascism and to lobby officials in individual cases. If officials did not do what she wanted, she threatened them with publicity. Often this threat worked where persuasion had not. Harold Nicolson, a National Labour MP, said this was why officials tended to hide behind a pillar when they saw her coming. Late in 1938, Rathbone formed a Parliamentary Committee on Refugees with three other MPs of various parties. Despite the "Parliamentary" designation, she funded all the activities herself, and the committee was soon meeting almost daily. In time, Rathbone would get two hundred MPs to pledge support for her work.

Rathbone wrote movingly about what she thought of trying to save refugees in the face of an indifferent or even hostile government and public. She felt it was "as though one stood hour after hour, day after day, with a small group of people outside bars behind which hordes of men, women and children were enduring every kind of deliberately inflicted physical and mental torture." The group scraped at the bars, and from time to time "a few victims are dragged painfully one by one through the gaps." But all the while, "we are conscious that streams of people are passing behind us unaware of or indifferent to what is happening, who could if they united either push down the bars and rescue the victims, or—much more dangerously—stop the torturers."

The wellspring of Rathbone's political activity was a deep sense of responsibility. In part, this responsibility came from what she considered the British government's betrayal of people and causes it had pledged to support. But there was another source as well. "Some people," she wrote, "apparently feel [responsibility] only for the evil they actually do; others feel guilty of every bit of evil in the world which they or their nations . . . fail to prevent, provided it was possible to prevent or try to prevent it without creating a greater evil . . . For Christians at least this view seems inherent in Christian teaching concerning our duty to our neighbor." The responsibility rested not only on the government but on individual citizens, "if we do not . . . exert every means we possess of influencing the government to change its policy."

Rathbone's work contributed to some easing of Britain's domestic refugee policy in the last year before the war, as the imminence of conflict stimulated a last desperate effort to get free of the dangerous regimes. By the end of 1939, Britain had admitted about fifty thousand refugees from Germany and another six thousand from Czechoslovakia. But the Royal Navy aggressively patrolled the eastern Mediterranean to block "illegal" Jewish migration to Palestine. Ships carrying refugees often responded by putting their passengers in rafts or small boats beyond Palestinian territorial waters and leaving them to row ashore. If the British authorities caught the migrants, they interned them in camps and counted the number against the quota.

The political logic that made Eleanor Rathbone an opponent of Chamberlain's appeasement and an advocate for refugees applied in the same way to Winston Churchill, who had a consistent record of support for Jewish refugees from Nazi oppression. Churchill advocated an immigrant and refugee quota for Palestine that was double what the Chamberlain government settled on in 1939, and he denounced the government's policy as yet another case of appeasement and betrayal. In the Balfour Declaration of 1917, the British government had committed itself to "look with favor" on a "Jewish National Home" in Palestine. But the government's 1939 White Paper insisted that it was *not* British policy that Palestine "should become a Jewish state." "What sort of National Home is offered to the Jews of the world," Churchill asked bitterly, "when we are asked to declare that in five years' time the door of that home is to be shut and barred in their faces?"

The fostering of Jewish immigration to Palestine had, in fact, been a signature policy of the League of Nations and the whole post–First World War liberal, international order—with all of its strengths and, sometimes, narrow European weaknesses. Its failure was a major failure of that world order. Churchill stressed the effect the new Palestine policy would have on British efforts to rally a coalition of democracies to face the dictators. "Can we—and this is the question—strengthen ourselves by this repudiation?" he wondered. "The despairing Jews will resist it. What will the world think about it? What will our friends say? What will be the opinion of the United States of America? Shall we not lose more . . . in the growing support and sympathy of the United States than we shall gain in local administrative convenience, if gain at all indeed we do?"

EARLY ONE MORNING, after nineteen days at sea, the Fürst family realized their ship's engines had grown quiet. They rushed up on deck. It soon became light. "We still lay far out before the great bay," Max wrote years later. "The blue sea, the irregular hustle and bustle of the harbor, the houses that seemed to climb the mountain, the yellow land and, behind it, the bluish shimmer of the mountain. We knew it was Mount Carmel. The sight was enchantingly beautiful, and we had time to marvel and admire it, as the ship would not land before noon." They had reached Haifa. They were safe.

Safe—but for someone with Max's thoughtful disposition, exile was never going to be easy. He knew that "many had gambled away their lives" by not moving quickly when there was a chance to emigrate.

He knew that it was not his fault that friends had been taken by the Gestapo and had died in Nazi prisons, in many cases friends whom he had inspired to take up political activity. But it was one thing to know this, another to feel it. One day, when he had reestablished his workshop in a cellar in Haifa, he looked up the stairs to the courtyard, almost blinded by the sunlight, to see an unfamiliar young woman at his door. "And you work here calmly," she said to him, "while half of your people are being killed?" At the time, he was angry and sent her away without saying anything. "What should I have said?" he wondered. "Should I have boasted that I had been in a concentration camp, and had only gotten out through luck?" But "the fishhook had gotten its barb into me. One is always responsible. The more we know, the more we have learned to think, the more hopeless it is to live and not be responsible for everything." His words were uncannily like those of Eleanor Rathbone. The German radical and the British reformer each understood that human beings are moral actors who make choices, and must be willing to take responsibility for the consequences of those choices.

Cläre Tisch had made a choice, too—to stay with the orphaned children when she could have emigrated. Nonetheless, Joseph Schumpeter renewed his affidavit of support for her in the summer of 1941. Cläre responded once again with gratitude: "You probably cannot imagine what a comforting feeling it is for me to know that there is someone there who wants to help me." But by this time there were new regulations for U.S. visas, and she was not sure she could get one.

Cläre wrote to Schumpeter again on November 8, 1941. "I am leaving Wuppertal the day after tomorrow," she told him, "and I still don't know what my new address will be. I also don't know if I will have an opportunity to let you know it right away." She assured him that "It gives me hope for the future into which I am now going, to know that when someday help is possible again, I can count on your help."

What she meant was that on November 10, she would be on a train of Jews being deported "east." Her destination was Minsk, in the German-occupied Soviet Union, where the Nazis had established a Jewish "ghetto."

They murdered Cläre soon after she reached Minsk. She was thirty-four years old.

PART TWO

MUNICH

8

"That's What I Want to Have!"

The chancellor has come to the German Army's training ground at Kummersdorf to see a demonstration of the latest weaponry. An ambitious and freethinking officer named Heinz Guderian relishes this opportunity to show the Führer what motorized units can do. Guderian has learned that Hitler is fascinated by the military possibilities of motorization, and at Kummersdorf, he orders several formations of tanks, motorcycles, and armored cars to go through their paces. Hitler is excited by what he sees. Watching Guderian's demonstration, he exclaims repeatedly, "That's what I need! That's what I want to have!" It is early 1934, but this is already a fateful moment for the later history of the Second World War.

Hitler is primed to be receptive to Guderian's ideas about tanks. Ten years earlier, he wrote about the "general motorization of the world" that in the "next war" will be "overwhelmingly decisive." He will soon tell a gathering of generals that "short decisive blows to the West and then to the East" will be necessary to secure the Lebensraum that Germany needs. Political radicalism and technological modernity merge: Hitler sees that the tank will be his instrument.

Ironically, Guderian has found his inspiration in the writings of British military theorists such as Basil Liddell Hart. He sees that the tank offers a way around the stalemate and slaughter of the First World War, when the incredible increase in the killing power of small arms and heavy artillery gave a big advantage to the defense. The technology to overcome the defense and return to a war of movement has been lacking. Now it is at hand. Sophisticated German military strategists have long known that against powers such as Britain, France, and the United States, Germany can win only a quick war. The tank, a weapon of fast-moving ground warfare, becomes the classic German weapon in the same way that the Spitfire is the classically defensive British weapon.

But just as Dowding has to overcome the Trenchardists to bring the Spitfire and radar to full development, Guderian has to fight more conservative thinkers in the upper reaches of the German Army. He knows that Blomberg is sympathetic. But he has to contend with "the rigidity" of others, most notably Ludwig Beck, the army chief of staff.

Guderian and Beck do not get along. (Actually, the abrasive Guderian gets on well with almost no one.) Guderian considers Beck "a calm, almost too calm, and thoughtful man of the old school," with "no understanding for modern technical matters." Guderian feels that Beck has chosen officers who agree with him to fill the important staff positions, creating "a barrier of reaction at the very center of the army." Beck is all about defense, or, as Guderian dismissively puts it, he is "a procrastinator in military as in political matters."

But things are not quite as Guderian claims. What is true is that Guderian is a Nazi, while Beck is a conservative traditionalist. During the Second World War, Guderian will fight enthusiastically for Hitler while Beck becomes a leading figure in the resistance. Guderian's later account of Beck is tinged by his anger at Beck's resistance work. In fact, in the 1930s, Beck has done more than most senior officers to bring tanks into the German Army. But for Guderian, the point about tanks is not whether they are present. The point is how they are to be used. He wants independent tank divisions that can move at their own fast pace and not be tied to the slogging foot soldiers. "Boot 'em, don't scatter 'em," is his motto. Beck, like most traditionalist German officers, thinks this idea is unproven, and so to rest Germany's security on it would be reckless.

Just as in Britain, there are logical connections between German military doctrine and foreign policy. Captain Liddell Hart observes that as a weapon of fast-moving war, the tank is the natural tool of the aggressor.

He encourages the British government to seek an outright world ban on tanks. Slow-moving war is in Britain's interest.

There is an even broader natural connection between Nazism and tanks, mirroring the one between Britain's peaceful liberalism and the Spitfire. Fascism, both in Italy and Germany, glorifies machines, speed, and aggression. The literary scholar and diarist Victor Klemperer writes about how in the middle of the 1930s, "The most memorable and frequent image of heroism [is] provided by . . . the race car driver." Bernd Rosemeyer, a race car driver who is killed in a crash in 1938, has for a time held a place in the popular imagination almost equal to the Nazi martyr Horst Wessel. When war begins in 1939, Klemperer finds that the decisiveness and will to victory of the race car driver translates smoothly into the popular image of the tank crewman.

And within the German Army there is a definite correlation: the more conservative and traditionalist officers such as Beck keep their distance from Hitler and are hesitant to embrace the idea of a fast-moving war of aggression. If Beck is not quite the adversary Guderian will later paint him, he nonetheless is skeptical about the tank's potential. Guderian claims that when he explains how he wants to use tanks in combat, Beck responds, "No, no, I don't want to have anything to do with you people. You move too fast for me." When a war game exercise in 1937 seems to prove that a rapid, daring tank thrust will really work, Beck gets the umpire to rule the outcome invalid. Another traditionalist officer tells Guderian that Panzer divisions—whole divisions consisting of tanks and operating independently—are "a utopian dream."

By contrast, the most Nazified units of the armed forces are also the most technologically up to date. These are the Waffen SS, or "armed SS," military formations under the command of Heinrich Himmler. Technically part of the Nazi Party rather than the army, the Waffen SS units are fully motorized well before the outbreak of war, when most German Army units are still relying on horse-drawn transport. When war comes, Allied forces will fear nothing quite so much as an SS Panzer division.

IF THE BRITISH were appalled at the way the First World War had gone, it is no surprise that the Germans felt worse. At least the British had won. For German politicians and soldiers, the First World War had been a trauma. Escaping from the strategic trap in which they had been caught and the defeat they had suffered in 1918 was their burning priority. But their solutions could hardly have been more different from the British ones.

Hitler's regime had no time for the careful economic concerns of Chamberlain's administration, or for the idea of the economy as a "fourth arm." Hermann Göring poured scorn on "bourgeois businessmen" who advocated "limitation of armaments [and] defeatism," revealing their "incomprehension of the foreign policy situation." Hitler wrote that "however well-balanced the general pattern of a nation's life ought to be, there must at particular times be certain disturbances of the balance at the expense of other less vital tasks." Economic policy had to take a backseat to the urgency of giving Germany the strongest army in the world.

Hitler and Göring certainly heard voices warning of serious economic consequences from their arms buildup—which might have included a falling stock market or, even more alarming after the chaos of the early 1920s, a return to hyperinflation. Sober-minded officials delivered such warnings repeatedly. As if he were channeling Chamberlain's cabinet, Finance Minister Count Lutz Schwerin von Krosigk warned Hitler in 1938 that "Every war in the future will be fought not only with military means but also will be an economic war of greatest scope," and so he felt duty-bound to warn Hitler of his "deep anxiety for the future of Germany." Krosigk was afraid that in the event of war, the British, understanding Germany's economic weakness and their own strength, would not bother to launch any military attack, but rather would "let Germany's economic weakness take effect" until the Reich collapsed under the pressure. But Hitler was certain of his priorities, and he brushed such warnings aside.

And if the trauma of the First World War had pushed the British to rediscover the virtues of a "limited liability" war fought with naval and air power, it had inspired German strategists to a redefinition of total war embracing the whole nation. The most prominent and influential German theorist of total war was a man who had been a pioneering practitioner of it between 1914 and 1918, the former second in command of the German Army, General Erich Ludendorff.

In 1935, Ludendorff published his book *Total War*, in which he claimed that the First World War introduced this new kind of conflict, and that henceforth all wars would be "total," meaning that "the moral and vital forces of the hostile populations" would be attacked "for the purpose of corrupting and paralyzing them."

Total war, said Ludendorff, had come about because of the rise of mass conscription and new methods of warfare, such as bombing from the air. Psychological factors were also important. "Aircraft . . . now throw not only bombs but also pamphlets and other propaganda material in the midst of the populations," he wrote, "and thanks to the increase of broadcasting, propaganda is carried among the enemy."

National politics had to change to match this new kind of war. "Like the totalitarian war, politics, too, must assume a totalitarian character," said Ludendorff. Even in peacetime, politics had to be "subservient to the conduct of war." Politics had to ensure "the highest output of a nation," and "should carefully consider the requirements and claims of the nation for the preservation of its existence in all spheres of life." One of those requirements was a new kind of egalitarianism and national unity. Already in 1921, Ludendorff had written that the "German Unity Front" he dreamed of must do away with "the antagonism between the middle class and the workers, between town and country, and the many other antagonisms and distinctions that weaken the German people."

In the 1920s and '30s, the terms *total war* and *totalitarianism* developed together. The German war veteran and writer Ernst Jünger was among the many intellectuals who saw, like Ludendorff, that a totalitarian state was fundamentally a state that was organized to fight a total war. To mobilize effectively for modern war, the "image of war" had to be "drawn in the peacetime order." Jünger insisted that this was now a mandatory process for all countries that made some claim on world power.

Hitler and Ludendorff probably first met in the spring of 1921, through Hitler's acolyte Rudolf Hess. Inevitably, the former general made a powerful impact on the former private first class, and Hitler began to adopt many of Ludendorff's ideas. That year, the Nazi newspaper the *Völkischer Beobachter* had only the highest praise for Ludendorff's book *Warfare and Politics*, and in 1923 the two men marched together in

Hitler's "Beer Hall Putsch," with Hitler calling Ludendorff "the general I idolize." Remarkably, even though in later years Ludendorff would turn sharply against Hitler and his party, Hitler's idolatry remained intact. Even in 1942, Hitler could still speak of wanting to have Ludendorff's mortal remains moved to a place of honor in Berlin. This is less surprising if we consider that the Third Reich, with its mass conscription, its ethos of classless egalitarianism for all non-Jewish Germans, its incessant propaganda and state control of all media, and its Four-Year Plan to harness the economy to the future war effort, was a point-for-point fulfillment of Ludendorff's ideas.

The scale of the German arms buildup in the 1930s was without any historical parallel, although Japan and the Soviet Union were following a similar path. In 1938, Germany spent five times the share of national income on armaments that the Kaiser's Germany had allocated to defense before the First World War, with a GDP that was 60 percent larger. As the historian Adam Tooze observes, this vast allocation of resources indicated how well Hitler understood the kind of effort it would take to overturn the Western democracies.

But this effort was too much for German society and its economy to bear, and the huge problems the armament drive created helped to push Germany toward war *sooner* than Hitler had wanted or planned. In 1936, Major General Friedrich Fromm, the head of the army's Central Administrative Office, foresaw that Hitler's plan for an army of 102 divisions by 1940 would cause exactly those problems of raw material supply and foreign exchange that a year later led to the convening of the Hossbach Conference. But even if materials were available, a large portion of Germany's available industrial plant would have to be quickly converted to manufacturing tanks and guns for the duration of the plan. And then what? If the factories were converted back to civilian use once the 1940 targets had been reached, there would be serious unemployment. If the factories kept making weapons, the army would continue to swell, and the government's financial problems, and the raw material shortages, would get even worse. Fromm's conclusion was clear: "Shortly after completion of the rearmament phase, the army must be employed, otherwise there must be a reduction in demands or in the level of war readiness." If the government did not intend to fight a major war by 1940, then the whole arms buildup was not only pointless, but also dangerously irrational. And so, the very logic of the huge buildup helped to push Hitler's regime toward war.

By the late 1930s, Germany was allocating 23 percent of its national wealth to military spending, as compared with 17 percent for France, 12 percent for Britain, and 2 percent for the United States. The Western democracies were nonetheless rearming and catching up with Germany—much faster than Hitler had imagined they would. German officials increasingly realized that to fight the British, the French, and possibly also the Americans, Germany would need to control oil and food from southeastern Europe and the Soviet Union. But to get these resources, it would also have to fight a war.

Hitler saw that the window of opportunity for his war was starting to close. It was time for the desperate gamble, the gamble on a fast war with tanks. As he put it in one address to his generals, "Our economic situation is such that we can only hold out for a few more years . . . We must act."

CZECHOSLOVAKIA HAD FEATURED prominently at the Hossbach Conference and in the new war plans that followed it. Hitler told Goebbels just before the Anschluss that Czechoslovakia would be "torn to pieces one day," and afterward he told Jodl that the Czechs' turn would come once Austria had been digested.

So it was not surprising that in the spring of 1938, Hitler's full attention turned to Czechoslovakia. The result would be an entirely new kind of crisis. Hitler's previous actions—departure from the League of Nations, rearmament and conscription, the militarization of the Rhineland, the takeover of Austria—were all things that any right-wing, nationalist German government would probably have tried to do sooner or later. Czechoslovakia was different. An assault on the Czech lands was something Hitler would have to carry out in the teeth of internal opposition from many of his diplomats and military commanders. The Czech crisis would be a long-running and potentially fatal catastrophe for Hitler's regime, for Europe, and for the world.

For one thing, Czechoslovakia was not a soft target. Though it had only fourteen million people, it possessed a relatively large and efficient army, and its borders with Germany lay in mountainous territory protected by a formidable string of fortresses. The army was backed by an extensive and sophisticated armaments industry, including the famous Skoda works of Pilsen. Czechoslovakia had formal treaties of alliance with the Soviet Union and France. Any attack on it raised the prospect of another world war.

There was also a crucial difference between what Hitler *said* he wanted to do in Czechoslovakia and what he actually wanted to do. The Germans of Czechoslovakia had been part of the ruling group in the old Austro-Hungarian Empire, and they were not happy about their new status as a minority in someone else's country. Hitler claimed to be nothing more than the protector of their rights and autonomy. He said he had no designs on the predominantly Czech and Slovak sections of the country. But at the Hossbach Conference and on many other occasions, he had made it clear to his military commanders that he wanted to destroy the entire state. This meant that for the first time, he was moving beyond the integration of ethnic Germans into one state and toward a very different kind of aggression.

Working in Hitler's favor, however, were Czechoslovakia's bitter internal divisions. These divisions offered a rich target to a hostile adversary: an aggressor could work on fostering and further inflaming those divisions as a way of bringing down the whole state. Ernst von Weizsäcker, the new state secretary at the Foreign Ministry, called this the "chemical" as opposed to the "mechanical"—in other words, military—approach to destroying Czechoslovakia. It was the chemical approach that Hitler set out to apply.

Here again, Hitler drew on tactics that had served him well in his own rise to power. Germany focused a flood of official propaganda on the injustices the Czech state allegedly imposed on its German minority. Real incidents of injustice could be exploited, however few they might be. Fake incidents were fabricated by Goebbels's propaganda machine. The Nazi strategy was to provoke violence between Czechs and Germans in order to portray the German community as the victim. If it was impossible to provoke an actual incident, the German media machine would conjure up a fake one.

Konrad Henlein, the leader of the pro-Nazi Sudeten German Party, traveled to Germany at the end of March 1938 to get his orders from Hitler, who told him that the Czech question would be "solved before very long." Henlein's job was to keep up a steady fire of demands on behalf of the Sudeten Germans against the Czech state. As Henlein himself expressed it, "We must always demand so much that we cannot be satisfied." Arriving at a better situation for Czech Germans was never the point. The point was to find a reason to destroy Czechoslovakia altogether. For Hitler, the worst outcome would be for the Czechs to give in to his demands. He reached back to his memories of the Austro-Hungarian Empire for the kinds of demands that national minorities had made then that the empire could never grant. He urged Henlein to call for separate German units within the Czech army.

Hitler wanted to do to Czechoslovakia what Austria had tried but failed to do to Serbia in 1914: isolate it so that an attack on it would not lead to a wider war. Only then would he invade and conquer the country. For this, the Nazis needed either a plausible pretext for invasion—something like the assassination of Austrian archduke Franz Ferdinand at the hands of terrorists backed by the Serbian intelligence service, which had set off the First World War—or a favorable moment in which the Western powers were distracted, perhaps by social tension in France or war in the Mediterranean, as Hitler had speculated at the Hossbach Conference. Keitel remembered that Hitler referred expressly to the 1914 assassination while planning strategy for Czechoslovakia. The German plan for propaganda and violence was calculated to weaken and discredit the Czech state both internally and in the eyes of foreign governments. Hitler also hoped that the construction of the "West Wall," a line of fortifications along Germany's border with France, would deter any attack from that direction.

At this point, an unexpected event upset Hitler's plans. Well into May 1938, Hitler had no specific time in mind for an attack on Czechoslovakia, other than "soon." In late April, he ordered Keitel to draw up plans for an attack. The draft Keitel produced contained what was presumably Hitler's instruction to him: "It is *not* my intention to smash Czechoslovakia by military action in the immediate future without provocation, unless an unavoidable development of the political conditions within

Czechoslovakia forces the issue, or political events in Europe create a particularly favorable opportunity which may perhaps never recur [emphasis added]." Then came "the weekend crisis."

On Friday, May 20, the Czech government reacted to news of a military emergency: credible reports that there were twelve German divisions massed on the Czech border. The defense minister, František Machnik, called up nearly two hundred thousand reservists, which meant that a force of nearly four hundred thousand well-trained and well-equipped Czech troops stood ready to meet a German invasion. An American military observer was impressed with the skill and resolve of the Czech forces. The whole country seemed ready to fight.

What had set this in motion? On May 18, the Czech military intelligence service received a report from a key German agent of extensive German mobilization along the border. It looked like what had just happened in Austria. The identity of this agent remains unknown, but he was close enough to the German Army or government that the Czechs took his information seriously. British intelligence, furthermore, initially confirmed what the Czechs feared was happening. The Czech domestic intelligence service reported that the German minister in Prague, Ernst Eisenlohr, had boasted that day that a German attack was coming soon.

However, on Saturday, May 21, František Havel, chief of the analytical section of Czech intelligence, began to get suspicious. There was too much information coming from too many sources. By Monday, Havel concluded that the information was fake. If so, however, it had been skillfully faked. The source knew a lot about the German armed forces and how they might really deploy for an attack.

But who was the source, and what was his motive? Hungary and Poland could benefit from a crisis over Czechoslovakia but not over the outbreak of war. There is no evidence that the information came from German intelligence. The historian Igor Lukes suggests that the most plausible suspect is the Soviet Union. Joseph Stalin had a clear motive. He feared a diplomatic arrangement at the expense of Czechoslovakia that would bring the German Army closer to his borders. He would have preferred a war that kept all the Western powers busy. The Soviet foreign intelligence service had an important resident in Prague, known to Czech intelligence as "Rudolf," who ran agents in Germany as well as in Czechoslovakia. Rudolf or one of his agents could have been the source.

If the origins of the story remain mysterious, the consequences of the Czech mobilization are clear. Hitler's new foreign minister, Joachim von Ribbentrop, reacted to it with his usual arrogant fury. He claimed that the "big mouths" in Prague were lying, and he told the Czech ambassador in Berlin that mobilization might bring about the very German invasion the Czechs were busy fabricating. The British ambassador, Sir Nevile Henderson, warned Ribbentrop that Britain would not stand aside in the event of a war with Czechoslovakia. Paul Schmidt, Hitler's interpreter, thought that Henderson's smooth and formal manner, "that of the perfect English gentleman, always somehow irritated both Ribbentrop and Hitler, who could not endure 'fine people.'" There was nothing diplomatic about Ribbentrop's response. He told the British envoy that "every German was ready to die for his country," and that if a war broke out between Germany and the Western powers, "it would be a war of aggression provoked by France, and Germany would fight, just as she did in 1914."

Even though intelligence reports soon cast doubt on the idea that Hitler had planned a May invasion, the British government became convinced that such plans had indeed been in the works and that only the resolve of Czechoslovakia and the Western powers had forced Hitler to back down. Chamberlain wrote to his sister Hilda that he did not believe the German ambassador's denials of a planned attack, adding that the weekend had been a "damned close run thing." A month later, using a metaphor he would return to again and again—and come to regret—Chamberlain wrote that the Germans had "missed the bus and may never again have such a favorable chance of asserting their domination over central & Eastern Europe."

"Anyone deliberately planning to madden Hitler could have thought of no better method" than suggesting that he had backed down in the face of resistance, Paul Schmidt wrote years later. In his rage, Hitler accelerated the timetable for an attack on Czechoslovakia. On May 28, he told his generals that instead of "solving" the Czech problem at some indeterminate point in time, he wanted the country wiped off the map by the autumn of 1938. The result was a revised plan of attack—still code-named "Case Green"—with a very different preamble. "It is my unalterable decision," Hitler said, "to smash Czechoslovakia by military action in the near future." For propaganda reasons, the Germans would find a "convenient apparent excuse" for the invasion.

THE POSITION HELD by Ludwig Beck, chief of the army's general staff, was one steeped in Prussian and German history and tradition, dating back to Prussia's Wars of Liberation against Napoléon's occupation in the years after 1806. Soldiers such as Beck revered the memory of Chief of Staff Helmuth von Moltke the Elder, who had led the Prussian Army through the wars of German unification, and his successor, Count Alfred von Schlieffen, even though a modified version of Schlieffen's plan for war had failed dismally in 1914. For most German officers, the army embodied the nation and the chief of the general staff had responsibilities reaching far beyond purely military affairs. He was another national leader, with the duty to advise the government on all political and diplomatic matters.

Beck believed deeply in this lofty idea of his office. He expected to give Hitler advice, and he expected Hitler to take it. As the crisis over Czechoslovakia arose, the worries Beck had first expressed upon seeing Hossbach's memorandum grew stronger. In the late spring and summer of 1938, Beck developed into the most persistent and scathing critic of Hitler's war plans. Just after the weekend crisis, Hitler invited his military commanders and senior Foreign Office personnel to a conference at the Reich Chancellery's Winter Garden. Beck responded with a remarkable display of self-confidence, rooted in the traditional status of the Prussian Army and its officer corps. "Please give the Führer my greetings," he told Hitler's army adjutant, "but I do not yet know whether I can come, because I have a lot to do." Beck attended the meeting nonetheless, and heard Hitler say that he wanted Czechoslovakia wiped off the map before the end of the year. "So, first we will take on the situation in the East," Hitler explained. "Then I will give you three or four years, and then we will bring order to the situation in the West." These words drove Beck to resist.

Beck's basic point was that Germany lacked the resources to fight a long war—but a long war was precisely what Germany's adversaries, Britain and France, were planning for. Germany would need at least three weeks to defeat Czechoslovakia, leaving its western border vulnerable to French and British attack. Even if Germany beat the Czechs on schedule and could somehow contain a Franco-British advance, the country would then be mired in a long war of attrition it would surely lose. Beck also believed that German public opinion would reject a war that was not clearly defensive.

Beck's criticisms of the Nazi regime's central policies grew increasingly blunt. "Different views on religious, racial, and national problems" abroad had led to "rejection, in part feelings of hatred toward today's Germany," he wrote, accurately identifying the main issues in the global crisis of democracy and the Second World War. The methods on which the regime relied—"bluff, nothing but lies in the press, play-acting"—created "an atmosphere of incredibility . . . so that even when something is actually true, it is no longer believed."

Beck's alarm mounted through the summer, as preparations for war advanced. He realized that Hitler's mind was closed to rational argument and that the only way to stop him was to overthrow him—a contravention of his long-standing belief that "mutiny and revolution are words that do not exist in the vocabulary of a German officer" (as he had told his deputy, Franz Halder, during the Fritsch crisis). For his part, Hitler grew increasingly irritated by Beck's criticisms and began to fume that the general was "fraudulent," telling his adjutants that Beck exaggerated French strength. Beck was full of "reactionary ideas" and wanted only to sabotage Hitler's plans. "What kind of generals are these that I . . . have to drive to war?" Hitler demanded. "If things were right, I would not be able to save myself from the generals driving *me* to war!"

As Beck realized that only removing Hitler from power could secure Germany's safety and Europe's peace, he discovered a separate line of resistance activity coming from the Foreign Office and the armed forces' intelligence service, the Abwehr. As the Czech crisis grew ever more acute, Hitler fell into open conflict with his own military, intelligence, and foreign policy officials.

THE OTHER LINE of resistance started with the intelligence officer Colonel Hans Oster. One of his fellow Abwehr officers recalled that everyone

in the Abwehr "who considered himself an opponent of National Socialism ran to Oster."

Fifty-one years old in 1938, Oster had served on the Western Front
and stayed in the army until being discharged in 1932 because of an affair
with another officer's wife. In 1933, he found his way into the Prussian
State Police under Hermann Göring, and from there to the Abwehr.
In late 1933, Oster met the ambitious young lawyer Hans Bernd Gisevius, who was about to be fired from the Gestapo. Gisevius told Oster
about Gestapo practices—above all, the abuse of political prisoners in
the concentration camps—and this began the process of Oster's disillusionment. His revulsion at the murders of the Night of the Long Knives
completed it. But it was the Fritsch-Blomberg affair that turned him
toward active rebellion. He became, as Gisevius remembered, "without
doubt the toughest and most determined fighter for law and freedom
that there was in Hitler's armed forces."

Oster thought that Fritsch's treatment had been a grievous insult to
the entire army. He had served under Fritsch in the 1920s and revered
his former commander. After the scandal, as he explained later, "I made
the Fritsch case my own." But there was also more to it. Oster, like a number of other officers, saw the Fritsch-Blomberg affair as a "cold coup d'état"
by the SS and Gestapo against the army. It was essential to resist. "Our
intentions were first of all to neutralize the *Reichsführer* SS [Heinrich
Himmler] and the Gestapo," said Oster.

Gradually, Oster became the center of a network of military and
intelligence officers, diplomats, and senior police officials who had concluded that Hitler's recklessness was driving Germany to disaster. They
all agreed that the Führer had to be stopped—if necessary, by removing
him from office. Oster began putting pressure on Beck to take his resistance beyond the circulation of acerbic memorandums.

From Oster, the lines of this network ran to several other Abwehr
officers—including the head of that service, the enigmatic admiral Wilhelm Canaris.

The Austrian intelligence officer Erwin von Lahousen had a strong
memory of reporting to Canaris after the Anschluss. As he recalled, he
greeted his new superior with his right arm raised in the Hitler salute.
Without saying a word, Canaris gently pushed Lahousen's arm down.

Lahousen later described Canaris as "the most difficult superior I have encountered in my thirty-year career as a soldier," but one with "intellectual and, above all, human qualities which raised him far above the military rubber stamps and marionettes that most of his colleagues and superiors were. He never struck me, Austrian that I am, as the typical German military man; rather he seemed a cosmopolitan in the uniform of a German admiral."

Like most military men, Canaris had originally welcomed Hitler's coming to power and shared many of Hitler's goals, until Fritsch's dismissal changed his mind. When disillusionment struck him, Canaris began to apply all his many gifts of trickery to bringing the system down. He liked to imagine, probably wrongly, that he was descended from a famous Greek admiral. True or not, he was widely considered to be a "cunning Odysseus," as Ernst von Weizsäcker remembered—and Weizsäcker thought Hitler shared this view, which explained Canaris's appointment as intelligence chief. Weizsäcker remembered that Canaris had a remarkable ability to get other people to talk without saying anything at all himself, and he could do this in six languages. Perhaps for this reason, Canaris was one of the few people to whom Weizsäcker could always talk without reservation. Their main subject of conversation was "the avoidance of war and the crushing of the Hitler-gang."

Canaris and Oster packed the Abwehr with men who had shown they were willing to resist the Nazis. Their recruits included two civilians whom Canaris had arranged to take into the Abwehr if war broke out, so that they could carry on resistance work while being shielded from other military deployment. One of these was the brilliant jurist Hans von Dohnanyi, the son of a Hungarian musician, connected by marriage with the prominent Bonhoeffer family. The other was the former Gestapo officer Hans Bernd Gisevius, who would go on to be one of the most important chroniclers of the anti-Nazi resistance.

The thirty-four-year-old Gisevius had once been outspoken in his contempt for Germany's democratic politicians, and had eagerly sought a job with the Gestapo when the Nazis came to power. What he witnessed in his brief time at the Gestapo—he was forced out after a few months—would fuel his passionate resistance work for the remainder of the Third Reich.

Gisevius was nakedly ambitious, pompous, and arrogant, and most of the resisters roundly disliked him. But he could give the resisters priceless access to senior police officers, particularly the head of the German criminal police Arthur Nebe (with whom he remained friendly, even after leaving the Gestapo) and the former Stormtrooper commander and later Berlin police chief, Count Wolf-Heinrich von Helldorff. Nebe and Helldorff had both been committed Nazis before 1933, and their switch to the resistance was likely opportunistic or the product of career frustration. But plotters of a coup need police and military forces on their side, and cannot always be too choosy about who those are. Certainly, Nebe and Helldorff knew the risks they were running. "You have no idea what torture is," Nebe told Gisevius once, while in a dark mood. "They squeeze everything out of you."

Ernst von Weizsäcker, the most senior official of the Foreign Office under Ribbentrop, was an altogether different person. Fifty-six years old, he was an insider's insider. His father had been prime minister of the state of Württemberg before the First World War, and Ernst had served in the navy before leaving to join the Foreign Office, where he rose rapidly. When Hitler named Ribbentrop foreign minister, Weizsäcker was a natural choice for the number two spot.

When Ribbentrop asked Weizsäcker to become state secretary, the two men had a frank talk about what the job would involve. In early March, Weizsäcker recorded in his diary that Ribbentrop had spoken of a "great program" that was "not to be fulfilled without the sword." If possible, Austria was "to be liquidated in 1938." Just over a month later, Ribbentrop went further. There would still have to be a few years of peace, Ribbentrop explained to Weizsäcker, in order for Germany to prepare. But there were "very expansive plans, especially for the East." These plans could not be carried out without British resistance. "Officially," said Ribbentrop, "we have to label Russia as the opponent, but in reality, everything will be oriented against England."

Weizsäcker claimed after the war that he had known nothing of the Hossbach Conference. Nor did he take seriously Ribbentrop's words about conquering land in "the East." The whole thing was too "fantastic," nothing but "confused romanticism," destined to fail when it encountered "sober reality" and "a clear warning from abroad."

But Weizsäcker was nonetheless disturbed by what he heard, and it strengthened his commitment to staying in office in an effort to contain the damage. After the Second World War, many ex-Nazi officials claimed that they had stayed in their jobs under Hitler only for this reason. Not all were telling the truth. Once the Nazis were gone and their officials were exposed to prosecution, "I fought the system from within" was an expedient defense. But many, particularly those in the resistance, felt genuinely obliged to choose this morally complicated role. Early in 1938, shortly after the Blomberg-Fritsch crisis broke, Gisevius ran into the recently dismissed ambassador Ulrich von Hassell. "I congratulated him," Gisevius remembered later, "for having successfully got himself kicked out." Gisevius meant that Hassell must have been relieved to be free of any responsibility for an increasingly wayward ship of state. But, Gisevius continued, "Hassell gave me a look of surprise," and "could not understand that I really meant my congratulations." Then Hassell explained something to Gisevius that made such an impression on the younger man that he thought about it "for years afterward." Someone who was in the opposition to a dictatorship, said Hassell, "must defend his official post with tooth and claw," and if he lost his job, he "must strive to get into the government again." Even a minor post could give a resister the chance to exert some influence. Looking back years later, Gisevius thought it was foolish for postwar moralists to write someone off just because he or she had been "paid by Hitler." After Hitler's destruction of political parties and labor unions, those were the only people who could offer meaningful resistance.

Like Beck, Weizsäcker was no pacifist and no opponent of German expansion. But also like Beck, he was an opponent of a war that Germany would surely lose and that, in any case, would cause appalling losses. "What keeps me going," he wrote in a letter in early July 1938, "is the thought that I have three sons of military age, and soon a captain as a son-in-law." If it was only about his good name, he added prophetically, "it would probably be better if I went fishing."

As THE CRISIS over Czechoslovakia mounted in the summer of 1938, Oster's and Halder's pressure began to have an effect on Beck, pushing him from drafting memos to thinking about a coup.

Beck, like most conservatives, had not started off opposing Hitler's goals or methods. A combination of patriotism and professional military disdain for Hitler's recklessness, however, drove him ever further into resistance. By July, Beck had concluded that "the time seems to be past, or at least it is [now] considerably more difficult," to persuade Hitler to drop his ideas through "objective reasoning and warnings." Beck advocated an active step on the road to rebellion: a strike by the army's commanding generals if Hitler refused to abandon his plans to invade Czechoslovakia. The generals, he thought, would "have the right and the duty before the people and before history to relinquish their offices" if Hitler neglected their advice. The army could carry out no military operations if all the commanders acted in solidarity. The justification for such a step, Beck wrote, was that "the survival of the nation" was at stake. The generals' "soldierly obedience has its limits where their knowledge, their conscience and their responsibility forbid the carrying out of an order."

Beck thought that the second half of September would be the right time for this drastic step, just after the annual Nazi Party Rally in Nuremberg. By this time, he assumed, stern warnings about the consequences of a German attack would be coming in from the French and British governments. Then he reconsidered and decided that the generals would have to take action in August. Beck was far from blind to the implications of what he was saying. The army would have to be ready to meet what he delicately called "internal tensions." His notes included these significant lines: "Corresponding orders are to be given. Witzleben [General Erwin von Witzleben, the Berlin garrison commander, firmly on the side of the resisters] is to be brought together with Helldorff." By this point, in sharp contrast to his attitude in February, Beck was now contemplating a coup d'état, probably followed by civil war. He wanted Berlin's military commander and chief of police squarely on his side.

On August 4, at Beck's urging and for the only time in the history of Nazi Germany, the general officer corps met on its own without Hitler to discuss Beck's idea of a strike. Beck read one of his harshly critical memos to the assembled officers. The tough and skeptical general Wilhelm Adam, who at that time was responsible for Germany's western defenses, spoke out in agreement with Beck. Walther von Brauchitsch, however, declined to present the speech Beck had written for him. And General Walther von Reichenau, an enthusiastic Hitler supporter, went straight to the Führer to report on what Beck had said.

At this critical moment, Beck decided he had had enough of Brauchitsch's unwillingness to press opposition to Hitler—"Brauchitsch left me in the lurch!" he complained—as well as Hitler's deafness to reason. He decided he had no choice but to resign. Other regime skeptics, such as Weizsäcker, tried unsuccessfully to talk him into staying at his post. At first Beck was put in command of troops guarding Germany's western borders, but a few months later he left the army altogether. Beck made one serious error: he agreed to Hitler's request that he keep his resignation quiet. This agreement robbed Beck's departure of whatever sobering effect it might have had for the wider public.

Even so, it had a sobering effect on many officers. "Beck's leaving really got to me," Fritsch would write in November to Hossbach. "But it is the way the system is today that an officer with such character cannot be tolerated." Beck himself was stoic. He assured Hossbach that their personal friendship would continue: "We will stay as we have been." About the loss of his job, he said, the main thing he missed was the horses.

ONE OF THE stranger features of the summer and fall of 1938 was the procession of Germans who traveled to Britain in a desperate effort to convince the Chamberlain government to stand firm against Hitler.

Beck, Weizsäcker, and Oster were the instigators of these visits. Weizsäcker, like Beck, had given up the idea that Hitler and Ribbentrop could be made to see reason. He decided that "We had to get rid of this leadership, somehow and sometime," and until then, "we had to put a spoke in the wheel of the runaway train, if not with normal methods, then undercover and secretly."

The emissaries all bore the same message: Hitler was determined to invade Czechoslovakia in the coming autumn; only firm warnings of a military response from Britain and France had any chance of deterring him; and if the Western democracies stood firm, the German resistance would have the chance it needed to remove Hitler from power.

In mid-August, Oster and Beck sent the elderly aristocrat Ewald von Kleist-Schmenzin to London. Beck told Kleist, "If you can bring me positive proof from London that England will go to war if we invade Czechoslovakia, then I will overthrow this regime." Kleist asked what Beck would consider "proof." "An open promise to support Czechoslovakia in the event of war" was Beck's response. In Britain, Kleist saw Churchill and Sir Robert Vansittart, who after being sacked as permanent undersecretary had been given a meaningless post as a foreign policy advisor to the Chamberlain administration. Kleist told Vansittart that war was "a complete certainty" unless the British government gave an explicit warning that there would be war if Hitler invaded Czechoslovakia. Hitler, said Kleist, was the real extremist who was driving everything forward. The other Nazi leaders were yes-men. The generals were opposed to war but felt powerless to stop it. Vansittart wrote a report for Lord Halifax on this meeting, and Halifax passed it to Chamberlain. But Chamberlain had just received contradictory advice from military circles in Berlin: precisely because Hitler was about to invade Czechoslovakia, it was crucial to make more concessions to him. Chamberlain told Halifax that Kleist simply wanted to stir up trouble, and "I think we must discount a good deal of what he says." The prime minister was not willing to go further than recalling Ambassador Henderson for "consultations." Kleist returned to Germany and reported that his mission had been a failure.

One of the most determined travelers was Carl Goerdeler. Goerdeler, another old-school conservative, had been the mayor of Leipzig and Hitler's price commissioner, but he had resigned in protest of Nazi policies to devote himself to the resistance. He tried to explain to Western leaders that Hitler took "appeasement" as a sign of weakness and that the policy was demoralizing for Germany's democratically minded opposition. He told a reporter from *The Times*—who passed the information on to the Foreign Office—that he had urged Fritsch to carry out a military coup and that Germany was close to financial collapse.

British leaders should have been under no illusions about the seriousness of Hitler's plans or the potential for internal resistance. But there were also sound reasons for not acting on the resisters' information. Goerdeler told Vansittart that Germany should be allowed to take over the Sudetenland. Kleist explained to Churchill that Germany needed a restoration of the monarchy and the return of the "Polish corridor," the territory that Germany had been forced to cede after the First World War to give Poland access to the Baltic Sea. Such messages only convinced the British that there was no real difference between Hitler and the old guard of conservatives who now opposed him. And sometimes the Germans' traditional conservatism ran up against its British equivalent. When Goerdeler mentioned the generals' hostility to Hitler, Vansittart objected to this "treasonable talk."

In fact, many British officials had concluded that the resisters were *worse* than the Nazis. The conservatives such as Goerdeler and Kleist wanted to resurrect the pre-1918 German empire, whose commercial, imperial, and naval rivalry with Britain had contributed to the outbreak of the First World War. At least Hitler did not seem to care about overseas colonies or building up a large navy—core British concerns. Why overthrow him to put the more dangerous old guard back in power?

On September 6, Theo Kordt, an official at the German embassy in London, went to 10 Downing Street to meet secretly with Lord Halifax and Horace Wilson, a close advisor to Chamberlain. Kordt was bringing a message that Oster had given to Kordt's brother Erich, who worked at the Foreign Office in Berlin. It was too dangerous for Erich to send the message to Theo in any written or telephonic form, so Erich had enlisted their cousin Susanne Simonis to memorize it and fly to London to see Theo. Thus, Theo Kordt became yet another German who told Halifax bluntly that Hitler was determined to invade Czechoslovakia and that Hitler's aggressive plans were based on his assumption that France would not honor its alliance treaty with Czechoslovakia.

Kordt explained that he represented military and political circles that would remove Hitler from power if the British refused to back down. His group believed that there would never have been war between Britain and Germany in 1914 if the foreign secretary, Sir Edward Grey, had announced clearly that Britain would intervene in a war between France and Germany (a debatable interpretation of the outbreak of the war, but one popular in Germany and shared by Chamberlain). It was crucial, said Kordt, that Chamberlain avoid repeating this error and announce clearly that Britain would go to war to defend Czechoslovakia. Kordt knew that such bluntness would be unusual British behavior. But the moment did not call for understatement. If Hitler continued to press for war, the commanders of the German Army would put an end to the Nazi regime.

Kordt thought Halifax seemed sympathetic, but the foreign secretary did not commit himself one way or another. In fact, Halifax pondered the matter carefully and consulted with Chamberlain. Reluctantly, Chamberlain approved sending a message along the lines that Kordt had requested. Halifax sent the message to the British ambassador to Germany, Sir Neville Henderson, who was in Nuremberg to attend the Nazi Party Rally. But the ambassador refused to pass it on to Hitler, on the grounds that Hitler was already of doubtful sanity and the message might push him over the edge. Rather than reprimanding or dismissing the ambassador for this breach of discipline, Chamberlain decided that Henderson was right and rescinded his authorization of the message.

ALMOST EVERYONE WHO met General Franz Halder, the man who had stepped into Beck's large shoes as army chief of staff, recorded the same impression: Halder seemed more like a professor or a schoolteacher than a soldier. Actually, the army had often thought the same thing. Early in his career, after Halder had run up a brilliant record at the Bavarian War Academy, the Bavarian Army planned to use him as an instructor. The First World War intervened. Later, as a staff officer between the wars, Halder was often responsible for developing training programs. By 1936, he was serving under Beck on the general staff. This gave Halder a front-row seat for the Blomberg-Fritsch affair. As with so many officers, the crisis was a turning point for Halder: it converted him not only to the opposition, but also to those willing to work toward a coup d'état. Halder had tried then to press Beck toward more decisive opposition. It was in this context that Beck had replied that the words *rebellion* and *mutiny* were not part of a German officer's vocabulary.

So, when Halder replaced Beck, the resistance plotters were initially enthusiastic. Even Beck said that Halder would be a more determined opponent of Hitler than he himself had been. Halder had been an anti-Nazi longer than anyone else in the army's upper ranks. As far back as 1919 or 1920, fellow officers had taken him to see Hitler speak in Munich. Halder hated what he saw, the man as well as the message. Years later, he claimed he had never changed his mind. When he became chief of staff, Halder told Brauchitsch that he was "determined to exploit every opportunity for fighting Hitler" that his new position offered.

When Gisevius met with Halder, probably on September 5, the civilian was so shocked by Halder's ringing denunciations of Hitler that he could not help thinking, "Isn't this man the general?" Moving in resistance circles as he did, Gisevius had heard plenty of angry denunciations of Hitler. "But I cannot recall having heard before or since so eloquent an outburst of stored-up hatred as Halder produced," he wrote later. Halder raged about "this madman, this criminal," the "bloodsucker" who was steering Germany to war because of his "sexually pathological constitution." Gisevius struggled to square this rage with the appearance of the man in front of him, whose brush cut, pince-nez, and severe expression made him look like "an obedient functionary." Later, Gisevius decided that he should have trusted his first impression of Halder. But in that moment, this firebrand of a general made Gisevius—himself known among the resisters as the most outspoken and intemperate of Hitler opponents—feel that he was altogether too moderate.

Gisevius and Halder agreed on how they should carry out their revolt. They would occupy the Gestapo headquarters and seize evidence of Nazi criminality. Thus armed, they would prosecute Hitler's henchmen. The army would step in to "restore order." But they differed on timing. Halder was an advocate of the "setback theory." This meant that he thought Hitler still enjoyed such strong support among Germans that there was little chance of successfully overthrowing him. His regime was too settled, his core of supporters too loyal, for Hitler to worry about any domestic threat. Halder calculated that only a major foreign reversal—a gamble that did not come off, an obvious and reckless risk of war that would be clear to all—could dent that popularity. When Hitler finally pushed the Western powers too far and they declared war, the resistance could strike. This was Halder's message to Gisevius. Until then, "the only thing for true patriots to do was to set their teeth, to get ready, and to keep under cover."

The civilians such as Gisevius and Goerdeler, however, were "unwilling to make the outbreak of a war an essential condition of our preparations," as Gisevius put it. War was too unpredictable. The civilians offered a compromise. "Suppose that we agreed to let things drift to the point of actual war, and that Halder for his part pledged himself to attempt the coup d'état as soon as Hitler irrevocably and irrefutably issued marching orders?" That Goebbels's propaganda constantly stressed Hitler's desire for peace played into the conspirators' hands, Gisevius wrote, "for even to mention the word 'war' was equivalent to treason." The memories of the First World War were too fresh in the minds of all Germans. "War meant bread cards, starvation rations . . . [and] hundreds of thousands of lives . . . In 1938 such things were simply inconceivable." But when Gisevius and Hjalmar Schacht, who had joined the conspirators, proposed this to Halder, they felt him beginning to back away from his earlier bold stance. Now Halder argued that everything might work out after all, that "the Western Powers might present Hitler with a free ticket to the East."

Yet, by the middle of September, both the coming of war and the launching of the plotters' coup seemed imminent. Goerdeler, Gisevius, and Schacht had worked out a plan with the Berlin military district commander Erwin von Witzleben. They would claim that Hermann Göring and Heinrich Himmler were themselves plotting a coup to force the vacillating Hitler into a war he didn't want. The army would then intervene against the Nazi machine, claiming to defend Hitler from this other coup. In this way, they hoped to avoid trouble with any soldiers who worried about their oath of loyalty to the Führer.

The conspirators were not quite sure what they should do with Hitler—or, rather, they had different and contradictory ideas about what to do with him. Gisevius thought that in the beginning they should be flexible, but that as soon as possible they should kill him. Halder wanted Hitler to be killed in a way that would disguise the army's involvement, to prevent any dangerous "stab in the back" myths developing—perhaps by putting a bomb in his train that they could blame on the British.

Beck and Hans von Dohnanyi, the supreme court judge who, like Gisevius, was connected to the Abwehr, wanted to put Hitler on trial to expose the scale of his crimes and misdeeds. They would also declare him insane, for which Dohnanyi's father-in-law, the distinguished neurologist Karl Bonhoeffer, was standing by.

The conspiracy also had its raiding party, under the command of Friedrich Wilhelm Heinz, a swashbuckling far-right terrorist from Weimar days who had soured on the Nazis and gravitated to the resistance. Witzleben and Oster commissioned Heinz to lead a squad of toughs who would break into the Chancellery and kill Hitler. Since Halder, Schacht, and Goerdeler would never agree to this, Heinz called his role "a conspiracy within the conspiracy." The plan was that Witzleben, Heinz, and their men would storm the Chancellery, Witzleben would demand Hitler's resignation, they would provoke an incident, and Heinz would kill the Führer.

On September 12, Hitler gave his much-awaited closing address at the Nuremberg Rally. He made a revealing connection between the democratic parties he had defeated to become German chancellor in 1933 and the hostile democracies of Britain and France in 1938. Before 1933, "many of our national comrades were forced to realize just how dishonest the political battle was" when the anti-Nazi parties claimed to be nationalist "yet were not reluctant to conspire with Marxist internationalists." Now Britain and France claimed to speak for democracy while opposing a Germany where "99 percent of the people" backed the government, while the Czechs engaged in brutal repression of their German minority. Germany, Hitler insisted, had made nothing but sacrifices for world peace. But these sacrifices had reached a limit.

"What we Germans demand is the right to self-determination," he said.

He made no explicit threat against the Czechs. But he warned that if the democracies continued to "accord their protection to the oppression of German men and women," the consequences "will be grave."

9

"Out of This Nettle, Danger"

Sir Edward Grey always keeps his cards very close to his chest. Shortly after he becomes British foreign secretary in 1905, he faces the question of whether Britain should form an alliance with France for protection against Germany. Britain and France have signed an "entente" (in 1904), but it is a loose arrangement that says nothing about Germany. Like most British statesmen, Grey does not want to be tied down to formal commitments. He wants to preserve British freedom of action. But with its rapidly growing navy, powerful army, and booming industrial economy, Germany is developing into a significant security threat, and it seems prudent for the British to make preparations. So, the military staffs of Britain and France meet and start planning what they will do if there is war with Germany. These meetings are kept secret from Britain's Parliament and public. Later, the Russians pressure the British to enter into similar secret naval talks. Eventually, word of these arrangements leaks, and there are questions in Parliament. In 1914, two members of Parliament ask Grey about the naval talks with Russia: Can he confirm they are happening? How will they affect relations with Germany?

Grey replies that there are no unpublished agreements "which would restrict or hamper the freedom of the Government, or of Parliament, to decide whether or not Great Britain should participate in a war."

Furthermore, there were no talks in progress that might change the situation.

This answer, of course, is highly misleading. Years later, Grey will admit this. "The answer given is absolutely true," he will say. "That criticism to which it is open is, that it does not answer the question put to me. That is undeniable." He draws a fine line. The nation should be told of any agreements that might "bind the country to action or restrain its freedom." But not of "military and naval measures to meet possible contingencies."

Grey's statement confuses the British public. It also confuses the German government. The Germans do not grasp how deeply committed Britain really is to the defense of France. After the war, many people, in Britain as well as Germany, think that if Grey had been more honest in communicating with the Germans, war could have been avoided. In 1938, the example of Grey is on everyone's mind. Chamberlain is determined not to make Grey's mistake. He wants to send clear signals to the German government, striking a balance between warning and moderation. After the May crisis, the Conservative member of Parliament Leo Amery writes in his diary: "It certainly does look as if Neville has succeeded in doing the very thing Grey failed to do in 1914, namely make Germany realize the danger of precipitate action."

IN LATE AUGUST, Neville Chamberlain began dropping hints of some mysterious plan he had devised to solve the Czech crisis should war appear otherwise inevitable. "I keep racking my brains," he wrote to his sister Ida in early September, "to try & devise some means of averting a catastrophe if it should seem to be upon us. I thought of one so unconventional and daring that it rather took Halifax's breath away. But since Henderson thought it might save the situation at the 11th hour I haven't abandoned it though I hope all the time that it won't be necessary to try it."

On Wednesday, September 7, Sudeten Germans rioted in the Czech town of Moravska Ostrava, and two Sudeten German Party parliamentary deputies were arrested. In response, Henlein and the Sudeten German Party broke off all negotiations with the Czech government.

That same day, an editorial in *The Times*, a paper widely understood to be the voice of Chamberlain's administration, suggested that the government of Czechoslovakian president Edvard Beneš should make the country more homogeneous "by the secession of that fringe of alien populations" who were "united by race" with the Germans. Although Chamberlain's government strongly denied using *The Times* for a statement of official policy, the editorial was taken everywhere to be precisely that. Goebbels commented, "One sees how far the English have already been driven into a corner." In a striking reflection of Hitler's real goals, he added, "But this solution, too, is unsatisfying in power-political terms. We must have Prague." Prague lay outside the Sudeten region, and thus symbolized control of all of Czechoslovakia, not just its German fringe. By September 9, the British government was getting intelligence that Germany was moving troops in the direction of the Czech border, and four days later, sources reported that all German embassies were being told that Hitler intended to invade Czechoslovakia on September 25.

Chamberlain thought that two things were essential for the success of his daring and mysterious plan: He needed to try it "just when things looked blackest," and "it should be a complete surprise." On the evening of September 13, "I saw that the moment had come and must be taken if I was not to be too late." He sent what he called "the fateful telegram" to Adolf Hitler, informing his cabinet only the following morning.

The telegram asked Hitler's permission for Chamberlain to fly to Germany to meet the Führer and talk in person about resolving the Czech crisis. The cabinet retroactively approved Chamberlain's step, "and then followed hours of waiting for the answer, for everything had to be transmitted to Berchtesgaden." Finally, on the afternoon of September 14, Hitler responded. His answer was yes.

Hitler was not happy about Chamberlain's gambit. "A turn that no one could have suspected," Goebbels noted. The propaganda chief's assessment of Chamberlain's strategy—no doubt reflecting Hitler's—was revealing. "The clever British are playing it safe. Creating a moral alibi for themselves. And sticking us with the war guilt, if it comes to a conflict." That was "not pleasant," but Hitler didn't have any choice; "he had to accept this visit." But in talking with Chamberlain, he would "keep his cards close to his chest."

In 1938, the term *summit meeting* had not yet been coined. World leaders very rarely met one another, and if they did, they never traveled by air to do so. Neville Chamberlain was sixty-nine years old and had been in an airplane only once before, fifteen years earlier (wearing a top hat for the occasion). The unprecedented drama of his flight to Germany was very much a part of his calculations about the journey's effects, on Hitler and the world.

"I must confess to some slight sinkings when I found myself flying over London and looking down thousands of feet at the houses below," he wrote to Ida a few days later. But he soon began to enjoy himself despite turbulence on the approach to Munich. He was received by Ribbentrop and the German ambassador to Britain, Herbert von Dirksen, along with "innumerable uniformed officials while a guard presented arms amidst the roll of drums." There was an enthusiastic crowd that greeted him with Nazi salutes and cries of "Heil!" As he had done for Halifax the year before, Hitler provided a special train to speed the visitors from Munich to Berchtesgaden. At every crossing, station, and from many houses, there were more Germans enthusiastically "heiling" the British prime minister.

A car took the British party from the Berchtesgaden train station to the Berghof. Hitler was waiting for them on the steps, "bareheaded and dressed in a khaki colored coat of broadcloth with a red armlet & a swastika on it & the military cross on his breast," Chamberlain would recall. "His hair is brown, not black, his eyes blue, his expression rather disagreeable, especially in repose and altogether he looks entirely undistinguished. You would never notice him in a crowd & would take him for the house painter he once was."

Hitler led Chamberlain to a small, bare room where they talked for three hours, with only Hitler's interpreter, Paul Schmidt, present. Schmidt remembered that "Chamberlain listened attentively, looking frankly at Hitler. Nothing in his clear-cut, typically English features, with their bushy eyebrows, pointed nose and strong mouth, betrayed what went on behind his high forehead . . . he dealt in lively manner with individual points" that Hitler raised.

"For the most part, H spoke quietly and in low tones," was Chamberlain's recollection. The dictator "poured out his indignation against the Czechs in a torrent of words so that several times I had to stop him and ask that I might have a chance to hear what he was talking about." Hitler's rage convinced Chamberlain that "the situation was much more critical than I had anticipated," and that Hitler might even be planning to give the order to attack almost immediately. Schmidt remembered that Hitler complained furiously of Czech violence and the mobilization of May, and insisted, "I shall not put up with this any longer. I shall settle this question in one way or another." Schmidt knew that when Hitler used the phrase "one way or another," it was "an extreme danger signal."

Chamberlain responded firmly, telling Hitler, "If I have understood you aright, you are determined to proceed against Czechoslovakia in any case," and adding after a pause, "If that is so, why did you let me come to Berchtesgaden? Under the circumstances it is best for me to return at once."

At this, Hitler calmed down and said that if the British government accepted "the principle of self-determination"—this meant secession of the Sudeten region from Czechoslovakia—then he was prepared to seek a negotiated solution. Hitler pointed out that the idea of a right to self-determination was not something he had invented, but had been "brought into being in 1918 to create a moral basis for the changes made under the Treaty of Versailles." Chamberlain responded that he could not give any assurance without first consulting his cabinet and the Czechs. "My personal opinion was that on principle, I didn't care two hoots whether the Sudetens were in the Reich or out of it," but a plebiscite would raise "immense practical difficulties." But Chamberlain offered to return to Britain, "hold my consultations & meet him again." Hitler regretted that Chamberlain would have to make two journeys, but would meet him next time near Cologne, to make the trip from Britain shorter. Hitler promised not to order an invasion until he had heard from Chamberlain, "unless some outrageous incident forced his hand"—not, in fact, much of a concession, as Hitler had ordered his military commanders to be ready to invade only by the end of the month. But, of course, Chamberlain could not know this. As they parted, Hitler became "much more cordial" and said he hoped to welcome Chamberlain back so that they could visit Hitler's teahouse at the top of the mountain.

Chamberlain concluded from this first encounter that "Herr Hitler's objectives were strictly limited," as Hitler had assured Chamberlain that "he was concerned with the German race" and "did not wish to include Czechs in the Reich."

"Hitler told me he felt he was speaking to a *man*" was the message Ribbentrop's secretary gave to Chamberlain's advisor Horace Wilson. The Germans understood Chamberlain's vanity, and knew that this calculated flattery would keep the prime minister well disposed toward Germany. Chamberlain boasted that Hitler "liked the rapidity with which I had grasped the essentials." The prime minister believed that he had "established a certain confidence which was my aim and on my side in spite of the hardness & ruthlessness I thought I saw in [Hitler's] face I got the impression that here was a man who could be relied upon when he had given his word." Here was the disastrous reaction to the work of Sir Edward Grey, the clearest illustration of Chamberlain's faith that he could meet the dictators, speak to them candidly, "man to man," and solve the critical problems without war—exactly what Grey had not been forthright enough to do in 1914.

Chamberlain added in a postscript, "I hear from a German source that I am the most popular man in Germany!" The Germans, he said, loved that he "came to save us from a war."

For all his vanity and self-satisfaction, Chamberlain was correct about the impression he had made on Hitler. Hitler described him to Goebbels as "an ice-cold old Englishman"—"cold" being the highest praise in his vocabulary. It was clear that Chamberlain's daring venture had crossed Hitler's plans. "His visit was not very convenient for the Führer," Goebbels recorded. Neither, in fact, was the route to a solution on which Chamberlain and Hitler had agreed. "But if it is being proposed in earnest, then at the moment we can't do much about it." The hope was that Prague would remain "intransigent"; "then there will be a complete solution"—by which Goebbels meant a German invasion. Revealing the German reliance on fabricated events and fake news, the propaganda minister noted that "since it has become a bit calmer [in the Sudetenland] new Czech excesses are coming today, they are due." Above all, "the panic bulletins from Czechoslovakia have to be increased."

THE BRITISH CABINET met on Saturday, September 17, to discuss the results of Chamberlain's journey and plan what to do next. Positions were fluid: most ministers were unsure of what to do, and at this point none could be classified as firmly pro- or anti-"appeasement." The next day, French prime minister Édouard Daladier and Foreign Minister Georges Bonnet came to London for consultations. The British had to work hard to convince the French to abandon the Czechs, work that Chamberlain described with an unusual flash of wit. "As so often in international discussions," he told the cabinet the next day, "the darkest hour was before lunch."

Ultimately, the French and British agreed on a joint message to the Czechoslovakian president, Edvard Beneš, that his country had to give up the Sudetenland, in its own interests and in the interests of European peace. The transfer could be by a plebiscite, but the message strongly recommended simply handing over to the Reich all areas with more than 50 percent German inhabitants, with final border determinations to be made by an international commission with Czech representation. In return, Britain would be willing to "join in an international guarantee" of the new borders. "Pretty stiff," Alexander Cadogan commented, "telling him [Beneš] to surrender."

The Czechs grudgingly agreed to this solution, and Chamberlain planned to return to Germany. Before he left, the cabinet agreed that if "Herr Hitler still adhered to the attitude that he must have an immediate settlement of the Hungarian and Polish minority questions [in Czechoslovakia] the Prime Minister proposed to say that he was unable to proceed further on the matter, and must return home to consult his colleagues." Cadogan thought that this point—that Chamberlain could not "champion Poles and Hungarians"—was "*essential*," and "I hope he'll stick to it."

Thus armed, Chamberlain again flew to Germany. The destination this time, as Hitler had promised, lay much closer to Britain: the spa town of Bad Godesberg, near Cologne. Here, Chamberlain stayed at the Hotel Petersberg, while the meetings were held across the Rhine, at the Hotel Dreesen.

Business began with Chamberlain's account of how he had gotten his cabinet, then the French, and finally the Czechs to agree to recognize the Sudeten Germans' right to self-determination. The British and French governments had prepared a plan for the transfer of Sudeten areas to

Germany and the drawing of a new border. Finally, the British and French governments would guarantee the new borders. In return for all this, Germany would sign a non-aggression pact with Czechoslovakia.

As Paul Schmidt recalled, "Chamberlain leant back after this exposition with an expression of satisfaction, as much as to say: 'Haven't I worked splendidly during these five days?'" But to the shock of nearly everyone in the room, Hitler replied, "quietly, almost regretfully, but quite definitely: 'I am exceedingly sorry, Mr. Chamberlain, but I can no longer discuss these matters. This solution, after the developments of the last few days, is no longer practicable.'" Chamberlain's mood was immediately transformed into anger, and Schmidt noticed that "his kindly eyes could gleam very angrily under their bushy brows." The prime minister said that he could not understand how Hitler could now say that the solution wouldn't work, when all the demands he had made the week before had been met. Hitler claimed that he could not make any deal with Czechoslovakia when Poland and Hungary still claimed disputed Czech territory—the very point Chamberlain and his cabinet had anticipated, and had agreed would be a reason to break off the negotiations. After several stormy negotiating sessions, Hitler said he was willing to wait until October 1 for the Czechs to evacuate the Sudetenland. This was enough for Chamberlain to give the Czechs a "memorandum" that Hitler had drafted—really an ultimatum. The meeting ended at two o'clock in the morning.

Chamberlain met his cabinet again on Saturday, September 24. "As usual," he told his colleagues, with no little understatement, "the discussion with Herr Hitler had been somewhat discursive." Yet Chamberlain seemed eager to make allowances for Hitler. Cadogan had been horrified by Chamberlain's tone in a meeting of the "inner cabinet" earlier that day: the prime minister was "quite calmly for total surrender." Cadogan thought Hitler had hypnotized Chamberlain. Duff Cooper agreed, noting that "Hitler has cast a spell over Neville." Cadogan was "still more horrified to find that P.M. has hypnotized H[alifax] who capitulated totally."

If he was credulous about Hitler, Chamberlain was in any event lucid and cold-eyed about the strategic realities. He had also thought very carefully about what a democracy could and should be willing to face when it came to war for a matter of principle. "If Czechoslovakia decided that she would fight," Chamberlain explained, "the result would almost certainly be that in future there would be no Czechoslovakia as it existed today or as it might exist if the present proposals were accepted." Even if Britain were to go to war now, "it would not be for the purpose of maintaining Czechoslovakia in its present form," because that was "impossible." The reason would be that the British reckoned "we could check Herr Hitler's ambitions more effectively by war now than by war hereafter. We must not lose sight of the fact that war today was a direct threat to every home in the country, and we must consider whether the protection which we could afford today to the people of this country against German bombs was as effective as the protection which we might be able to offer in the future"—a reasonable position in view of the rapid development of air defenses then under way. Chamberlain told the cabinet that as his plane had returned from Godesberg, he had flown up the River Thames to London and "imagined a German bomber flying the same course." He had wondered "what degree of protection we could afford to the thousands of homes which he had seen stretched out below him," and concluded that "we were in no position to justify waging a war today in order to prevent a war hereafter." The calculation about the value of delay, like the strategy of maneuvering Germany into assuming blame for the outbreak of any war, was always an important element of Chamberlain's thinking.

But the mood in Britain, even within the British cabinet, was starting to stiffen. A crucial development started with Cadogan, who was disgusted by the tone Chamberlain and Halifax had taken at a meeting just after Godesberg. Cadogan found Halifax "happily défaitiste-pacifist." Cadogan wasn't sure if the cabinet was deluded or just did not understand the issues. "Pray God there will be a revolt," he thought, and noted that he had given Halifax "a piece of my mind." He thought it had had no effect.

But it had. Halifax always seemed to be caught between his Christian principles and his political pragmatism. This was why Churchill had sardonically dubbed him the "Holy Fox." That night, one side of his nature rebelled against the other. Halifax told Cadogan the next morning, "Alec, I am very angry with you. You gave me a sleepless night. I woke at 1 and never got to sleep again. But I came to the conclusion that you were right, and at the cabinet, when the P.M. asked me to lead off, I plumped for refusal of Hitler's terms."

The scene in the cabinet had been dramatic. What Halifax said had stunned Chamberlain and the rest of the ministers. Quietly but emotionally, Halifax explained how "he had found his opinion changing somewhat in the last day or so." The previous week, he had hoped that agreeing to a transfer of the Sudetenland overseen by an international commission and following a plebiscite would not just be yielding to force. Now he was having doubts. There was also the important factor of Hitler's honesty. Halifax "could not rid his mind of the fact that Herr Hitler had given us nothing and that he was dictating terms, just as though he had won a war without having had to fight." From there, he moved to a still-more-fundamental point: "So long as Nazism lasted," the cabinet meeting minutes record him as saying, "peace would be uncertain." Halifax did not think it would be right to pressure the Czechs to accept Hitler's terms. "We should lay the case before them. If they rejected it, he [Halifax] imagined that France would join in, and if France went in we should join with them."

After this, Chamberlain passed Halifax a quickly penciled note: "Your complete change of view since I saw you last night is a horrible blow to me, but of course you must form your opinions for yourself." He added a vague threat of resignation: if the French insisted on "dragging us in," Chamberlain did not think he could "bear responsibility for the decision." Halifax replied with a note of his own: "I feel a brute— but I lay awake most of the night, tormenting myself and did not feel I could reach any other conclusion at this moment, on the point of coercing [Czechoslovakia]." Chamberlain could not resist adding a sharp response: "Night conclusions are seldom taken in the right perspective."

Now it was clear that most of the ministers were no longer willing to believe Hitler's promises. The argument in cabinet came down to a moral insistence on standing with Czechoslovakia against a pragmatic recognition that there was little practical aid that Britain and France could offer, and a war would probably end with worse consequences for the Czechs than Hitler's demands. But this time, the French also insisted on standing firm.

Chamberlain proposed writing one more letter to Hitler putting forward the idea that the arrangement that the Czechs had accepted should form the basis for an international commission to resolve the crisis. "This further move would once more demonstrate to the world how hard we had tried to preserve peace. If it was unsuccessful, we should lose nothing by it, and it would help to consolidate world opinion in our favor." Horace Wilson would take the letter to Hitler. If it failed to move the Führer—and Chamberlain did not think it would—Wilson would inform Hitler that France would go to war over Czechoslovakia and that Britain would then likely join in. The cabinet agreed.

NOW THE BRITISH Government and the British people seemed to be steeling themselves for war. On September 23, Halifax had cabled Chamberlain, "Great mass of public opinion seems to be hardening in sense of feeling that we have gone to the limit of concession and that it is up to the Chancellor [Hitler] to make some contribution." Three days later, the National Labour MP Harold Nicolson recorded in his diary that "my first sight of the war of 1938" was a poster reading "City of Westminster: Air Raid Precautions: Gas Masks Notice." His "second sight" was workmen digging air raid trenches in Green Park.

The Foreign Office issued an official statement in which the crucial line read, "If in spite of all efforts made by the British Prime Minister a German attack is made upon Czechoslovakia the immediate result must be that France will be bound to come to her assistance, and Great Britain and Russia will certainly stand by France." Churchill claimed in his memoirs that he had drafted this statement along with Reginald Leeper, the Foreign Office press secretary, and the text has become known as the Leeper telegram. The government began planning wartime food and oil distribution and the evacuation of children from cities, along with the distribution of gas masks and the digging of trenches and air raid shelters that Nicolson noticed. The armed forces were put on alert. The cabinet agreed that Chamberlain would speak to the country by radio on September 27, and at Churchill's suggestion, Parliament was recalled for September 28. Chamberlain agreed to mobilize the Royal Navy and to announce this measure in his radio address. Horace Wilson was sent to Germany with a letter for Hitler in the same terms as the Leeper telegram: "The French Government have informed us that, if the Czechs reject the Memorandum and Germany attacks Czechoslovakia, they will fulfill their obligations to Czechoslovakia. Should the forces of France in consequence become engaged in active hostilities against Germany, we shall feel obliged to support them."

Horace Wilson visited Hitler in Berlin on Monday, September 26. They talked for nearly an hour, but when he got to reading Hitler the second paragraph of Chamberlain's letter—saying that the Czech government had refused Hitler's "proposals"—Hitler flew into a rage, threatened to "smash" Czechoslovakia, and shouted that "we will all be at war next week." At that point, incredibly, Wilson decided that it would not be "appropriate" to read the warning of possible British intervention. He feared that Hitler would take this as an "ultimatum" and that the speech the Führer was to deliver that evening would become even more extreme. This was a reversion to the habits of Sir Edward Grey.

War now seemed both certain and imminent. On Monday evening, Hitler spoke to a crowd of Nazi activists, sprinkled with many foreign diplomats and journalists, at the Sportspalast in Berlin. Goebbels introduced him, closing with words that would become a Nazi slogan: "Führer, command. We will follow!"

Hitler's speech made clear the depth of his hatred for the Czechs and especially for President Beneš. But it was just as clear that his hatreds and resentments ran far wider—to the whole post–First World War settlement, the new democracies, the world's international institutions. It was authoritarian leaders he liked. He spoke of the good relations he had established with the Polish government and its late dictator Marshal Józef Pilsudski, relations he could never have established with a democracy: "For these democracies, dripping all over with peace rhetoric, are the most blood-thirsty of all warmongers. Democracy did not reign in Poland, one man did!" His agreement with Pilsudski had been a deed "truly in the service of peace, worth substantially more than the idle talk in the League of Nations' Palace in Geneva." When he spoke of the annexation of Austria, he complained sarcastically, "Have we not witnessed it time and time again how in the eyes of democracies a plebiscite becomes irrelevant and even detrimental to their cause the moment it does not produce the desired results?"

As for Czechoslovakia, he insisted that the Sudetenland was "the last territorial demand I shall make in Europe." But Beneš stood in the way. Beneš, said Hitler, was "the 'father of the lie.'" What he meant was the "lie" that there was any such thing as a Czechoslovak nation. Instead, the Czechs had simply annexed Slovakia. And "since this state did not appear to be a viable structure, they simply took three and a half million Germans in clear defiance of the rights and desires of the Germans for self-determination." That didn't suffice, either, so the Czechs "took another million of Magyars, adding a number of Carpatho-Russians and several hundreds of thousands of Poles." The resulting state existed "contrary to the clear desire and will of the nations thus raped and in clear defiance of their right to self-determination." Now, despite the lurid atrocities that Hitler accused the Czechs of carrying out against the Germans, Beneš "sits in Prague and is comfortable believing: Nothing can happen to me. England and France will always back me."

Hitler summoned up just enough grace to thank Chamberlain for his efforts to resolve the crisis. But there was nothing gracious about the end of this performance. The American reporter William Shirer was there to broadcast the speech for CBS News. He described Hitler as "shouting and shrieking in the worst state of excitement I've ever seen him in." Shirer thought that "for the first time in all the years I've observed him," Hitler simply "completely lost control of himself." After Hitler sat down, Goebbels jumped up again and shouted, "One thing is sure: 1918 will never be repeated!" He meant—as Hitler had often said—that Germany would never again surrender as it fell apart from internal divisions. Now, Shirer observed that Hitler looked up at his propaganda minister, "a wild, eager expression in his eyes, as if those were the words which he had been searching for all evening and hadn't quite found. He leaped to his feet and with a fanatical fire in his eyes that I shall never forget brought his right hand, after a grand sweep, pounding down on the table and yelled with all the power in his mighty lungs: 'Ja!' Then he slumped into his chair exhausted."

Shirer and others who heard this wild outpouring of hatred against the Czechs, against democracy, and against the international order would have been surprised by Hitler's plans for the speech. Earlier in the day, he had told Goebbels that his speech would "be very clever and build golden bridges to London and Paris." He added that he had to lend Chamberlain support in British domestic politics.

When Hitler was finished, the crowd sang an old patriotic song from the wars against Napoléon. But Shirer thought it was a "curious audience, the fifteen thousand party *Bonzen* [party hacks] packed into the hall." They applauded and echoed Goebbels's "Führer, command! We will follow!" But "there was no war fever. The crowd was good-natured, as if it didn't realize what his words meant."

This audience was in any case not representative of Berliners. That became clear the next day, when Hitler tried to stage a repeat of the patriotic enthusiasm of 1914. He ordered some of his motorized troops to parade through Berlin. Shirer went out near dusk to the corner of Unter den Linden and the Wilhelmstrasse, the center of the government district. "I pictured the scenes I had read of in 1914 when the cheering throngs on this same street tossed flowers at the marching soldiers, and the girls ran up and kissed them," he wrote. But now he watched as Berliners leaving their shops and offices at the end of a day's work "ducked into the subways, refused to look on, and the handful that did stood at the curb in utter silence unable to find a word of cheer for the flower of their youth going away to the glorious war." It was, he thought, "the most striking demonstration against war I've ever seen." A policeman shouted that Hitler was reviewing the troops from the balcony of his Chancellery a few blocks down the Wilhelmstrasse. Shirer went to have a look and found "there weren't two hundred people in the street or the great square of the Wilhelmplatz. Hitler looked grim, then angry, and soon went inside, leaving his troops to parade by unreviewed." The experience burned itself into Hitler's mind.

On Tuesday morning, Horace Wilson went again to talk to Hitler. Under cover of a good deal of diplomatic flattery—on the "magnificent reception" that had greeted Hitler's speech of the night before—he was there this time to deliver a stern warning. He did so, as he told the cabinet later that day, "very slowly," making a deliberate effort to phrase the message as Chamberlain himself would have. If Czechoslovakia accepted the German "memorandum," Wilson told Hitler, all well and good. But if not, and if Germany attacked Czechoslovakia, France would "fulfill her treaty obligations to Czechoslovakia," and "Britain would feel herself obliged to support France." Hitler objected that this meant that France would attack Germany. Wilson insisted that the French government had chosen its words very carefully, and he repeated that the French would "fulfill their treaty obligations."

Diplomacy was usually lost on Hitler, who exploded in a rage that this would mean war within six days and that he would "destroy" Czechoslovakia. Wilson seemed to want to continue the conversation, but Ambassador Henderson hustled him out of the room. Wilson nonetheless parted by promising Hitler that he would "still try to make those Czechs sensible."

That evening, Chamberlain spoke to the British people over the BBC. He began by referring to all the letters he had received in recent days—not only from Britain but "from France, from Belgium, from Italy, even from Germany." He had found them heartbreaking, both in their anxiety over the prospect of war and "their intense relief when they thought, too soon, that the danger of war was past."

When Chamberlain had accepted the leadership of the Conservative Party, he told his listeners, he had known what he was in for, and he had gotten it. "If I felt my responsibility heavy before, to read such letters has made it seem almost overwhelming." He followed this with a revealing observation: "How horrible, fantastic, incredible it is that we should be digging trenches and trying on gas masks here because of a quarrel in a faraway country between people of whom we know nothing." No American isolationist could have said it better.

Then came Chamberlain's ideas about how a democracy should think about war and peace: "However much we may sympathize with a small nation confronted by a big and powerful neighbor, we cannot in all circumstances undertake to involve the whole British Empire in war simply on her account," he said. "If we have to fight it must be on larger issues than that. I am myself a man of peace to the depths of my soul. Armed conflict between nations is a nightmare to me; but if I were convinced that any nation had made up its mind to dominate the world by fear of its force, I should feel that it must be resisted. Under such a domination life for people who believe in liberty would not be worth living; but war is a fearful thing, and we must be very clear, before we embark on it, that it is really the great issues that are at stake, and that the call to risk everything in their defense, when all the consequences are weighed, is irresistible."

This ambivalent performance stimulated a lot of anger among those who wanted stronger opposition to Nazi aggression. Duff Cooper was irritated that Chamberlain had made "no mention of France," nor spared "a word of sympathy for Czechoslovakia." Chamberlain had saved his sympathy, he thought, only for Hitler. But he was particularly furious that the prime minister had said nothing about the mobilization of the fleet, as the cabinet had agreed that he would.

Chamberlain's tone probably reflected the alarming advice he had received from the military chiefs of staff earlier that day. "It is our opinion," they told him, that "no pressure that Great Britain and France can bring to bear, either by sea, on land, or in the air, could prevent Germany from . . . inflicting a decisive defeat on Czechoslovakia." Czechoslovakia could be saved only indirectly, by "the defeat of Germany" as "the outcome of a prolonged struggle, which from the outset must assume the character of an unlimited war." And there was a further danger: if Italy and Japan were to enter this war on Germany's side, then Britain would be faced with a commitment "which neither the present nor the projected strength of our defense forces is designed to meet," placing "a dangerous strain on the resources of the Empire."

WHEN HANS BERND Gisevius and the other conspirators learned of Chamberlain's first visit to Hitler at Berchtesgaden, they could not believe the news. "But to our horror we found that it was true," Gisevius remembered. They convinced themselves that this was a purely tactical move on Chamberlain's part, that the British were "temporizing in order to 'pass the ball' to our generals" and to put Hitler even more clearly in the wrong. They kept working on their coup plans—and in fact, worried more about Hitler losing his nerve and backing down than they did about Chamberlain. When it became clear that Chamberlain really had come to negotiate, Gisevius felt that "we of the 'pro-West' party had been proved fools."

Yet, when news of the outcome of Bad Godesberg broke, Gisevius and his friends "felt a tremendous sense of relief." With war now looming, the mood in Germany changed. Perhaps Hitler was not so infallible. "As the news got around," Gisevius wrote, "a wave of disappointment, indignation, and panic spread through Germany. Never before had the Germans spoken so freely and vituperatively. Strangers talked to one another on the streets. The fearful shock could be read plainly in people's faces."

The resisters kept doggedly to their plans, through a network running from Oster's office to the OKW, police headquarters, and the Foreign Office. The tension was taking its toll. "For the first and the last time in this life," Gisevius remembered, "I nearly quarreled with Oster because of his increasing pessimism." Oster thought the Western powers were going to give in. Gisevius told him that for such defeatism, he deserved a post in Goebbels's propaganda ministry. But Oster was an intelligence officer and had better sources of information, including reports from Göring's telephone-tapping Office of Research. Tomas Masaryk, the Czech ambassador in London, reported to Prague on wires that ran through Germany. Masaryk, said Gisevius, "was not only well informed but unfortunately extremely indiscreet during those dreadful hours."

Nonetheless, by Tuesday everything was ready to go: Hitler was set to launch his invasion, Britain and France were prepared to go to war, the plotters were about to carry out their coup. That night, Heinz met with his group of commandos to get ready for their attack on Hitler's Chancellery. Erich Kordt had gotten a plan of the building for the raiders, and had agreed to make sure the doors would be open. Canaris had told the Abwehr officer Helmuth Groscurth to distribute rifles and explosives to the group. Heinz calmly told his men that whatever happened, whether or not Hitler and his bodyguard resisted, they should provoke a disturbance and kill Hitler. In the small hours, he gathered his squad together at the Army High Command office.

Despite the rising tension, and the German people's evident lack of enthusiasm for war, Hitler's terms remained uncompromising. This was good news for the plotters. Oster got ahold of a last letter from Hitler to Chamberlain refusing all moderation. On Wednesday morning, Gisevius took the letter to Erwin von Witzleben, the Berlin military district commander, who in turn took it to Halder. Now that Halder had "unequivocal 'proof'" that Hitler really was aiming for war, Gisevius wrote, "tears of indignation" ran down his cheeks. "Bold rebel that he was, he was amazed that Hitler could have played him so false as not to inform him of his real plans." The determined Witzleben insisted that it was time to "take action." But Brauchitsch refused to give a final order to launch the coup until he had paid one more visit to the Chancellery to see where things stood. "While Brauchitsch set out for the Wilhelmstrasse," Gisevius continued, "Witzleben rushed back to his military district headquarters. 'Gisevius, the time has come!' he told me excitedly." Gisevius returned to Abwehr headquarters. There, Oster was waiting to give Heinz and his squad the final orders to move on the Chancellery.

But that was where things stayed.

THE DECISION FELL on Wednesday morning, September 28, a day that Jodl called "the hardest" and Wiedemann "the most exciting day I had ever experienced in the Reich Chancellery." A crowd of ambassadors, ministers, and officers filled the building. Veterans of Hitler's Chancellery often described how business got done in the Führer's presence: everyone in constant motion, walking up and down the room with Hitler, the courtiers offering their own opinions. Weizsäcker wrote about how "usually there was a kind of standing colloquium, in which whoever was there participated, the posse of adjutants included." Ribbentrop pressed Hitler toward war; Göring pleaded for caution. "From my corner of the room," Schmidt recalled, "I closely watched the actors in this tense battle . . . I observed from Hitler's reactions how, very gradually, the balance tilted in favor of peace."

That morning in Rome, Mussolini had received the British ambassador, who had urged the Duce to arrange an international conference over Czechoslovakia. Mussolini's foreign minister and son-in-law, Count Galeazo Ciano, tried to telephone Ribbentrop, but reached only Kordt and would not condescend to speak to anyone less than the foreign minister. Mussolini called his Berlin ambassador, Bernardo Attolico. "This is the Duce, do you hear?" he said. Mussolini told Attolico that he wanted to accept the British proposal for a conference, and he instructed his ambassador to see Hitler. "Tell him what I've told you. Hurry, hurry!" Attolico telephoned Erich Kordt. Their common language was English, so Attolico said, "Kordt, I have a personal message from Il Duce. I must see the Führer at once, very urgent, quick quick." Kordt told him to come to the Chancellery. Attolico began by assuring Hitler that Mussolini would stand by him no matter what he did, but added, "The Duce is, however, of the opinion that it would be wise to accept the British proposal, and begs you to refrain from mobilization." Mussolini's proposal was for a four-power conference—the Germans, Italians, French, and British. This prodding from his ally brought Hitler back from the edge. It is likely that he was starting to worry that this time British and French resistance was real. And then there was the distressing result of the military parade of the previous day. "Tell the Duce I accept his proposal," Hitler said quietly.

In fact, Hitler had been coming under pressure over the past two days. One source was a telegram from President Roosevelt urging him "not to break off negotiations looking to a peaceful, fair and constructive settlement." Alongside the main message were some carefully phrased but striking elements. Roosevelt wrote that while "the supreme desire of the American people is to live in peace," in the "event of a general war they face the fact that no nation can escape some measure of the consequences of such a world catastrophe"—a veiled threat of American involvement. Roosevelt noted as well that "every civilized nation of the world voluntarily assumed the solemn obligations of the Kellogg-Briand Pact of 1928 to solve controversies only by pacific methods."

Hitler told Göring a few weeks later that he had had two reasons for backing down and consenting to one more meeting: doubt about the willingness of the German people to go to war—which even Goebbels had had the nerve to stress to him—and worry that Mussolini would leave him in the lurch.

The conspirators were still waiting anxiously for word that Hitler had ordered the invasion. "We could not understand why neither Brauchitsch nor Halder sent word," wrote Gisevius. "The minutes passed into hours of unutterable suspense; and then the sensational report crashed down upon our heads. The impossible had happened. Chamberlain and Daladier were flying to Munich. Our revolt was done for."

WALKING TO THE House of Commons on Wednesday afternoon, Harold Nicolson watched a group of children feeding pigeons. "Those children ought to be evacuated at once," his companion told him, "and so should the pigeons." Nicolson also saw a crowd setting flowers at the base of the Cenotaph, the memorial for British soldiers killed in the First World War. "The crowd is very silent and anxious," Nicolson wrote. "They stare at us with dumb, inquisitive eyes."

What happened in the House of Commons that day was as tense and dramatic as any movie. Chamberlain was due to tell the House of all that he had done to prevent war—at a moment when everyone expected war to break out in the next day or two. A little after three o'clock, he rose slowly and spread the notes of his speech on the box in front of him. The house was unusually crowded: among the visitors in the Diplomatic Gallery was the American ambassador, Joseph Kennedy, who had brought his son John for the occasion. The members, so often unruly, watched in hushed expectancy as Chamberlain prepared to speak. The only disturbances came from the messengers who brought telegrams and telephone message slips to the members. Churchill received so many that they were held together with an elastic band.

Speaking, as *The Times* reported, "in a clear voice, which was sometimes low but never faltered," Chamberlain delivered a chronology of the events that had led to the crisis. The members already knew what had happened in August and most of September, and Chamberlain's recitation of familiar material had the effect of increasing the tension. Finally, he referred to the cabinet meeting of September 23, and his listeners realized that he had now moved into territory they did not yet know. He began speaking of "yesterday morning," and as Harold Nicolson wrote, "we were all conscious that some revelation was approaching." "I glanced at the clock," Nicolson wrote. "It was twelve minutes after four. The Prime Minister had been speaking for exactly an hour." Then Nicolson noticed that "a sheet of Foreign Office paper was being rapidly passed along the Government bench. Sir John Simon interrupted the Prime

Minister and there was a momentary hush. He adjusted his pince-nez and read the document that had been handed to him. His whole face, his whole body, seemed to change."

What had happened was that at three thirty, Nevile Henderson had telephoned from Berlin. Cadogan took the call. Henderson said that Hitler had invited Mussolini, Daladier, and Chamberlain to Munich for a conference for the next day. "Dictated message," Cadogan noted, "and ran with it to the House. Fished H[alifax] out of Peers' Gallery and we went along to behind Speaker's Chair and sent it to P.M." *The Times*'s reporter watched as the message was passed from Halifax to Lord Dunglass, Chamberlain's parliamentary private secretary, and from him to Sir John Simon, who gave it to Chamberlain.

Members of the House of Lords, who were listening to the speech by way of a microphone feed, heard Chamberlain ask Simon, "Should I tell them now?" Simon said he should. Chamberlain picked up the thread of his speech. "That is not all," he continued. "I have something further to say to the House yet. I have now been informed by Herr Hitler that he invites me to meet him at Munich tomorrow morning. He has also invited Signor Mussolini and Monsieur Daladier. Signor Mussolini has accepted and I have no doubt Monsieur Daladier will also accept. I need not say what my answer will be."

Virtually all members of the House responded with enthusiastic cheers. Among the few exceptions were Winston Churchill, Anthony Eden, and Leo Amery, who, in the words of the historian Robert Seton-Watson, "held aloof from the demonstration, realizing the dire consequences which the House was preparing for itself." Harold Nicolson did not rise to cheer, either. He watched as Churchill offered Chamberlain deliberately ambivalent good wishes. "I congratulate you on your good fortune," said Churchill. "You were very lucky." Nicolson thought that Chamberlain, who had been showing "great satisfaction and even greater self-satisfaction," did not like Churchill's message "at all."

That night, Lord Dunglass heard Annie Chamberlain say to her husband, "I want you to come back from Germany with peace with honor," adding "you must speak from the window like Dizzy did." She was referring to Prime Minister Benjamin Disraeli's triumphant return from the Congress of Berlin in 1878. This would prove to be fateful advice.

■ ■ ■

AFTER THIS, THE meeting at Munich was almost an anticlimax.

On Thursday morning, as Chamberlain drove once again to Heston airfield, his route was lined by cheering crowds. Chancellor of the Exchequer Sir John Simon had urged the cabinet to see Chamberlain off, and they were nearly all there. Before getting on the plane, Chamberlain gave a few words to the assembled press and well-wishers. Characteristically, he offered a quote from Shakespeare: "When I come back I hope I may be able to say, as Hotspur said in *Henry IV*, 'Out of this nettle, danger, we pluck this flower, safety.'"

The conference was held at the so-called Führerbau, one of the new Munich buildings Hitler had commissioned. It stood (and still stands, now a music academy) at the Königsplatz in north-central Munich, near the famous Glyptothek and Lenbachhaus Museums. It is a long three-story building designed by Ludwig Troost. French ambassador André François-Poncet thought it "a characteristic specimen of Hitlerian architecture," repudiating "detail, ornament, curve, and roundness of form, seeking to impress by the Doric simplicity of its lines and the massive aspect of its proportions." The interior resembled "some mammoth modern hotel furnished by a professional interior decorator."

Chamberlain was the first to arrive, accompanied by Horace Wilson and William Strang, a senior Foreign Office official. The French party of Daladier, François-Poncet, and Alexis Léger, head of the French Foreign Ministry, soon joined them. Mussolini came last, with Count Ciano.

Things got under way at 12:45. Given the frantically rushed conditions under which the conference had been brought together, it was no surprise that it was poorly organized. No one took an official record, no one chaired the meetings, there was no agenda. Rather than sitting at a conference table, as François-Poncet remembered, the delegates were "grouped in a semi-circle around a vast fireplace, the British on the left, the Italians and Germans in the center, the French on the right." Weizsäcker recalled that the "conversation was disorderly, springing from one subject to the next. Only Chamberlain tried to bring a bit of order to the discussion."

Hitler thanked everyone for coming and explained the issues as he saw them. "He speaks calmly," Ciano noted, "but from time to time he becomes agitated and then he raises his voice and pounds his fist into the palm of his other hand." Hitler claimed that the very existence of Czechoslovakia threatened European peace. He made wildly exaggerated statements about the violence Czechs were meting out to Germans in the Sudetenland, and about the flood of refugees into Germany, which he claimed "had risen to 240,000." Chamberlain and Daladier thanked Hitler for convening the meeting and agreed that a speedy, though peaceful, solution was essential. Then Mussolini proposed to base all discussions on a document that, as Ciano wrote, "in reality was telephoned to us the evening before from the embassy as representing the wishes of the German government." Weizsäcker, Neurath, and Göring had together drafted the plan the day before.

For the last time in his career, Mussolini was the real star of the show. With "his great genius" and "strong will," the adoring Ciano wrote, Mussolini "dominates and the others join around him." Less sycophantic observers saw it almost the same way. Weizsäcker thought that Hitler had not yet "freed himself from Mussolini's influence," and François-Poncet remembered how "standing at his [Mussolini's] side, Hitler gazed intently upon him, subject to his charm and as though fascinated and hypnotized. Did the Duce laugh, the Führer laughed too; did Mussolini scowl, so scowled Hitler." The experience left the veteran ambassador with the impression that "Mussolini exercised a firmly established ascendancy over the Führer." The Duce spoke French, German, and English, if not always very well, and so was the only leader who could talk to all the others without a translator. He combined, Weizsäcker thought, "the practice of parliamentary negotiation with an autocratic manner of expression." François-Poncet remembered him as "squat, laced into his uniform, the features of a Caesar, patronizing, completely at ease as though in his own house."

In the early afternoon session, after Hitler's tirade against the Czechs, Daladier stepped in to pose what François-Poncet called "the crucial question": did the conference want Czechoslovakia to exist or not? If the point of the conference was only to dismember Czechoslovakia, then Daladier felt that he "had no business in this place." But if the point was to find a way to ensure the future of Czechoslovakia, then he was ready to take up the issue "in a spirit of reciprocal concession and collaboration." Mussolini showed a flash of diplomatic ability, saying that Daladier had misunderstood Hitler's idea and that everyone "wished to consolidate and to respect the existence of the Czechoslovakian state."

The conference broke for lunch at 3:15. Hitler took Mussolini and Ciano to his apartment. The French and British delegations went to their hotels. At 4:30, things started up again. Unlike in the first session, this time a crowd of officials and ambassadors joined in, and there were more witnesses to what happened. François-Poncet wrote that still there was little order or agreement: "For want of directive, the discussion proved difficult, confused, and interminably long. Hampered by the necessity of a double translation, it kept constantly changing its topic and ceased whenever a contradiction arose. The atmosphere grew thicker and heavier." With evening coming on, the British took the lead and produced a typewritten memo proposing an agreement, drafted by Wilson and Strang. After a break to translate the document into the other languages, debate continued. The French tried to put controls on the territories that could be transferred to Germany following a plebiscite. Hitler opposed this, but finally gave in. The Italians and Germans refused to issue any "guarantee" of Czechoslovakia's new borders until the claims of the Hungarians and Poles had been dealt with. Eventually, they promised to give such a guarantee once these claims had been met. By 1:30 a.m., an agreement had been reached.

The settlement provided for a German occupation of the Sudetenland starting two days later and to be completed by October 10. Britain, France, and Italy agreed to guarantee that the Czechs would comply. An international commission consisting of representatives of the four Munich powers plus Czechoslovakia would work out "the conditions governing the evacuation." German forces could occupy the territory in four stages, while the international commission would work out occupation of any further Czech territory. The commission would also determine in which territories a plebiscite should be held. These two points—the phases of the occupation and the international commission determining where plebiscites would be held—were the major differences from Hitler's demands at Bad Godesberg, and thus the concessions that British and French diplomacy had managed to extract from him. Plebiscites were to be held by the end of November. The commission would also make a final determination of boundaries.

"Everyone is satisfied," Ciano noted, and tersely recorded the end of the conference: "Signing, handshakes, departure."

There was one more important step. "I asked Hitler about 1 in the morning while we were waiting for the draftsmen whether he would care to see me for another talk," Chamberlain later wrote. Hitler "jumped at the idea & asked me to come to his private flat." Chamberlain paid this visit early the next morning. He brought a document he had asked William Strang to draft for him, avowing the desire of the British and German people "never to go to war with one another again." Chamberlain explained his strategy to Dunglass, emphasizing once again the importance he placed on maneuvering for American favor: "If he signs it and sticks to it that will be fine, but if he breaks it that will convince the Americans of the kind of man he is."

Chamberlain and Hitler "had a very friendly & pleasant talk" that morning on issues ranging from Spain to southeastern Europe to disarmament. "At the end I pulled out the declaration which I had prepared beforehand and asked if he would sign it," Chamberlain wrote. "As the interpreter translated the words into German Hitler frequently ejaculated Ja! Ja! And at the end he said Yes I will certainly sign it. When shall we do it. I said now & we went at once to the writing table & put our signatures to the two copies which I had brought with me."

The Munich settlement unleashed an enormous surge of relief across Europe. From one day to the next, war had gone from being imminent to being, perhaps, a distant prospect. Reflecting on the trip home from Munich, Ciano wrote that "from the Brenner Pass to Rome, from the king to the peasants, the Duce receives welcomes as I have never seen." Daladier had expected a hostile response upon his return to Paris, but he found the roads lined with a cheering crowd whose number was estimated at half a million. "The people are crazy," he said to Léger, with the worldly cynicism appropriate to a French leader.

"Even the descriptions of the papers," Chamberlain wrote to Hilda, "give no idea of the scenes in the streets as I drove from Heston to [Buckingham] Palace. They were lined from one end to the other with people of every class, shouting themselves hoarse, leaping on the running board, banging on the windows & thrusting their hands into the car to be shaken." There was a huge crowd outside 10 Downing Street as well. It was here that Chamberlain took his wife, Anne's, advice and stepped out onto the balcony in emulation of Benjamin Disraeli. "This is the second time in our history a prime minister has returned from Germany bearing peace with honor," he told the crowd. "I believe it is peace for our time."

10

"Living at the Point of a Gun"

Radio listeners hear a weather report followed by an announcement: "We now take you to the Meridian Room in the Hotel Park Plaza in downtown New York, where you will be entertained by the music of Ramón Raquello and His Orchestra."

The Spanish-flavored dance music plays for a few moments. But soon the broadcast is interrupted for a bulletin from "Intercontinental Radio News." An observatory reports strange gas explosions on the surface of Mars. With this, the listeners are returned to Ramón Raquello's orchestra. Soon, however, the radio station is bringing its listeners an interview with "Professor Richard Pierson, famous astronomer," from the "Princeton Observatory." Pierson tells the interviewer—an intrepid reporter named Carl Phillips—that he can't explain the explosions.

The bulletins keep coming. The "National History Museum" in New York reports a shock "of almost earthquake intensity" near Princeton. There are reports of a "huge, flaming object" hitting the ground near Grover's Mill, New Jersey. Carl Phillips makes his way there from Princeton with remarkable speed, and tries to "paint for you a word picture of the strange scene before my eyes." What he sees is not a meteorite, but a large metal cylinder. He interviews a farmer who has seen the object crash in his fields. The situation grows steadily more alarming. A bizarre creature crawls out of the cylinder. As Phillips describes the scene, the creature uses a kind of flame thrower to kill the police and bystanders that surround it. Finally, there is a dull thud as Phillips's microphone hits the ground. Then, only silence.

After that, the crisis spreads rapidly. New Jersey is placed under martial law and troops are mobilized, only to be slaughtered by the mysterious creature. The "Secretary of the Interior" speaks from Washington—not identified by name and sounding remarkably like President Roosevelt. He assures the nation that while the threat is grave, Americans will contain it "with a nation united, courageous and consecrated to the preservation of human supremacy on this earth." But artillery and bombers can't stop the aliens. The attackers use heat and poison gas. Soon they have reached New York City, as millions of people stream out to Long Island or Westchester, trying to escape. Reports come in of Martian landings across the country.

The panic across the United States—real panic, not part of the broadcast—is extraordinary. Perhaps six million people are listening as the Columbia Broadcasting System sends these reports into the ether. More than a million people do not notice or hear the introduction announcing that this is a production by the young Orson Welles's Mercury Theatre. They don't ponder all the terms and descriptions that are slightly off—the "Hotel Park Plaza" located "downtown," the "Intercontinental News Service," the "National History Museum." They do not seem skeptical about the Martians' ability to travel from Mars to Earth, land in New Jersey, destroy several army units, and lay waste to New York City inside forty-five minutes. People rush into the streets. If they have cars, they race out of town; if they have children, they frantically try to find them.

It is October 30, 1938.

The world is a nervous place, the United States no less than anywhere else. The Munich crisis has only just passed. In those tense September weeks, American radio listeners got used to alarming news bulletins breaking in on sporting events or dance music concerts. Many are still thinking about war, and about Germans. "The war talk has us so upset," one person tells (actual) Princeton professor Hadley Cantril, who spends the days and weeks after the broadcast studying the reaction. "Conditions are so unsettled since Chamberlain went to see Hitler." People know that the technology of aviation is making huge strides. "I feel that with new devices on airplanes, it is possible for foreign powers to invade us. I listened to every broadcast during the European crisis," says one of Cantril's interviewees. "I had the idea that the meteor was just a camouflage," says another. "It was really an airplane like a Zeppelin that looked like a meteor and the Germans were attacking us with gas bombs." Some people even think about the victims of Nazi persecution. "The Jews are being treated so terribly in some parts of the world," one person tells Cantril. "I was sure something had come to destroy them in this country."

A young playwright named Howard Koch has written the script for Welles's broadcast. Later, Koch will explain how seriously Welles takes the project—the play and its effects make what Welles considers an urgent point. Koch himself is skilled at burying a message under the surface of a script. A few years later, he will become one of the screenwriters for the immortal film Casablanca. It will be Koch who gives Humphrey Bogart's character, Rick Blaine, his backstory: running guns to Ethiopia and fighting in the Spanish Civil War on the Loyalist side. No one in the film explicitly spells out Rick's political affiliation. But in 1930s America, only a Communist would have this résumé.

Orson Welles thinks a lot about the new medium of radio, how it can convey information—and how it can deceive people. He is inspired by an incident in Britain a few years before: in 1926, with labor tensions high and a general strike looming, the BBC broadcast "reports" of a mob trying to destroy the Houses of Parliament, turning a trench mortar on Big Ben, hanging a cabinet minister, and ultimately sacking the BBC studios— returning in between bulletins to a dance band playing at the Savoy Hotel. Many listeners believed the reports. As his own broadcast proceeds, Welles knows exactly what is happening. A CBS official confronts him to say, "You're scaring people to death, please interrupt and tell them it's only a show." But Welles is defiant: "They're scared? Good, they're supposed to be scared. Now let me finish."

A few days after the broadcast, the pioneering journalist Dorothy Thompson puts her finger on the point. "The greatest organizers of mass hysterias and mass delusions today," she writes, "are states using the radio to excite terrors, incite hatreds, inflame masses, win mass support for policies, create idolatries, abolish reason and maintain themselves in power." She thinks that Welles has "made a greater contribution to an understanding of Hitlerism,

Mussolinism, Stalinism, antisemitism, and all the other terrorism of our times, more than will all the words about them that have been written." Her point strikes even closer to home than she knows. Hadley Cantril, the most thorough student of the panic, will go on to work with the Roosevelt administration and British intelligence to shape American opinion in favor of entering the war—and to shape it covertly.

FOR ALL THE cheering crowds that greeted Neville Chamberlain and Édouard Daladier on Friday, September 30, 1938, the immediate aftermath of Munich seemed to bring only regret, shame, sadness—and fear. Daladier told his aides, "Don't have any illusions. This is only a respite, and if we don't make use of it, we will all be shot." Count Ciano recorded that even while the document was being signed, André François-Poncet went red in the face and exclaimed, "See how France treats the only allies that remained faithful to her!" Even Chamberlain wrote that the day at Munich had been "one prolonged nightmare." Much like Daladier, as he drove through cheering crowds with Lord Halifax at his side, he muttered gloomily, "All this will be over in three months." He was exhausted after his return to London and repaired to the prime minister's official country house, Chequers, for the weekend. "I came nearer there to a nervous breakdown," he told his sister, "than I have ever been in my life." But he knew he had to pull himself together, "for there is a fresh ordeal to go through in the House." Starting on Monday, the House of Commons would debate the Munich accord.

Munich was the main event on the path to war. For the countries involved, Germany and Italy, France and Britain—and for the important countries that weren't directly involved, the Soviet Union and the United States—Munich was the crucial turning point that fundamentally changed how political and military leaders thought about what they were doing and where they were going. There was a paradox here, too. Munich was the result of a Herculean effort, mostly by Chamberlain, to preserve the peace. But it marked the last moment at which most people thought war could be avoided. After Munich, everything speeded up. The dive into war become ever sharper and more unmistakable.

For the smaller countries of Europe, too, particularly those in the vulnerable zone of central and eastern Europe, Munich was a disaster. The Western abandonment of Czechoslovakia was like a small stone that caused a landslide. The betrayal of an ally made the Western democracies unattractive partners for everyone else. Furthermore, the loss of the Sudetenland made what remained of Czechoslovakia all but indefensible. That meant that other countries in Germany's path—such as Poland and Romania—had lost a reliable ally. France's security, too, had relied on its allies in the east. The weakening of Czechoslovakia was a roundabout way of weakening France as well. And British security depended on France.

Not surprisingly, there was considerable bitterness in eastern Europe after Munich. The Bulgarian ambassador in Moscow told his French counterpart that "in all the little countries of Europe" the day was one of "distress and mourning." He warned that these countries could now "only seek the protection of Germany and submit ourselves to its wishes." President Beneš was even blunter: "It's a betrayal," he said, "which will be its own punishment."

Also unsurprisingly, Winston Churchill and the small circle of his followers in Parliament were in a funereal mood when news of the Munich settlement came in. On the evening of September 29, Churchill was at the Savoy Hotel for a meeting of the "Other Club," a political dining circle that he helped to found in 1911. As the hour grew late and most of the club's members had made deep inroads in the Savoy's wine cellar, the mood turned ugly. Already there were accurate reports of the terms of the settlement. "I was extremely depressed," Duff Cooper noted in his diary. "It seemed to me that we might as well have accepted the Godesberg ultimatum and have done with it." Churchill directed his anger at Duff Cooper and Walter Elliot, the two cabinet ministers present, wondering how "honorable men with wide experience and fine records in the Great War" could "condone a policy so cowardly." Duff Cooper and Robert Boothby, a Churchill protégé, attacked the pro-Chamberlain editor of the *Observer*, J. L. Garvin, so fiercely that he stormed out in a rage and did not return to the Other Club until after the Second World War. Duff Cooper decided he would resign from the cabinet, and Churchill growled that at the next general election he would "speak on every socialist platform in the country against the government."

Churchill left the party well oiled and supported by Richard Law, the son of the late prime minister Andrew Bonar Law. As they passed an open door leading to one of the hotel's restaurants, they heard sounds of loud laughter. "The restaurant was packed," Law said later, "and everyone was very gay. I was acutely conscious of the brooding figure beside me. As we turned away, he muttered 'those poor people! They little know what they will have to face.'"

ON MONDAY, OCTOBER 3, Chamberlain had to face the House of Commons. The day began with Duff Cooper's speech announcing his resignation from the cabinet. In any crisis in foreign affairs, he explained, Britain should explain its intentions clearly and firmly. Chamberlain's government had failed to do this. "The Prime Minister has believed in addressing Herr Hitler through the language of sweet reasonableness," Duff Cooper told the House, whereas "I have believed that he was more open to the language of the mailed fist." Even the warnings in the two days before Munich had not been enough. "That is not the language which the dictators understand," Duff Cooper continued. "Together with new methods and a new morality they have introduced also a new vocabulary into Europe. They have discarded the old diplomatic methods of correspondence . . . They talk a new language, the language of the headlines of the tabloid press, and such guarded diplomatic and reserved utterances as were made by the prime minister . . . mean nothing to the mentality of Herr Hitler or Signor Mussolini."

But by far the most powerful words in this debate came from Winston Churchill. One of the most brilliant speeches in this extraordinary orator's career, it illustrated above all the distance he had traveled since the early 1930s, when he had often expressed contempt for democracy. Perhaps this change reflected political calculation. Churchill certainly knew that his political constituency was now coming as much from the left's desire to resist fascism as it was from the right's imperial outlook. Since 1936 he had been working more and more with left-leaning politicians and advocates of the League of Nations, an institution that most Conservatives disliked. He was a core member of the "Focus Group," a cross-party alliance whose slogan was "arms and the covenant"—in other words, rearmament to meet the Nazi menace coupled with a determined commitment to the covenant of the League of Nations.

There was something else, too. It was in the wake of Munich that Churchill demonstrated beyond any doubt his profound understanding of world affairs, his fully intact moral compass, and with all this, his powerful claim on leadership. For years there had been as much to say for Chamberlain's cautious, pragmatic, and traditionally British strategic thinking as for Churchill's more romantic and warlike approach. But now the positions were reversed. It had been clear since the meeting at Godesberg that Chamberlain's policy had become morally as well as strategically bankrupt. The first important sign of this was Halifax's revolt in the cabinet. Churchill's speech was the second sign. It now fell to this imperially minded aristocrat to demonstrate how a democracy should respond to a totalitarian threat.

Under the cover of polite words about his "pleasant relations" with Chamberlain, Churchill began "by saying what everybody would like to ignore or forget but which must nevertheless be stated," which was that "we have sustained a total and unmitigated defeat, and that France has suffered even more than we have."

He acknowledged Chamberlain's "immense exertions" in the service of peace, and yet for all this, "the utmost he has been able to gain" for Czechoslovakia was that "the German dictator, instead of snatching his victuals from the table, has been content to have them served to him course by course." With caustic wit and shrewd accuracy, Churchill argued that the differences between Hitler's demands at Berchtesgaden and Godesberg and the settlement of Munich amounted to nothing more than that "£1 was demanded at the pistol's point. When it was given, £2 were demanded at the pistol's point. Finally, the dictator consented to take £1 17s. 6d. [93.75 percent of £2, as British money was then denominated] and the rest in promises of goodwill for the future."

Churchill understood that Germany threatened not just one country, but much of the globe, along with the international institutions that the democratic world had established. The alternative to appeasement at Munich would have been a multinational alliance—arms and the covenant. "France and Great Britain together, especially if they had maintained a close contact with Russia, which certainly was not done, would

A man who would not be bullied: Armed forces adjutant Friedrich Hossbach with his boss, Adolf Hitler.

The military high command in 1937: Werner von Blomberg (minster of war), Hermann Göring (commander in chief of the Luftwaffe), Werner von Fritsch (commander in chief of the army), and Erich Raeder (commander in chief of the navy) meet with Hitler.

"Laden with responsibility and almost melancholy": Ludwig Beck, chief of the general staff of the German army.

An unlikely army officer and even more unlikely communist: Mikhail Tukhachevsky, one of the Red Army's most brilliant generals.

"What went on in Number One's brain?": Soviet premier Vyacheslav Molotov and NKVD chief Nikolai Yezhov flank Joseph Stalin in 1937.

"What an influence a woman can exert": Eva von Blomberg, née Gruhn.

Trying to flee the wilderness: Winston Churchill campaigns to hold his seat in the general election of 1935.

"You must remember that you don't know anything about foreign affairs": Neville Chamberlain as chancellor of the exchequer in the 1930s.

"Friendliness and a desire for good relations": Lord Halifax (second from right) visits Germany in November 1937 for an international hunting exhibition, with Hermann Göring (second from left) and British Ambassador to Germany Sir Nevile Henderson (right).

"Not so much as the twitching of a muscle": Franklin Delano Roosevelt with his aide Louis Howe just after the shooting of Chicago mayor Anton J. Cermak in February 1933.

"Just the kind of bloody silly name they would think of": R. J. Mitchell, designer of the Spitfire.

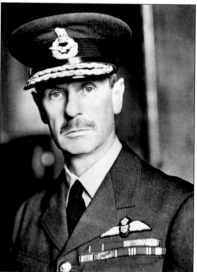

Architect of Britain's survival in 1940: the quiet visionary Hugh Dowding, the head of Royal Air Force Fighter Command.

"Our essentially businesslike tradition in the conduct of war": The military strategist Basil Liddell Hart contemplates the British way of warfare.

Anschluss: Hitler enters Vienna, March 14, 1938.

"I made the Fritsch case my own": German intelligence officer Hans Oster.

At the center of the resistance from first to last: Hans Bernd Gisevius, a civil servant and intelligence officer who played a major role in opposing Hitler.

"These are Prussian officers!": The seldom-very-resolute Franz Halder (left), who succeeded Beck as chief of the general staff, and Walther von Brauchitsch, who succeeded Fritsch as commander in chief of the army.

"Out of this nettle, danger": Chamberlain, Benito Mussolini, and Italian foreign minister Galeazzo Ciano at the Munich Conference.

"Peace with honor . . . Peace for our time": Chamberlain brandishes his agreement with Hitler upon returning to Heston Aerodrome, September 30, 1938.

"The last territorial claim I will make in Europe": German forces enter the Sudetenland, October 1938.

"They're supposed to be scared!": Orson Welles in the studio broadcasting "The War of the Worlds," October 30, 1938.

"The president's attack dog": Secretary of the Interior Harold Ickes introduces Roosevelt in Chicago for the "Quarantine Speech," October 5, 1937.

"Sad and slightly embittered": The image of George Washington surveys the Bund rally at Madison Square Garden, February 20, 1939.

"There is nothing at all that is without political bias": Propaganda Minister Joseph Goebbels in Vienna, with Arthur Seyss-Inquart of the Austrian Nazi Party at left.

"I know how much the German nation loves its Führer": Molotov (now Soviet foreign minister) and Stalin stand behind German foreign minister Joachim von Ribbentrop as he signs the Non-Aggression Pact, August 23, 1939.

Where it began: The radio transmitter at Gleiwitz, Upper Silesia, the site of a faked border raid, Germany's rationale for the invasion of Poland on September 1, 1939.

Planning what follows "the final destruction of the Nazi tyranny": Roosevelt and Churchill meet at Placentia Bay, August 11, 1941.

have been able . . . to influence many of the smaller States of Europe," including Poland. Such a firm alliance would also have given encouragement to the internal resistance in Germany—as Churchill knew well from his own contacts, although of course he was careful not to disclose too much in his speech. But the British government had taken too isolationist an approach and refused to declare well beforehand that it would join in an international defense of Czech sovereignty against unprovoked aggression. This had led to a tragic paradox: "His Majesty's Government refused to give that guarantee when it would have saved the situation, yet in the end they gave it when it was too late, and now, for the future, they renew it when they have not the slightest power to make it good."

Now the liberal democratic world order was fatally weakened. "All is over," Churchill lamented. "Silent, mournful, abandoned, broken, Czechoslovakia recedes into the darkness. She has suffered in every respect by her association with the Western democracies and with the League of Nations, of which she has always been an obedient servant." The strategic position of Britain and France had been overturned. "We are in the presence of a disaster of the first magnitude which has befallen Great Britain and France." The other countries of central and eastern Europe would move away from the weakened democracies and make what terms they could with Germany. In that region there were ministers and governments that were pro-German, "but there was always an enormous popular movement in Poland, Rumania, Bulgaria and Yugoslavia which looked to the Western democracies and loathed the idea of having this arbitrary rule of the totalitarian system thrust upon them, and hoped that a stand would be made. All that has gone by the board." He could not resist bitterly adding, playing on Chamberlain's radio address of September 27, "We are talking about countries which are a long way off and of which, as the Prime Minister might say, we know nothing."

Here Churchill demonstrated his thorough understanding of how the crisis of liberal democracy in central Europe posed an increasing danger to democracies everywhere. It was telling that he spoke directly of the contrast between "democratic" and "totalitarian" countries, when even many of the British politicians who agreed with Churchill about

Munich—such as Duff Cooper—still framed the issue in terms of traditional balance-of-power politics, not ideology. "Many people," Churchill
continued, "no doubt, honestly believe that they are only giving away
the interests of Czechoslovakia, whereas I fear we shall find that we
have deeply compromised, and perhaps fatally endangered, the safety
and even the independence of Great Britain and France." And, Churchill argued, this raised in turn the deeper question of how a democracy should deal with totalitarian adversaries. "You have to consider the
character of the Nazi movement and the rule which it implies," he said.
"The Prime Minister desires to see cordial relations between this country and Germany. There is no difficulty at all in having cordial relations
with the German people. Our hearts go out to them. But they have no
power. You must have diplomatic and correct relations, but there can
never be friendship between the British democracy and the Nazi Power,
that Power which spurns Christian ethics, which cheers its onward
course by a barbarous paganism, which vaunts the spirit of aggression
and conquest, which derives strength and perverted pleasure from persecution, and uses, as we have seen, with pitiless brutality the threat of
murderous force. That Power cannot ever be the trusted friend of the
British democracy."

These words embodied not only strategic good sense, but a bright
beam of moral clarity focused on the dim post-Munich landscape.
Churchill ended his speech with another burst of passionate eloquence.
He did not begrudge "our loyal, brave people" the "natural, spontaneous
outburst of joy and relief when they learned that the hard ordeal would
no longer be required of them at the moment; but they should know
the truth." The truth was that the government had neglected British
defenses, and that "we have sustained a defeat without a war, the consequences of which will travel far with us along our road; they should
know that we have passed an awful milestone in our history, when the
whole equilibrium of Europe has been deranged, and that the terrible
words have for the time being been pronounced against the Western
democracies: Thou art weighed in the balance and found wanting." He
concluded with a last, grim warning. "And do not suppose that this is
the end. This is only the beginning of the reckoning. This is only the first
sip, the first foretaste of a bitter cup which will be proffered to us year by

year unless by a supreme recovery of moral health and martial vigor, we arise again and take our stand for freedom as in the olden time."

A time would soon come when Churchill's words would galvanize his country and half the world to resistance against tyranny. But in October 1938, that time had not yet arrived. Much of the press was critical of his speech. The *Daily Express* dismissed it as an "alarmist oration" that had weakened his influence within the Conservative Party. *The Times* said that Churchill had "treated a crowded House to prophesies which made Jeremiah appear an optimist." Nor was Churchill's influence in Parliament strong. Neville Chamberlain and the Conservative Party's parliamentary whips could still intimidate their caucus. Only two dozen Conservative members abstained rather than support Chamberlain's policies, and even with the Labour and Liberal opposition largely against Munich, Chamberlain won the vote handily, 366–144. The *Manchester Guardian* observed that "it would take a revolt of 200, not 20, Tories to disturb this Government."

HANS BERND GISEVIUS still hoped that something could be salvaged from the wreck of the plot, but Erwin von Witzleben made it clear to him that the army would never revolt "against the victorious Führer." A few days later, Gisevius, Hjalmar Schacht, and Hans Oster "sat around Witzleben's fireplace and tossed our lovely plans and projects into the fire," Gisevius later recalled. "Chamberlain saved Hitler" was his bitter summation.

This wasn't just Gisevius's view. Ambassador Nevile Henderson wrote to Halifax a week after Munich: "By keeping the peace, we have saved Hitler and his regime."

But Hitler was no happier with the settlement, and his anger seemed to grow the more he brooded on it. He hadn't wanted a deal. He had wanted a war. Chamberlain's diplomacy had cheated him of it. His anger poured out in a speech at Saarbrücken just over a week after Munich. The rest of the world, he growled, had refused to recognize that the right of self-determination applied to Germans, too. "These international citizens of the world"—his way of characterizing the French and British politicians who had just made so many concessions to him—"have sympathy for every criminal who is brought to justice in Germany," but were "deaf to the suffering of ten million Germans." Even today, he continued, "this world is still filled with the spirit of Versailles."

Chamberlain's efforts to bring a fundamental change in Anglo-German relations had not netted him much. Germany's "only real friend" abroad, said Hitler, was Benito Mussolini. Hitler then, grudgingly, mentioned the "two other statesmen"—without giving their names—"who had taken the trouble of finding a way to peace." But the real lesson of the whole crisis was that Germans had to be ready to defend themselves. The statesmen who had been at Munich might well want peace. "But they govern in countries whose inner construction makes it possible that they could be replaced at any time, to make room for others who do not have peace so much in view. And these others are there. In England it would only be necessary, instead of Chamberlain, for Herr Duff Cooper or Herr Eden or Herr Churchill to come to power, because we know with certainty, that it was the goal of these men to immediately start a new world war." In the background, he continued, there was the "Jewish international enemy," and on top of that, fake news—"the power of a certain international press, that lives only from lies and defamation."

In the fall of 1938, however, the potential British opponents whom Hitler had so accurately identified were a small and demoralized band with little following in Parliament or the country. At the end of the year, the Conservative Party organization made a determined effort to get rid of a critic, by forcing Churchill out of his House of Commons seat through "deselection"—holding a vote of party members in the constituency on whether he should still have the Conservative nomination for that seat, similar to what in the United States is now called "primarying" a member of Congress. Churchill had to work hard to secure his political survival. In a similar attack, the Conservative Party's central office succeeded in deselecting another stern critic, the Duchess of Atholl, who then lost a by-election for her seat. Chamberlain was exultant.

MUNICH BROUGHT JUST as big a change in attitude for Franklin Delano Roosevelt as it did for most of the European leaders.

Before Munich, Roosevelt had suffered from ambivalence about how to respond to Nazi aggression. Privately he was scathing, both about the brutality of the Nazis and the weakness of the British and French. After Chamberlain's first visit to Hitler, Roosevelt told his cabinet with disgust that Chamberlain was after peace at any price, and that Roosevelt expected Britain and France would betray Czechoslovakia and then "wash the blood from their Judas Iscariot hands." But, typically, he would commit himself publicly to very little. On September 8 and again on September 12, French foreign minister Georges Bonnet invited Roosevelt to intervene as an arbitrator. Roosevelt did not respond. He did tell a French visitor, "You may count on us for everything except troops and loans"—the very things the Allies would most need from the United States.

On September 19, as the Sudeten crisis seemed to be moving inexorably toward war, Roosevelt pondered how he could best influence the European situation. He wanted to get a message to the British and French governments, but thought "the time has passed for speeches on my part." He told Henry Morgenthau Jr. that "I guess my best bet is the old boy up at the British embassy."

So, that afternoon, Roosevelt asked Sir Robin Lindsay, the British ambassador in Washington, to come see him. Roosevelt "emphasized the necessity of absolute secrecy," Lindsay reported home in the early hours of September 20, and that "nobody must know that I had seen him." Roosevelt did not even tell the State Department of the meeting.

What did the president want to say with this desperate need for secrecy? It was that he thought the Anglo-French note to Czechoslovakia recommending acceptance of the demands Hitler had made at Berchtesgaden was the "most terrible remorseless sacrifice that had ever been demanded of a state," and it would "provoke a highly unfavorable reaction in America." In his typical style, Roosevelt explained that he "would like to do or say something to help but was at a loss to know what . . . He would be afraid to express disapproval of German aggression lest it might encourage Czechoslovakia to vain resistance. He thus felt unable to do anything and thought at his press conference tomorrow . . . he would confine himself to refusing to make any comment at all."

Roosevelt outlined three different scenarios for what might happen next. Of course, Czechoslovakia might accept the German demands.

Roosevelt thought this unlikely. The second possibility was that there would be war. Roosevelt offered Lindsay his advice on how Britain and France should fight, which was strikingly similar to the ideas of Captain Liddell Hart. Roosevelt thought the Allies would lose a war that they conducted "on classical lines of attack." They would "suffer terrific casualties and would never get through." So, instead, they should "carry it on purely by blockade and in a defensive manner ... The Powers should close their own frontiers to Germany, stand on an armed defensive and call on all other States adjoining Germany to adopt the same line of non-intercourse." Lindsay noted, "It is possible that this is what was in the President's mind when he talked about 'quarantine' in his Chicago speech." Roosevelt suggested that the democracies not even declare war on Germany, which would allow him to evade the provisions of the Neutrality Act. In the kind of statement that would have horrified, but not surprised his isolationist opponents, Roosevelt explained he had "wide latitude" to interpret the act.

There was also, the president suggested, a third possibility. He told Lindsay that this was the heart and the most secret part of his message. Roosevelt would be willing to call for an international conference (thus reviving the idea that Chamberlain had torpedoed earlier in the year) to resolve all contested international borders. He would himself attend—so long as the conference were not in Europe. The Azores might be a possibility. He also stressed that it was "almost inconceivable" that American troops would ever be sent to Europe. As Churchill was risking the end of his political career by passionately and forlornly fighting against the Munich accord, this was as far as Roosevelt would go. He warned Lindsay that if word of his advice leaked, "he would almost be impeached and the suggestion would be hopelessly prejudiced."

In mid-September, then, Roosevelt's feelings about the best strategy for handling German aggression seemed to lie somewhere between appeasement and containment. In fact, when he heard that Hitler had agreed to the meeting at Munich, he sent a terse cable of congratulations to Chamberlain: "Good man."

But in the wake of Munich, Roosevelt seemed to rethink the problem and began to take a more openly hawkish position toward Germany—and to take real action to meet the Nazi menace. The drama of Munich had finally convinced Roosevelt that Hitler was an implacable enemy on whom all reason, and all negotiating, was wasted. A new tone came into his public and private statements, and U.S.-German relations grew markedly colder. "There can be no peace," Roosevelt said in a radio address a month after Munich, "if the reign of law is to be replaced by a recurrent sanctification of sheer force." He went on to list four other conditions under which there could "be no peace," including the repeated "threat of war" and the "dispersion all over the world of millions of helpless and persecuted wanderers." By December, when Germany threatened to sever diplomatic relations with the United States, Roosevelt could tell Undersecretary of State Sumner Welles, "It would not hurt us . . . So what?"

One of Roosevelt's worries involved the security of all of the Americas, so he began actively working to strengthen ties to Latin American countries and to shore up anti-Nazi feeling in the region. In speeches, he began to stress more and more that America had a role as the leader of the democratic world. He instructed his ambassador to Paris, William Bullitt, to start working on assembling an anti-Hitler alliance of the democratic states, with quiet promises of American support in the forms of arms and aircraft. This strategy, too, represented a claim to American leadership of the democratic world, and a clear rejection of Chamberlain's appeasement. However discreet, even secret, some of Roosevelt's moves were, the point was not lost on Hans-Heinrich Dieckhoff, Germany's ambassador in Washington, who was convinced that it was since Munich that Roosevelt had begun to stand firmly against Hitler.

Trying to build a democratic alliance was one practical step. There were two other important elements to Roosevelt's thinking in the post-Munich atmosphere. They revealed how he thought the United States should operate as a leader of the world's democracies. One involved a diagnosis of what might become democracy's next crisis. The other was about how a leader like Roosevelt could talk to Americans about the predicament they faced.

OVER THE CHRISTMAS season of 1938, Roosevelt worried about the rapid rise in tensions with Germany in the last two months of the year.

He worried about the threat Germany posed to the United States and to democracy in the world, and about how to meet that threat. He and Eleanor had their grandchildren with them for the holidays, and there were movies every night in the White House, but the president kept slipping away to dictate, revise, and dictate again. He was getting ready to deliver his State of the Union message to Congress on January 4, and he felt that this time the stakes were much higher than usual.

"In reporting on the state of the nation," his speech began, "I have felt it necessary on previous occasions to advise the Congress of disturbance abroad and of the need of putting our own house in order in the face of storm signals from across the seas." This was another such occasion.

"We know what might happen to us of the United States," he continued, "if the new philosophies of force were to encompass the other continents and invade our own." Americans could "not afford to be surrounded by enemies of our faith and our humanity." The world "has grown so small and weapons of attack so swift that no nation can be safe in its will to peace so long as any other powerful nation refuses to settle its grievances at the council table."

Roosevelt had a serious point to make about the proper response to such a threat. "If another form of government can present a united front in its attack on a democracy, the attack must be met by a united democracy." Could America compete with the dictatorships while still remaining "within our American way of life, within the Bill of Rights, and within the bounds of what is, from our point of view, civilization itself?" In other words, could a democracy face the Nazi menace, and possibly a total war against that menace, and remain a democracy?

The president was touching on a question that, over the next two years, would worry him more and more. There was a term for the scenario Roosevelt had conjured up. It was coined in 1937 by a versatile political scientist, lawyer, and communications theorist (and Yale professor of sociology) named Harold D. Lasswell. The term was *garrison state*.

The garrison state, Lasswell said, was what was likely to happen when a modern industrial nation mobilized for total war. The garrison state was a totalitarian state. "In the garrison state all organized social activity will be governmentalized . . . there will be no organized economic, religious, or cultural life outside of" the "duly constituted" state agencies. There would be no unemployment. Not to work would be a breach of military discipline. For anyone who did not fit in to this society, there would be "but one alternative—to obey or die."

In Germany, Erich Ludendorff had seen "the nation in arms" as the path to a better future. For Lasswell, the garrison state was a nightmare dystopia. "It is clear that the friend of democracy views the emergence of the garrison state with repugnance and apprehension," he said. But the garrison state might become "unavoidable."

Lasswell was not alone in his concerns. Back in 1925, the columnist Walter Lippmann had written, "Possibly a war can be fought for democracy; it cannot be fought democratically . . . in the presence of danger, where swift and concerted action is required, the methods of democracy cannot be employed."

There was a conservative and anti-Roosevelt version of the garrison state idea, meant as a critique both of Roosevelt's supposed power-grabbing and his supposed willingness to involve the United States in a foreign war. Former president Herbert Hoover was one spokesman for this anti-Roosevelt version. "Any major war," said Hoover, "means that our country must be mobilized into practically a Fascist government." Hoover worried that "a war to save liberty would probably destroy liberty," because "personal liberty and free economic life are not built for modern war." Anti–New Deal business leaders said much the same kind of thing, as did Roosevelt's pro-appeasement ambassador in London, Joseph Kennedy.

But liberal-minded anti-Nazis who saw the danger of the garrison state also saw, as Roosevelt did, the only viable alternative: to preserve its own democracy, America would have to help save democracy elsewhere, especially in Britain and western Europe. As far back as 1917, Walter Lippmann had coined the term "the Atlantic community," by which he meant the "profound web of interest" that united "Britain, France, Italy, even Spain, Belgium, Holland, the Scandinavian nations, and Pan America" as nations forming "one community in their deepest needs and their deepest purposes." Roosevelt recognized that if Hitler conquered western Europe, Americans "would be living at the point of a gun . . . to survive in such a world, we would have to convert ourselves permanently into a militaristic power."

Roosevelt's foreign and domestic policy in this period amounted to a desperate search for a way around dystopia—neither surrendering to fascism nor having to become a garrison state to meet it. He sought nothing less than a response to the Nazi menace that would allow the United States to remain a democracy.

The first wing of this strategy was to ensure that American democracy remained vibrant enough to compete with its Communist and Fascist challenges. In a 1936 message to Congress, Roosevelt had called the New Deal "an effort to restore power to those to whom it rightfully belong(s)." The government had to step in to prevent powerful economic interests from usurping the liberties of the people and create a democracy strong enough to head off the grievances that could lead to Fascism or Communism. Roosevelt was not, he said, fighting "a war against want and destitution and economic demoralization. It is more than that; it is a war for the survival of democracy." On the eve of the 1938 midterm elections, the president warned voters, "If American democracy ceases to move forward as a living force, seeking day and night by peaceful means to better the lot of our citizens, Fascism and Communism, aided, unconsciously perhaps, by old-line Tory Republicanism, will grow in strength." Dictators kept the "conveyer belts" of economic progress moving only "at a terrible price to the individual and to his civil liberty." The New Deal, he said, "has been trying to keep those belts moving without paying such a price."

The second element of Roosevelt's strategy involved the structure of American defense forces. Here, as his advice to Ambassador Lindsay at the time of Munich suggested, he followed a Liddell Hart–style strategy, a hyper version of "the British way in war." He sought to emphasize the navy and the air corps and shift American arms away from ground forces. This was a strategy rooted in American, as well as British, historical and cultural patterns, and the logic of the world of the 1930s.

As we have seen, the total war doctrine, and the totalitarianism, of Nazi Germany (and also of the Soviet Union) was particularly focused on the development of massive ground forces, a logical approach for continental countries whose major national security threats would reach them by land—and whose political systems favored such a force structure. Soviet military commander Mikhail Tukhachevsky had poured scorn on the idea that the Soviet Union should focus on its navy, and dismissed officers who disagreed with him as pseudo-Marxists. British and American historical experience suggested that countries with the luxury of defending themselves by sea or air power had a better chance of remaining internally free. There was a long history of soldiers being used as tools of internal repression. Navies and air forces can't do crowd control.

Britain and America were alike in being protected (if to different degrees) by water. They were alike in having political and cultural traditions that were resolutely civilian and antimilitarist. They were alike in having a strong faith in technological solutions to problems. For all these reasons, Britons and Americans found the idea of a national defense that relied on naval and air power deeply appealing. Air forces required fewer personnel than mass ground armies. This meant that relying on them would keep casualties low, while inflicting all the damage on the enemy.

This point was critical for democracies in the aftermath of the First World War. The massive losses of that war had come in ground battles such as Verdun, where the German and French armies had together suffered nearly three-quarters of a million casualties, or the Somme, where in just one day (July 1, 1916), and mostly one hour, the British lost twenty thousand men. In the interwar years, most politicians doubted that democracies would ever tolerate this scale of loss again. Air and sea warfare would never generate Verdun-style mass casualties, at least not to the combatants. Strategic bombing, in particular—bombing the enemy's cities, the enemy's civilians—was a way of winning a war by making the other side do the dying.

Fittingly, the United States led the world in the development of an aircraft that could carry out strategic bombing effectively. The prototype of a radically new kind of bomber, the Boeing B-17, first flew in 1935. The B-17 was a modern, all-metal monoplane, a four-engine heavy bomber that could fly at 250 miles per hour and carry 2,500 pounds of bombs for 2,260 miles. It entered service in 1937. The British would have nothing to equal it until 1942. The Germans would never have anything like it.

The U.S. Navy had never built up to the limits it was permitted under the Washington Naval Treaty of 1922 and the London Naval Treaty of 1930. One of Roosevelt's first actions in office was to order the construction of four cruisers, two aircraft carriers, sixteen destroyers, four submarines, and several auxiliary cruisers, "the greatest batch of fighting ships yet ordered in a single day," in the words of the historian Justus Doenecke. Then, between 1935 and 1939, the air corps budget nearly tripled, rising from $30 million to $83 million.

Roosevelt, much like Chamberlain, was an imaginative thinker about air warfare. The Munich settlement had come about as it had, he thought, because of the weakness of British and French air power in the face of German—a weakness that the United States shared. In November 1938, Roosevelt explained how much Munich had changed his thinking, and how he saw the solution to the Nazi menace. "I am not sure now I am proud" of having urged Chamberlain to negotiate before Munich, he admitted. "When I write to foreign countries," he continued, "I must have something to back up my words. Had we had this summer 5,000 planes with the capacity immediately to produce 10,000 per year, even though I might have had to ask Congress for authority to sell or lend them to the countries in Europe, Hitler would not have dared to take the stand he did."

Roosevelt's words shone a clear light on his "Atlantic community" thinking. American security rested on Britain and France; air power was essential for Britain and France to be able to defend themselves against the Nazis; this meant the United States needed greater air power as well. The specter of the garrison state lurked in the background. The United States, Roosevelt told his military commanders, needed "a huge air force so that we do not need to have a huge army to follow that air force"; for the United States to send large ground forces to Europe was "undesirable and politically out of the question." In the run-up to Munich, he told his cabinet how he would conduct a war if he were Chamberlain—not attacking on the ground, but using a naval blockade and bombing Germany. Secretary of the Interior Harold Ickes recorded the president making the point that "this kind of war would cost less money, would mean comparatively few casualties, and would be more likely to succeed than a traditional war by land and sea."

So it was that the United States made critical contributions to a uniquely Anglo-American conception of modern war. Where the Germans and the Soviets stressed winning through totalitarian control of one's own civilian population, coupled with a model of a fast-moving ground war based on tanks, the Anglo-American version put much more emphasis on air power and on scoring the knockout blow through intense bombing of enemy population centers. Army Air Corps training manuals of the 1930s began to speak of winning not only by destroying the enemy's industrial system, but also by using bombs to shatter the morale of the enemy population. Air commanders believed that this was possible and, further, that a breakdown of civilian morale would inevitably lead to a country's military defeat. Roosevelt thought that "the morale of the German people would crack under aerial attacks much sooner than that of the French or the English."

American leaders based this judgment on what they considered to be historical evidence. The airmen thought that the defeat of the Confederacy in the Civil War and of Germany in the First World War had rested on breaking civilian morale. Ironically, this meant that they agreed with Hitler and Ludendorff that Germany's 1918 defeat had not started with defeat in the field, but rather, with the breakdown of morale at home. Here again, Anglo-American ideas had the same starting point as German and Soviet ones. But they reached a very different conclusion.

But any war, even the kind of high-tech airborne war that Roosevelt imagined, would need solid popular support. As a master communicator, Roosevelt had a strategy for how to convey to Americans the need to confront the dictatorships.

FRANCES PERKINS, ROOSEVELT's secretary of labor and the first woman to hold cabinet office in the United States, once listened as a young reporter questioned the president on his political ideology. Was he a Communist? Was he a capitalist? Was he a socialist? To all these questions Roosevelt responded, with a mixture of puzzlement and surprise, "No."

"Well, what is your philosophy, then?" the reporter asked.

"Philosophy? Philosophy?" the president sputtered. "I am a Christian and a Democrat—that's all."

Perkins added, "Those two words expressed, I think, just about what he was."

It was what he was in foreign as much as domestic affairs. As Roosevelt struggled to find the right response to the Nazi menace, he turned increasingly to a synthesis of Christianity and democracy—indeed, he began to argue that Christianity defined democracy, in opposition to the totalitarian dictatorships. This was the second critical element in Roosevelt's thinking as 1938 turned to 1939. How could a modern leader explain the facts of life of world affairs to a democratic electorate? The historian Ky Woltering has shown that a stark dichotomy between Christianity and totalitarianism was a central feature of American rhetoric and policy in the early Cold War, particularly in the democratic reshaping of West Germany. But the rhetoric of the Christian-totalitarian dichotomy did not begin with the Cold War. It began with Roosevelt. It fit his philosophical orientation as "a Christian and a Democrat."

Roosevelt knew that support for a more muscular foreign policy was heavily concentrated in the deeply Christian South, not in the diverse urban North. He knew as well that Catholics, particularly in the large Italian and Irish immigrant communities, tended to be skeptical of foreign involvement—not least because of the atrocities Loyalists had inflicted on priests and nuns in the Spanish Civil War. The Christian-totalitarian dichotomy offered him a persuasive way to explain to such people why democracies had to take a stand against totalitarianism.

Roosevelt explained the dichotomy in his 1939 State of the Union address. "Storms from abroad," he said, "directly challenge three institutions indispensable to Americans, now as always. The first is religion. Religion is the source of the other two—democracy and international good faith." International good faith he defined as "a sister of democracy" that "springs from the will of civilized nations of men to respect the rights and liberties of other nations of men."

Freedom of religion was, for Roosevelt, the very essence of democracy. "Where freedom of religion has been attacked, the attack has come from sources opposed to democracy. Where democracy has been overthrown, the spirit of free worship has disappeared. And where religion and democracy have vanished, good faith and reason in international

affairs have given way to strident ambition and brute force." "An ordering of society," he continued, "which relegates religion, democracy and
good faith among nations to the background can find no place within
it for the ideals of the Prince of Peace. The United States rejects such an
ordering, and retains its ancient faith."

Then came something close to a call to action. "There comes a time
in the affairs of men when they must prepare to defend not their homes
alone, but the tenets of faith and humanity on which their churches,
their governments and their very civilization are founded. The defense
of religion, of democracy and of good faith among nations is all the
same fight. To save one we must now make up our minds to save all."

OVER THE WINTER of 1938–1939, the Roosevelt administration fell
into an increasingly angry dispute with Hitler's regime. The dispute was
about nothing less than the meaning of democracy and religious freedom. It began with the violence of Kristallnacht, and grew sharper in
December with a characteristically fierce speech by Harold Ickes.

Ickes never worried too much about making friends and was sometimes known as "the president's attack dog." But he always deployed his
combative temperament on the side of the underdog. In the 1920s he had
served a brief stint as president of the Chicago branch of the NAACP, and
as a lawyer he had taken cases on behalf of workers, Native Americans,
Jews, and African Americans. As Roosevelt's secretary of the interior,
he would famously arrange for the African American contralto Marian
Anderson to sing at the Lincoln Memorial in 1939 after the Daughters
of the American Revolution barred her from Constitution Hall.

On December 18, 1938, Ickes spoke at the annual Hanukkah banquet
of the Cleveland Zionist Society. He started with some very blunt words
about the barbarism of Nazi antisemitism. The medieval era scarcely
offered an appropriate comparison for the Nazis, he said, because it
had been a time of slow improvement: "To seek a true comparison it is
necessary to go back into that period of history when man was unlet-
tered, benighted and bestial." He went from there to a fierce criticism of
Charles Lindbergh and Henry Ford, both of whom had accepted honors
from the Nazi regime. "How," Ickes wanted to know, "can any American

accept a decoration at the hand of a brutal dictator who, with that same hand, is robbing and torturing thousands of fellow human beings?" Lindbergh and Ford were "free citizens of a free country" who had "obsequiously accepted tokens of contemptuous distinction at a time when the bestower of them counts that day lost when he can commit no new crime against humanity."

These words were certainly more than enough to anger the German government. But what followed was more important. Ickes placed Nazi antisemitism within the broader global crisis of democracy, linking religious freedom and economic democracy as the core of anti-Nazi politics. "Let us never forget," said Ickes, "that the recrudescence of antisemitism in the world today is a symptom of the decline of democracy. We know that the emancipation of the Jew in the Western World came with the rise of democracy. We know that it is in lands where democracy has ceased to work that intolerance has raised its ugly head and has turned its malevolence upon the Jews and other helpless minorities."

It was not enough simply to protest antisemitism, for "antisemitism is but a symptom." What he meant was that it was a symptom of the social and economic evils that gave rise to dictatorship in the first place. "We must reach down," said Ickes, "and deal with those conditions which have caused men and women to yield their democracy to a dictatorship. We must see to it that democracy works, not to the economic advantage of a few, but for the well-being of the many." Jews could not be safe if democracy was not safe. This meant that "if the economic system does not operate fairly one cannot assume that the victims of economic injustice will be fair or just when they seek to place the responsibility for their misfortune. Nor is it likely that the beneficiaries of special privileges will hesitate to divert the wrath of their victims away from themselves to some other group which can conveniently be made to serve as a scapegoat."

America could not expect to be immune to the global democratic crisis. "Fascism is an ever-present threat, even here in America," Ickes warned. "Every intelligent man and woman knows that the danger that threatens America is the same that has already engulfed other countries." For homegrown fascists, America's diverse society offered not just Jews, but also African Americans and many recent immigrants as targets. These people had "only to remember back a few years when the hooded figure of the Ku-Kluxer harassed them."

The point came back to religious freedom and the rights and freedoms of minorities. With every fascist advance, "we see fleeing, helpless minorities, stripped of their possessions and not knowing where they can go to start life all over again, be they aged or sick or of tender years." In Europe, the fascist tide had hit Jews the hardest, although "Catholic priests and even Lutheran ministers, who insisted upon the rights of freedom of worship, have learned, to their cost, how brutal and ruthless a dictator can be." "Personally," Ickes concluded, "I wish that the gates of America might be thrown welcomingly wide open to the political refugees of any country."

The reaction to Ickes's speech in the American press was generally positive, but it kicked off a diplomatic storm with Germany. It had been clear enough since 1933 that the Roosevelt administration did not think much of the Nazi regime, although at a formal diplomatic level, relations had remained amicable. Roosevelt's 1937 "quarantine" speech might have marked a tentative step on the road to conflict, but he had not followed it with action. At the end of 1938, however, Munich and the violence of Kristallnacht changed the situation dramatically. Here, in case there had been any doubt, was a demonstration before the entire world that hateful words led straight to violence. Roosevelt told a press conference that he had not thought such things were possible in the twentieth century. He recalled the U.S. ambassador from Berlin, and Hitler responded by ordering his ambassador home from Washington as well. Neither country would have an ambassador in the other's capital until after the Second World War.

This was the context for Ickes's bare-knuckled address in Cleveland. His speech, as he wrote a few days later, "so outraged Germany as to create an acute diplomatic situation between that country and the United States." The German chargé d'affaires filed an official protest and asked the U.S. government to disavow the speech. The Roosevelt administration refused. Undersecretary of State Sumner Welles, after speaking with the president, replied that Ickes's words had reflected the "overwhelming opinion" of Americans.

Hitler was highly attentive to the foreign press. His state secretary,

Otto Meissner, presented him each morning with a selection of translated extracts—not summaries—from foreign papers. Hitler was particularly interested in foreign leaders. As he was not otherwise very conscientious about paperwork or other official duties, this concern with the press tellingly reveals his insecurity and image-consciousness.

This image-consciousness in turn explains the rage the German press vented on Ickes. Ickes surmised that the German government was still reluctant to attack Roosevelt directly, so he offered a perfect surrogate. Of course, the German press—which operated under the careful, daily direction of Goebbels's Propaganda Ministry—made much of the fact that Ickes had given the speech to a Zionist society. But the Nazis found Ickes's commitment to individual liberty and civil rights even more important, stressing his ties to the American Civil Liberties Union, "the important auxiliary troops of Jewish Communism in the USA." Under the headline "America and Germany," the *Völkischer Beobachter* wondered why the Roosevelt "regime" was so determinedly building up its armed forces. "Would Roosevelt like to exercise police power over the entire world?"—a reference to Theodore Roosevelt's claim that the United States could exercise international police power over all the Americas. By contrast, the *Völkischer Beobachter* had only kind words for Republicans and isolationists.

This transatlantic confrontation took another step forward when Roosevelt gave his State of the Union address. The reaction in the German press was fierce and telling. Roosevelt was trying to define democratic opposition to totalitarianism; the Nazis responded by trying to drain the legitimacy from his arguments. It helped that Senator Key Pittman of Nevada, the chair of the Senate Foreign Relations Committee and an important if not always reliable ally of the president, had advocated the use of naval blockades against the dictators with the blunt argument "Why shoot a man when you can starve him to death?" This allowed the Nazis to push back against the main theme of Roosevelt's speech. The *Völkischer Beobachter* claimed that what American politicians understood by "civilization," "peace," and "good faith" amounted to "the death by starvation of defenseless women and children, as was also the goal of 'humanitarian' Wilson-America even after the end of the World War."

The Nazi press poured scorn on the American democratic freedom that Roosevelt contrasted to dictatorship: American "freedom" was only "a paper freedom, that through a truly grotesque uniformity of life" was "converted into its opposite." Even under the German "dictatorship"—the *Völkischer Beobachter* put the word in scare quotes—there was more variety and color in the life of every German community than in the United States. And of course the criticisms were heavily laced with antisemitism. An article citing a publication put out by the American fascist group the Silver Shirts bore the headline "USA Under Jewish Dictatorship," with the subheading "It's crawling with Jews around Roosevelt and Ickes."

The Nazis had come to power on January 30, 1933, and it had become an annual tradition on that date for Hitler to give a speech with something of the character of an American president's State of the Union address. The week before the speech, Goebbels met with an advisor to Father Coughlin, the right-wing American radio priest, who told him that "America is at its core more antisemitic than we believe it to be." Coughlin wanted the Nazis to give a "positive declaration in favor of Christianity." When Goebbels told Hitler about this meeting, Hitler agreed to "go into this question" in his upcoming speech. Hitler also vowed that he would "give the Americans a good talking to."

Hitler's two-and-a-half-hour speech was a response to Roosevelt and to Ickes—a "hard polemic against America," as Goebbels put it, and a "crystal-clear argument on the church question." Like Roosevelt, Hitler offered a narrative of how his nation had been resurrected from chaos and disaster in 1933 to triumph in 1938. Hitler was now for the first time speaking to the Reichstag of "Greater Germany," meaning that it included representatives from Austria and the Sudetenland as well as what Germans now called the "old Reich."

Hitler poured scorn on democracy: "The so-called democratic freedom to live to the full according to one's persuasions and instincts," he said, led only to "a squandering of the existing wealth of the creative potential of the individual and to his ultimate paralysis." In an echo of Ludendorff, he argued that "a national community instilled with discipline and obedience can far more easily mobilize the forces necessary to secure the survival of its own people."

Coming from someone who could simply have reveled in the triumphs of the past year, much of Hitler's speech was surprisingly bad-tempered. No doubt thinking of Ludwig Beck and others who had tried to restrain him, he complained of "men whom neither the greatest of calamities nor earthshattering upheaval can incite to inner reflection or induce to spiritual action." The past year had taught him that "in a critical hour, one man of action"—no doubt he meant himself—"weighs more than one thousand sophisticated weaklings," among whom he certainly included Beck. He singled out those Western democratic politicians who had irritated him by "feeding the flame of hatred against so-called totalitarian states." They were "Mr. Duff Cooper, Mr. Eden, Churchill [and] Mr. Ickes." And in response to Roosevelt's linking of Christianity and democracy, Hitler denied that "National Socialist Germany is a state hostile to religion." In Germany, he insisted, "no one has yet been persecuted for his religious orientation, nor will anyone be persecuted for this reason."

Even by Hitler's standards, this was a remarkably dishonest claim. For his part, Ickes was delighted to be placed alongside Eden, Churchill, and Duff Cooper. "He called us warmongers," Ickes wrote in his diary. "Naturally, I felt flattered that Hitler should have singled me out for attack."

The culmination of Hitler's speech—and the passage that has been most often quoted and remembered—was what Hitler called his "prophecy."

This "prophecy," too, was rooted in the exchange between the Americans and the Germans about democracy and faith, and shaped by Hitler's assumption that the Roosevelt administration opposed him only because it was in thrall to American Jews. He had often been a prophet before, Hitler claimed, and he had often been laughed at before ultimately being proven right. "Today I will again be a prophet: If international finance Jewry in and outside Europe should succeed once again in driving the nations into a World War, then the result will not be the Bolshevization of the earth and thus the victory of Jewry, but rather, the elimination of the Jewish race in Europe."

In the years that followed, Hitler would have more and more occasion to refer to this chilling "prophecy."

ONE OF THE great "what ifs" of Munich is whether things might have gone differently if the Western democracies had done more to bring in the Soviets.

This is something Churchill, for all his anticommunism, had very much wanted to do. In March 1938, he told the Soviet ambassador to Britain, Ivan Maisky, that "the only reliable means to restrain this beast"—Hitler's Germany—would be a "grand alliance" that included the Soviet Union. Churchill's priorities were very clear: he told Maisky that "today the greatest menace to the British Empire is German Nazism," not Soviet communism. He explained that he was doing what he could do to bring about such an alliance. At the beginning of September, with the crisis over Czechoslovakia looming, Churchill again lobbied Maisky, telling him of his "plan." Should the talks over Czechoslovakia break down, Britain, France, and the Soviet Union would deliver a joint ultimatum to Germany emphasizing that an attack on the Czechs would mean war with all. Maisky, on his own initiative, was also using Churchill as a back channel to get information to Halifax— and thus to the prime minister.

But Chamberlain took a much more jaundiced view of "the 'Grand Alliance,' as Winston calls it." Churchill's idea looked appealing, said Chamberlain, until "you come to examine its practicability." Then its attraction vanished. Chamberlain thought the Soviets were doing nothing more than "stealthily and cunningly pulling all the strings behind the scenes to get us involved in war with Germany," a prospect that "looked black indeed." Of course, it was Chamberlain's view and not Churchill's that prevailed in 1938. And as in other cases, the prime minister had a point, even more than he could then know.

The Soviet Union had an alliance treaty with Czechoslovakia, related to its alliance with France, through which it promised to aid in the defense of Czechoslovakia if France did as well. There were some obvious logistical problems with this arrangement. The Soviet Union did not border Czechoslovakia, and its military forces could reach it only by crossing Poland or Romania. Fearing the Soviets as much as the Germans, neither country was excited about this prospect.

The British and French made no serious effort to involve the Soviets in the Czech negotiations of September 1938. Nonetheless, Stalin mobilized troops along his western border and told them their mission was the defense of Czechoslovakia. What these troops might actually have done in the event of war is another question. Even President Beneš, desperate to secure Soviet aid, was not sure what it might entail. "They naturally play their own game," he told his secretary. "We cannot trust them completely either. If they get us into it, they will leave us twisting in the air." And in fact, the Soviets responded with silence to every Czech plea for aid.

This was because Stalin had his own agenda, which had nothing to do with the Czechs, and certainly nothing to do with defending democracy against Nazism. Stalin's agenda began with his deeply paranoid understanding of the rest of the world, a paranoia that his intelligence services and even their notorious British agents fed. During the Munich crisis, John Cairncross and Guy Burgess, young diplomats and two of the "Cambridge Five" group of Soviet spies, passed Foreign Office documents to their controllers. These documents helped reinforce Stalin's delusion that the British were appeasing Germany only to "lure" it into attacking the Soviet Union. Stalin's anti-British fixation joined his lingering hatred of Poland from the war of 1919–1921, and his resentment of Romania.

Out of these ingredients Stalin forged a distinctively paranoid understanding of what would make the Soviet Union secure. A few years later, during the Second World War, he told the Yugoslav partisan representative in Moscow, Milovan Djilas, "This war is not as in the past; whoever occupies a territory also imposes on it his own social system. Everyone imposes his own system as far as his army can reach. It cannot be otherwise." There is no reason to think Stalin's views were any different in 1938 or 1939. In fact, in 1936 the French general staff had asked the Soviet military attaché in Paris how the Soviet Union would help France if Germany attacked. The answer was blunt: "By attacking Poland."

Stalin's paranoia led him to see eastern Europe and the Baltic as a potential protective barrier between his country and the capitalist

West. Above all, he wanted to be able to deploy troops in places such as Romania and Poland. This goal was consistent over decades and was the fundamental factor in Stalin's foreign policy. It didn't matter who the potential enemy might be, or the potential ally, for that matter.

As the Czech crisis blew up, the Soviets partially mobilized five army groups, four of them on the Polish border. On September 15, they began an ethnic cleansing campaign against Poles in border areas of Ukraine. "Poles should be completely destroyed," ran the order. The point was almost certainly to remove any threat of a "fifth column" before a hostile Soviet invasion of Poland. There would have been no need to destroy Poles "completely" if the Red Army were simply going to pass through Poland on its way to Czechoslovakia or Germany—and then leave again.

It was the same with Romania. The territory of Bessarabia (today mostly the independent Republic of Moldova) had been part of Imperial Russia, but had been awarded to Romania in the peace settlement following the First World War. Stalin wanted it back. The fifth partially mobilized Soviet Army group was deployed on the border with Bessarabia. On September 22, a report from the Romanian border noted that the Soviets had established many new observation and reconnaissance posts and, as in western Ukraine, were removing ethnic Romanians from the border area. As a route to Czechoslovakia for Soviet military forces, Romania was completely unsuitable. Its road and rail infrastructure was poor, and all its double-tracked rail lines were in the south, whereas the route from the Soviet Union to Czechoslovakia ran through the north of the country. No Romanian rail line at all ran to Slovakia. Whatever that Soviet Army group was doing on the Bessarabian border, it wasn't there to defend the Czechs.

In any case, the aftermath of Munich was as sobering for Stalin as it was for Roosevelt and Chamberlain. Suddenly, Stalin was confronted with a world every bit as threatening as the one his paranoid fantasies and mendacious excuses had conjured up. Germany had come a step closer to his frontier. Japan loomed as a danger on the far-eastern side of the giant Soviet Union. And even Poland began to take on the contours of a threat once again.

No sooner had the Munich accord been signed than Poland issued its own ultimatum against Czechoslovakia, demanding the territories of

Teschen and Freistadt, which had substantial Polish populations. The Czechs conceded. Of course, Poland was an old enemy of the Soviet Union. Now it looked like it might be going over to the side of the dictators. The Soviets issued a veiled warning: Poland contained six million Ukrainians and two million Belorussians. Who was to say, the threat implied, that the Soviets might not seek their own "Munich" at Polish expense?

But of course, Germany was a vastly bigger worry for the Soviets, big enough to change Stalin's policies fundamentally. So only a few days after this warning, the Soviet government started issuing hints to the Poles about a common defense against the Nazis. In the coming year, the allegiance of Poland would be very much in play in European diplomacy: Germany, the Western democracies, and the Soviet Union would all compete for it. And the fact that Poland's political direction had become an item of serious concern in the foreign offices of Europe inevitably meant that the Soviets were pulled into European affairs. Stalin might prefer to be an isolationist, but after Munich, this was no longer an option. He, too, would have to pick a side: with the democracies or with Germany.

Another fundamental change was coming. Stalin's Terror had been raging through the Soviet state, the Red Army, and the Communist Party since 1936. He had attacked precisely those institutions that were vital to defense and national security: the foreign affairs commissariat, a third of whose staff had been executed or imprisoned; the NKVD's foreign intelligence service, which had been gutted; and of course the officer corps of the Red Army. Now, in the wake of Munich, Stalin announced an official inquiry into arrests carried out by the NKVD. In late November, Nikolai Yezhov, the head of the NKVD and Stalin's main instrument in the Terror (which the Russians called the *Yezhovshchina*), was replaced by Lavrentiy Beria. Yezhov would now have to bear the blame for the Terror that Stalin was ostentatiously rejecting. In the coming year, he would be arrested and confess to all the usual kinds of crimes: treason and "wrecking." Early in 1940, he would get the executioner's bullet he had given so many others.

The end of the Terror offered some bizarre experiences to the officers and officials who survived it. The brilliant and courtly general Konstantin Rokossovsky had been arrested in June 1937, just as Tukhachevsky and his fellow officers were executed. It didn't help Rokossovsky that his father was Polish, putting him into one of the most endangered categories of the Terror. (Ethnic Poles were twelve times as likely to be arrested as non-Polish Soviet citizens and, once arrested, almost certain to be shot.) His interrogators beat and tortured him, but remarkably, Rokossovsky refused to sign a confession that he had spied for Poland or Japan. Somehow, Stalin's men never got around to shooting him. Early in 1940, he was released and restored to his command. There is a story that just after his release, Stalin called him and said, "Well, Rokossovsky, I don't seem to have seen you around for some time. Where did you get to?" Rokossovsky explained patiently, "I was arrested, Comrade Stalin. I was sitting in prison."

"A fine time you chose to go to prison!" was the dictator's reply.

11

"A Dissemination of Discord"

The event is controversial before it begins. Mayor Fiorello La Guardia and the American Civil Liberties Union do not approve of its purpose, but insist it should be allowed to go forward. The unlikely pairing of an American Legion post and the Trotskyist Socialist Workers Party think it should be banned. A Legion official explains that he has received "literature" showing that speakers at the rally will urge that civil liberties be limited to "white gentiles." Followers of Father Coughlin call out to the police, "You'll have plenty of arrests tomorrow night."

It is February 20, 1939. The pro-Nazi German American Bund is celebrating George Washington's birthday two days early with a massive rally—twenty thousand supporters—at New York's Madison Square Garden. The New York City Police Department assigns 1,745 officers to protect the Bundists, one of its largest deployments ever.

Outside the Garden are perhaps ten thousand anti-Nazi protesters (some of the police claim it is more like one hundred thousand), who engage in running battles with the officers. The journalist Dorothy Thompson ventures inside the Garden and finds "a hall decorated with American flags and faced by an enormous portrait of George Washington," whose expression looks "sad and slightly embittered." Chairs have been set where the ice surface would normally be, and they are full. When a procession carrying flags and banners enters, everyone stands and gives straight-armed Hitler salutes. At the front of the hall the thirty-two-foot-tall Washington stands flanked by American flags (Betsy Ross and modern) and swastikas. The Bund has its Stormtroopers, too; they are called the Order Division. They wear gray uniforms, and like their brown-shirted German equivalents, they are there to intimidate opponents. In 1931, Thompson saw a Nazi rally in Berlin's Sportspalast and finds little difference here. Listening to a speech by the Bund's public relations director, Gerhard Kunze, she feels she heard it all in Berlin. Every word Kunze says is "made in Germany by the Nazis," who are openly conspiring against democracy.

Thompson hears speakers insist that America is a republic, not a democracy. They rebrand American ideals as "white gentile ideals." They want German racial laws introduced into the United States. They want to prevent any diplomatic collaboration between the United States, Great Britain, and France. They advocate "an organized boycott of 'Aryan' citizens against all other American citizens not of 'Aryan' race." Thompson learns "what I had already heard in Berlin, that all of our press, our finance, our government and our cultural life are in the hands of Jews and that the Jews are Communists." The Bundists refer to the president of the United States as "Rosenfeld." The crowd boos his name and jeers at the mention of other liberals or Jews close to Roosevelt: Harold Ickes, Frances Perkins, Harry Hopkins, Supreme Court justice Felix Frankfurter. They cheer, though, for Father Coughlin, Benito Mussolini, and Adolf Hitler.

At one point, Thompson laughs derisively at something Kunze has said. She is immediately "seized by two policemen" and also "set upon by a husky uniformed stormtrooper." The policemen inform her that the right of freedom of assembly does not include the right to laugh at a public speaker.

One man goes further than laughing. Isadore Greenbaum is a twenty-six-year-old hotel employee from Brooklyn. As Bund leader Fritz Kuhn is speaking, telling the crowd that the Bund wants the "American government to be returned to the American people who founded it," that it desires a "socially just, white gentile-ruled United States," Greenbaum tries to rush the stage. He is stopped by six hefty Stormtroopers. They beat him savagely. One of them grabs Greenbaum's hair and throws him across the stage. Kuhn watches impassively; the crowd roars its approval of the beating. The police take Greenbaum to night court, where he is charged with disorderly conduct. Only after that is he allowed to see a doctor.

Yet the Bundists clearly feel that they are the real victims of oppression. Kunze complains that "there is no free radio for white men," and demands that radio stations "cease giving the people the trash of the Cantors, Winchells and Bernsteins and give them instead the voice of one who speaks American without an accent." Fritz Kuhn, who certainly does not speak "American without an accent," complains there is a "campaign of hate" against the Bund and that most people know him only through the "Jewish-controlled press" as a "creature with horns, a cloven hoof, and a long tail."

"If," Dorothy Thompson concludes, "this democracy allows a movement, the whole organization and pattern of which is made by a government openly hostile to the American democracy, to organize, set up a private army and propagandize on this soil, we are plain saps." Thompson is married to the writer Sinclair Lewis, the author of a 1935 novel about American fascism entitled It Can't Happen Here.

THE CRISIS OF democracy of the 1930s was not only a matter of democracy failing where it had been newly achieved, in central and eastern Europe. It was not only a matter of the long-established democracies such as Britain and America confronting the menace of Hitler's Germany. The crisis also reached inside democracy's heartlands. The Nazi menace lurked at home as well as abroad.

The Great Depression had wrought more havoc on the economy of the United States than on that of any other country, with the possible exception of Germany. Between 1929 and 1933, American GDP fell by more than a quarter, while the value added by manufacturing fell by half. The official unemployment rate reached 24.9 percent. Half of all banks failed, and international trade fell by 60 percent. Almost at a stroke, the optimism about growth, prosperity, and the good life that had long characterized American society—and particularly in the Roaring Twenties—was gone. The future suddenly looked darker, more dangerous, and poorer. But as devastating as the economic effects were on individual lives and attitudes, the economic crisis alone did not create the somber mood of the 1930s. In Europe, a mixture of nationalism, racism, insularity, and skepticism about the rationality of human beings had threatened democracy and sparked a desire for authoritarian politics. The same things were happening in the United States.

Many people doubted that the democratic system was equal to solving twentieth-century problems. Two days after Hitler came to power, as Roosevelt waited for his own inauguration, he received a visit from the columnist Walter Lippmann. "The situation is critical, Franklin," Lippmann told the president-elect. "You may have no alternative but to assume dictatorial powers." Roosevelt's New Deal was conceived as a desperate effort to save American democracy.

As in Europe, America's crisis of democracy also rested on an angry rejection by many, perhaps most, Americans of the First World War and its outcome. This attitude brought in turn a desperate desire by many Americans to insulate the country from the rest of the world. It was in this atmosphere that President Woodrow Wilson failed in 1919 and 1920 to persuade the nation, and particularly the Senate, to approve American membership in the League of Nations. The Republican senator William Borah of Idaho spoke for many when he said the League would imperil "what I conceive to be the underlying, the very first principles of this Republic," above all "the right of our people to govern themselves free from all restraint, legal or moral, of foreign powers."

The mention of "foreign powers" brought in another point. As in Europe, America's crisis of democracy was about racial and ethnic conflict. Madison Grant, one of the leading American advocates of the new "science" of eugenics, provided a good example of how tightly antidemocratic politics and racism were tied together: he blamed the French Revolution of 1789 for "the dogma of the brotherhood of man," which contradicted his notions of racial hierarchy, and he used the term *democratic institutions* as an insult.

During the 1920s, admittedly, there was a split between elite and grassroots opinion when it came to international affairs. The jazz-age United States was far from idle on the world stage, launching such initiatives as the Dawes and Young Plans in 1924 and 1929 to restructure German reparation payments, and the Kellogg-Briand Pact in 1928 in an effort to outlaw war altogether. But when the Great Depression struck, Americans more decisively turned their backs on the world. The New Deal itself represented an effort to "insulate" America from international influences.

The widespread American hostility to any form of international engagement in the interwar years fit comfortably with a heightened and racialized nationalism. This had been brewing before the First World War, especially as advocates of limiting immigration encountered the idea of eugenics. The war gave a dramatic boost to such notions. So did the Bolshevik Revolution in Russia, and the fears of Communist subversion elsewhere in the world that followed it. In response, many Americans began to cling ever more tightly to the idea that being American meant being of British or northern European stock. To people who thought this way, the influx of immigrants around the turn of the century from southern and eastern Europe would fatally damage America's "Anglo-Saxon" or "Nordic" character, while bringing with it dangerous foreign ideologies.

In this atmosphere, the Ku Klux Klan rose again, climbing to a membership of between four and five million. Unlike during the Reconstruction era, the Second Klan spread to the North and West. Its orientation was often as anti-Catholic and antisemitic as it was antiblack. What it offered was a new compound of Protestantism, white supremacy, and nationalism—the same mixture that had fueled the Nazis in Germany.

Of course, this effort to redefine Americanism around Protestantism and Anglo-Saxon or Nordic "whiteness" had serious implications for African Americans even apart from the rebirth of the Klan. From the late nineteenth century, across the American South, a combination of special taxes, literacy tests, and residency requirements had nullified the protections of the Fifteenth Amendment, so that by 1938, only about 4 percent of African Americans in the South could vote. Discriminatory laws were often accompanied by brutal violence. Between 1900 and 1930, nearly two thousand African Americans were lynched. Federal antilynching legislation was stymied in Congress by the power of Southern members, who had a particular lock on the Democratic Party and thus effectively a veto (in this case through filibuster) on legislation.

By the 1930s, the Klan had receded, but new organizations arose to promote the idea of a white, Protestant (or at least Christian), antisemitic

America. These included the German American Bund and the Silver Legion of America, which featured Nazi-style uniforms and their own versions of Stormtroopers. Father Charles Coughlin of Detroit spread antisemitic hate to a huge radio audience, and his Christian Front followers amounted to another kind of Brownshirt. Long before the celebrated aviator Charles Lindbergh became the star speaker of the America First Committee, these groups proclaimed "America First" as their policy. They had very different constituencies, and their ethnic and religious differences meant that they could never unite effectively. But they all aimed to keep the United States out of any European war and to defeat Franklin Roosevelt.

The racism that lay behind the Johnson-Reed Act, segregation, and the rise of the Klan and the other far-right groups was at the core of America's crisis of democracy. It also connected the American crisis to the European one. The assertion of nationalism and isolationism against globalization was common everywhere, even to the New Deal. Hitler was a close student of developments in the United States. He was a great admirer of Madison Grant's book *The Passing of the Great Race*, which influenced the Johnson-Reed Act and appeared in a German translation in 1925. In *Mein Kampf*, after a tirade about Germany's careless immigration policies, Hitler praised the United States as the "one country" that "simply excludes certain races from naturalization." Hitler recognized the Johnson-Reed Act as a cautious step on the road to America's becoming a *völkisch* (racist and extreme nationalist) state. When the Nazis took power, they looked to American immigration and citizenship laws, and laws banning racially mixed marriages, as models. American influence (particularly the Jim Crow laws in the South) even lay behind the infamous Nuremberg Laws of 1935.

Hitler and the Nazis certainly didn't need tutorials in hate from Americans or from anyone else. But when they went looking for ways to apply their hatred, they found in American racial laws the "classic example."

LEGALIZED HATRED WAS not the only zone of common German American experience in the crises of the 1930s. The irrationality of human beings, and the ways in which politicians and businesspeople could profitably exploit that irrationality, was another.

The most prominent American commentator on this theme was the influential newspaper columnist Walter Lippmann, who had first learned about propaganda from work he had done drafting American messages directed at German soldiers in the First World War. Lippmann saw that a mass press could spread legends and lies that millions of citizens would believe: that angels saved the British Army at the Battle of Mons, that Russian soldiers arrived in Britain with snow on their boots, that the Germans crucified prisoners of war. The first fruit of his concern was a short book called *Liberty and the News*, in which Lippmann coined a phrase that would resonate many years later and in very different hands: the increasing importance of public opinion in modern democracies, he argued, put "a premium upon the manufacture of what is called consent." Then he paid a visit to newly fascist Italy and was drawn to write two more highly influential books: *Public Opinion* (1922) and the even more pessimistic *The Phantom Public* (1925).

The size of the American electorate had doubled since 1896 (and would soon have tripled), and the complexity of social and political problems had increased proportionately, which meant that few citizens could bring informed judgment to many of these questions. But there was an even worse problem: perhaps *no one* could make rational judgments about human affairs. All perception, Lippmann thought, was subjective. "We do not first see, and then define, we define first and then see," he wrote. Stereotypes, mostly cultural in origin, set the definitions. This led Lippmann to a very serious problem: if all this were true, then there were no facts, only different cultural judgments masquerading as facts.

This was bad news for a democratic system that depended on its voters' ability to find and accurately understand information. Given that the public was not competent to make decisions, politicians had to flatter it into thinking it was. This meant that deception and dishonesty had become central to the workings of democracy. "Public men had to accustom themselves to telling the public only a part of what they told themselves," said Lippmann. The new breed of demagogic politicians filled Lippmann with contempt. In 1927, he voiced his scorn for the mayor of Chicago, "Big Bill" Thompson, who had won office by catering

to the "very lowest prejudices" of the people. "How long can popular government endure," Lippmann wondered, "on a foundation of this kind?"

Something had to fill that space between the vast numbers of new
voters and the even vaster facts of the world's complexity. In Hitler's
Germany, that thing was frankly dubbed "propaganda." In the United
States and other democracies, it bore the gentler name "public relations."

This new field was born in part out of the experience of wartime
propaganda and partly out of the corporate response to the muckraking
journalism of the years before the First World War. One of the pioneers
of American public relations, Ivy Lee, had been a reporter before he
switched to helping Standard Oil and Bethlehem Steel improve their
images. Lee bluntly demonstrated the disregard for verifiable reality
that his job required: in speeches in the mid-1920s—approvingly citing
Lippmann—he argued that facts did not exist. "The effort to state an
absolute fact is simply an attempt to achieve what is humanly impossible," he said. "All I can do is to give you my interpretation of the facts."
No one could be unbiased: "All of us are apt to try to think that what
serves our own interests is also in the general interest. We are very prone
to look at everything through glasses colored by our own interests and
prejudices." Lippmann saw this as a deeply worrying problem. For Lee,
it was a business opportunity. He did not limit himself to representing
American businesses: in the 1920s, he represented the Soviet Union,
and in the 1930s, the giant German chemical conglomerate IG Farben.

This was the point at which the new profession of public relations
slid into the other new profession of political consulting. Here the pioneers were the Californian husband-and-wife team Clem Whitaker and
Leone Baxter, who in 1933 founded a firm called Campaigns Inc. Like
Ivy Lee, Whitaker and Baxter had no interest in anything as quaint as
"facts" or "truth." And they understood they were living in something
new: a society of consumers, not citizens. "Every voter, a consumer;
every consumer, a voter" was their mantra.

Whitaker and Baxter did not think their consumers were very
bright. Political campaigns had to have a simple theme. "A wall goes up
when you try to make Mr. and Mrs. Average American Citizen work or
think," said Whitaker. Repetition was good. So were rhyming phrases.
Honesty and factual accuracy were entirely beside the point. After they

had orchestrated the defeat of the radical muckraker Upton Sinclair's 1934 bid to be governor of California, Baxter admitted the irrelevance of their own campaign's claims. But she added a verbal shrug: "We had one objective: to keep [Sinclair] from becoming Governor."

Whitaker and Baxter lived a very long way from Hitler and Germany's stormy politics. But they and the German dictator had strikingly similar ideas about persuading people. Hitler wrote *Mein Kampf* just as Lippmann was fretting about the fitness of modern humans to be democratic citizens, and as Lee, Whitaker, and Baxter were learning to make money out of the problem. For his part, Hitler thought that German centrist politicians of his time were failing because they lacked the instincts for "moving and influencing the masses." "The mass of humanity as such is lazy and cowardly," he wrote, and capable at best of passive acceptance of an idea. They could never be reached with the written word. You could reach them better with "the picture in all its forms up to film," because "here a man needs to work with his brains even less." With one glance he has gotten the point. Gut feelings—"instinctive disgust, deeply felt hatred"—were much more important and harder to change than opinions about facts. Wrong ideas "can be gotten rid of with instruction," said Hitler, "resistance from a gut feeling never."

Hitler had the same low opinion of general public intelligence. "The broad masses of the people are not made up of diplomats or professors of constitutional law," he wrote, but of "a mass of human children prone to doubt and insecurity," ruled by "sentiment rather than by sober reasoning." Like Whitaker and Baxter, he drew this conclusion: "Propaganda must limit itself to a few themes and repeat them endlessly . . . perseverance is the first and most important condition of success."

Just as Ivy Lee and Campaigns Inc. were not worried about the truth of their promotions, Hitler understood that lies could play an important role in politics. Here, as in his other observations on propaganda, he showed a cynical but shrewd appreciation of how dishonesty functions in political campaigns. A successful campaigner, Hitler wrote, focuses on telling big lies, and does not bother with small ones, for "in the bigness of the lie there is always a certain element of credibility." The "broad masses of the nation can always be more easily corrupted in the depths of their hearts than that they consciously or voluntarily become wicked," so "in the primitive simplicity of their nature they more readily fall victims to the big lie than to the small lie, since they themselves often lie about small things, yet would still be ashamed to tell a big lie," and so "they cannot at all believe that others could have the impudence to distort the truth so infamously." The kicker was that, once out there, the lie could never be entirely erased. "Even if the true facts are given to them, they will still doubt and hesitate for a long time and will assume that at least some part of it is still true. For precisely this reason, some residue of the most impudent lie will always remain behind, a fact that all the great liars and lying organizations of this world know only too well."

Certainly, Hitler knew it well. Like Ivy Lee and Campaigns Inc., he was interested in the opportunities offered by the masses' gullibility. Nazism wallowed in the irrationality and anti-intellectualism it exploited. The first goal of this wallowing was to spray contempt on Nazi opponents. But the ultimate goal was to get the German people ready for war.

Hitler repeatedly vented his contempt for experts and intellectuals— except, occasionally, when they praised him and flattered his fragile ego. But mostly, he scorned what he saw as the individuality and the disloyalty of intellectuals. "When I look at our intellectual classes," he mused in November 1938, "—unfortunately we need them, otherwise one day we could, I don't know, exterminate them or something." Goebbels expressed the same contempt alongside a rejection of "objectivity" like that of Ivy Lee. "There is nothing at all that is without political bias," he said. "The discovery of the principle of absolute objectivity is the privilege of German university professors—and I do not believe that university professors make history."

Goebbels drew an important and revealing lesson from Orson Welles's "War of the Worlds" broadcast. Early in 1939, as German-American relations headed toward a new low point, Goebbels wrote that the American people were victims of a campaign "by certain unscrupulous world-provocateurs . . . One can see just how far this provocation goes from the fact that today public opinion in North America can fall for the crudest deception. An American radio station need only broadcast a fantastical radio play about a Martian invasion of the American continent and a large part of the American people are virtually gripped by panic. That is the consequence of this infamous lying and unconscionable agitation." Goebbels, too, thought that people could be made to believe anything.

It remained for Hitler to explain clearly the real point of pouring propaganda over the credulous masses. On November 10, 1938, the day after Kristallnacht, he returned to the Führerbau on Munich's Königsplatz, where the Munich Conference had been held six weeks before. He was there, in theory, to thank Germany's newspaper publishers and many of its reporters for their coverage of the Sudeten crisis. Really, he had something much grimmer to say.

Hitler was still worrying about the obvious lack of enthusiasm for war that the German people had shown in September. Since he had come to power, he explained, circumstances had forced him to speak only of peace. Only in this way had it been possible for him to win back Germany's freedom. But "obviously" this "peace propaganda" had its "dubious side," Hitler said: the German people had actually started to believe it.

It was now necessary "to gradually reorient the German people psychologically and slowly make clear to it that there are things that, if they cannot be carried out with peaceful methods, must be carried out with violence." This was, Hitler said, largely a matter of presenting "certain foreign political events" in such a way that the "inner voice of the people gradually begins to cry out for violence."

Hitler had no doubt that "the people" would do so if things were put to them in the right way. It was up to the press to propagandize the people into war. "We have to bring the whole German people to this. They must learn to believe so fanatically in the final victory that, even if we sometimes suffer defeats, the nation . . . will consider them from a higher point of view: that is temporary." The decisive point was that the nation "closes ranks behind the leadership." That, said Hitler, would make him proud, and would be "an enormous relief."

To ACHIEVE THAT "closing of ranks," Hitler always hammered home the threat of "foreigners"—whether they were real foreigners in France or the Soviet Union or German citizens whom he wanted to exclude from the country, such as Jews. The arrival of threatening foreigners was the universal and pervasive fear of the 1930s. Those foreigners could be abstract or fictional, like the Martians in Orson Welles's radio play. But they could also be very real. The Bund's goose-stepping Stormtroopers were one example of something foreign and threatening. So, in a different way, were migrants and refugees. And so were agents of foreign governments and foreign intelligence services.

Nazi police and intelligence forces spread a lot of fear in the democracies in the 1930s. The philosopher Theodor Lessing, Jewish and liberal, a brilliant and resourceful critic of German nationalism, fled into exile in Czechoslovakia in 1933. Sudeten German Nazi agents found him there and murdered him. In 1935, Nazis abducted the investigative reporter Berthold Jacob from Switzerland. Jacob had reported on secret German rearmament during the Weimar period and had been imprisoned for treason even before the coming of Hitler. After the Nazi takeover, he kept up his reporting from a sanctuary in the still French-controlled Saarland.

Also in 1935, two German émigrées in London, the former Social Democratic Reichstag deputy Mathilde Wurm and the left-wing journalist and activist Dora Fabian, were found dead in the apartment they shared in London. A coroner's inquest ruled that their deaths were suicides, but there were many reasons to be skeptical of this finding and to suspect that German agents were behind these deaths as well. Fabian had been actively involved in investigations of Hans Wesemann, a socialist German émigré whom the Gestapo had "turned" and who had been responsible for the abduction of Berthold Jacob, among others. Fabian and Wurm's apartment had been broken into twice, and no one who knew them thought they were plausible candidates for suicide. The coroner found that Fabian had killed herself over heartbreak at the end of an affair with the German emigré Karl Korsch, but the only evidence for that claim came from Korsch himself, whom other emigrés in London suspected of being a Nazi agent—and why should Wurm kill herself over Fabian's heartbreak? The police investigation, as many critics pointed out, had been sloppy. The case caused a media sensation in the United Kingdom, stimulating fears that Nazi terror was spreading to the British Isles. The Labour MP Ellen Wilkinson wrote that after the second break-in, she had urged Fabian to go the police, saying, "This isn't Nazi Berlin." Fabian had only smiled bitterly and replied, "The greatest asset the Nazi agents have is that no one, neither police nor one's friends, will *believe* that anyone can do the things here that we have proof they do."

There was institutional organization behind these efforts. In 1933, the Gestapo ordered all German police forces to prepare lists of émi-grés with a particular focus on leading Communists, pacifists, Social Democrats, and "members of the Jewish intelligentsia." The secret police built up a network of agents abroad for surveillance of refugees. Usually the agents were themselves German, sometimes working for the police because of blackmail, sometimes simply for money. The German For-eign Office also set up a new branch, the Referat Deutschland, to keep tabs on émigrés. The Nazi Party had its Auslands-Organisation, which actively organized pro-Nazi Germans living abroad.

It was alarming enough that Nazi agents might rob from, abduct, or even murder people living in democratic countries. Perhaps more alarming was that the Nazis might interfere actively in democratic poli-tics and possibly even swing election outcomes. Franklin Roosevelt was well aware of this danger. "We have learned," he said in his State of the Union address in 1939, "that long before any overt military act, aggres-sion begins with preliminaries of propaganda, subsidized penetration, the loosening of ties to goodwill, the stirring of prejudice and the incitement to disunion." It was a theme he kept up. In a fireside chat of May 1940, he would warn that attack could come through "a dissemination of dis-cord," in which "a group that may be sectional or racial or political" is "encouraged to exploit its prejudices through false slogans and emotional appeals. The aim of those who deliberately egg on these groups is to create confusion of counsel, public indecision, political paralysis and eventually, a state of panic." A few months later, in his famous "Arsenal of Democ-racy" fireside chat, he warned that the "evil forces which have crushed and undermined and corrupted so many others are already within our own gates," and there were "American citizens, many of them in high places, who . . . are aiding and abetting the work of these agents."

In the late 1930s and during the first years of the Second World War, the German Foreign Office ran an extensive American operation that lobbied dozens of U.S. senators and representatives and used them to spread German propaganda. The head of the network was George Sylvester Viereck, a German American who in various ways had been spreading pro-German propaganda since before the First World War. His operations had three main goals: to convince Americans that Germany was unbeatable; to push lawmakers to support neutrality; and to maintain German-American trade. Spreading disinformation was key to these efforts. The politicians who were useful to Viereck were strongly isolationist in sentiment, such as the New York State congressman Hamilton Fish, and sometimes cash-strapped, such as Senator Ernest Lundeen of Minnesota, to whom Viereck promised that collaboration would prove "more profitable both politically and financially than anything that you yourself can do." Viereck actually worked directly out of Lundeen's office. The result of his efforts was that Lundeen and Fish (and others in Congress) used the floor of the House and Senate to spout the propaganda of a hostile foreign power. Through the congressional privilege of franking, Viereck was also able to distribute offprints of these speeches by the hundreds of thousands at American taxpayer expense.

Shortly before Lundeen was killed in a plane crash in 1940, Viereck assured him that a looming investigation was just a "witch hunt." In fact, as files declassified only in 2013 show, it was a British intelligence operation that ran Viereck to ground. The British leaked information on his activities to the press and to American authorities. Viereck was charged under the Foreign Agents Registration Act. That was effectively the end of his operation.

The German government also intervened heavily in the 1940 U.S. presidential election, spending millions of dollars in an effort to secure the Democratic nomination for someone friendly to Germany—the labor leader John L. Lewis was the Germans' main hope—and when it became clear that Roosevelt would again be the Democratic nominee, the German government tried desperately to get his Republican challenger, Wendell Willkie, elected instead. The German embassy in Washington spent thousands of dollars on travel expenses for Republican congressmen so that they would make sure there was an isolationist plank in the GOP platform—failing to understand that no American ever pays any attention to the party platforms—and also paid for full-page newspaper ads demanding "Stop the march to war!"

It is to stop foreign influence of this type that states have intelligence services, and the intelligence and police work in Britain and the United States in the 1930s was generally good enough—if not always much more than good enough—to keep Nazi agents from doing the worst things. But a particularly difficult challenge emerges when a leader simply doesn't want to hear accurate intelligence about adversaries or, even worse, when he himself becomes someone the intelligence services consider unreliable. This was the problem Neville Chamberlain began to pose for the British services late in 1938.

Like most countries, Britain had a foreign intelligence service (known as the Secret Intelligence Service, SIS, or sometimes as MI6), run by the Foreign Office, and a domestic intelligence service (known as MI5), under the authority of the Home Office. The Nazi menace was, of course, the primary responsibility of SIS. But as it happened, MI5 had an outstanding agent within the German embassy in London who supplied high-grade intelligence on the Nazis.

The agent was a remarkable figure named Wolfgang Gans Edler Herr zu Putlitz, the scion of an aristocratic Brandenburg family. Putlitz had served in the First World War and had joined the German diplomatic service in 1925, after earning a doctorate in economics in Berlin and studying at Oxford. By the late 1930s, he was in charge of the consular department at the London embassy. A passionate anti-Nazi, Putlitz seems to have worked both for Soviet and British intelligence in the 1930s. He communicated with MI5 through another remarkable agent, Jona von Ustinov, always known by his nickname, Klop (Russian for "bedbug"). Despite the name and nickname, Klop was German, though his wife was Russian. He was fired from his job as the press officer at Germany's London embassy when he refused to prove he was not Jewish. He gained British citizenship and became a journalist in London—and an agent of MI5. Klop's excellent contacts in the Berlin embassy, including Putlitz, made him extremely useful to the British. The MI5 officer Peter Wright wrote many years later that the information Klop got from Putlitz was "possibly the most important human-source intelligence Britain received in the pre-war period."

The team of Putlitz and Klop supplied documents such as reports from the Nazi Auslands-Organisation in Britain. From these reports MI5 received advance warning of such moves as the remilitarization of the Rhineland and the invasions of Austria and Czechoslovakia. Putlitz believed that Hitler meant what he had said in *Mein Kampf* about eastward expansion. The consequence was that appeasement was futile. MI5 adopted this view from 1936 on. Klop's son, Peter Ustinov (who as a stage and film actor would become much more famous than his father), also got in on the espionage act. Young Peter was in school with the son of German ambassador Joachim von Ribbentrop and reported on how enthusiastically Ribbentrop's son drew scenes of war and destruction.

SIS and MI5 carried on a ferocious rivalry. The famous SIS officer and "Cambridge spy" Kim Philby remembered years later that SIS had greeted the end of the Second World War with relief because its officers could now "get back to fighting the real enemy, MI5." So it is not surprising that SIS did not see the German threat the same way. While information from Klop led MI5 to urge the government to stand firm at Munich, SIS advocated forcing the Czechs to accept Hitler's terms. In the aftermath of the Munich settlement, MI5 produced a report based on information from Putlitz and Klop that, in the words of the historian Christopher Andrew, amounts to "probably the first (albeit implicit) indictment of government foreign policy by a British intelligence agency." To ensure that the report got Chamberlain's attention, MI5 included information about Hitler's scorn for Chamberlain: the Nazi dictator was said to have called Chamberlain an "asshole" and mocked his trademark umbrella.

But the response was not what MI5 had hoped. Recently declassified documents from Britain's Foreign Office tell the story. In late November 1938, MI5's sources delivered the alarming information that the press officer at the German embassy, Fritz Hesse, was meeting secretly with Chamberlain's press secretary, George Steward. MI5 also secured a report from Hesse to Ribbentrop describing one of Hesse's meetings with Steward. According to this report, dated November 25, 1938, Steward had told Hesse, "There was an urgent desire to take now a further visible step along the line laid down in the Munich agreement," and he was proposing an agreement on "humanizing warfare, particularly aerial warfare." Such an agreement should be negotiated personally and in secret between Chamberlain and Hitler, without involving the

Foreign Office. Steward assured Hesse that "some of the worst agitators against Germany have had a spoke put in their wheel"—which probably referred to Churchill and other appeasement critics, whom Chamberlain was trying to force out of Parliament. Hesse wanted to know "what I am to do in case the Führer wishes to pursue this doubtless officially inspired proposal," adding that the suggestion was "another sign of how great the wish for understanding with us is here in England and is also evidence . . . that Great Britain is ready during the next year, to accept practically everything from us and to fulfill our every wish."

Chamberlain's office, then, was not only communicating secretly with the German government, but was also discussing with the Germans the plans to sideline British critics of Chamberlain and Germany. Alexander Cadogan, who received this information from MI5, was not sure whether, and what, he should tell Halifax. He thought Halifax would feel he had to confront Chamberlain with these reports. If Chamberlain denied any knowledge of the contacts and "made a scapegoat of somebody," Halifax would probably accept the explanation and keep working. But if Chamberlain "stuck to his guns" on negotiating with the Germans, Cadogan thought Halifax would resign.

Cadogan also wondered about the effect on Chamberlain. "He would probably think his policy of 'appeasement' had been torpedoed by the wicked anti-German Foreign Office," Cadogan concluded. Chamberlain would try to "clip the wings" of the Foreign Office and meanwhile keep on with his clandestine dealings. If Halifax resigned, Cadogan feared that Chamberlain would install a "dummy" as foreign secretary and take SIS under his own control. Cadogan also thought it was possible that Chamberlain might be forced to call an election, which would be fought between appeasers and anti-appeasers. The Germans, seeing that Chamberlain might lose, would launch a war right away. Chamberlain's supporters would blame this outcome on the anti-appeasers, and the result would be a bitterly divided nation facing a desperate war with Germany.

Nonetheless, Cadogan concluded that he had to tell Halifax. The result in fact was that Chamberlain made a "scapegoat" of someone else. Halifax accepted this, perhaps grudgingly, and things went on their way.

Chamberlain stuck stubbornly with appeasement, even as its returns seemed to be growing fewer and fewer.

LIKE BRITAIN AND the United States, France could not remain untouched by the 1930s crisis of democracy. With French institutions less hallowed by tradition, democracy in France was in fact under much greater internal danger than in the English-speaking countries. In the 1930s it looked at times to be going the way of the German democracy of the Weimar Republic.

German democracy had been undermined in part by violence between organized groups of right and left that the state could not control. Something similar erupted in France in February 1934. The lingering horror of the First World War, the economic malaise of the 1930s, and a sense that scandal and corruption were endemic to French institutions seemed to shake the stability of the French state. The ideological extremes grew ever farther apart. The French Communist Party was strong and growing. In response, there were French radical right groups that copied the style of the Italian Fascists and German Nazis, with colored uniforms and jackboots: groups such as the Jeunesses Patriotes (Patriotic Youth) and the Croix-de-Feu (Cross of Fire). On the night of February 6, the passions and anger overflowed on the streets of Paris as these groups took to the streets and violence erupted between the gangs of the right and those of the left. That night, eighteen people were killed and as many as fourteen hundred wounded.

Unlike in Germany, however, the moment passed and, for a time, national confidence seemed to improve with the economy. The right-wing violence of 1934 sparked a countermobilization on the left. The parliamentary elections of 1936 produced a majority for the parties of the center and left—the Radical Socialists (a wildly misleading name, as the party was really centrist), the Socialists, and the Communists. The leader of the Socialist Party, a Jewish intellectual named Léon Blum, took office as premier.

Blum came into office with ideas, similar to those of Franklin Roosevelt, for what he called "Republican defense": the preservation of democracy at home through social justice as part of the resistance to Nazism abroad. He named three women to positions as undersecretaries at a time when French women still could not vote. But Blum's administration soon ran into trouble with the contradictions in its program. Like the Baldwin and Chamberlain governments, Blum's cabinet decided not to intervene to save its sister Popular Front in the Spanish Civil War. The problem Blum's government faced with Germany was only a variation on the same theme. The goals of the Popular Front were to pursue peace and democracy while resisting fascism—but what if choosing peace meant accepting fascism, or opposing fascism meant war? Blum never found a good answer to that conundrum. And Blum's premiership provoked the same kind of countermobilization on the right that the events of February 1934 had provoked on the left. Perhaps no French right-wingers ever really cried out, "Better Hitler than Blum!" as many believed, then and later. But for the nationalist right, a Jewish socialist as the leader of France was the reddest of red flags. Charles Maurras, the guiding spirit of the nationalist and antisemitic movement Action Française, called Blum "a man to shoot but in the back." A right-wing parliamentarian voiced his disgust that "this old Gallo-Roman nation" was to be governed by a "subtle Talmudist."

Blum's government managed both to launch a serious rearmament program and to push some of its social reform legislation (including a forty-hour work week and paid vacations for industrial workers). But the French Senate had a much more conservative composition than did the lower house, the Chamber of Deputies. In June 1937, Blum lost a vote in the Senate and decided to resign.

The political polarization and mutual paranoia in France grew ever more severe. The left had thought the events of February 1934 were an attempted fascist coup d'état. When the Popular Front came to power, it was the right that feared an imminent Communist revolution. The fact that the Radicals had been pulled into the orbit of the Socialists and the Communists opened up a political space among the kinds of people the Radicals had always represented, who now felt abandoned: peasants, small-business owners, and low-level white-collar workers, what the French call *les classes moyennes*.

François de La Rocque had been the leader of the quasi-fascist veterans' organization Croix-de-Feu since 1929. In 1936, the government banned the Croix-de-Feu; in response, de La Rocque formed a new political party, the Parti Social Français (French Social Party, PSF). The PSF, too, had at least some of the elements of fascism, mixed with elements of traditional political conservatism. De La Rocque's party grew rapidly and, by the end of the 1930s, had a membership of around a million, more than the Communists and Socialists combined. There is little doubt that if there had been an election after 1936, the PSF would have won it.

Not only was there no election, but Édouard Daladier, who took up the office of prime minister in April 1938, began to govern in a manner that resembled the Germany that had slipped into Hitler's grasp in 1932 and 1933. In order to get his program passed without worrying that the left or right might throw him out of office again, Daladier got the Chamber of Deputies and the Senate to grant him the power to rule by executive order for four months. This power was later repeatedly renewed. The three German chancellors before Hitler had ruled through such orders under the authority of the Reich president. The orders could have been overturned by the Reichstag (or parliament), but never were, because the Social Democratic Party feared that the only alternative to rule by executive order was rule by Hitler. When Hitler came to the chancellorship anyway, he got the Reichstag to do what the Chamber and Senate later did for Daladier: vote him the power to rule by decree—except in Hitler's case, for four years, not four months. To be sure, Daladier was not Hitler. But the precedent was hardly encouraging. As in Germany in 1932 and 1933, it revealed a parliamentary system that could no longer function properly in an emergency, or perhaps at all.

BRITAIN ALSO HAD its homegrown Fascists, notably Oswald Mosley and his British Union of Fascists (BUF). For a time, Mosley had the support of a prominent newspaper publisher, Lord Rothermere, and his mass-circulation *Daily Mail*. But the BUF stayed small and did not even contest the 1935 election, which relegated it to insignificance. To many Britons in the late 1930s, the really alarming trend in politics was the dictatorial conduct of the government they already had.

Light-years away from the ineffectual, umbrella-toting weakling of legend, the real Neville Chamberlain was a formidable figure, with authoritarian instincts covering a very thin skin. Chamberlain was cursed with a famous father and half brother. His family had always seen him as the third and least significant of the Chamberlain politicians. The patriarch, Joseph Chamberlain, one of the dominant figures of late-Victorian British politics, had not planned for his younger son to have a political life at all, and the family treated Neville with condescension when he got there anyway. When Neville was already five years into his role as chancellor of the exchequer and the leading figure in Stanley Baldwin's cabinet, his half brother, Austen, warned him, "Neville, you must remember that you don't know anything about foreign affairs." Neville complained that Austen "always finds it difficult to realize that I am no longer his little brother."

These experiences contributed to a brittle defensiveness, perhaps even an inferiority complex, that spelled trouble when Chamberlain moved into the prime ministership in 1937. The veteran journalist James Margach recalled years later that what happened to Chamberlain "vividly demonstrated what power can really do to a man . . . When I knew him first . . . he was the most shy, kindly, generous-minded and warm-hearted of men . . . But when he became prime minister . . . he became the most authoritarian, intolerant and arrogant of all the premiers I have known."

In fact, many Britons worried that Chamberlain's administration was becoming a mild, British version of fascism, one that might become less mild in the event of war—a British version of the garrison state that haunted Roosevelt. George Orwell wrote to a friend in 1937 that "Everyone with any imagination can foresee that fascism . . . will be imposed on us as soon as the war starts." In his 1939 novel, *Coming Up for Air*, Orwell imagined a British police state as the direct result of renewed foreign conflict—a foretaste of his more famous gloomy prophecy *Nineteen Eighty-Four*—with "the air-raid sirens blowing and the loud speakers bellowing that our glorious troops have taken a hundred thousand prisoners . . . the posters and the food queues, and the castor oil and the rubber truncheons and the machine guns squirting out of bedroom windows."

Neville Chamberlain had only contempt for the opposition and was utterly intolerant of criticism, whether from within his own party or without. Even before he became prime minister, a senior Conservative official worried that "There is a widespread feeling among people that Mr. Chamberlain is an autocrat at heart, and that if he were to take Mr. Baldwin's place as P.M. we should be taking a step away from democracy." Once Chamberlain had moved into the top job, a dissident Conservative member of Parliament complained that under Chamberlain's rule, "the Conservative party machine is even stronger than the Nazi party machine. It may have a different aim, but it is similarly callous and ruthless." John Colville, who was Chamberlain's assistant private secretary, found that Chamberlain could respond even to the mildest criticism with a violent fury "which I could never have expected in such a cold man." Chamberlain, Colville thought, "likes to be set on a pedestal and adored, with suitable humility, by unquestioning admirers."

Chamberlain's quick, clear mind, his brittle shyness, and his unwillingness to suffer fools made him an abrasive parliamentary performer. He neglected most of the usual parliamentary courtesies and went after his opponents aggressively in debate. Chamberlain's loyal supporters complained that the opposition was "making us all out as fascists," but in fact the changeover from Baldwin's administration marked a dramatic lurch back toward partisan conflict. After a year of Chamberlain, even Baldwin was angry that his successor had moved away from the centrist consensus of the years before 1937. Chamberlain's government was "swinging to the right," and Baldwin worried that there "never can be a national foreign policy as long as he is there."

What Chamberlain wanted was a national foreign policy on his terms and his terms alone. His aggressiveness extended to management of the press. Margach called him the first prime minister to apply modern techniques of media management on a large scale. He had no time whatsoever for reporters' criticism. Often, he would not answer questions spontaneously, demanding advance notice instead. Threats and intimidation were his usual response to negative coverage, even to probing questions. When asked a question he didn't like, his response was usually a "haughty sneer," followed by a hint that the reporter's employer would not appreciate his "unpatriotic" attitude. Sometimes Chamberlain would just stare coldly and then bark "next question, please." A question about Nazi persecution of Jews was likely to elicit the response that the reporter had fallen prey to "Jewish-Communist propaganda."

Ironically, nothing angered Chamberlain more than the press calling him a dictator. Margach remembered Chamberlain summoning several reporters to 10 Downing Street, where they found him "white with fury." He banged the table and snarled, "I tell you that I'm not dictatorial, I'm not autocratic, I'm not intolerant, I'm not overpowering. You're all wrong, wrong, wrong, I tell you. I'm the most relaxed and understanding of people. None of you, I insist, must ever say I'm dictatorial again." That the press was "wrong" or even dishonest was a frequent Chamberlain complaint. In a cabinet meeting in 1939, he raged that press criticisms were only a "mass-produced and artificial agitation which bore no relation to any spontaneous feeling of indignation in the country." The reason the press was so "unpatriotic" lay in its "degeneration."

Chamberlain knew how to mix a bit of carrot with the stick. He would pick out certain journalists to favor, somehow giving them the idea that they had become special insiders with a share of power. Of course, the price of such treatment was that the reporter had to support Chamberlain's policy. The strategy worked, and got much of the British press to suspend its critical faculties altogether. One commentator found that some of Chamberlain's statements at press conferences were so patently untrue and contrary to all evidence that many civil servants could not understand why the press accepted them without independent verification. Harold Macmillan, at the time a dissident Conservative member of Parliament, and a future prime minister himself, had a scathing opinion of his fellow Conservatives that applied to some of the press as well: "If Chamberlain says that black is white, the Tories applaud his brilliance. If a week later he says that black is black after all, they applaud his realism. Never has there been such servility."

A dramatic illustration of Chamberlain's authoritarian tendencies, and the consequences of crossing them, came in a parliamentary debate of August 2, 1939. Chamberlain wanted to adjourn the House of Commons until October. But war was clearly looming, and many in the opposition, and even some among his own supporters, feared he would use the interval to negotiate another craven deal with Hitler. The debate that followed turned unexpectedly into an impassioned forum on the state of British democracy and its role in the world.

By this time, it was Winston Churchill who had become one of the strongest voices for British democracy. Churchill focused on the significance for the world of what happened in Britain's Parliament. "This House is sometimes disparaged in this country," he said, "but abroad it counts. Abroad, the House of Commons is counted, and especially in dictator countries, as a most formidable expression of the British national will and an instrument of that will in resistance to aggression." He put forward a scathingly sarcastic criticism of the Chamberlain government's arrogant dismissal of the legislative branch. "It is a very hard thing, and I hope it will not be said, for the Government to say to the House, 'Begone! Run off and play. Take your gas masks with you. Do not worry about public affairs.' Leave them to the gifted and experienced Ministers who, after all, so far as our defenses are concerned, landed us where we were landed in September last year"—in other words, at the time of Munich. He closed his speech with an appeal for national unity and for turning away from partisan rancor, something that would become an ever-more-central pillar of his message.

After Churchill spoke, the debate developed into one about the proper relationship between the executive and legislative branches. Richard Law argued that it would be wrong and even unconstitutional to criticize opponents of the adjournment for showing lack of confidence in the prime minister. But then, in fact, the thin-skinned Chamberlain, with the nastiness that criticism always drew from him, did just that. He poured scorn on his opponents, saying that their speeches showed them to be "very badly in need of a holiday." And then he did precisely what Law had begged him not to do. "If you distrust [the government]," he said, "and show it by your vote, very well; it is a vote of no confidence in the Government, and no confidence in the Prime Minister in particular."

These words were too much for a young Conservative MP named Ronald Cartland. Cartland was in his first term in Parliament, but he had already demonstrated a fearless independence that looked likely to cut his parliamentary career short. Chamberlain's vindictiveness and unwillingness to seek unity pushed Cartland beyond endurance. His short speech became the sensation of the day's debate.

"I am profoundly disturbed by the speech of the Prime Minister," said Cartland. The members would soon be heading out to their constituencies. In the country at large there was "a fantastic and ludicrous impression, as everybody on both sides of the House, with perhaps one exception, knows," that "the Prime Minister has ideas of dictatorship." The speech that Chamberlain had made in this debate, said Cartland, along with his refusal to listen to all proposals for a shorter recess, "will make it much more difficult . . . to try and dispel that idea."

It would be easy for Chamberlain, "when the whole of democracy is trying to stand together to resist aggression, to say that he had tremendous faith in this democratic institution." Here, Cartland, who was thirty-two years old and a reserve officer, added a poignant note: "We are in the situation that within a month we may be going to fight, and we may be going to die." It was "much more important . . . to get the whole country behind you rather than make jeering, pettifogging party speeches which divide the nation . . . I frankly say that I despair when I listen to speeches like that to which I have listened this afternoon."

Cartland had spoken for only a few minutes. But his scathing criticisms of Chamberlain caused a sensation—and a backlash that ironically confirmed his point. A few years later, Harold Nicolson called Cartland's speech "the greatest of all heresies." Several members had heckled when Cartland said that some might soon be going to die. With a "flame of indignation," Cartland had spat out, "It is all very well for you . . ." Nicolson felt that "its effect was galvanic and I have seldom felt the temperature rise so rapidly." After dinner, he found that "the lobbies were still humming." One member told him that "Ronnie Cartland has ruined his chances with the Party but he has made his parliamentary reputation."

But Chamberlain easily won the vote, and the knives were out for Cartland. The *Evening Standard* ran a headline: "Premier Calls for List of MPs Who Did Not Vote Last Night. They Will All Be Blacklisted." If, in fact, few had much to fear, the story nonetheless reported that "the case of Mr. Ronald Cartland is regarded as being different because of his criticism of the Prime Minister." Twenty Conservative MPs asked that the party whips take "severe measures" against Cartland. This meant that Cartland, like Churchill and the Duchess of Atholl a few months before, was being lined up for "deselection."

With his impenetrable self-righteousness, Chamberlain claimed that his critics had been angry only because his case was "unanswerable," and he went so far as to complain that opponents "who have the thinnest skins" think "they should be allowed to throw mud to their heart's content." As for "Master Cartland," Chamberlain hoped "he has effectively blotted his copybook" with his constituency. The prime minister was "taking steps to stimulate local opposition." He thought Cartland had always been "a disloyal member," but now "he made a personal attack on me," and even if the Conservatives ended up losing the seat, "I would rather do that (temporarily) than have a traitor in the camp."

The war intervened before Chamberlain could destroy the young man's political career. But Cartland's predictions were right. On May 30, 1940, he was killed in action fighting in France. He was the first member of Parliament to die in the Second World War.

PART THREE

WAR

12

"I Have to Tell You Now . . ."

As he broods about the outcome of the Munich conference, Adolf Hitler draws two important conclusions. The first is that the Western leaders are truly as weak as he has thought. The second is that he did not need to hold the Munich Conference at all. He could have had the war he wanted against Czechoslovakia. The British and the French would have backed down and abandoned their ally.

Hitler is, more than ever, angry at those diplomats and military officials whose timidity has robbed him of his triumph. On February 1, 1939, Ernst von Weizsäcker notes in his diary that the "thesis" that Britain and France would have stayed out of a war under all circumstances "is now official." Actually, Weizsäcker himself thinks the democracies would have gone to war, however unhappily, had there been no Munich settlement. He now has to "suffer under the reproach of defeatism," but this does not bother him too much given that "in the end the Führer preferred my un-bloody solution." Hitler's armed forces adjutant Rudolf Schmundt, who has replaced the much more strong-minded Hossbach, tells his fellow officer Hermann Teske at the end of February that it is "a great pity that war hadn't come" over the Sudetenland. If it had, it would have "strengthened the position of the armed forces, particularly the army, with the Führer and the people—which was unfortunately necessary." Through "unsteadiness—especially *on the part of the generals—much trust has been shaken." Hitler has "spoken about this very often in downright bitter terms." Not surprisingly, says Schmundt, Hitler singles out Ludwig Beck for criticism.*

Hitler hardly keeps it a secret that his program of expansion is only beginning. Even before his first meeting with Chamberlain at the Berghof, he had told Weizsäcker and Ribbentrop that if the Czechs ceded the Sudetenland, "then [the rest of] Czechia itself will just come later, for instance, next spring." After Munich, he orders the army to plan an invasion of what remains of Czechoslovakia.

Hitler has had enough of people trying to contain him. At the end of January, Joseph Goebbels, who almost always channels Hitler's views, notes that he has had a long debate with Hitler's Wehrmacht adjutants. "In the armed forces things are not by a long shot what they should be," Goebbels complains.

By early 1939, the most important remaining civilian official seeking to limit what Hitler is doing is the Reichsbank chief, Hjalmar Schacht. More and more, Schacht is coming into conflict with Hitler about the funding of armaments, Hitler's drive for autarky, and even, Schacht claims, about Jewish policy.

On January 7, Schacht and seven other governors of the Reichsbank submit a memo to Hitler insisting that the Reich can maintain its financial balance, and prevent inflation, only by scaling back its armaments drive. The memo is blunt. "The reckless expenditure of the Reich represents a most serious threat to the currency," Schacht and his colleagues warn. "The tremendous increase in such expenditure foils every attempt to draw up a regular budget; it is driving the finances of the country to the brink of ruin despite a great tightening of the tax screw, and by the same token it undermines the Reichsbank and the currency." Schacht and his fellow governors conclude that "the time has now come to call a halt."

There is no doubt what Hitler thinks of this. One official reports to Schacht that when Hitler sees the memo, he explodes: "This is mutiny!" Joseph Goebbels thinks that Schacht has "virtually tried to blackmail the Führer." The banker is a "rogue and a Freemason," says Goebbels, and it is "high time" that he is "put on ice."

Late on the evening of January 19, Schacht is summoned by telephone to a meeting at the Chancellery for nine o'clock the following morning.

He knows that this is an unusual hour for Hitler, who rarely goes to bed before two or three and so seldom receives anyone until at least eleven. A later phone call puts the time back to 9:15, leading Schacht to suspect that Hitler is nervous about the meeting. Hitler is always uncomfortable with people of real accomplishment—as the arrogant Schacht regards himself.

The next morning at the Chancellery, Hitler announces without pre-amble, "I have called you in order to hand you your dismissal as President of the Reichsbank." Schacht accepts the written notice wordlessly. Hitler seems discomfited by this lack of reaction. "You don't fit into the National Socialist picture," he explains. Again, Schacht says nothing. Hitler seems embarrassed and tries again: "You have refused to allow your officials to be examined by the party organs with a view to establishing their political reliability." Schacht has often insisted that he has to be free to pick his own assistants, and seeing no point in putting forward this explanation once again, he continues to keep his silence. Hitler takes another tack. "You criticized the events of November Ninth before your employees." This is a reference to a speech Schacht gave at a Christmas party in which he openly condemned Kristallnacht. This time, Schacht responds with a deft jab: "If I had known that you approved of those happenings, I might have kept silent." This is enough for Hitler. He dismisses Schacht with the words "I'm too much upset to talk to you anymore now." Without a further word he escorts Schacht to the Chancellery door.

By EARLY 1939 there was little doubt that war was coming in Europe, and coming soon. What was not clear was who would be fighting whom.

Back in 1928, Hitler had speculated about a future alliance between Germany, Britain, and Italy for a war against the Soviet Union. A decade later, Hitler's preferred scenario was to recruit Poland as a junior part-ner for that war against communism. But here, for the first time, he ran up against real resistance from a central European state.

Poland in the 1930s was, as the historian Stephen Kotkin put it, "a nasty regime sandwiched directly between two nastier ones." Under the hero of the Polish-Soviet War, Marshal Pilsudski, and his heirs, Poland had become an authoritarian and nationalist state with antisemitic leanings. But it was not as authoritarian, nationalist, or antisemitic as

Hitler's Germany, and not as brutal as Stalin's Soviet Union. Poland's policy was to try to keep itself upright by balancing between its nastier neighbors: good relations with both if possible, no alliance with either, and certainly no alliance with one against the other.

In early January, Hitler met at Berchtesgaden with the Polish foreign minister Józef Beck. Hitler wanted Poland on his side. He also wanted the free city of Danzig returned to Germany, and some sort of arrangement for the "Polish Corridor"—the strip of former German territory that gave Poland access to the Baltic—although here Hitler struck a flexible tone and said he was open to a solution using "entirely new methods." In exchange, he was willing to offer Poland territory from Soviet Ukraine, which Germany and Poland would presumably soon conquer. Hitler also held out the idea of a resolution of the "Jewish Question." But the Poles, reasonably enough, did not trust Hitler's promises. They also resented the Nazi Jewish policies that had created a refugee problem in Poland. Beck met with Ribbentrop the next day, at which time the German foreign minister invited Poland to join the Anti-Comintern Pact, the German-Italian-Japanese alliance aimed at the Soviet Union. Beck again politely declined, and insisted that Poland wanted "peaceful neighborly relations" with the Soviet Union, although he hinted that perhaps Polish policy might change. "I asked Beck whether he had given up Marshal Pilsudski's aspirations in this direction, that is, toward the Ukraine," Ribbentrop recorded. Laughing, Beck replied that "they [the Poles] had even been in Kiev and that these aspirations were doubtless still alive today."

Ribbentrop traveled to Warsaw on January 25 to try again with Beck. Again, the Polish foreign minister politely declined the German bargain—the return of Danzig in exchange for territory in Ukraine. Exasperated by Beck's refusal to make any concessions on Danzig (and hence access to the Baltic Sea), Ribbentrop wondered why the Poles were so stubborn, and he insisted, "The Black Sea is also a sea." He then told the German ambassador in Warsaw, "It will be necessary to change the order of problems and first settle other matters."

Ribbentrop meant that if the Poles would not go along with Hitler's war for eastern expansion, Germany would have to attack Poland to get to the Soviets. But this might bring France, and then perhaps Britain and even the United States, into a war against the Reich. This vision of encirclement, which Hitler believed had been Germany's downfall in the First World War, merged with his antisemitic fantasies. Only the Jews could be behind such an anti-German plot—Jews who had previously backed the British and American governments to resist Germany, and who had also encouraged Poland to be uncooperative. This fantasy about a Jewish conspiracy joining Western democracy to Eastern communism had been behind Hitler's "prophecy" of January 30.

The looming but undefined war took on sharper contours with an event that formed the next crucial point after Munich in the path to war: Hitler's annexation of Bohemia and Moravia in March 1939.

THE CZECH LANDS of Bohemia and Moravia were rich in industry, particularly defense industries. Their geography made them strategically crucial. For Hitler, possession of Bohemia and Moravia was another step on the road to the ultimate prize and the ultimate enemy, the Soviet Union.

To get control of the Czech lands, the Nazis used Slovakia as a cat's paw, carefully fostering its desire to break with Czecho-Slovakia—the hyphen was added to the country's name after Munich. On March 14, 1939, the Slovakian prime minister Father Jozef Tiso, under German pressure, proclaimed the independence of Slovakia. Then he asked that Germany "protect" his new state from the Czechs. Meanwhile, the Czech president, Emil Hacha, who had succeeded Beneš, asked to come to Berlin to meet with Hitler, arriving that very evening. He was subjected to the kind of bullying and intimidation that Hitler had meted out to many others, such as Austrian chancellor Schuschnigg the year before. Hacha fainted, or perhaps even suffered a mild heart attack. A shot of stimulant revived him. He then agreed to hand his country over to Germany as a "protectorate." The next day, the Nazis were in Prague.

Taking control of the Czech lands was a fateful step. For the first time, Hitler had violated not just the pre-Nazi-era treaties he had always sworn to overturn, but an agreement he himself had signed not six months before. Contrary to all his prior public statements, the annexation did more than bring Germans into a unified Reich. It was an act of aggression against people who were clearly not German. The crucial question for Western leaders had always been whether Hitler's goals were limited. Now they had their answer.

Not that the answer registered immediately in London or Paris. In the House of Commons, Chamberlain struggled to argue that Hitler's move had not violated the Munich accords. It was just that it "had not been contemplated" by the countries who signed that deal. French foreign minister Georges Bonnet and Senator Henry Bérenger told the British ambassador in Paris that the breakup of Czechoslovakia simply showed that the country for which they had almost gone to war in September had never been "viable" anyway and that the less they were involved in the crisis the better.

A firmer line began, as it had the previous September, with Halifax. The foreign secretary convinced Chamberlain that he had to take the occupation of Prague more seriously. On March 17, Chamberlain gave a speech in his hometown of Birmingham in which he insisted that Britain would go to war to stop another country from trying "to dominate the world by force." Halifax pushed for more. Various intelligence and diplomatic reports hinted at an imminent German attack on Poland or Romania. On March 31, Chamberlain announced in the House of Commons that "in the event of any action which clearly threatened Polish independence, and which the Polish Government accordingly considered it vital to resist with their national forces, His Majesty's Government would feel themselves bound at once to lend the Polish Government all support in their power." A week later, Italy launched a surprise attack on Albania, after which the French and then the British extended similar guarantees to Romania and Greece. The Chamberlain government reversed its 1937 decision against sending ground troops to France. British and French military staffs began planning joint operations in the event of war with Germany, and for the first time ever in peacetime, the British government introduced a draft for its army.

The war of 1939 might have been Germany and Poland against the Soviets, with the Western democracies neutral. It might have been Germany against the democracies, with Poland and the Soviet Union neutral. Further variations were also possible. But it was around Poland that a looming but vague war began to take definite shape.

The Germans tried one last time for a Polish alliance. On March 21, Ribbentrop told the Polish ambassador in Berlin, Józef Lipski, that Hitler "was becoming increasingly amazed at Poland's attitude"—meaning its unwillingness to join a German campaign against Bolshevism and to trade Danzig for Ukraine. Lipski did not hear this as a threat that the Germans would do to Poland what they had done to the Czechs. And in fact, on March 25, Hitler emphasized to Walther von Brauchitsch that he did not want to settle problems with Poland by force, in part because he did not want to "drive Poland into the arms of Britain."

But Hitler's occupation of Prague had set off a chain reaction: the British guarantee of Poland, followed by Foreign Minister Józef Beck's visit to London to discuss relations. The Germans saw Beck's visit as a definitive sign that the Poles had gone over to the British side. Hans Bernd Gisevius recorded that Hitler flew into an intense rage when he learned of the British guarantee, and vowed, "I'll cook them a stew that they'll choke on." On April 3, Hitler ordered that "Case White," the plan for the invasion of Poland, be ready for September 1.

The British guarantee to Poland was well intentioned and brave. It was also poorly thought through. Poland was militarily weaker and less defensible than Czechoslovakia would have been in 1938. But there was an even bigger problem. If the Germans could not force the Poles into an alliance against the Soviet Union, the British and French were about to learn they could not have both Warsaw and Moscow as alliance partners—even assuming that this was what they wanted.

WHEN NEVILLE CHAMBERLAIN "peered across the distance toward the Kremlin," wrote the great British historian A. J. P. Taylor, "he saw there faces which reminded him of the Opposition front bench." Taylor was explaining why Chamberlain did not try very hard to secure an alliance with the Soviet Union in 1939. As always, he wrote with mocking irony. But he wasn't wrong.

Chamberlain disliked the Soviet Union, its ideology, and its leaders at least as much as he disliked Nazi Germany. He did not think British interests would be well served by an alliance with Stalin. Part of the reason lay in his estimate of Soviet military capacity. "I must confess to the most profound distrust of Russia," he wrote to his sister Ida in late March. "I have no belief whatever in her ability to maintain an effective offensive even if she wanted to." In what seems like comical understatement, he added, "And I distrust her motives which seem to me to have little connection with our ideas of liberty and to be concerned only with getting everyone else by the ears." An alliance with the Soviets would complicate Britain's other important international relationships. The Soviet Union, Chamberlain complained, was "both hated and suspected by many of the smaller states notably by Poland Romania and Finland so that our close association with her might easily cost us the sympathy of those who would much more effectively help us if we can get them on our side."

Chamberlain was prim and fussy in his choice of words. But he was right. Any arrangement with Stalin would have to come at the expense of the smaller nations of central and eastern Europe and the Baltic—the same nations Hitler threatened and Britain was now pledging herself to defend.

The harsh reality, which twentieth-century history illustrated again and again, was that either Germany or Russia was going to dominate central and eastern Europe. There wasn't a third possibility. In 1943, Sir William Strang, who had been head of the Foreign Office's Central Department at the time of Munich, wrote bluntly after much hard experience that "it is better that Russia should dominate eastern Europe than that Germany should dominate western Europe." In other words, Germany posed a threat in both directions—east toward the Soviet Union, but also west toward Britain—whereas the Soviets (seemed) only to menace their near, eastern, neighbors. Thus, Britain had to prefer the Soviet domination of eastern Europe to the German option. It is difficult to call Chamberlain's reluctance to accept this in 1939 morally inferior to Strang's cold realpolitik of a few years later.

But in 1939, Britain had to pick one or the other, and with the knowledge then available, it was not so easy to identify the lesser evil. Germany and the Soviet Union were both potential threats to their neighbors. The Soviet Union preached an ideology of worldwide revolution and was at least trying to be a threat to every capitalist state, whether near or far. Its intelligence services carried out a much more extensive range of operations around the world, including subversion and terrorism, than did their German equivalents.

While Hitler's and Stalin's regimes were both brutal and inhumane to a degree without precedent in human history, before 1939, between the famines of the early thirties and the Terror of the later thirties, Stalin had killed far more people than had Hitler. Nor was this simply a matter of killing real or imagined political opponents. The historian Timothy Snyder observes that by the end of 1938, Stalin had killed a thousand times more people because of their ethnic origins than had Hitler—and for all Hitler's much more overt antisemitism, to that point Stalin had even killed more Jews. The Nazi Holocaust, the fruit of Hitler's "prophecy," still lay in the future.

If Nazi Germany really was the "ultimate enemy," as British intelligence put it, only the Soviet Union could offer enough military strength to stop the Germans in eastern Europe. But the price of this defense for Poland, the Baltic states, Finland, and Romania was likely to be subjugation or even annexation by the Soviets. Chamberlain's government was under no illusions about this. This was the dilemma facing the British in 1939.

To make matters worse, Poland's refusal of the German embrace now gave Hitler an urgent reason to come to terms with Stalin, if he was going to have the war he wanted when he wanted it.

Shrewd observers had long seen this possibility. Even in April 1938, Edvard Beneš had told a Romanian diplomat that "if Russia is separated from the Western Powers," it was possible that "we will see Hitler collaborating with the Soviets." Beneš knew that in such a case, Poland, Czechoslovakia, and Romania would be "absolutely at the disposal of [these] two Great Powers."

The mistrust between the Soviets and the Western democracies was already enormous. Stalin did not believe the democracies would ever accept the existence of the Soviet Union, and so he automatically distrusted any promises they might make. His fear was that British policy actually aimed at a deal with Germany to turn Hitler's aggression to the east. British conduct, from Halifax's visit to Hitler through the Munich settlement, had given Stalin grounds for his suspicions. His intelligence agencies diligently fed his paranoia with stories of British treachery.

The British nurtured the same kinds of doubts about Soviet policy, with better reason. "I cannot rid myself of the suspicion," Chamberlain wrote to Ida, "that they are chiefly concerned to see the 'capitalist' Powers tear each other to pieces while they stay out themselves." He was worried by cabinet colleagues who said that "if we don't agree Russia & Germany will come to an understanding, which to my mind, is a pretty sinister commentary on Russian reliability."

For all these reasons, negotiations between the British, the French, and the Soviets about forming an alliance against Hitler dragged from April to August. Meanwhile, there were signs of diplomatic movement between the Soviets and the Germans. At the beginning of May, Stalin sacked his foreign minister, Maxim Litvinov—cosmopolitan, Western-oriented, and Jewish—and replaced him with Vyacheslav Molotov, who was none of those things. Stalin's dismissal of Litvinov was a close parallel to Hitler's sacking of Neurath the year before: the dictator got rid of someone whose views he did not like and found a more congenial replacement. Dismissing a Jewish minister was also a clear offering to the Nazis.

More information came from the very indiscreet Karl Bodenschatz, Hermann Göring's adjutant. He told the French air attaché that "something is going on in the East." Hitler was going to "talk to Russia," and "perhaps we will see a fourth partition of Poland." The new French ambassador in Berlin thought this was reliable information because Bodenschatz had a good track record, having "let us know last February 26 that Bohemia and Moravia would soon be scratched from the map of Europe."

By now, the scale of the danger was starting to get through to the Poles. On May 10, Soviet deputy foreign commissar Vladimir Potemkin met in Warsaw with Polish foreign minister Józef Beck and reported later to Molotov that "through a detailed analysis of the balance of power in Europe and the possibility of effective Franco-British aid for Poland, Beck was led to recognize that without the support of the USSR, the Poles cannot defend themselves." But Beck seems to have spoken out of turn, because the next day, the Polish ambassador in Moscow went to see Molotov to "apologize" for "imprecise" information: Poland could not accept an alliance with the Soviet Union, nor even a Soviet guarantee of its border.

Round it went in the weeks that followed, in a grim atmosphere of fear and mutual mistrust. All sides now worried that their potential partner might be dealing with the other side. All sides worried about the mess they would be in if such an opposite partnership came to pass. The differences were that the French, British, and Soviets desperately wanted to avoid a war, while Hitler desperately wanted to get one going. The democracies gave at least some thought to the ethics of their position; the dictatorships, none. After a meeting with Halifax, the Soviet ambassador in London, Ivan Maisky, complained that British leaders suffered from a "complete failure to grasp the psychology of such men as Hitler and Mussolini." English gentlemen, he said, could not understand that "aggressors have an entirely different mentality! Those who would like to understand the aggressor mentality would do better to look to Al Capone as a model." That Maisky's boss was also just such a gangster did not invalidate his point.

Poland's refusal to let Soviet troops cross Polish territory to get at Germany was one obstacle to a deal between the Soviets and the West. The Soviets also wanted "guarantees" for the sovereignty of the Baltic states, ostensibly to keep Germany out. But as the Soviet ambassador reported from Paris, to the Western powers, such guarantees looked more like giving the Soviets "a free hand in the Baltics." In May, Alexander Cadogan noted that the Soviets proposed "including Finland among the states to be guaranteed," which was "an enlightening comment on the Soviet proposals—the Finns simply won't have any guarantee from the Soviets."

The British tried to get around the problem in late May by suggesting that Britain, France, and the Soviet Union all agree simply to comply with their obligations under Article 16 of the League of Nations Covenant. This was the provision requiring that League members come to the aid of other members against an aggressor. Molotov's response revealed the Soviets' priorities. On May 28, he announced that talks with Germany for a commercial treaty were about to resume.

In June, Molotov insisted that a list of countries the Soviets would "help" had to be included in any alliance treaty, or there was no deal. On July 1, he added another element: "indirect aggression" by the Germans, which could include moves such as inducing the Czech surrender, should be included as one of the triggers for the alliance. A definition of "indirect aggression" should be put into a secret protocol along with a list of states to be "protected." As such a definition Molotov suggested "a reversal of policy in favor of the aggressor." Chamberlain's government understood exactly what this "protection" would mean. Looking back in October 1939, Halifax told a gathering of Conservative members of Parliament that Britain had been right not to buy a Soviet alliance at the price of the freedom of the Baltic states.

Nothing about these negotiations made Chamberlain any more eager for a Soviet alliance, or less resentful that Halifax had pressured him into pursuing one. In late July, he complained to Ida, "We are only spinning out the time before the inevitable break comes, and it is rather hard that I should have to bear the blame for dilatory action when if I wasn't hampered by others I would have closed the discussion one way or another long ago." On July 23, in an effort to break the impasse, the French, British, and Soviets all agreed to conduct military talks before going back to work on the political agreement.

Throughout the spring and summer, the Germans had pursued the Soviets, who remained cool to the Nazi advances. But Soviet frustration with the democracies mounted as the West refused to concede what the Soviet Union considered most essential to its security: control of eastern Europe and the Baltic. Finally, on August 2, Ribbentrop said the magic words. He called in Georgii Astakhov, chargé at the Soviet embassy in Berlin, and told him, "There is no basis for the enmity between our countries." They could talk about "all problems connected to territory from the Black Sea to the Baltic." A few days later, Astakhov reported to Molotov that he was getting hints that the Germans wanted to "express their disinterest . . . in the Baltic (outside of Lithuania), Bessarabia, Russian Poland . . . and renounce any aspirations toward Ukraine." In return they wanted the Soviets to renounce any interest in Danzig and former German Poland. "Obviously," Astakhov wrote, "conversations of the kind proposed by the Germans can only proceed in the absence of an Anglo-Franco-Soviet agreement." Later in August, the German ambassador in Moscow, Count Friedrich-Werner von der Schulenburg, insisted to Molotov that Hitler was ready to agree to anything the Soviet Union wanted.

By this time, the British and French had put together a team of officers for talks in Moscow about military arrangements. But the British still seemed to be trying to delay the business as much as possible. The British and French officers traveled to Moscow by a slow steamer. The Foreign Office offered a lot of excuses for this decision: No British or French commercial airline flew to the Soviet Union. The British did not want to use RAF planes because the right types were not available in sufficient numbers, or were too uncomfortable. Fast naval cruisers lacked appropriate cabins. Thus, it came down to slow steamers. There were other, unstated problems. Neither the British nor the French wanted to chance crossing Germany by air. The French in any case wanted the arrival of their delegation to be inconspicuous, to minimize the embarrassment if the talks did not go well. For the Soviets, though, these excuses could only strengthen the suspicion that the democracies were in no way serious about an alliance.

The head of the French delegation was the highly competent and forward-thinking general Joseph Édouard Aimé Doumenc. In charge of the British team was Admiral Sir Reginald Plunkett-Ernle-Erle-Drax, whose name, however unfairly, somehow added to the farcical quality of the talks. The lead Soviet negotiator was Kliment Voroshilov, the people's commissar for defense and thus a much higher-ranking person than his visitors. When the talks began on August 12, Doumenc and Drax found Voroshilov likable, but this could not smooth over the difficulties. A revealing exchange during the third day of meetings drove the point home.

Voroshilov asked repeatedly how the French and British imagined Soviet troops should aid Poland, Romania, or Turkey against an attack. Doumenc explained that it would be up to those countries to defend themselves. If they requested Soviet aid, Moscow could supply it. Doumenc asked Voroshilov if he found this point clear. "No," the people's commissar replied. The others laughed, as if Voroshilov were making a joke. But he wasn't. "Forgive my frankness," he said, "but we are speaking soldier to soldier." He did not understand how Soviet forces were to be deployed "in the common effort." Drax answered lamely that Poland

and Romania would be happy to know Soviet troops were available and would surely ask for Soviet support if they were attacked. Voroshilov said he wanted a clear answer. "These questions are essential for the USSR," he said; "everything else is subordinate." If the questions were not resolved, there was no point in continuing the talks. Drax said it was a political question that lay beyond the competence of the military men.

Voroshilov had made it very clear what the Soviet interest really was. If Poland or Romania were attacked by the Germans and requested Soviet help too late, he explained, they would be crushed, and the defensive point of the alliance would be lost. This was crucial. Stalin defined Soviet security by how much space there was between his country and an aggressor. He wanted control of the Baltic and eastern Europe to provide a zone of safety for his own country. But the democracies wouldn't bite. The parties agreed to limp along, discussing other aspects of military planning, but the sessions broke down on August 17 with this critical issue unresolved. When the delegations met briefly on August 21, Voroshilov proposed a longer adjournment because, supposedly, senior Soviet officers had to leave for annual maneuvers.

The Western delegations were housed near a building that had once been the Austrian embassy. On August 18, the visitors noticed frantic activity in the neighboring house. The Soviets were making it ready for another set of visitors. Drax and Doumenc would soon discover who the new guests were.

By August, Hitler was in a much bigger hurry than the complacent British to reach a deal with the Soviets. The British and French guarantees to Poland, coupled with Hitler's own insistence on starting the war that fall, meant that he had only days to make a deal with Stalin. If he did not invade Poland by early September, the fall rainy season would render a modern mechanized campaign impossible.

This put Stalin in the driver's seat. Weizsäcker complained that "the cunning Slavic peasants there want to raise our offer," although he urged that the Germans "be more explicit in Moscow about a partition of Poland." Stalin told Voroshilov to make sure that the democracies were blamed for the failure of their talks.

Remarkably, it was not until August 20 that Drax received written confirmation of his authority to negotiate on behalf of the British government. The day before, Molotov had given a draft of a Soviet-German non-aggression pact to the German ambassador in Moscow. On August 20, Hitler responded with a personal note to Stalin, accepting the draft terms but begging that Stalin receive Ribbentrop on August 22 or 23 to finalize the "supplementary protocol" the Soviets wanted but had not further defined.

Stalin ordered Voroshilov to take a break from his talks with the British and French and go duck hunting. On August 21, he responded to Hitler: "The people of our countries need peaceful relations with each other." He invited Ribbentrop to Moscow for August 23. When the news arrived at the Berghof, Hitler ordered the opening of champagne, although as a nondrinker, he didn't touch it himself.

Now Hitler was confident his war was on. The next morning, he spoke to his military commanders. The war had to come now, he told them. "There will never again in the future be a man with more authority than I have," he explained, whereas the enemy leaders were "below the average," "no personalities." Hitler would give some kind of propaganda reason for starting the war, "no matter whether it is plausible or not." He worried only that "at the last moment"—as before Munich—"some swine or other will yet submit to me a plan for mediation."

When Ribbentrop arrived in Moscow, he found the city decked out in swastika flags. At his meeting with Stalin, Ribbentrop told a joke that was making the rounds in Berlin: it was said that Stalin himself would soon join the Anti-Comintern Pact. Stalin proposed a toast to Hitler, saying that he knew "how much the German nation loves its Führer." He gave his word of honor that the Soviet Union "would not betray its partner." The record does not indicate whether Ribbentrop made the same promise in return.

The pact had its public and its secret sides. Publicly, Germany and the Soviet Union promised not to go to war with each other for ten years. A secret "additional protocol" defined German and Soviet spheres of influence—meaning areas that one side could conquer without the other objecting. Finland, Latvia, and Estonia fell to the Soviets; Lithuania, to Germany. (The agreement was later modified to give Lithuania to the Soviets as well.) Poland was to be divided "approximately" at the Narew, Vistula, and San Rivers. Unsurprisingly, Bessarabia went to the Soviets. Nazi Germany had given Stalin what the British and French would not.

Ribbentrop had wanted to include a preamble about the "natural friendship" between Germans and Soviets, but here Stalin was more realistic. "For many years now," he told Ribbentrop, "we have been pouring buckets of shit on each other's heads." Stalin thought public opinion needed a little more time to adjust before the dictatorships became so effusive with one another.

HITLER DID NOT believe that the democracies would ever declare war on him. But he kept repeating his fear that "some emotional acrobat" would ruin his plans with "weak-diaper proposals." This was the trauma that Neville Chamberlain had inflicted on him at Munich. With the signing of the Molotov-Ribbentrop Pact, Hitler's script was written. His police duly created a highly implausible propaganda pretext for invading Poland—a fake Polish raid on the German radio transmitter at the border town of Gleiwitz, the town from which Franz Bernheim had challenged Hitler's antisemitic laws in 1933. Early on the morning of September 1, German forces crossed into Poland from East Prussia, Pomerania, Silesia, and Bohemia. The Nazi war had begun.

Now the question was *when* would war begin for the democracies? The British and French governments had pledged aid to Poland, but even in the face of the German invasion, they hesitated. It took a democratic revolt to drive Neville Chamberlain to war.

On Friday, September 1, Chamberlain told the House that it was "time for action," but then he said only that he was waiting to see if the Germans would give an assurance that their forces would leave Poland. The British government had given Germany a warning that it would fulfill its obligations to Poland—but with no time limit. Bafflement, discontent, and shame began to grow among politicians of all parties. What clearer case of aggression could there be, what clearer grounds to rush to Poland's aid? The frustration and rage overflowed the next day, when the House held an unusual Saturday sitting. Astonishingly, Chamberlain told the House that the British government had received no response from Germany, perhaps because the Germans were considering "a proposal which, meanwhile, had been put forward by the Italian Government, that hostilities should cease and that there should then immediately be a conference between the Five Powers, Great Britain, France, Poland, Germany and Italy." Munich again—as, ironically, both Hitler and British anti-appeasers feared.

The next speaker was the deputy Labour leader, Arthur Greenwood, an indifferent orator who was about to have the one great moment of his political career. When he rose to speak, he was greeted by cheers from the Labour and, to his considerable surprise, Conservative benches alike. A little unsteadily, Greenwood told his colleagues he would "speak what is in my heart at this moment." At this, the maverick Conservative Leo Amery called out in exasperation, "Speak for *England*, Arthur!"

This outburst astonished the House. For decades, Amery had been a friend of Chamberlain. He owed his parliamentary career to Chamberlain's political machine. Now the prime minister turned around in his seat to stare in shock at his protégé. Amery knew he had just ruined any chance of ever entering Chamberlain's cabinet.

And Greenwood spoke for England. "I wonder how long we are prepared to vacillate," he said, "at a time when Britain and all that Britain stands for, and human civilization, are in peril. Every minute's delay now means the loss of life, imperiling our national interests" and— responding to an interjection from Conservative Bob Boothby—"the very foundations of our national honor." When Greenwood sat down, the cheers came once again from both sides of the House.

It was clear that the House of Commons and Chamberlain's cabinet were at the point of mutiny. There would be no Munich this time. That night, the cabinet agreed to send a last ultimatum to the Germans, with a time limit of eleven o'clock the next morning.

ON SUNDAY, SEPTEMBER 3, fifteen minutes after the expiration of that ultimatum, Neville Chamberlain took to the airwaves to tell the British people that war had come again. His first words were moving, even heartbreaking, the despair evident in his voice, but the tone restrained and dignified.

"This morning," he began, "the British Ambassador in Berlin handed the German Government a final note stating that, unless we heard from them by 11 o'clock that they were prepared at once to withdraw their troops from Poland, a state of war would exist between us." And then it came: "I have to tell you now that no such undertaking has been received, and that consequently this country is at war with Germany." The long pause after this fateful sentence only heightened the effect. It is easy to imagine millions of people in Britain listening, stunned, their throats tightening, memories of the horrors of the last war and of lost loved ones crowding into their minds.

But then Chamberlain's habitual self-absorption overcame him. As he prepared to send his countrymen and women into an abyss of death and grief for the second time in a generation, he told them, "You can imagine what a bitter blow it is to *me* that all my long struggle to win peace has failed. Yet I cannot believe that there is anything more or anything different that I could have done and that would have been more successful" (emphasis added).

The comedian Spike Milligan, who grew up in a poor district of London, gave a sarcastic account of Chamberlain's inability to lead the British people out of class division to wartime national unity. "A man called Chamberlain, who did Prime Minister impressions, spoke on the wireless," Milligan remembered years later. "He said, 'As from eleven o'clock we are at war with Germany.' (I loved the WE.)" In the same vein, A. J. P. Taylor remembered a tone-deaf poster from early in the war: "*Your* Courage, *Your* Cheerfulness, *Your* Resolution Will Bring *Us* Victory" (emphasis added). Working-class Britons who remembered the betrayed promises of social reform after 1918—returning veterans had been promised "homes for heroes" in a program that soon fell victim to government budget-cutting—could easily imagine that once again working people were being asked to die to preserve the privileges of the elite.

Even pessimists were surprised by what quick work the German forces made of Poland. The Poles fought proudly and with great courage, but they were in a hopeless position. The Luftwaffe destroyed the

Polish Air Force in the first days of the campaign. Poland had few tanks, and its cavalry could do nothing to stop the German armored forces. The final blow came on September 17, when the Soviets, giving further proof of Stalin's long-held intentions, invaded from the east. Warsaw surrendered on September 27. The Polish government never officially surrendered the country as a whole, but the Germans wiped out the last military resistance on October 6. About seventy thousand Polish soldiers had been killed fighting the Germans, and another fifty thousand fighting the Soviets. German losses were much fewer, but far from minor: fourteen thousand killed and around thirty thousand wounded.

With the coming of war, Chamberlain had had to bow to overwhelming public and political pressure and offer Churchill a place in his cabinet. That place, in fact, was Churchill's old post from the Great War—first lord of the Admiralty. (A famous radio signal went around the Royal Navy that day: WINSTON IS BACK.) For the next eight months the working relationship between the two old rivals ran far more smoothly than could ever have been expected, due largely to Churchill's loyalty and sense of duty. But the obvious and constant contrast between the two men opened up a problem for Chamberlain.

A sign of things to come was a remarkable mid-September letter from Roosevelt to Churchill. It is highly unusual, even improper, for a head of state to open up direct communications with a minister of another state. But this is what Roosevelt did. This could only be a reflection of his low opinion of Chamberlain, which had probably begun with Chamberlain's rejection of Roosevelt's diplomatic overture in January 1938 and gained force with the Munich settlement. It also suggests that the perceptive Roosevelt sensed, like Hitler, that Churchill was going to be prime minister before long.

"It is because you and I occupied similar positions in the [First] World War," Roosevelt began, "that I want you to know how glad I am that you are back again in the Admiralty." With the barest nod to diplomatic convention, Roosevelt continued that he wanted Churchill "and the Prime Minister" to know "that I shall at all times welcome it if you will keep me in touch personally with anything you want me to know about." Churchill dutifully checked with Chamberlain and secured the prime minister's approval to enter into correspondence with the president of the United States. One of the most intriguing and productive political relationships in history was launched.

To his great moral credit, Chamberlain hated war intensely. And of course, he had strained every muscle to keep it from coming. But this left him ill-equipped to be an effective war leader. In the early part of the war, the British people, and even Chamberlain's government, did not seem very sure what they were fighting for. In late September, even Lord Halifax and Alexander Cadogan could not decide what Britain's war aims should be. After Stalin claimed his share of Poland, they could not talk of liberating Poland without going to war against the Soviet Union. What if they made the war about getting rid of "Hitlerism" only to have Hitler turn his regime over to Göring? Nor could Chamberlain give any direction. A week after the war broke out, he said, "What I hope for is not a military victory—I very much doubt the possibility of that—but a collapse of the German home front." This was not much of a strategy, and it was certainly never going to inspire anyone.

By contrast, Winston Churchill, so long in the political wilderness, now found his stock rising. The day Britain declared war, he had given the House of Commons a ringing statement of the war's meaning: "We are fighting to save the whole world from the pestilence of Nazi tyranny and in defense of all that is most sacred to man . . . It is a war . . . to establish, on impregnable rocks, the rights of the individual, and it is a war to establish and revive the stature of Man." It was becoming increasingly clear, even to many Chamberlain supporters, that these were the words of a wartime leader.

The indomitable Eleanor Rathbone had written Churchill the year before to say that "There is a great longing for leadership and even those who are far apart from you in general politics realize that you are the one man who has combined full realization of the dangers of our military position with belief in collective international action against aggression." In the fall of 1939, she convened an all-party Parliamentary Action Group, which became the main instrument for those seeking more effective leadership. Members of the group who wrote memoirs later, and most male historians, have never given Rathbone the credit she deserves for finding that leadership. But through her efforts, by October 1939, parliamentarians such as Duff Cooper and Leo Amery were quietly discussing plans to overthrow Chamberlain and bring Churchill to the premiership.

Six relatively uneventful months followed the defeat of Poland, the interval known ever since as the "Twilight War" or the "Phony War." So long as the war stayed quiet, Chamberlain could keep a lid on internal dissent. But Hitler's war would not stay quiet.

13

"These Are Prussian Officers!"

I am Prussian, know ye my colors? . . .
That my fathers died for freedom's sake
Know ye, thus my colors spake.

Bernhard Thiersch and August Neithardt
"Das Preussenlied," 1830–1832

The "Preussenlied," at one time the anthem of the kingdom of Prussia, is still well known to officers in 1940. To be a Prussian officer involves accepting a stern code of behavior. Frugality, honor, duty, and above all sacrifice are its essential elements. It is the code of a poor northern country created out of barren, sandy soil by repeated acts of will, depending on its armed forces to rise into the top table of European powers. The first words of the song sum it up: the singer honors the memory of his "fathers"— seemingly, all his forefathers—who died in the service of Prussia's black- and-white banner. And by making the colors his own, he stoically accepts that he will meet the same fate.

Prussian officers all know the code and believe they abide by it, but it is a flexible set of principles that can be applied according to taste. This is above all true when it comes to obeying orders, especially the orders of the king.

Military history has always been a core subject of Prussian officer train- ing and of general staff studies. The commanders of the past, particularly those wreathed in the glory of the wars against Napoléon and for German unification, live in this historical memory. They are not only touchstones of Prussian identity. The commanders of the past are role models for conduct in the present.

The obvious role model for stoic acceptance of orders is supplied by Friedrich Wilhelm von Seydlitz. Seydlitz is a commander of cavalry in the army of Prussia's celebrated king Frederick the Great. He is credited with developing the cavalry as an effective branch of Frederick's services. At the disastrous Battle of Kunersdorf in 1759, Frederick himself is in command on the battlefield as the Prussians face the Russians and Austrians. As the battle progresses, Frederick orders Seydlitz and his cavalry to attack. Seydlitz leads the charge. It goes disastrously. The casualties are heavy, and Seydlitz is seriously wounded. A bit later, Frederick wants another cavalry attack. Seydlitz tries to talk him out of the idea, as it will involve a frontal assault on fortified positions in the teeth of artillery fire. But Frederick insists, and the cavalry attacks. The result is an even worse slaughter than on the first attack, with the Prussian ranks breaking and the Prussian cavalry even trampling its own infantry. Seydlitz expected this result, but he does not question the king's order. He becomes the model for one kind of adherence to the Prussian code: selfless obedience to commands, even if they seem foolish, even if they seem murderous. "That my fathers died for freedom's sake . . ."

But officers of the latest generation have an alternative model for applying the Prussian code to royal commands. It comes from a later military commander, Count Johann David Ludwig Yorck von Wartenburg. In 1806, Prussia is soundly defeated by Napoléon's army. The kingdom is forced to give up much of its territory, and French troops occupy Berlin. King Frederick William III passively accepts his subordination to Napoléon.

Not so his army commanders, above all Count Yorck. They become part of a reform movement that seeks to create a new, modern, vital Prussia that will be able to rise again and defeat Napoléon. In 1812, Napoléon invades Russia, and his invasion soon turns into a disastrous defeat. The Prussian reformers see that their opportunity has arrived. In December 1812, Yorck signs the Convention of Tauroggen, in which Prussia allies itself with Russia against France. Under its terms, Yorck agrees to have his troops stand aside and let Russian forces enter Prussia to pursue the French.

King Frederick William, however, has not agreed to Tauroggen. Yorck and other officers—including Carl von Clausewitz, who will later write the world's most influential book on the theory of warfare—are freelancing. This means the agreement they have signed amounts to treason. But they adhere to the Prussian code in their way. Early in January, Yorck sends a letter to the king. "As long as everything went in the accustomed way," he writes, "the loyal servant was bound to follow circumstances— that was his duty." But circumstances have changed, and "duty likewise demands that this situation, which will never occur again, be exploited." Yorck is not only speaking as the king's loyal servant, he insists: "These words are almost universally the words of the Nation; a declaration from Your Majesty will breathe life and enthusiasm back into everything and we will fight like true old Prussians and the throne of Your Majesty will stand rock-solid and unshakeable for the future." Yorck is waiting only to hear from the king "whether I should now advance against the true enemy, or whether political conditions demand that Your Majesty condemn me." He waits for an answer in a "spirit of loyal dedication, and I swear to Your Majesty that I shall meet the bullets as calmly at the place of execution as on the field of battle."

Yorck is following the code: he, too, will gladly die for his colors and for freedom's sake. But there is something else here: the one higher law than the king's will is the voice of the "nation." In 1813, this is a new idea. But the point will linger. Yorck becomes a hero. Prussia's superpatriotic historians will celebrate his memory (even if they conspicuously downplay the extent of his rebellion). Berlin has a Yorckstrasse and a Tauroggener Strasse. The point for soldiers in 1940: In special circumstances, duty to the nation may outweigh duty to the ruler. It may even call for the commission of treason. German officers in that year will have a lot to think about.

FROM THE AUTUMN of 1939 into early 1940, there was a sustained argument in the German High Command about how to fight the war and, in a broader sense, about what kind of country Germany should be. This was fundamentally one argument with two branches. The first branch placed most of the generals on one side and Hitler on the other about whether to launch an offensive against the Western powers. The second was an argument among the generals, with Hitler taking one side, about what that offensive should look like. The second argument had much deeper implications than were obvious on the surface.

On October 6, 1939, when it was clear that Poland had been completely defeated, Hitler gave a speech declaring that it was the "mission of [his] life" to bring the German and British people together. That he had not so far succeeded was due to the hostility of "some of the British statesmen and journalists," a hostility that had "shaken" him. He mentioned Churchill by name several times, but not Chamberlain, who was still the prime minister. With this warm-up, he proposed a peace conference "to determine the fate of this continent for decades to come."

But Hitler didn't wait for a response from the British or French. On October 9, he issued "Directive Number 6 for the Conduct of the War." The directive made plain that Hitler thought time was working against the Germans: the Western democracies would only grow steadily stronger. He therefore ordered preparation of an attack on the "northern wing of the Western Front through the areas of Luxembourg, Belgium, and Holland" at "as early a date as possible." The ambitions of the attack were relatively limited. The goal was "to defeat as strong a part of the French operational army as possible" and to gain territory in the Netherlands, Belgium, and northern France to provide air bases within easy striking range of Britain, and security for the vulnerable Ruhr industrial region.

The army commanders were horrified, particularly by the phrase "as early a date as possible." Even Walther von Reichenau, the most pro-Hitler of the generals, called the idea of an immediate western offensive "virtually criminal." The more opposition-minded officers and civilian resisters worried that war against the West would put an end to any thoughts in Britain and France that there was a difference between the German people and their government. For the democracies, the war would become an all-out struggle against all Germans, making it impossible for the opposition to get rid of Hitler and settle the war on acceptable terms. To put this another way, the war would become total—the way Ludendorff had meant total war.

Ludwig Beck played a role in the resistance once again, if this time from the sidelines. At the end of September, he summed up his thoughts in a pessimistic memorandum written to persuade army commanders of the hopelessness of their position. "Germany stands, at the moment, at the beginning of a world war," he wrote. The defeat of Poland did not much matter. All that this victory had really achieved, Beck thought, was to bring the Soviet Union onto the stage, and this would in the end prove disastrous for Germany. Fighting Britain meant fighting a world war, which meant fighting a naval war. Germany was in no way equipped to do this. Beck suspected the United States and its resources would become an ever-larger factor in the war, and he described Roosevelt as "one of the grimmest opponents of the Third Reich."

Beck thought that Britain and its allies would try to win by avoiding ground conflict and instead would wear Germany down with a naval blockade. He concluded that it was not possible for Germany to arrive at a good peace settlement, the purpose of all wars. Ironically, at just this time, Liddell Hart, always a proponent of naval blockades, also advocated a compromise peace on the grounds that Britain had no rational path to victory. A few days later, Beck added that even scoring a decisive victory over the Allied armies in France would not win the war, if Britain were still able to operate against Germany.

If the strategic situation looked much the same to thoughtful people on both sides of the lines, so did the moral foundations of political action. Many, perhaps most, of the German officers and civilians who tried to resist Hitler did so because they, like Roosevelt, saw Christian faith and Nazism as irreconcilable. "Good churchgoers," Hans Bernd Gisevius thought, "had no option but to resist the totalitarian state." Hans Oster's resolution and unflappable good cheer "sprang from his unshakable trust in God." "Come what may," Oster once wrote to his son, "we fear only the wrath of God that will fall upon us if we are not clean and decent and do not do our duty." The resistance work of Abwehr chief Admiral Canaris, Gisevius wrote, also "sprang from a well-thought-out philosophy of life and a deep religious faith."

This kind of faith inspired an even more surprising driver of resistance: Wilhelm Ritter von Leeb, one of Germany's most senior, most important, and most respected generals.

Leeb was a forbidding-looking man with a shaved head and hawk-like features dominated by fierce and penetrating eyes. He had never made much effort to conceal his disdain for the Nazis, always going out of his way to avoid ceremonial occasions when prominent Nazis were present. He was a devout Catholic, whom Nazis often dismissed as the "parson-general." Leeb's faith was the basis of an active conscience. After the war, while an American prisoner, he noted in his diary that for All Souls he had "gone to mass for Alfred [his son] . . . and all the soldiers who fell under my command."

Leeb had been one of the generals dismissed in the purge following the Blomberg-Fritsch crisis. He was brought back to service temporarily for the occupation of the Sudetenland, and then permanently on the outbreak of war in 1939, when he was put in command of all forces on the Western Front.

Like many senior officers, Leeb thought Germany would lose the war, and his desire for peace was heightened after his son Alfred was killed in action in Poland. As Leeb's biographer Georg Meyer observes, "The father wanted to spare other parents the loss of their children," while "the Christian felt Hitler's war to be unjust." In late September, Leeb suggested that the Germans could release all "unnecessary" units from the Western Front, which would demonstrate Germany's desire for peace. The idea drove Hitler into a rage.

Shortly after the defeat of Poland, Leeb wrote a memo with a long title to Walther von Brauchitsch: "The Outlook for and the Effects of an Attack on France and England Through Violation of the Neutrality of Holland, Belgium, and Luxembourg." More informally, Leeb called his memo "The Folly of an Attack."

Never one to mince words, Leeb began, "Deep worry about our future presses me to take up the pen." He thought that unless an attack on Britain and France resulted in the complete destruction of their military strength, it would only enrage them and drive them to fight to the bitter end. Like most German officers, Leeb admired the "toughness" of the British and, a little more grudgingly, of the French. He believed it was impossible for the Germans to degrade French and British military power to the point that the Allies would make peace. The main reason was that it would be impossible to launch a surprise attack: the German preparations would be visible to the Allies, and with the efficient French rail network, they could quickly move forces to where they were needed.

In a passage that made clear how even in Hitler's Reich, commanders had to think about public opinion and public morale, Leeb wrote that the attack on Poland had "called forth no enthusiasm at all like that of 1914 in the German people." Instead, "wide, thinking circles asked themselves whether no other solution than war was possible." People with no critical judgment might still accept that the war had to go on, but even they would find enthusiasm giving way to "disappointment and depression," because "the whole people yearns for peace." Leeb doubted that Germans would believe "the insistence of the Führer, that war had been forced on him by the intransigence of Britain and France." In other words, one of Hitler's most senior generals claimed that the war was both unnecessary and unpopular, and that Hitler was lying about the point of it.

Brauchitsch probably had Leeb's memo on his mind when he met with Halder on October 14 to talk about strategy. Brauchitsch thought the generals had three choices: they could attack in the west as Hitler had ordered; they could wait and see what happened; or they could bring about "fundamental changes." "Fundamental changes" was a euphemism for regime change. The generals were back where they had been the year before: they thought Hitler was driving Germany to ruin, and so they were contemplating a military coup d'état. Not that they were happy about the prospect: they worried that overthrowing the regime would create a weakness the enemy would quickly exploit. Nonetheless, it was their duty to explain the military prospects to Hitler "soberly" and urge him to find a peaceful resolution.

There was another reason that some officers were pondering "fundamental changes" in the autumn of 1939. The full barbarity of Nazi rule was unfolding in the conquest and occupation of Poland. Partly with locally organized paramilitary forces and partly with the Einsatzgruppen, special killing squads made up of SS and police personnel, the Germans set out on a spree of mass murder, targeting Polish aristocrats, intellectuals, clergy, and Jews. They murdered approximately 65,000 people in Poland in the last three months of 1939.

Units of the regular army committed atrocities as well. But some of the senior army officers were horrified and began to complain. Most of these officers were also involved in the resistance. One was the intelligence officer Helmuth Groscurth. Groscurth, forty-one years old and the son of a pastor, was the very embodiment of the Prussian code. On one occasion, frustrated by the way Halder and other senior officers lost their nerve when dealing with Hitler, Groscurth vented his scorn in his diary: "What conditions! These are Prussian officers! A chief of the general staff is *not* to break down!" In fact, Chief of Staff Halder was not Prussian; he was Bavarian. It says a lot about the power of the Prussian code that officers from other regions gladly took it up—and were *expected* to take it up.

The same stern principles and deep religious faith also made Groscurth a fearless opponent of Nazism, on a moral as well as a practical level. The year before, after Kristallnacht, he had written, "One has to be ashamed to be German." One week after the beginning of the campaign in Poland, Oster told Groscurth about some remarks by Heinrich Himmler's SS deputy Reinhard Heydrich. Heydrich had complained that military courts worked too slowly. He wanted Polish aristocrats, clergy, and Jews simply to be shot in masses without any judicial proceeding. What Groscurth learned about these atrocities drove him from passive disgust to active efforts to bring down Hitler's regime—applying the Prussian code like an extreme Yorck and not a Seydlitz.

Groscurth launched a formal complaint about the Polish atrocities. Ultimately, the army demanded jurisdiction over the occupation regime in Poland in order to put a brake on the killings. Hitler's response was a predictable expression of his zoological anarchism. "A hard racial struggle cannot be subject to any law," he said. The German occupiers would have to act in a way that was "incompatible with our usual principles." Hitler wanted Poland to be nothing but a region for slave labor, with all potential leaders eliminated and living standards kept to the absolute minimum. He wanted the population to be killed off by attrition. After twenty years, Hitler explained, "hard work, hunger and pestilence will have completed their devil's work."

A remarkable episode followed. On October 23, Colonel General Johannes Blaskowitz took up his duties as the commander of German occupation troops in Poland. Soon he found that soldiers of all ranks were coming to him to complain about atrocities. Blaskowitz was a resolutely unpolitical soldier and not a resister like Groscurth or Oster. But, like Groscurth, he was a pastor's son, and something of that moral grounding seems to have stayed with him. In November, he submitted a memo to Brauchitsch about what he had learned, keeping the tone neutral and focusing on the problem of maintaining discipline among the troops. But even a dry statement of the facts had a powerful impact in Berlin, where it circulated among senior officers. Brauchitsch, as usual, would not submit the memo directly to Hitler, sending it instead through Hitler's army adjutant Gerhard Engel. And it was to Engel that Hitler vented his rage over Blaskowitz, complaining of the "childish attitudes" of army commanders and insisting that he could not fight a war with "Salvation Army methods."

Blaskowitz was undeterred. In February 1940, he delivered to Brauchitsch a second memo, very different in tone. It is likely that Abwehr chief Wilhelm Canaris wrote some or all of it. But Blaskowitz was determined enough to put his name to it. Clearly, its arguments were pitched pragmatically to maximize the chance of persuading key Nazi leaders to do the right thing. It is "mistaken," the memo read, to slaughter "a few tens of thousands of Jews and Poles, as is happening at the moment." To do so could not kill the idea of the Polish state or "get rid of" the Jews. It would only give grounds for enemy propaganda. The slaughter of Jews drew sympathy among the Catholic Poles, such that a hostile alliance would form between Jews, Poles, and the Catholic Church, "our arch-enemies in the eastern area." But "the most severe damage" which the Polish atrocities would do to Germany would be the "measureless brutalization and moral decay" that would "spread like a plague" among the German soldiers. Blaskowitz attached deposition transcripts from several German soldiers who had witnessed atrocities carried out by the police, to illustrate "what barbarity these beasts are capable of." The soldiers did not understand how such atrocities could go unpunished.

This memo forced Heinrich Himmler to do some damage control. In March, he pointedly told a gathering of army commanders in Koblenz that "I am doing nothing the Führer does not know." In the face of this not-so-veiled threat, the officers made no overt complaints. That spring, Blaskowitz was dismissed from his position in Poland, and Himmler went out of his way to harm the officer's career from then on.

For the handful of dissident officers, rage and disgust about the atrocities in Poland became tied to their opposition to an assault in the west.

Through October and November, as Hitler insisted on an immediate western offensive, the conspirators worked toward a coup d'état. Halder's attitude fluctuated just as it had the year before. When Groscurth met Halder on October 31, the chief of staff spoke of arranging "accidents" for a number of Nazi leaders, including Göring and Ribbentrop. With tears in his eyes, he added that for weeks he had gone to see "Emil" (the officers' disrespectful nickname for Hitler) with his pistol in his pocket, "in order to have the chance of blowing him away." The plotters disagreed about what exactly they wanted to do: simply kill Hitler and a few other Nazis and hope that after that, all would be well, or follow up the assassination with an organized seizure of power. Halder favored the first option, believing there was no one available who could take Hitler's place. Groscurth urged the second, pointing to men such as Beck or Goerdeler, who had the stature to lead the state at least for a time.

In the first days of November, the unpredictable Halder found his courage again. Plans for a coup were ready. On November 3, Groscurth told Gisevius that the coup was on. Halder had given him the authorization to warn Beck and Goerdeler that they should stand ready from November 5 on.

Hitler had ordered the offensive against the west to start on November 12. On November 5, he was to have a last meeting at the Chancellery with Brauchitsch to discuss the plans. The day was a torment for the conspirators, much like September 14 or September 28 of the previous year. As they waited for orders to launch the coup, Gisevius remembered, "We were, of course, as ready as we should ever be. All of us were fearfully tense and eager." But the day went by without word of what had happened between Brauchitsch and Hitler, and, Gisevius recalled, "We had become slightly uneasy. Had the decision been postponed again?"

Halder, who went with Brauchitsch to the Chancellery but waited outside the room while the commander spoke to Hitler, had prepared his chief with arguments against an attack in the west. Replacements had not yet been integrated and trained. Some of the officers were "weak." Much equipment was still in need of repair. The meeting lasted only twenty minutes and did not go well. Hitler insisted that the issues between Germany and the democracies could be settled only militarily. Brauchitsch tried to explain that there had been some examples of "indiscipline" among the troops, resembling the days when the army had broken down in 1918. This was the wrong thing to say to Hitler. He flew into a rage. He demanded specifics: What had happened? In which units? What had been done about it? He wanted death sentences for all breaches of discipline.

It got worse. The army wasn't ready to fight only because it did not want to fight, Hitler raged. "I know the spirit of Zossen," he growled, "and I will destroy it." Zossen was the base outside Berlin from which the army general staff worked. Brauchitsch left the meeting pale and shaken. "Please do not hold it against me," he begged Halder. "I know you are dissatisfied with me. When I confront this man I feel as if someone were choking me and I cannot find another word."

"A discussion with [Hitler] about these things is just not possible," Halder concluded—a point he must surely have noticed before. Halder understated his level of panic. "At Zossen," Gisevius wrote, "everybody was in the throes of a general nervous crisis. Perhaps this is putting it too moderately; it was more like a state of panicked confusion." Hitler's remark about the "spirit of Zossen" suggested that he knew about plans for a coup. Halder ordered the destruction of all documents relating to it. He told Groscurth bluntly that "the offensive will be made." There was no alternative, as "the people and the army are not united." Halder added, "[T]he forces that were counting on us are no longer bound. You understand what I mean." He meant that Goerdeler and Beck could stand down. It was two years to the day since the Hossbach Conference.

"These indecisive leaders are disgusting," Groscurth complained bitterly. It was a view that Prussians more inclined to follow Yorck than Seydlitz would continue to hold. A few years later, Hossbach himself would vent his rage on Halder in a bitter letter: the "immorality of the supreme army command" had contributed to all the misfortune that had come over Germany. To start the war had meant to lose the war, Hossbach insisted. "There was demonstrably no doubt about this in the general staff of the army up to August 28, 1938, the day of your assumption of office."

Halder's and Brauchitsch's loss of nerve spelled the end of any attempt at a coup in 1939. The senior intelligence officer General Kurt von Tippelskirch told Groscurth that there would be no chance of pushing Brauchitsch to act. "We just have to go through this valley," he said.

On November 23, Hitler summoned a group of senior army, navy, and air force officers to the Chancellery to hear another long tirade. He told his audience that he was "irreplaceable" and followed this with the insistence that "I am convinced of my powers of intellect and of decision . . . The fate of the Reich depends only on me . . . I have the greatest experience in all armament questions . . . No one has ever achieved what I have achieved." The point was to intimidate the opposition. Hitler vowed that he would "annihilate" any resistance.

A few officers, such as Groscurth and the tough, salty Leeb, did not want to give up, at least on the idea of stopping a western offensive. Leeb tried to get the other army group commanders in the west to join him in a joint resignation or at least a joint protest to Hitler. One responded that "this went a little too far," so the generals decided instead to "delay as long as possible the beginning of the attack."

Leeb took one more step. In December, Groscurth briefed him on the atrocities in Poland. The same day, Leeb drafted a letter to Halder. "It is reported from many sides," he wrote, "and, it seems to me, credibly, that the conduct of the police in Poland is unworthy of a civilized nation." Leeb thought Brauchitsch had been ineffective in dealing with the crimes. This had only strengthened Leeb's own "desire for a fight, and this fight cannot be avoided." Not everything could be spoken of, Leeb wrote delicately, but "You know, my dear Halder, that the army, if it is led decisively, is in every direction the strongest power factor."

But by this time Hitler had thoroughly intimidated Halder and Brauchitsch, and without them, resistance from the army could go nowhere. The Gestapo started tapping the Leeb family telephone and opening the general's mail.

THE ARMY'S PESSIMISM about an attack in the west infected the operational planning. The senior officers, such as Halder and Brauchitsch, were not playing to win; they were playing not to lose. The first plans the army High Command drew up, under the code name Case Yellow, aimed only to extend the German front lines and gain ground in the Netherlands and Belgium. Scarred by memories of the First World War, they could not imagine a bigger victory than that.

They were probably right about the likely fate of a fall 1939 offensive. The irony is that as their pessimism contributed to delaying the attack, and as they flirted with plans to remove Hitler from power, they inadvertently set up the conditions in which the army would score a stunning victory against its commanders' own expectations. This victory would in turn make Hitler untouchable, at least while its glow lasted.

The attack in the west would now have to wait for the spring of 1940. Hitler gave his generals one caveat: a stretch of clear, cold winter weather, with good visibility for the Luftwaffe, could give the Germans an opportunity to strike earlier. Such weather in fact came in January. By the middle of the month, everything seemed ready. The date of the attack was set for January 17. The Army Group B war diary recorded that after eleven postponements, the great day was finally at hand. They were wrong: there was a twelfth postponement.

This was partly because fog and snow returned. More dramatically, it was because a staff officer from the Seventh Airborne Division had chosen to fly across Belgian territory carrying critical deployment plans. Bad weather forced his plane to make an emergency landing, and he wasn't able to burn the plans. The German commanders had to assume that the Belgians had passed them on to the British and French—as in fact they had.

Hitler had never been happy with the High Command's cautious ideas anyway. When Halder and Brauchitsch presented their plan to him on October 25, he objected that he had always wanted the attack to strike south of the Meuse River, and then head west and northwest so that "the enemy marching into Belgium" could be "blocked and eliminated." Brauchitsch and Halder were astonished, and argued every point vigorously with Hitler for the next six hours. After the generals had left, Hitler complained to Wilhelm Keitel that their plan was nothing but a replay of Germany's First World War "Schlieffen Plan." "You won't get away with an operation like that twice running," said Hitler. "I have quite a different idea and I'll tell you about it in a day or two." A little while later, Keitel continued, "the Führer told me with some great pleasure that on this particular strategic issue he had had a long personal discussion with General von Manstein, who had been the only one of the army's generals to have had the same plan in view, and this had greatly pleased him."

In 1939, General Erich von Manstein was serving as chief of staff to the senior general Gerd von Rundstedt, the commander of Army Group A, which was stationed along the border with Belgium and Luxembourg. Later, as a field marshal, Manstein would become one of the most important commanders on the Eastern Front. Most of the other German commanders of the Second World War considered him the ablest among them, a brilliant field commander and operational planner. He was also arrogant and did not suffer fools gladly. His personal prickliness often got in the way of his career. He and Halder could not stand each other. Even Hitler's support for Manstein was only ever grudging. "The man is not my kind," Hitler told Engel, but, he added significantly, "he knows what he is doing."

Manstein and Heinz Guderian had similar views on the kind of war Germany needed to fight. Both were frustrated by the timid plans germinating in the offices of the High Command. "One day in November [1939]," Guderian remembered later, "Manstein asked me to come to see him and outlined his ideas on the subject to me; these involved a strong tank thrust through southern Belgium and Luxembourg toward Sedan . . . and a consequent splitting in two of the whole French front." The Germans would send their tanks through the dense Ardennes Forest. Once they had broken through to open country, they would turn northwest and drive for the Channel coast. British and French forces would be cut off and trapped in Belgium. Manstein called the plan the "sickle cut," for the curving line of the tanks' advance. Guderian spent some time with the maps and thought back to his own experiences in the region during the First World War. He assured Manstein that his idea would work, so long as the attacking formation had enough armored and motorized units—ideally, all the armor Germany could deploy. Manstein remembered it the same way. Guderian, he said, was "on fire for our plan."

Their cautious superiors were not. The High Command did not want to allocate more than one or two tank divisions to Manstein's breakthrough. Manstein insisted that to succeed, the attack would need every available tank. Instead of granting his wish, the High Command

punished the original thinker. In late January 1940, Manstein was transferred from Rundstedt's staff to the command of an army corps deployed
in Germany. He was in no doubt that his transfer was the product of
top-level irritation with his persistence in pushing his ideas.

This wasn't just a debate about a military plan. It was about fundamental political positions. It was about what kind of country Germany
was supposed to be and how it should fit into the world. Leeb and Beck
had one answer to this question. Hitler, Manstein, and Guderian had
another. Halder and Brauchitsch were much closer in outlook to Leeb
and Beck, and it is likely that they presented cautious and pessimistic plans to Hitler because they wanted to deter him from an attack in
the west altogether. Behind that was their view that the war itself was
both illegitimate and likely to end in disaster. And they objected to the
crimes that Hitler's kind of war—aggressive, fast-moving, reckless, even
desperate—had already brought and would inevitably continue to bring
with it.

Hitler's search for something different, however, reflected the radicalism of his regime. The fact that the High Command tried to shunt
Manstein off to a junior field command where he would have no role in
operational planning illustrates how they saw the stakes of the argument.
In the fall of 1939, the top High Command positions were occupied
mostly by officers who opposed fighting a war against the democracies.

Manstein was proposing the kind of attack that Guderian had been
advocating for years: one that could allow Germany to win before its
enemies brought their greater wealth to bear. Against powers with
imperial, global reach and resources, such as France and Britain—and,
in the background, America—Germany could win only by taking huge
risks. From the very beginning, this had been the essential premise of
Hitler's political movement and of his regime: the point had always been
to break out of the world economic dominance of Anglo-American
capitalism, with whatever desperation was required. Guderian and
Manstein understood this well.

Hitler was increasingly irritated by the High Command's caution.
His army adjutant Engel recorded his rage over Halder and Brauchitsch,
who "deliberately sabotage his ideas," but Hitler felt "he would come out
on top, even if he wasn't a trained general staff officer." Hitler ranted to

Engel that he had to get rid of Brauchitsch because he needed optimists around him, not pessimists. Yet he refused to accept Brauchitsch's resignation when it was offered.

Manstein needed to circumvent the chain of command to get to Hitler. It was probably Hitler's armed forces adjutant Rudolf Schmundt, Hossbach's successor, who arranged a covert meeting. On February 4, Schmundt had returned from a visit to Koblenz enthusiastic about conversations he had had there with Rundstedt and Manstein. Schmundt told Engel that Manstein's plan "contained the same opinion regarding the best concentration of forces . . . as that continually advocated by the Führer." The next day, Schmundt told Hitler what he had heard in Koblenz and suggested that Hitler bring Manstein to Berlin. "F[ührer] agreed at once," Engel recorded, "but ordered both Schmundt and myself not to mention this proposed conference to [Brauchitsch] or Halder."

Manstein was duly summoned to Berlin on February 17 for a breakfast with Hitler for officers newly appointed to command positions, among them Erwin Rommel. At the end of the breakfast, Hitler pulled Manstein aside for a private conference in his study. There "he asked me to present my views on the conduct of the western offensive," Manstein remembered later. Manstein did not know how much Schmundt might already have filled Hitler in on the plan, but "in any case I had to admit that he was astonishingly quick to grasp the points which our Army Group had been advocating for months. He agreed completely with my explanations." This wasn't just Manstein's ego at work. Engel found that Hitler was "thrilled" by Manstein's ideas.

Three days later, Hitler issued new orders for the attack. They followed Manstein's ideas exactly. Now Case Yellow was something very different from what it had been. Hitler's Germany had turned a crucial corner.

14

"Let Us Go Forward Together"

First Lord of the Admiralty Winston Churchill's mind is working furiously as always: seeing possibilities in the near future, imagining the unconventional response that could win the war for Britain. He wonders if the Germans might defeat France, requiring Britain to carry on the war alone. "But even if we were single-handed," he decides, "as we were in the days of the Napoleonic wars, we should have no reason to despair of our capacity—no doubt we should suffer discomfort and privation and loss—but we should have no reason to despair of our capacity to go on indefinitely."

He believes the path to victory is not the brutish one of fighting the whole weight of the German Army in a war of attrition. "The position of both armies is not likely to undergo any decisive change," he writes, "although no doubt several hundred thousand men will be spent to satisfy the military mind on the point." There has to be a more elegant way—a more British way. "Are there not other alternatives than sending our armies to chew barbed wire in Flanders?" he wonders. Soon his fertile mind has hit upon such an alternative: opening another front in the Middle East.

It is not 1940. It is 1914.

Turkey has just entered the war on the side of Germany. In late November, Churchill proposes using the Royal Navy to force the Dardanelles strait, which connects the eastern Mediterranean to the Sea of Marmara, between the Gallipoli peninsula and the mainland of Asia Minor. Once the British control the strait, they can sail battleships into the Sea of Marmara and shell the Turkish capital of Constantinople, or land troops there. They will easily be able to send supplies to embattled Russia. They might be able to knock Turkey quickly out of the war. They can open a Balkan front against the Austro-Hungarian Empire, and even against Germany. With the bulk of the German Army in the west, and the Austrians unable to beat even Serbia, the operation could be a war-winner.

No one thinks it will be easy. The Dardanelles strait is forty-one miles long and, in places, only a mile wide. There are Turkish fortifications and heavy guns on both sides. The waters are mined, and strong currents run from the Black Sea through the Sea of Marmara to the Dardanelles, making it difficult for minesweepers to operate. Churchill thinks the strait can be forced using obsolete and expendable battleships. "Importance of results would justify severe loss," he cables the Mediterranean naval commander. A little later, he writes that he would "not grudge a hundred thousand men" for the success of the mission.

It is a typical Churchill idea: bold, imaginative—and risky. It all goes badly from the start. On March 18, 1915, the Royal Navy moves into the strait. The cost is one French and two old British battleships sunk and several more damaged. The navy retreats in disarray. The British cabinet decides to combine the naval operation with a land campaign to secure the Gallipoli peninsula, but there is a fatal delay of five weeks before the ground operations can be launched. It is not until April 25 that four divisions of British, French, Australian, and New Zealand troops can be landed on the peninsula. By then it is too late. The Turks have had plenty of warning to strengthen their defenses. Turkish troops are commanded by a highly talented general named Mustafa Kemal, who as Kemal Atatürk will later rise to become the first president of postwar Turkey. The British naval and army commanders in the area are all second-rate. A senior officer on the British planning staff writes to a friend that if the operation fails, "It will be a very serious business. I am afraid it was started without being thought out in consequence of some heated impulse of Winston Churchill, who could not be content with the limited opportunities that the Germans give the Fleet." The friend who receives this letter is the mayor of Birmingham, Neville Chamberlain.

The Allies' casualties from the landings are heavy, and the Gallipoli mission soon bogs down in exactly the sort of trench warfare it was meant to avoid. Eventually, the Allied troops have to be withdrawn, the mission given up as a failure.

Even before the withdrawal, Gallipoli has cost Winston Churchill his job, though its failure is by no means only his fault. He is not responsible for the ground troops, nor for the planning of their operations, nor for the delay in the landings, nor for the inadequate numbers that are pried away from the Western Front. It is really for political reasons that he is made to carry the blame. Churchill has loved every minute of commanding the Royal Navy. His demotion to the meaningless cabinet position of chancellor of the Duchy of Lancaster—where his only real responsibility is appointing magistrates—is a cruel blow. Later, his wife, Clementine, will write, "I thought he would die of grief."

The ever-loyal Clementine also writes an anguished letter to Prime Minister H. H. Asquith. Her husband, she insists, "has the supreme quality which I venture to say very few of your present or future cabinet possess, the power, the imagination, the deadliness to fight Germany." It is not the last time Churchill's pugnaciousness will form a stark contrast to the listless approach of cabinet colleagues, even of a prime minister.

But Gallipoli will be a millstone around Churchill's neck for a very long time. Whenever other politicians condemn his recklessness or lack of judgment, it will be Gallipoli they talk about. This will remain so until another amphibious operation goes terribly wrong, another operation which Churchill has planned and commanded as first lord of the Admiralty. But this other operation will have a very different effect on his career.

WHEN THE GERMANS invaded Norway in the early morning hours of April 9, 1940, an aide went to awaken King Haakon VII. "Majesty, we are at war!" said the aide. "Against whom?" was the king's laconic response.

Well might he have wondered. Through the autumn of 1939 and the spring of 1940, both the British and the Germans had been pondering various schemes for violating Norwegian neutrality. The Germans wanted to establish naval bases to break out of the British stranglehold on the North Sea. The British wanted to open a route to aid Finland in its desperate war against the Soviet Union. (As yet further confirmation of his real designs, Stalin had invaded that country on November 30.) The British also wanted to block German shipments of Swedish iron ore from the area around Gällivare. In March, Finland surrendered, though on relatively advantageous terms, as its forces had performed much better than those of its Soviet adversary. Churchill still wanted to grab the iron ore fields but lost the debate in the cabinet. He eventually won approval for a mine-laying operation in Norwegian waters to block German ships. A British expedition sailed for Norway on April 5.

The day before, Chamberlain had made an unfortunate speech declaring that by not attacking the west thus far, Hitler had "missed the bus." He hadn't. Before the British expedition could reach Norway, the Germans struck. As German soldiers moved into Denmark, the navy carried troops to landings at Oslo and key Norwegian ports such as Trondheim and Narvik, where the Germans were helped by a garrison commander who supported the pro-Nazi Norwegian Vidkun Quisling.

The British should have been able to use their vast naval superiority to land troops and to bottle up the German attack in Norway. Instead, what followed was a spectacular display of disorganization and incompetence at all levels of the British forces and government. Plans were changed and changed again. British troops landed at Narvik only to become stuck in the snow. They were withdrawn after achieving nothing. An effort to take Trondheim also foundered. Some of the problems lay with incompetent officers, some with the lack of central direction of the war effort. This was Chamberlain's fault. But Churchill could not escape some of the blame. The operations were largely conducted by the Royal Navy, for which he was responsible. He ignored intelligence warnings in the days before April 9 that the Germans were gathering for an attack on Norway. And he, too, changed his mind repeatedly about the timing and direction of Norwegian operations.

By contrast, although the Germans had faced longer odds—their forces had to be carried great distances in the teeth of superior naval power—they had operated with daring and efficiency. To be sure, they had suffered serious losses to a navy that was small to begin with. Yet they had won.

For Britons whose memories reached back to the First World War, this latest naval fiasco looked a lot like Gallipoli. Although blame for that disaster was widely shared, it had almost ended Churchill's political career. Now, in a twist of extraordinary historical irony, Norway, a disaster for which Churchill was largely to blame, would have a very different effect on his fortunes. The perceptive Clementine Churchill told her husband later, "Had it not been for your years of exile & repeated warnings re. the German peril, Norway might well have ruined you."

Discontent with Chamberlain's government was growing, and the dissidents were becoming bolder as the prime minister's dictatorial style finally caught up with him. He had tried several times since the outbreak of the war to broaden his government by including meaningful participation from the Labour Party. But Labour always refused these invitations. The Labour members of Parliament hated Chamberlain, remembering, as one put it, how he had treated them "like dirt" when things were going better for him. Clement Attlee, the party's cool, crisply competent leader, said in a speech, "The time will come when the nation will demand a change, and when that time comes, we are ready." His colleague Herbert Morrison was blunter. He told the *Daily Mail*, "I am going to reserve the right to get rid of Chamberlain as soon as I jolly well can."

By the beginning of May, the Conservative member of Parliament Henry "Chips" Channon found there was a lot of talk that "Winston should be Prime Minister as he has more vigor and the country behind him." Churchill was being "lauded by both the Socialist and Liberal oppositions" and "being tempted to lead a revolt against the PM."

Tempted he must have been, but Churchill remained loyal. When Harold Macmillan told him, "We must have a new prime minister, and it must be you," Churchill replied gruffly that he had signed on for the voyage and he would stick with the ship. "But I don't think he was angry with me," Macmillan remembered.

Nonetheless, in that first week of May, a political crisis was brewing. Chamberlain gave another complacent speech on May 4, trying to claim that Norway had been a British victory. The members of the House, Harold Nicolson recorded, knew "that this is simply not true," and "if Chamberlain believed it himself, then he was stupid. If he did not believe it, then he was trying to deceive." There was a good deal of talk that David Lloyd George might come back as prime minister to save the day, as he had in 1916, when he had replaced the worn-out Asquith. Nicolson did not think much of this idea, but he did not know who could take Chamberlain's place. "Eden is out of it. Churchill is undermined by the Conservative caucus. Halifax is believed (and with justice) to be a tired man. We always say that our advantage over the German leadership principle is that we can always find another leader. Now we cannot."

On May 7, the Labour Party put forward a motion to adjourn the House of Commons. In itself, this was a routine matter. But May 1940 was not a routine time. Just as the adjournment debate the previous August had exploded into a debate on Chamberlain's authoritarian tendencies, everyone understood that the debate on this motion would be about Norway and Chamberlain's conduct of the war.

The debate turned out to be the most dramatic and important in British parliamentary history.

"The House is crowded," Harold Nicolson noted, "and when Chamberlain comes in, he is greeted with shouts of 'missed the bus'"—the kind of savage sarcasm of which British parliamentarians have always been eminently capable. There was much more to come.

The Conservative backbencher Admiral Sir Roger Keyes came "dressed in full uniform with six rows of medals," Nicolson recorded. This imposing figure proceeded to make "an absolutely devastating attack" on the conduct of the Norway operations, to which the members listened "in breathless silence." Keyes concluded by calling bluntly for Churchill to become prime minister: "I have great admiration and affection for my right honorable Friend the First Lord of the Admiralty. I am longing to see proper use made of his great abilities. I cannot believe it will be done under the existing system." Nicolson thought it was "by far the most dramatic speech I have ever heard," and when Keyes sat down, there was "thunderous applause."

Something still more dramatic was coming. Leo Amery had long been a gadfly Conservative, mostly on the party's far right. It was Amery who had astonished the House on September 2 when he called on Arthur Greenwood to "Speak for *England.*" Now he entered the debate as members who had gone for dinner rushed back to the chamber—and as the House filled, he knew the members were following his words with growing approval. Amery opened by pointing squarely to the stakes of this debate, and of the war itself, for democracy: "The whole of Parliament has a grave responsibility at this moment," he said. "For, after all, it is Parliament itself that is on trial in this war. If we lose this war, it is not this or that ephemeral Government but Parliament as an institution that will be condemned, for good and all." He, like Keyes, offered a devastating critique of the competence of Chamberlain's government. "We cannot go on as we are," he warned.

Amery concluded with a historical analogy between the performance of British troops so far in the Second World War and the similar low fortunes of Oliver Cromwell's Parliamentary troops in the English Civil War of three hundred years before. When he was preparing his speech, he had remembered another quotation from Cromwell. "I doubted whether this was not too strong meat," Amery remembered, "and only kept it by me in case the spirit should move me to use it as the climax to my speech." But as he felt he "had the House with me," he found himself "going on to an increasing crescendo of applause . . . I cast prudence to the winds and ended full out with my Cromwellian injunction."

What he said ranks with the most resonant words ever uttered in the House of Commons. "We are fighting to-day for our life, for our liberty, for our all . . . This is what Cromwell said to the Long Parliament when he thought it was no longer fit to conduct the affairs of the nation: 'You have sat too long here for any good you have been doing. Depart, I say, and let us have done with you. In the name of God, go.'"

The impact was stunning. Amery was right when he wrote, "I may or may not have made better speeches before, but I certainly have never made one that was so effective both at the moment and in its consequences." Lloyd George told Amery afterward that he had never heard a more dramatic climax to a Commons speech. But more important, as Amery noted, "it settled the fate of the Government."

The debate was scheduled to continue on Wednesday, May 8. Churchill was in a strange position. The events of the previous year had vindicated his long, lonely stand against Hitler and against the appeasers. Everyone in politics knew this. But he was now serving as a senior figure in the appeasers' government. And, of course, the Norwegian debacle had come on his watch. In speaking on behalf of Chamberlain's government, he would have to strike a very difficult balance. His supporters were sensitive to this problem. "Our chief anxiety concerned Churchill," Macmillan remembered. "We were determined to bring down the Government, and as every hour passed, we seemed more likely to achieve our purpose. But how could Churchill be disentangled from the ruins? If the chief issue of the first day had been the overthrow of the Government, the chief anxiety of the second was the rescue of Churchill."

When the debate opened again, Herbert Morrison made official what had only been implied the day before: Labour wanted a vote of censure on Chamberlain's government. Chamberlain replied, in his arrogant and solipsistic way, that he would call on his "friends" in the house to support him. Many members thought this was in very bad taste, but it was the former prime minister David Lloyd George, seventy-seven years old and rousing himself for what turned out to be his last significant speech in a Commons debate, who delivered a devastating rebuttal. Lloyd George and Chamberlain had intensely disliked each other—far more than Churchill and Chamberlain disliked each other—since the First World War. Lloyd George had gotten some advice before the debate: to get under Chamberlain's skin and make him lose his temper; this always caused the prime minister to say something foolish. So armed, Lloyd George now delivered the final cut in this long duel. "It is not a question of who are the Prime Minister's friends," he pointed out. "It is a far bigger issue." Chamberlain had appealed for sacrifice, Lloyd George noted. "I say solemnly that the Prime Minister should give an example of sacrifice, because there is nothing which can contribute more to victory in this war than that he should sacrifice the seals of office."

Lloyd George also worked to protect Churchill. When Churchill proudly and honorably insisted on bearing his full measure of responsibility for Admiralty decisions, Lloyd George responded that Churchill "must not allow himself to be converted into an air-raid shelter to keep the splinters from hitting his colleagues."

But however difficult the task—defending Chamberlain effectively enough for decency and honor, but not so effectively as to close off his own chances of becoming prime minister—Churchill's pugnacious spirit could rise to it. "One saw at once," Chips Channon thought, "that he was in [a] bellicose mood, alive and enjoying himself, relishing the ironical position in which he found himself: i.e. that of defending his enemies, and a cause in which he did not believe."

Members did not have to think back very far to remember Churchill's scathing criticisms of Chamberlain's policies. Now many of Chamberlain's erstwhile allies were melting away, and Churchill, who had the strongest moral claim to criticize the prime minister, spoke for him instead. Many politicians in Churchill's situation, brooding on the slights they had endured from a rival, would have savored the chance of vengeance. Instead, Churchill showed character fit for high leadership. He spoke for reconciliation. He took up Chamberlain's unfortunate reference to his "friends." "He thought he had some friends," came the Churchillian growl, "and I hope he has some friends. He certainly had a good many when things were going well." He closed with an appeal for unity. "I say, let pre-war feuds die; let personal quarrels be forgotten, and let us keep our hatreds for the common enemy. Let party interest be ignored, let all our energies be harnessed, let the whole ability and forces of the nation be hurled into the struggle, and let all the strong horses be pulling on the collar. At no time in the last war were we in greater peril than we are now, and I urge the House strongly to deal with these matters . . . in accordance with the dignity of Parliament."

Throughout his time in office, Chamberlain had relied heavily on his chief whip, the hatchet-faced David Margesson, to enforce party discipline and crush dissent in the Conservative caucus. Now, Nicolson thought, "the weakness of the Margesson system is displayed by the fact that none of the Yes-men are of any use whatsoever [in parliamentary debate] whereas all the more able Conservatives have been driven into the ranks of the rebels."

In any case, the Margesson system had broken down. Despite the fiercest effort of Margesson's whips, when the vote came on the censure motion, 33 Conservatives and 8 non-Conservative supporters of the government voted in favor of it. Sixty more Conservatives abstained. The result was 281 for Chamberlain's administration and 200 against. If all the Conservatives had voted for Chamberlain, he would have won by 213 votes, not 81. When the result was announced, there were loud cries of "Go! Go! Go!" aimed at Chamberlain. He had not won by enough. The vote was really a moral defeat.

Chamberlain thought first about restructuring his government as a coalition, bringing in Labour. But the Labour Party's leaders told him bluntly that they would not serve in any administration he led, though they would serve under another Conservative.

In a private meeting on the late afternoon of May 9, in the presence of only Halifax, Churchill, and Margesson, Chamberlain said that either Churchill or Halifax would have to become prime minister. Halifax thought Chamberlain made it plain that he, Halifax, was the one "mentioned as the most acceptable," particularly by the Labour leaders who would have to be included in a new administration. Churchill remembered it a little differently. He thought that Chamberlain assumed that his, Churchill's, pugnaciousness in the previous day's debate might have alienated Labour and given the advantage to Halifax. In any case, Chamberlain went on to say that the question was "Whom he should advise the King to send for after his own resignation had been accepted?"

"Usually I talk a great deal," Churchill remembered, in words that no one would have disputed, "but on this occasion I was silent . . . As I remained silent a very long pause ensued. It certainly seemed longer than the two minutes which one observes in the commemorations of Armistice Day. Then at length Halifax spoke." In fact, according to new information uncovered by the British writer Geoffrey Shakespeare, before Halifax spoke, it was Margesson who intervened decisively, arguing that only Churchill could be the man of the hour. And then Halifax spoke. "I said it would be a hopeless position," as he told the story later, referring to the prospect of his becoming prime minister. "If I was not in charge of the war (operations) and if I did not lead in the House, I should be a cypher. I thought Winston was a better choice. Winston did *not* demur. Was very kind and polite but showed that he thought this the right solution."

"By the time [Halifax] had finished," Churchill continued, "it was clear that the duty would fall upon me—had in fact fallen upon me. Then for the first time I spoke. I said I would have no communication with either of the opposition parties until I had the King's commission to form a Government. On this the momentous conversation came to an end, and we reverted to our ordinary easy and familiar manners of men who had worked for years together and whose lives in and out of office had been spent in all the friendliness of British politics."

That was where things stood on the evening of May 9—with Churchill poised to take the premiership, subject to word from the Labour leaders. This was an extraordinary and sudden transformation. The man who had come within a hair of being driven from politics in late 1938 for his ferocious opposition to the Munich accord now had power almost within his grasp.

But an even greater shock was coming.

"THE SUN IS shining, the column waits at the edge of a forest . . . There is the noise of motors, sometimes flyers, early in the first light great squadrons. We are waiting for the road to be clear." So wrote Erich Kuby, a soldier in the First Signals Company of the Third Motorized Division of Rundstedt's Army Group A. Kuby's company was waiting to cross into Luxembourg.

A little before dawn on the morning of Friday, May 10, 1940, German bombers crossed into France. At 4:45, air-raid sirens went off at Vincennes, and soon they were heard all over Paris. Units of Fedor von Bock's Army Group B crossed into Belgium and the Netherlands. At first, the Allies took Army Group B's attack for the main German offensive. But, in fact, Bock's forces were carrying out an enormous diversion. The point was to lure the British and French armies into Belgium, so they could be cut off and surrounded by the Manstein-Guderian "sickle cut," as yet undetected and unsuspected by the Allies.

No one woke up the Allied commander in chief, French general Maurice Gamelin, until six thirty. By this time, the Belgian and Dutch governments had sent official requests to the Allies for military aid. The Allies responded with their long-prepared plan. To meet the expected German attack in the Low Countries, the best of the Allied forces—nine British and twenty-nine French divisions—began moving to the Dyle River in Belgium. The Luftwaffe did not try to stop them. No one paused to wonder about this, and certainly no one considered the possibility that the Allied armies were going right where the Germans wanted them.

These dramatic events almost derailed the change of government in London. "At about ten o'clock Sir Kingsley Wood [at that time, holding the cabinet office of lord privy seal] came to see me," Churchill recalled. Wood had just seen the prime minister. "He told me that Mr. Chamberlain was inclined to feel that the great battle which had broken upon us made it necessary for him to remain at his post." Wood told Chamberlain bluntly that, on the contrary, "the new crisis made it all the more necessary to have a National Government, which alone could confront it, and he added that Mr. Chamberlain had accepted this view."

At a war cabinet meeting late that afternoon, Chamberlain confirmed that he would go. He had now heard definitively from the Labour leaders that they would not serve in any coalition under him, but would "take their share of responsibility as a full partner in a new Government, under a new Prime Minister, which would command the confidence of the nation." Chamberlain said he would see the king and resign that evening. According to the minutes, he said nothing about who his successor would be.

When Chamberlain went to see King George VI, the king consoled his prime minister on how "grossly unfairly" he had been treated. "We then," the king recorded, "had an informal talk over his successor." The king "of course" proposed Halifax, but Chamberlain explained why that could not be. "Then I knew that there was only one person whom I could send for to form a Government who had the confidence of the country, & that was Winston," the king recalled. "I asked Chamberlain his advice, & he told me Winston was the man to send for."

It was Churchill's turn to see the king. In his memoirs, Churchill relayed this dramatic moment with a light touch. "His Majesty received me most graciously and bade me sit down. He looked at me searchingly and quizzically for some moments, and then said, 'I suppose you don't know why I have sent for you?' Adopting his mood, I replied, 'Sir, I simply couldn't imagine why.' He laughed and said, 'I want to ask you to form a Government.' I said I would certainly do so."

Churchill promised to send the king at least five names of cabinet ministers that very evening, and he wasted no time in doing so. He immediately confirmed with Attlee and Greenwood that Labour would participate in his administration, making it a truly national coalition in a way that the Conservative-dominated "National" governments of the 1930s had never been. To shore up Conservative support—Churchill was painfully aware how much resentment of him still lingered in the Conservative caucus—he asked Neville Chamberlain to stay on as lord president of the council and Lord Halifax to remain as foreign secretary. Furthermore, he offered these old appeasers, along with Attlee and Greenwood, places in the tight, five-man war cabinet he created to run the war effectively. Churchill also named himself to a new position, minister of defense, so that he would have coordinating power over all aspects of the war.

At the age of sixty-five, Winston Churchill had gained an office he had aspired to all his life, and one that just a year before had seemed permanently beyond his grasp. With his peculiar intuition, Adolf Hitler had always sensed that *this* man was his most dangerous antagonist. Angry but also worried references to Churchill had been cropping up in Hitler's speeches for years. Now it was Churchill who faced the dictator as the Phony War gave way to one that was all too real.

Churchill did not try to minimize the hardships that lay ahead. In his first speech as prime minister, he told the nation that he had "nothing to offer but blood, toil, tears and sweat." He warned his countrymen and countrywomen, "We have before us an ordeal of the most grievous kind. We have before us many, many long months of struggle and of suffering." But his unfailing buoyancy was there, too. "I feel sure that our cause will not be suffered to fail among men," he said. "Come then, let us go forward together with our united strength."

Here was something new, a world away from the gloomy solipsism of Chamberlain's speech on the outbreak of war. Democracy now had what it had lacked all through the 1930s: not only a passionate and peerlessly eloquent voice, but one speaking from a position of power.

Something else had arrived with Churchill. Throughout the 1930s, the dominant tone in British politics had been set by the National Governments, under first Ramsay MacDonald, then Stanley Baldwin, and then Chamberlain. The first two had been cautious, timid administrations, hugging the political center, always looking for the safest course.

Under Chamberlain, the government's tone had started to take on a disturbing authoritarianism. All this time, the outsiders had been people like Churchill on the right, along with some disgruntled Liberals and the left of the Labour Party. By the late 1930s, these groups were beginning to coalesce around anti-Nazism, and just as Churchill found more democratic ways to articulate his policies, Labour began to see the point of defense spending, and strong-minded independents such as Eleanor Rathbone recognized that Churchill would be the most effective democratic leader. When Churchill's coalition came to power, the outsiders were suddenly the insiders. It was an epochal change in British politics, clearing the way not only for an effective defense against Hitler, but also, in the years that followed, profound social reform that would go a long way toward making Britain a better home for more of its people. Churchill's cabinet, not entirely by his own wishes, would become the chrysalis for a new political consensus lasting until the 1980s. In 1940, Britain experienced a political change that was the mirror image of the change in Germany: when the German military plot faded away in confused irresolution and Manstein got Hitler to approve his plan of attack, Germany became more fully Nazified than it had been before. Britain under Churchill became more fully democratic.

Just days before, Harold Nicolson had complained that British democracy could not seem to find its leader. But now it had. And it had done so through a triumphant affirmation of that democracy. Amery, at the start of his speech on May 7, had stressed the democratic stakes of the debate. The debate's outcome brought in a government that was not only more competent and more energetic than its predecessor—and vastly more inspiring—but one that truly represented all of Britain's people as perhaps no British government had before. As the historian Jonathan Schneer writes, "Britain, the mother of parliaments, was showing the world democracy in action. That was worth fighting for, and even worth dying for. Germans could make no such demonstration."

Churchill's competence and buoyant confidence as a war leader had brought him to his country's highest office. He knew what he could do. A famous passage in his memoirs records his feelings on the night he became prime minister: "As I went to bed at about 3 a.m.," he remembered, "I was conscious of a profound sense of relief. At last I had the authority to give directions over the whole scene. I felt as if I were walking with destiny, and that all my past life had been but a preparation for this hour and for this trial . . . I was sure I should not fail."

CHURCHILL WOULD NEED every bit of that confidence in the weeks and months that followed. No British prime minister—probably no leader of any country—had ever come to office in the midst of a greater disaster.

Manstein's "sickle cut" succeeded beyond the wildest hopes of German commanders. Guderian's tanks poured through the Ardennes in days and crossed the Meuse at Sedan, where the Prussians had decisively defeated the French in 1870. With only open country ahead of them, they turned northwest and drove for the English Channel. Within five days of the beginning of the battle, French premier Paul Reynaud—who had replaced Daladier in March—was certain his country had lost: "We have been defeated," he told Churchill on the telephone on May 15. Within two weeks, the Germans had split the British and French armies, cut off the forces that had moved so confidently into Belgium, and forced the British into a panicky retreat to the Channel port of Dunkirk. Here, contrary to almost everyone's expectations, the British managed to rescue most of their army and some of the French forces as well. This was, as Churchill said, a deliverance for Britain and for himself, too—before the evacuation had proved successful, he had had to convince his cabinet to decide to continue the war, not knowing if any troops would make it back from France, over the opposition of Halifax (but with the support of Chamberlain).

With the British gone and Case Yellow a resounding success, the Germans launched the second part of their operation, Case Red, against a disorganized and stunned French Army. The widespread belief that the French did not fight with determination is an utter falsehood. In just a few weeks of May and June, French forces suffered 124,000 dead and 200,000 wounded, an enormous figure for such a short time and one that could not have been reached if they had not been fighting valiantly. The Germans did not outnumber the Allies; nor, generally, did they have better weapons, or even more tanks. What they had was better leadership, better tactics, better nerve, and better luck. On June 17,

France, now under the leadership of the elderly First World War marshal Philippe Pétain, asked for an armistice. Hitler traveled to the Forest of Compiègne for the signing, which took place in the very railway car in which Germany had signed the Armistice in 1918—it had been brought out of a museum for the purpose. Hitler's Germany had done in six weeks what the Kaiser's Germany had not been able to do in nearly four and a half years of war.

The defeat of France marked a revolution in world affairs. It was the point of transition from one world order to another, from the European and imperial system of the last four centuries to a more globally diverse order in which non-European powers—above all, the United States and the Soviet Union—would be the anchors. France's army had been a key to the defense strategies of both Britain and the United States. With France gone, the English-speaking democracies had to carry out a quick rethinking.

For Churchill, the response was obvious. He knew, although he never said this publicly, that Britain had no path to victory over Germany without having the United States as a full military ally. According to his son, Randolph, Churchill came to this revelation even before France had surrendered. One morning in mid-May, as the French crisis was unfolding, Randolph went to see his father and found him shaving. Churchill told his son to sit down and read the papers while he "hacked away" with his old-fashioned razor. After a few minutes, Churchill turned to his son and said, "I think I see a way through . . . I will drag the United States in."

For the next eighteen months, trying to "drag the United States in" was more or less Churchill's job description. As the disaster grew ever grimmer in the early summer of 1940, he took advantage of the opening Roosevelt had given the previous September to dispatch some blunt messages to the president. As early as May 15, in his first cable to Roosevelt after becoming prime minister, Churchill warned that "the scene has darkened swiftly," and he shrewdly began hinting at the thing that certainly worried Roosevelt the most: the specter of America as a garrison state. "If necessary we shall continue the war alone, and we are not afraid of that. But I trust you realize, Mr. President . . . that you may have a completely subjugated, Nazified Europe established with astounding swiftness and the weight may be more than we can bear." A few days later, Churchill was blunter still. His government would never surrender to the Nazis, he assured the president. But he could not vouch for a successor, and then "you must not be blind to the fact that the sole remaining bargaining counter with Germany would be the fleet." If Britain were "left by the United States to its fate," no one could blame British leaders who "made the best terms they could for the surviving inhabitants." A former assistant secretary of the navy, as Roosevelt was, could understand right away that a Germany that gained control of the Royal Navy would be a mortal threat to the United States.

Churchill's message struck home. On June 10, Roosevelt gave the commencement address at the University of Virginia. "Some indeed still hold to the obvious delusion," he told the students, "that we . . . can safely permit the United States to become a lone island in a world dominated by the philosophy of force." Such an island, said Roosevelt, represented "a helpless nightmare of a people without freedom, a people lodged in prison, handcuffed and hungry." To prevent this from happening, "we will extend to the opponents of force the material resources of this nation."

The German victory in France seemed to be a vindication of the aggressive, daring Nazi approach to war, a desperate gamble against the superior resources of the Allies. It looked as if Hitler, Guderian, and Manstein had been right, and that Beck, Leeb, and the other cautious generals had been wrong. But Beck and Leeb were not wrong. They had seen what Liddell Hart saw: if the Allies could manage not to lose a short war, their superior resources and control of the seas would make German victory in a long war unlikely. The sophisticated air defenses that people such as R. J. Mitchell, Hugh Dowding, and Neville Chamberlain had created allowed Britain to escape an early defeat. Britain's survival in 1940 in turn allowed Roosevelt the time he needed to prepare the United States for war—and to prepare American opinion to join the war.

Once Hitler dragged the Soviet Union into the war against him, the point became even clearer. The historian Paul Kennedy has recently noted that Britain, the Soviet Union, and the United States, to different degrees, held a critical advantage that France or Poland (and Germany itself) could not match: their vital resources were protected by either water or a huge land mass. This was a strategic problem that all the daring and skill of the Mansteins and Guderians could not solve.

TWO OF THE men who had tried to slow down the rush to war did not see much of the struggle when it came.

In spite of all he had been through and the dishonor he had suffered at Hitler's hands, Werner von Fritsch rushed to the colors on the outbreak of war. He was named a supernumerary officer of the Twelfth Artillery Regiment for the attack on Poland. It seemed to some of his fellow officers that he went out of his way to find danger, volunteering for special assignments and sometimes venturing far ahead of the front lines. On September 22, 1939, while Fritsch was on a reconnaissance mission, shrapnel or a machine gun bullet hit him in the thigh and severed his femoral artery. A junior officer tried to bind the wound, but Fritsch told him, "Just leave it." He bled to death within a minute.

Fritsch had visited Ludwig Beck just before going to the front, and Beck, too, had felt in no doubt that Fritsch was looking for "an upright death." When he heard of Fritsch's fate, Beck lamented that "the number of men . . . whose thinking and outlook was the same as mine was never large, and is growing ever smaller." Oddly—it was early in the war, and the hatreds had not yet bitten deeply—even the BBC paid tribute to Fritsch as one of the last of the chivalrous and high-minded Prussian soldiers, and then played the classic German song lamenting a fallen friend, "I Had a Comrade." Beck heard the broadcast, and it brought him to tears.

Neville Chamberlain was depressed and bitter after Churchill supplanted him, although he worked hard and loyally in Churchill's cabinet. "All my world has tumbled to bits in a moment," he complained to Hilda in mid-May, and a month later, "There is no pleasure in life and no prospect of any." The prospects would darken still more. He began to feel abdominal pain in the middle of June. A month later, he admitted to his sisters that he was in "considerable trouble with my inside which hasn't been working properly for a long time & is getting worse." He had surgery on July 29. The doctors informed him that it had gone well and he would not need more surgery. Remarkably, they did not tell him the full truth: they had found that he was dying of bowel cancer.

Still unaware of his real condition, Chamberlain returned to London on September 9 and tried to go back to work. He soon realized he could not keep going. At the end of September, under some pressure from Churchill, he resigned his cabinet office and his leadership of the Conservative Party. Only then did he learn the truth of his condition. He was told he had between three months and a year to live.

In mid-October, he told U.S. ambassador Joseph Kennedy that he wanted to die. "I saw my father live 8 years after a stroke," Chamberlain explained, "and often wish[ed] he were dead." Kennedy was about to return to the United States. "This is goodbye," Chamberlain told the ambassador. Chamberlain died in his sleep on November 9. He had declined Churchill's offer of a knighthood, wanting to die, like his father, simply as "Mr. Chamberlain."

Three days later, the House of Commons paid tribute to the fallen leader. Churchill's eulogy ranks among his most eloquent speeches. Human beings, he said, were unable "to foresee or to predict to any large extent the unfolding course of events," which was just as well, for "otherwise life would be intolerable." "In one phase men seem to have been right, in another they seem to have been wrong. Then again, a few years later, when the perspective of time has lengthened, all stands in a different setting . . . History with its flickering lamp stumbles along the trail of the past, trying to reconstruct its scenes, to revive its echoes, and kindle with pale gleams the passion of former days." No one, in short, could ever avoid the cycle of being judged right and wrong—a fact that few knew better than Churchill.

Chamberlain's project had failed. But the hopes that had guided him "were surely among the most noble and benevolent instincts of the human heart—the love of peace, the toil for peace, the strife for peace, the pursuit of peace, even at great peril and certainly to the utter disdain of popularity or clamor." This fact, said Churchill, "will stand him in good stead as far as what is called the verdict of history is concerned."

History has not been kind to Chamberlain. But Churchill was right in ways he himself would never have wanted to admit. We see the outbreak of the Second World War in 1939 as a vindication of Churchill's long and lonely struggle against appeasement, and correspondingly, as the final and damning verdict on Chamberlain's policy. We see it this way because of the shocking outcome of 1940—the swift defeat of France—which we then assume to have been inevitable. But the dramatic German victory of 1940 was in fact a chancy, even unlikely outcome. After all, Beck and Leeb saw the strategic questions much the same way as did Liddell Hart and Chamberlain. The German commanders expected the war to be a long struggle in France, resembling the last one. If that had happened, the policies of the 1930s would look very different from how they look to us now. In any case, in the longer term, the Second World War provided a substantial vindication of most of Chamberlain's strategy: rearmament, particularly in the air; a deemphasizing of the ground war component of British forces; and respect for the economic health that was the wellspring of military strength. In the longer term, the Second World War lived up to Beck's and Leeb's fears, and Chamberlain's hopes.

Chamberlain had many faults, both personal and political: vanity, self-absorption, and thin-skinned intolerance of dissent and criticism. But he also bequeathed Britain the means of its survival in 1940: the Spitfire and the radar chain. He explained his actions to Joseph Kennedy in words that Roosevelt would have heartily endorsed: "A democracy will not wake up until the danger is imminent. Leaders have to wait until public opinion is formed and then try to be a little ahead." He had done this, for instance, by introducing conscription in 1939. And he did one other thing: as even Goebbels had foreseen, by trying so hard to avoid a war, Chamberlain made it clear that when war came, there could be no doubt on whom the blame fell. Britain could enter the war united, with the increasing moral and practical support of the United States. Chamberlain himself knew this well: "That consciousness of moral right," he noted, "which it is impossible for the Germans to feel, *must* be a tremendous force on our side."

THE FIRST FEW years of the Second World War went badly, even disastrously, for the Allies. Apart from the successful air defense in the Battle of Britain in the summer and fall of 1940—in which Mitchell's Spitfire and Hugh Dowding's sophisticated air defense system saved the country and much else—Britain experienced nothing but defeat, often crushing and humiliating defeat, until it routed Erwin Rommel's Afrika Korps at the Battle of El Alamein in October 1942. The United States and the Soviet Union also began their wars with defeats. It was well into 1943 before the Allies could look with confidence toward a likely victory.

But something important had changed since the mid-1930s. Then, it had seemed to many that democracy had no answer to the new cult of the dictators: democracy was too slow and inefficient to handle modern problems like the crisis of the Great Depression. The Depression had also discredited liberal internationalism and ushered in a world in which an increasing number of people thought the solutions to their problems could only be national, a matter of closing themselves off from the rest of the world, whether in trade or migration flows. The racism and nationalism that so profoundly shaped politics in that time also gave anti-internationalism a powerful boost.

It is easier to see now that some fundamental trends in the world were starting to work against the drift away from democracy. The growing worldwide trend toward individualism and consumerism and the breakdown of deference to authority spelled trouble for every kind of dictatorship. Even Hitler had problems with it. The Cold War Communist dictators of eastern Europe would have even more, and it would ultimately bring them down, while also complicating life for democratic leaders. But in the shorter term, it was necessary for the democracies to thread a very delicate needle: to overcome individualism sufficiently to mobilize for war against the totalitarian dictatorships without themselves becoming garrison states. It was the historical service of Churchill and Roosevelt that they saw how to do this. But it is important to understand that both of them had to work out their programs as acts of improvisation, dealing with vast new circumstances—modern total war, the threat of totalitarian regimes, a new kind of mass democracy, the trend toward individualism—while trying to survive in the day-to-day competition of regular politics.

The recipes these two leaders arrived at were remarkably similar. A central component of them was the "Christian-totalitarian dichotomy," which began appearing in Roosevelt's speeches in 1939. Churchill, too, used this kind of language. In his famous "Finest Hour" speech of June 18, 1940, Churchill insisted that the looming Battle of Britain would be a battle for "the survival of Christian civilization." If Britain won this battle, then "all Europe may be free and the life of the world may move forward into broad, sunlit uplands." If it lost, "then the whole world, including the United States, including all that we have known and cared for, will sink into the abyss of a new Dark Age made more sinister, and perhaps more protracted, by the lights of perverted science."

In his January 6, 1941, State of the Union address, sounding as if he were already at war, Roosevelt reminded Americans that they could not "fight by armaments alone" without a solid understanding of the way of life they were defending. "In the future days which we want to make secure," he said, "we look forward to a world founded upon four essential human freedoms." These were "freedom of speech and expression," "freedom of every person to worship God in his own way," "freedom from want," and "freedom from fear." All these freedoms, said Roosevelt, were to apply "everywhere in the world." And "that kind of world," he added, "is the very antithesis of the so-called new order of tyranny which the dictators seek to create with the crash of a bomb."

Here was the democratic response to the Nazi menace. It had taken time to get there. There was nothing inevitable about the process: with different leaders, or with chancy political, technological, or military events going a different way, it might not have come at all. But it had come nonetheless.

"The End of the Beginning"

The hard-bitten German immigrant arrives in Missouri. "Unpleasant conditions in the homeland," he recalls later, "and, I would like to say, an in-born ambition, had driven me across the ocean to the United States, where the conditions for the advancement of an ambitious young man were in those days far better and more favorable than they are today." Although he is dubbed a "greenhorn," a rookie in the wide-open spaces of the new continent, he quickly proves his skill with both rifle and horse, and is taken on by surveyors to venture out into the wilds beyond what is then the frontier town of St. Louis. There he gets to know the Native Americans, particularly one Winnetou, the "great chief of the Apaches." He becomes very close to this noble chief, "the best, most loyal, and most self-sacrificing of all my friends, a true example of the race from which he came."

But in his years in America, he is a witness to the genocidal brutality that the European newcomers mete out to Winnetou's people, as the new United States stretches out across the American continent. "It is a cruel law," he says, "that the weaker must give way to the stronger." There is no doubt that the land had belonged to the native peoples, but "it was taken from them." And "everyone who has read the history of the 'famous' Conquistadores knows what streams of blood thereby flowed, and what cruelties occurred." The settlers of North America, he continues, have merely followed the Conquistadores' example. "The white man came with sweet words on his lips, but at the same time with a sharp knife in his belt and a loaded rifle in his hand." Sometimes he "bought" the land from its inhabitants, but either didn't pay at all or paid with "worthless exchange goods." He administered "the creeping poison of firewater," along with diseases, such as smallpox, that could depopulate entire villages. There is no doubt about it. Winnetou's people are dying out.

The hard-bitten immigrant is called Old Shatterhand. He is the hero of one of the best-selling series of novels ever written in German, by the convict-turned-writer Karl May. When he publishes these stories in 1893, May has never seen the North American continent. But this doesn't keep his stories from achieving a phenomenal popularity that they will still enjoy many decades later. Young Germans of Adolf Hitler's generation are entranced by May's tales. Later, Hitler will recall that when he first encountered the writings of Karl May, "I was overwhelmed! I threw myself into him immediately which resulted in a noticeable decline in my grades." As supreme commander of Germany's armies, he urges his generals to pay attention to the resourceful combat tactics that Winnetou deploys— particularly when he is arguing with them about the plans for Case Yellow—and makes sure a special edition of May's works is published for soldiers at the front. Among his own prized possessions is a complete set of May's writings in an expensive vellum edition. The books show a good deal of wear, and at least a few are always by his bedside. When the news from the front lines is mostly bad, Hitler's friend and architect, Albert Speer, finds that Hitler turns to May's writings to restore his courage—"like the Bible for elderly people."

It is through Old Shatterhand's eyes that Hitler first sees the United States. Physically, he will never follow in Old Shatterhand's footsteps. But he can echo the German pioneer's reflections on America. Three hundred years ago, Hitler tells crowds in 1927, New York was just a fishing village. Then "more and more people moved west and took possession of a new world." This process did not happen "through peaceful discussion," but rather, with the use of "firearms and not least of fire water." Through Old Shatterhand, Hitler has learned something about how Lebensraum can be conquered with genocide. It is not for nothing that in 1940 and 1941, as he sets out to conquer eastern Europe, he travels on a train called "Amerika."

But Hitler doesn't see just Old Shatterhand's America, either. Hitler understands, sometimes fearfully, the modernity and power of America in his own time. In 1939, he watches a film of New York City taken from the air. As press chief Otto Dietrich will remember, he is both impressed and intimidated by the city's "enormous vitality and powerful progressive impulses." He wants to develop Hamburg, Germany's port to the world, so that it projects the same spirit. He plans to build the largest suspension bridge in the world there, accompanied by huge skyscrapers, including one inspired by New York's Chrysler Building. He admires Henry Ford not just for the carmaker's virulent antisemitism, but also for his innovations in production and wage policy.

America serves Hitler as a model, a stimulus, a warning. He doesn't want America as an enemy. But in 1940 and 1941, he knows with ever greater certainty that this is the predicament he faces: the struggle between his nationalist, imperialist autarky and American democratic capitalism is coming to a head.

FOR A FEW weeks from mid-June to mid-July 1940, after the fall of France and before the Battle of Britain, Hitler thought his war was definitively over. On June 15, two days before France called for an armistice, he ordered the reduction of his army from 155 divisions to 120. "The enemy's imminent collapse," he explained to Halder, meant that "the army's task is complete and we can carry out the restructuring of enemy countries into the basis of the new peacetime order at our leisure." Hitler thought the air force and the navy could carry on the war against Britain "by themselves." The soldiers of 35 divisions, a very major force, could simply be sent home.

But six weeks later, Hitler changed course and ordered planning to begin for a massive invasion of the Soviet Union. Clearly something important had happened around the middle of July.

On July 19, Hitler called the Reichstag into session to expound on the recent victories. As always in his major speeches, he reached back and gave a narrative of recent history, starting with the injustices of the Treaty of Versailles and the democratic, liberal order the Allies had sought to establish after the First World War. (Hitler called it the

"Jewish-capitalist chains of a pluto-democratic thin class of exploiters.") He complained that in the First World War, Germany had been "very terribly led," unlike now. He announced a long list of promotions for senior officers and concluded with what he called "an appeal to reason" for Britain to give up and end the war.

On the same day, in what was finally an un-sphinxlike move, Franklin Delano Roosevelt spoke by radio to the Democratic National Convention in Chicago to accept the party's nomination for a third term as president.

"The fact which dominates our world is the fact of armed aggression," he said in an unusually blunt summation of the international situation. The war that had developed in Europe, claiming France and leaving Britain alone to face the Nazis, was "not an ordinary war." It was "a revolution imposed by force of arms," which "proposes not to set men free but to reduce them to slavery." The defense against the Nazi menace was a twofold task. "One must be accomplished, if it becomes necessary, by the armed defense forces of the nation." The other task was one he had touched on in earlier speeches, and which had been the foundation of the New Deal since 1933. It was "to make our federal and state and local governments responsive to the growing requirements of modern democracy." This meant equalizing the distribution of wealth and liberalizing and broadening "the control of vast industries." He tarred his isolationist opponents with the brush of appeasement: "If our Government should pass to other hands next January . . . we can merely hope and pray that they will not substitute appeasement and compromise with those who seek to destroy all democracies everywhere, including here." In a tone similar to Churchill's "Finest Hour" speech, Roosevelt claimed that the stakes of the war were "the continuance of civilization as we know it versus the ultimate destruction of all that we have held dear—religion against godlessness; the ideal of justice against the practice of force; moral decency versus the firing squad; courage to speak out, and to act, versus the false lullaby of appeasement."

Roosevelt's speech was taken very seriously in Germany. The Nazi regime heard it as virtually a declaration of war. In fact, the Germans seemed much surer of Roosevelt's enmity than he probably was himself. The former German ambassador to the United States, Hans-Heinrich

316 THE NAZI MENACE

Dieckhoff, described Roosevelt's speech as an expression of "fanatical hatred" in which "the president declares the totalitarian countries to be the enemy and stigmatizes not only their domestic conditions, but above all the dangers of an external expansion of their ideologies ... Although he does not mention any nation by name, it is plain that he is aiming at Germany, Italy, Japan, and also Soviet Russia ... Never has Roosevelt's complicity in the outbreak and the prolongation of this war come out so clearly as in the speech ... The speech shows how clearly we have always judged Roosevelt." Dieckhoff thought that Roosevelt's rejection of National Socialism was rooted in the "English ideological" and "New York Jewish climate."

The Italian foreign minister, Count Ciano, had just arrived that day in Berlin. Meeting with Ribbentrop before Hitler's "Appeal to Reason" speech, Ciano formed the impression that the Germans were "hoping and praying that [Hitler's] appeal [to the British] will not be rejected." Ciano was then a witness to the "unconcealed disappointment" when late that same evening, the "first cold English reactions" to Hitler's speech were broadcast.

More was coming. Churchill adroitly assigned Lord Halifax, still serving as foreign secretary, the task of responding to Hitler. In a speech on July 22, Halifax referred specifically to Roosevelt's address of three days before: the British picture of a free Europe had been "drawn once again in bold outline by the President of the United States." The churchgoing Halifax devoted much of his speech to outlining the Christian-totalitarian dichotomy. Hitler was nothing less than the Antichrist, "which it is our duty as Christians to fight with all our power." Here again he drew in the Americans, "that great people" who "pray for our victory over this wicked man" because "the foundations of their country, as of ours, have been Christian teaching and belief in God."

Hitler now found himself confronted both with unexpectedly tough British resistance and increasing American enmity. These facts explain what he did next and why he did it.

On July 21, 1940, Hitler met with his top commanders and told them to "take up the Russian problem." The United States was also on Hitler's mind—as an enemy. "America can supply England and Russia," he told his commanders. This seems more than a little puzzling. The United

States and the Soviet Union were officially neutrals after all, the latter virtually a German ally. Hitler's air assault on Britain, a necessary warm-up to invading the island, would not even fully begin for a few more weeks. But Hitler's thoughts were already turning toward the Soviet Union and the United States. The reason has to do with the essence of Nazism and of its assault on the world of the mid-twentieth century.

On July 13, Franz Halder had briefed Hitler on the current invasion plans for Great Britain. Hitler explained that he was most concerned with the question of why Britain refused to seek peace. He thought the British were holding out hope that the Soviet Union might yet switch sides and replace France as Britain's powerful continental ally. Hitler also worried that a direct military defeat of Britain would not do the Germans any good, because the British empire could never fall into German hands. A crushing British defeat would only strengthen the United States and Japan. A week later, Hitler told Walther von Brauchitsch that Britain was hoping for a "turnaround in America." So Hitler ordered the commander in chief of his army to start thinking about an attack on the Soviet Union, to knock out Britain's last hope and to make Germany strong enough to resist any attack from America.

On July 31, Hitler met with his top military commanders again at the Berghof and once again made these points about Britain, the United States, and the Soviet Union. His conclusion was clear: "Russia must be taken care of. Spring 1941."

Back in January 1939, several things had come together in Hitler's mind: the rage he felt over Ickes's and Roosevelt's biting criticisms, his frustration with the Munich settlement, his enduring fixation on Churchill, and the murderous antisemitism that caused him to link Anglo-American democracy with Soviet communism. The result was his "prophecy" about how a world war of Germany against finance capital *and* communism would bring the annihilation of the Jews. A year and a half later, the process repeated itself. Confronting British and American hostility, Hitler concluded that the path to defeating the democracies ran through crushing the Soviet Union.

The invasion that would come to be known as Operation Barbarossa began on June 22, 1941. It was the largest military operation in human history, with more than three million soldiers in the invasion force. It was also the largest criminal action in human history. The planning became increasingly barbaric as it developed. The Germans looked to occupy the Baltic states, Byelorussia, Ukraine, and European Russia, driving out most of the inhabitants except those "needed" for slave labor, and starving the rest. The plans, in fact, called explicitly for starving people to death by the tens of millions. Infamous orders—the "Barbarossa Decree," the "Commissar Order"—made it clear that German soldiers and police forces would violate every possible norm of civilized conduct in their genocidal treatment of Soviet civilians and soldiers alike. Millions of Soviet prisoners of war would die in German captivity, mostly from starvation. What we know today as the Holocaust developed in step with these other forms of barbarity.

JUST WEEKS AFTER German tanks rolled into the Soviet Union, Roosevelt and Churchill met in person for the first time (at least since 1918, a meeting that had irritated Roosevelt and that Churchill did not remember), at Placentia Bay, off the coast of Newfoundland. The main product of their meeting was the Atlantic Charter, a plan for a liberal, democratic, and peaceful world to follow what the Charter bluntly called the "final destruction of Nazi tyranny."

As with so much else in the story of how the democracies responded to the Nazi menace, little about the Atlantic Charter was planned or clearly thought through. Roosevelt and Undersecretary of State Sumner Welles thought it would be important to cap the meeting with a statement of principles. Revealingly, they were worried that the British might formally recognize the Soviet gains from the Molotov-Ribbentrop Pact in order to preserve their one effective ally. But the Americans were astute enough to realize that the kind of statement they wanted would be a challenge to the British Empire, and so it would be tactically wise to get the British to write the first draft. Sumner Welles's British counterpart, Alexander Cadogan, took care of this task. Later in the war, Churchill and Roosevelt would distance themselves from the Charter, oddly pointing out that they had never actually signed it. And yet the Charter they cobbled together became one of the founding documents of the postwar democratic world order.

The Atlantic Charter turned Roosevelt's "four freedoms" into alliance policy. In it, the two leaders spoke of "the right of all peoples to choose the form of government under which they will live," "freedom from fear and want," and an international "system of general security." They vowed to work toward "economic advancement" and "social security." Early in 1942, Britain, the United States, the Soviet Union, and twenty-five other states signed a declaration calling themselves the United Nations—Roosevelt came up with the term as Churchill was visiting the White House at the end of 1941—and expressly adopting the Atlantic Charter as their statement of policy. The victory of the United Nations over the Axis would grant a liberal democratic international order its second chance, after the first chance had failed so dismally in the crisis of the 1930s. The Atlantic Charter thus became the founding document of the world organization that, in the twenty-first century, is still called the United Nations.

We should not let lofty sentiments blind us to uglier realities. Much of what Roosevelt and Churchill proclaimed at Placentia Bay was shadowed by hypocrisy. Churchill presided over an empire that denied freedom, and sometimes meted out brutal treatment, to many of its African and Asian subjects. He accepted the Charter only because Britain's weakness obliged him to follow the American lead. Roosevelt, for his part, forced the Charter on the British because he feared that leaving them and the Soviets to formulate war aims would only lead to a replay of the secret treaties and shady dealings of the First World War. Roosevelt's own record was far from unblemished. New Deal legislation had always depended on the votes of Southern segregationists, and during the war he was willing to make only the most halting steps toward equal treatment for African Americans. He also became steadily less interested in helping European refugees, including Jews, as the war advanced.

But proclaiming a noble goal often has unintended effects. Once the principle has been released, it cannot be contained. That Thomas Jefferson owned slaves has not kept his "inalienable rights" of "life, liberty and the pursuit of happiness" from inspiring every American movement for greater freedom and human rights. The Atlantic Charter was like this, too. More than half a century after its drafting, Nelson Mandela wrote that the Charter "reaffirmed faith in the dignity of each human being and propagated a host of democratic principles." The Charter and the Allies' fight "against tyranny and oppression," he said, had been an inspiration for the African National Congress and for all Africans seeking freedom. The point was just as clear to British imperialists worried about India. "We shall no doubt pay dearly in the end for all this fluffy flapdoodle" was Leo Amery's gloomy reaction to the Atlantic Charter. Amery was by then secretary of state for India in Churchill's cabinet. The "fluffy flapdoodle" was all that talk about "peoples choosing their own form of government."

Certainly, the dictators were in no doubt about what the Atlantic Charter's principles meant for them. When British foreign secretary Anthony Eden met Stalin in early December 1941, he told the Soviet leader that recognizing his gains from the Molotov-Ribbentrop Pact would violate the Charter's principles. Stalin replied angrily, "I thought the Atlantic Charter was directed against those people who were trying to establish world domination. It now looks as if the charter was directed against the USSR."

But the most fateful reaction came from Hitler.

Hitler's Luftwaffe adjutant Nicolaus von Below remembered that Hitler "flew into a passion of rage" when he heard about the Charter, and "was particularly upset by point six which promised 'the final destruction of the Nazi tyranny.'" But through his rage, Hitler also recognized that the democracies had come up with some dangerous propaganda. On August 18, four days after the Charter had been made public, Goebbels flew to Hitler's East Prussian headquarters and found the Führer ill and suffering from nervous strain. Hitler told Goebbels that it was only because of the rising tide of antisemitism in Europe that they had been able to dispose of the "dangerous dynamite" of the Atlantic Charter so easily. This linking of antisemitism and the Charter was an important clue to Hitler's thinking.

In mid-August 1941, the invasion of the Soviet Union was still going well, if already not quite as well as Hitler and his commanders had expected. Nonetheless, Hitler looked optimistically to a future in which the Soviet Union would be beaten and the British would come to their senses, get rid of Churchill, and finally, in a burst of passionate anti-Americanism, join him for a war against the United States. Then, on August 14, British deputy prime minister Clement Attlee read the Atlantic Charter over the airwaves. With one blow, Hitler's strategy had fallen apart. The point of invading the Soviet Union had been to remove Britain's last ally. Now Britain seemed firmly allied to the United States. This also meant that the British would never join him in a struggle with the New World for global supremacy.

Back in 1939, Hitler had issued his "prophecy" that the coming of a world war against both the democracies and the Soviets would bring "the annihilation of the Jewish race in Europe." And so it was no coincidence that in the wake of the Atlantic Charter, the Nazi regime began to move toward genocide. In their conversation about the Atlantic Charter on August 18, Hitler and Goebbels decided that from then on, German Jews would have to wear a yellow star conspicuously on their clothing. A steady drip of heightened persecution followed. The most alarming came at the end of October: a decree from Heinrich Himmler blocking most Jews from emigrating from any territory controlled by Germany. It is hard to imagine any reason for this decree that doesn't reflect a plan to murder the Jews who were now trapped in Hitler's Europe.

IT WAS WITH the Atlantic Charter that the democracies most clearly set out the goals they were pursuing. It was with Operation Barbarossa and the Holocaust that the Nazi regime became most fully itself. Violently extreme nationalism, antisemitism and other forms of racism, the desire to build an autarkic Germany as a shield against the liberal democratic world and against Soviet communism—these things had always been at the heart of the Nazi program. Hitler had explained his goals many times, not least at the Hossbach Conference and in his "prophecy" speech. Yet these goals also evolved. That evolution took place in the course of years of confrontation with the democracies—where, in turn, a very different vision grew out of the experience of confronting Nazism. In 1941, the two visions were fully formed. Operation Barbarossa, the Holocaust, and the Atlantic Charter were their expressions.

The democracies (and their unlikely ally, Stalin) were then still a long way from victory. Millions would have to suffer and die before, as Churchill put it, "every trace of Hitler's footsteps, every stain of his infected, corroding fingers" would be "sponged and purged and, if need be, blasted from the surface of the earth." But there had been a decisive change since the dark years of 1937 and 1938. Churchill and Roosevelt knew what they were fighting for. They could spell out a vision of a future world, the world after victory, that their people found compelling. In time, it would happen. So, if not yet the end, 1941 was, to quote Churchill once again, at least "the end of the beginning."

NOTES

PREFACE: THE CRISIS OF DEMOCRACY

4   **many fine scholars have done before:** Piers Brendon, *The Dark Valley: A Panorama of the 1930s* (New York: Vintage, 2000); Donald Cameron Watt, *How War Came: The Immediate Origins of the Second World War* (London: Heinemann, 1989); Richard Overy, *The Twilight Years: The Paradox of Britain Between the Wars* (New York: Penguin Books, 2009), to give just a few examples.

1. REICH CHANCELLERY, EARLY EVENING

9   **He is nervous:** Joachim Fest, *Plotting Hitler's Death: The Story of the German Resistance* (New York: Metropolitan Books, 1997), 36–38; Kirstin A. Schäfer, *Werner von Blomberg—Hitlers erster Feldmarschall: Eine Biographie* (Paderborn: Schöningh, 2006), 104.

9   **His new war minister:** Andreas Wirsching, "'Man kann nur Boden germanisieren'. Eine neue Quelle zu Hitlers Rede vor den Spitzen der Reichswehr am 3. Februar 1933," *Vierteljahrshefte für Zeitgeschichte* 49, no. 3 (July 2001): 540–42, 545; Fest, *Plotting Hitler's Death*, 36–38.

10   **He starts with a message:** Wirsching, "Boden," 545–48.

11   **This last is the part:** Wirsching, "Boden," 523–24, 542–45.

11   **A few years later:** Nicholas Reynolds, *Treason Was No Crime: Ludwig Beck, Chief of the German General Staff* (London: William Kimber, 1976), 83.

11   **"talking to the wall":** Schäfer, *Blomberg*, 104.

12   **"He'll get a few surprises":** Wirsching, "Boden," 349.

12   **On Friday, November 5:** Weather maps and forecasts, *Berliner Tageblatt*, November 4, November 5, November 6, 1937.

12   **The Führer and chancellor:** "Hossbach Memorandum," doc. 503, in J. Noakes and G. Pridham, *Nazism 1919–1945,* vol. 3, *Foreign Policy, War and Racial Extermination: A Documentary Reader* (Exeter, UK: University of Exeter Press, 2001), 70–72.

13   **When the meeting convened:** Friedrich Hossbach, *Zwischen Wehrmacht und Hitler: 1934–1938,* 2nd ed. (Göttingen: Vandenhoeck und Ruprecht, 1965), 9.

13   **A fellow officer:** Karl-Heinz Janssen and Fritz Tobias, *Der Sturz der Generäle: Hitler und die Blomberg-Fritsch Krise 1938* (Munich: C. H. Beck, 1994) 12; Hossbach, *Zwischen Wehrmacht und Hitler,* 9.

13   **But Hossbach was equally blunt:** Hossbach, *Zwischen Wehrmacht und Hitler,* 9, 21–22, 33–34.

14   **Hossbach thought Hitler would listen to advice:** Hossbach, *Zwischen Wehrmacht und Hitler,* 32.

14   **But Hossbach was coming to realize:** Hossbach, *Zwischen Wehrmacht und Hitler,* 22, 31.

15   **"For him, desks":** Baldur von Schirach, quoted in Stephen Kotkin, *Stalin: Waiting for Hitler, 1929–1941* (New York: Penguin Press, 2017), 586.

15   **Hitler "disliked reading files":** Fritz Wiedemann, *Der Mann, der Feldherr werden wollte* (Velbert: Blick und Bild Verlag, 1964), 69.

15   **Hitler imposed his own rhythms:** Hossbach, *Zwischen Wehrmacht und Hitler,* 17–18, 32, 43.

15   **Yet, with stunning speed:** Benjamin Carter Hett, *The Death of Democracy: Hitler's Rise to Power and the Downfall of the Weimar Republic* (New York: Henry Holt, 2018).

16   **The pace of the German arms buildup quickened:** Adam Tooze, *The Wages of Destruction: The Making and Breaking of the Nazi Economy* (New York: Penguin Books, 2007), 37, 219–37.

17   **The nub of the crisis:** Tooze, *Wages of Destruction,* 236–38.

18   **But Hitler was in a hurry:** John Lukacs, *The Duel: The Eighty-Day Struggle Between Churchill and Hitler* (New Haven, CT: Yale University Press, 2001), 17; Ian Kershaw, *Hitler, 1936–1945: Nemesis* (New York: W. W. Norton, 2000), 83–84.

18   **From the moment Hitler entered:** Hossbach Memorandum, Noakes and Pridham, *Nazism,* 73.

18   **"The German racial community":** Hossbach Memorandum, Noakes and Pridham, *Nazism,* 73.

19   **Blomberg, fifty-nine years old:** Harold C. Deutsch, *Hitler and His Generals: The Hidden Crisis, January to June, 1938* (Minneapolis: University of Minnesota Press, 1974), 8–9; Schäfer, *Blomberg.*

19   **Werner von Fritsch was as different:** Johann Adolf Graf von Kielmannsegg, *Der Fritschprozess 1938: Ablauf und Hintergründe* (Hamburg: Hoffmann und Campe, 1949), 15–26; Fritsch, Memo, February 1, 1938, BA-MA, N24/29, *Nachlass Hossbach.*

20   **From their beginnings in the 1920s:** Hett, *Death of Democracy,* 109–11.

20   **Hitler expressed grave doubts:** Hossbach Memorandum, Noakes and Pridham, *Nazism*, 74.

21   **"two hate-filled antagonists":** Hossbach Memorandum, Noakes and Pridham, *Nazism*, 75.

22   **solved only by "force":** Hossbach Memorandum, Noakes and Pridham, *Nazism*, 76–77.

22   **the British had already written off Czechoslovakia:** Hossbach Memorandum, Noakes and Pridham, *Nazism*, 78–79.

22   **Blomberg and Fritsch protested:** Hossbach, *Zwischen Wehrmacht und Hitler*, 188.

22   **Foreign Minister Neurath protested:** Hossbach, *Zwischen Wehrmacht und Hitler*, 189.

23   **In later years:** Hossbach quoted in Kielmannsegg, *Fritzschprozess*, 33; Friedrich Hossbach, "Ein Beitrag zur Wahrheit," September 23, 1946, BA-MA N24/273, *Nachlass Hossbach*.

23   **Hossbach also remembered:** Hossbach, *Zwischen Wehrmacht und Hitler*, 120.

23   **But Hossbach remembered the expression:** Hossbach, *Zwischen Wehrmacht und Hitler*, 119–20.

23   **Everything was different now:** Both Raeder and Blomberg said after the war that they had *not* taken Hitler's words seriously on November 5, either (see Kershaw, *Hitler, 1936–1945: Nemesis*, 861n282), but this was at a time when they faced actual or possible prosecution for conspiring in plans for a war of aggression, and they had every interest in downplaying the meeting. The contemporary evidence from late 1937 reveals genuine surprise and alarm on the part of many senior military commanders at what Hitler was saying.

24   **"Again and again":** Kielmannsegg, *Fritschprozess*, 34.

24   **Fritsch repeated to Hitler:** Hermann Gakenholz, "Reichskanzlei 5. November 1937," in Richard Dietrich and Gerhard Oestreich, *Forschungen zu Staat und Verfassung. Festgabe für Fritz Hartung* (Berlin: Duncker & Humbolt, 1958), 471ff.

24   **"fine, clever countenance":** Ernst von Weizsäcker, *Erinnerungen* (Munich: Paul List Verlag, 1950), 172.

25   **after becoming chief of staff:** Beck's position was originally called head of the Truppenamt, or "Troop Office," as the Versailles Treaty forbade the creation of a German general staff, and thus of a "chief of the general staff." His position was renamed in 1935 to reflect its real nature. Ernest R. May, *Strange Victory: Hitler's Conquest of France* (New York: Hill and Wang, 2000), 33–34.

25   **war was a last resort:** "Die Lehre vom totalen Kriege," in Ludwig Beck, *Studien*, ed. Hans Speidel (Stuttgart: K. F. Koehler, 1955), 258.

25   **a "devastating" effect:** Hossbach, *Zwischen Wehrmacht und Hitler*, 191.

25   **Major changes to Europe's human geography:** Klaus-Jürgen Müller, *General Ludwig Beck: Studien und Dokumente* (Boppard am Rhein: Harold Boldt Verlag, 1980), 499 (hereafter cited as Müller, *Beck Dokumente*).

25   **With even more contempt:** Müller, *Beck Dokumente*, 501.

25   **as Beck wrote:** Müller, *Beck Dokumente*, 500.

25   **The French intelligence service:** François-Poncet to Delbos, November 6, 1937, *Documents Diplomatiques Français*, 2. Serie, Tome 7, 343–44; Paul Paillole, *Notre espion chez Hitler* (Paris: Éditions Robert Laffont, 1985), 107–9.

26   **Hitler's response:** Hossbach, *Zwischen Wehrmacht und Hitler*, 191. In German practice, initials do not necessarily indicate approval, but presumably Blomberg would have commented on any errors he had noticed.

2. THE MEANING OF GLEIWITZ

27   **Franz Bernheim lives in:** Philipp Graf, *Die Bernheim-Petition 1933: Jüdische Politik in der Zwischenkriegszeit* (Göttingen: Vandenhoeck und Ruprecht, 2008), 10–12, 133; Bernheim Petition to the League of Nations, *American Jewish Year Book*, 1933–34), 78.

28   **The Western democracies:** Graf, *Bernheim Petition*, 34; Mark Mazower, *Dark Continent: Europe's Twentieth Century* (New York: Vintage Books, 2000), 41–42.

28   **The Polish Minority Treaty:** *Minorities Treaty Between the Principal Allied Powers and Poland, 1919*, in Clive Parry, ed., *The Consolidated Treaty Series* (Dobbs Ferry, New York: Oceana Publications, 1969), vol. 225, 412–24; Mark Mazower, "The Strange Triumph of Human Rights, 1933–1950," *Historical Journal* 47, no. 2 (2004): 382.

29   **The victors had no intention:** Mazower, "Strange Triumph of Human Rights," 382; Margaret MacMillan, *Paris 1919: Six Months That Changed the World* (New York: Random House, 2001), chap. 23, "Japan and Racial Equality."

29   **There is also a strong dose:** Graf, *Bernheim Petition*, 43–44.

29   **Remarkably, there is no minority treaty:** Graf, *Bernheim Petition*, 11; "Bernheim Petition to the League of Nations," *Jewish Yearbook* 1933, 74.

30   **In June 1933:** "Bernheim Petition to the League of Nations," *Jewish Yearbook* 1933, 74, 82–83; "Minority and Refugee Questions Before the League of Nations," *Jewish Yearbook* 1934–1935, 89.

30   **From 1933 to 1937:** Graf, *Bernheim Petition*, 245.

31   **The word could mean a lot:** Mazower, *Dark Continent*, 100; Michael Bess, "Wide World of Racisms," in *Choices Under Fire: Moral Dimensions of World War II* (New York: Vintage Books, 2006), 21–41.

32   **Benito Mussolini:** Quoted in Winston Churchill, *The Gathering Storm* (Boston: Houghton Mifflin, 1948), 305–6.

32   **The 1921 census:** Elisabeth Bakke, "The Making of Czechoslavakism in the First Czechoslovak Republic," in Martin Schulze Wessel: *Loyalitäten in der Tschechoslowakischen Republik 1918–1938. Politische, nationale und kulturelle Zugehörigkeiten* (Munich: R. Oldenbourg Verlag, 2004), 24n3.

32   **In Czechoslovakia:** Karl Bosl, ed., *Die erste Tschechoslowakische Republik als multinationaler Parteienstaat: Vorträge d. Tagungen d. Collegium*

Carolinum in Bad Wiessee vom 24.–27. November 1977 u. vom 20.–23. April 1978 (Munich: Oldenbourg, 1979).

32   **Many political thinkers:** Mazower, *Dark Continent*, 57.

33   **Orthodox economics taught:** Robert O. Paxton and Julie Hessler, *Europe in the Twentieth Century*, 5th ed. (Boston: Cengage Learning, 2011), 266.

33   **economic policies that move *away*:** Paxton and Hessler, *Europe in the Twentieth Century*, 273.

33   **The weakness of the Western democracies:** Paxton and Hessler, *Europe in the Twentieth Century*, 301.

34   **"So long as these people imagine":** Mazower, *Dark Continent*, 55.

34   **a characteristic British attitude:** "Collective Neutrality," *The Times*, August 10, 1936.

35   **Colonel Hossbach would observe:** Hossbach, *Zwischen Wehrmacht und Hitler*, 89.

35   **"zoological anarchist":** Timothy Snyder, *Black Earth: The Holocaust as History and Warning* (New York: Tim Duggan Books, 2015), 241.

35   **"It should never":** Quoted in Mazower, "Strange Triumph of Human Rights," 384.

36   **"Everything that I undertake":** Hitler to Carl Burckhardt, August 11, 1939, quoted in in Kershaw, *Hitler: 1936–1945: Nemesis*, 898n118. Kershaw expresses skepticism about the quote's authenticity, although it is consistent with many similar statements by Hitler.

3. "IN THE CIRCLE OF GUILT"

37   **an unlikely army officer:** Shimon Naveh, "Tukhachevsky," in Harold Shukman, ed., *Stalin's Generals* (New York: Grove Press, 1993), 258.

37   **But when his family falls on hard times:** Naveh, "Tukhachevsky," 259; John Erickson, *The Soviet High Command: A Military-Political History, 1918–1941* (London: Frank Cass, 2001), 55–56.

37   **In the nearly three years:** Naveh, "Tukhachevsky," 259–62.

38   **Tukhachevsky's rise continues:** David R. Stone, "Tukhachevsky in Leningrad: Military Politics and Exile, 1928–1931," *Europe-Asia Studies* 48, no. 8 (December, 1996): 1372.

38   **One of Tukhachevsky's good connections:** Naveh, "Tukhachevsky," 262–63.

38   **Tukhachevsky lives well:** Yuri Slezkine, *The House of Government: A Saga of the Russian Revolution* (Princeton, NJ: Princeton University Press, 2017), 318; Kotkin, *Stalin: Waiting for Hitler*, 412.

38   **a powerful presence:** Simon Sebag Montefiore, *Stalin: The Court of the Red Tsar* (New York: Alfred A. Knopf, 2004), 221–22; Erickson, *Soviet High Command*, 72.

38   **Tukhachevsky is ruthless:** Richard Pipes, *A Concise History of the Russian Revolution* (New York: Vintage Books, 1996), 349–50; Stone, "Tukhachevsky in Leningrad," 1366; Montefiore, *Stalin*, 222.

39   **His original mind:** Naveh, "Tukhachevsky," 265–66.

39   **an avid reader of Machiavelli:** Kotkin, *Stalin: Waiting for Hitler*, 428, 493; Robert C. Tucker, *Stalin in Power: The Revolution from Above, 1928–1941* (New York: W. W. Norton, 1990), 379.

39   **one of Stalin's spectacular "show trials":** Igor Lukes, "Stalin, Benesch und der Fall Tuchatschewski," *Vierteljahrshefte für Zeitgeschichte* 44, no 4 (October 1996): 530–32.

39   **Stalin and his spy agency:** Lukes, "Stalin, Benesch," 531–53; Tucker, *Stalin in Power*, 383; Nikolai Abramov, "The New Version of the 'Tukhachevsky Affair,'" *New Times* 13 (March 23–April 3, 1989): 36–39; Coulondre to Delbos, June 28, 1937, *Documents Diplomatiques Français*, 2. Serie, Tome 6, 225–28.

39   **Rumors have been going around:** Tucker, *Stalin in Power*, 432–33.

40   **the Politburo orders Tukhachevsky's demotion:** Robert Conquest, *Stalin: Breaker of Nations* (New York: Penguin, 1992), 200; Kotkin, *Stalin: Waiting for Hitler*, 411; Abramov, "New Version of the 'Tukhachevsky Affair,'" 36–39.

40   **"Among the rulers of our time":** Conquest, *Stalin*, 183; Robert Conquest, *The Great Terror: A Reassessment* (New York: Oxford University Press, 1990), 64. Interestingly Stalin's most recent biographer, Stephen Kotkin, makes something close to the opposite point, stressing Stalin's volubility. Kotkin, *Stalin: Waiting for Hitler*.

40   **He liked to foster:** Conquest, *Stalin*, 129; Conquest, *Terror*, 56, citing Nikita Khrushchev's memoirs.

41   **Stalin read voraciously:** Kotkin, *Stalin: Waiting for Hitler*, 1–2, 417, 839.

41   **approximately 5.5 million:** Timothy Snyder, *Bloodlands: Europe Between Hitler and Stalin* (New York: Basic Books, 2010), 53.

41   **In December 1934:** There has been a Reichstag fire–like debate over the Kirov assassination. For the more traditional view that Stalin was behind Kirov's murder, see Robert Conquest, *Stalin and the Kirov Murder* (New York: Oxford University Press, 1989). The most recent research suggests that Stalin was not involved: see Matthew E. Lenoe, *The Kirov Murder and Soviet History* (New Haven, CT, and London: Yale University Press, 2010).

41   **"We are a hundred years behind":** Kotkin, *Stalin: Waiting for Hitler*, 74.

42   **Soviet leaders saw themselves:** Silvio Pons, *Stalin and the Inevitable War, 1936–1941* (London: Frank Cass, 2002), xi–xii.

42   **This fear could easily slide:** Snyder, *Bloodlands*, 111, 96, 470n37; Terry Martin, "The Origins of Soviet Ethnic Cleansing," *Journal of Modern History* 70, no. 4 (December 1998): 813–61.

42   **A Nazi diplomat:** Conquest, *Stalin*, 224.

42   **Stalin's notorious chief prosecutor:** Conquest, *Stalin*, 198.

42   **This approach was not very far:** Vassily Grossman, *Life and Fate* (New York: New York Review Books, 2006), 578–79.

42   **There were also some remarkable parallels:** This is the theme of the late Alan Bullock's last great work, *Hitler and Stalin: Parallel Lives* (New York: Vintage, 1993).

42   **In Stalin's case:** Conquest, *Stalin*, 3–4.

43   **"a grey blur"**: Quoted in Stephen Kotkin, *Stalin: Paradoxes of Power 1878–1928* (New York: Penguin Press, 2014), 176.

43   **"the most outstanding mediocrity"**: Conquest, *Terror*, 61.

43   **Winston Churchill called**: Winston Churchill, "The First Month of War," Radio Broadcast, October 1, 1939, in Robert Rhodes James, ed., *Winston S. Churchill: His Complete Speeches 1897–1963*, vol. 6, 1935–1942 (New York and London: Chelsea House Publishers, 1974), 6161.

43   **Its agents, like Nazi agents**: See Christopher Andrew and Vasili Mitrokhin, *The Sword and the Shield: The Mitrokhin Archive and the Secret History of the KGB* (New York: Basic Books, 2001), especially chaps. 3–5.

44   **There was an internal debate**: Pons, *Stalin and the Inevitable War*, 134–45.

44   **Stalin used the threat of war**: Kotkin, *Stalin: Waiting for Hitler*, 376–77, 397, 414–28; Tucker, *Stalin in Power*, 383–84, 434–35.

44   **among the half dozen officers**: Kotkin, *Stalin: Waiting for Hitler*, 412.

44   **This meant torture**: Tucker, *Stalin in Power*, 435.

44   **Stalin addressed the military council**: Kotkin, *Stalin: Waiting for Hitler*, 414–21.

45   **Tukhachevsky and the other officers**: Tucker, *Stalin in Power*, 434–38; Kotkin, *Stalin: Waiting for Hitler*, 423–25.

45   **Tukhachevsky's last words**: Tucker, *Stalin in Power*, 440.

45   **the court sentenced Tukhachevsky**: Conquest, *Stalin*, 201; Abramov, "New Version of the 'Tukhachevsky Affair,'" 36–39.

45   **In early 1937**: Kotkin, *Stalin: Waiting for Hitler*, 378–79.

45   **Hitler followed the fate**: Joseph Goebbels, entry for July 10, 1937, *Die Tagebücher von Joseph Goebbels*, ed. Elke Fröhlich (hereafter cited as *TBJG*), Teil 1, Bd. 4 (Munich: K. G. Saur, 2000), 215.

46   **just one of the developments**: Andreas Krämer, *Hitlers Kriegskurs, Appeasement und die "Maikrise" 1938: Entscheidungsstunde im Vorfeld von "Münchener Abkommen" und zweitem Weltkrieg* (Berlin: Walter de Gruyter, 2014), 31.

46   **In June 1937**: Pons, *Stalin and the Inevitable War*, 82–85.

4. "WE ARE LOOKING FOR A PROGRAM"

47   **He is in his study**: Martin Gilbert, *Winston S. Churchill*, vol. 8, *Never Despair, 1945–1965* (Hillsdale, MI: Hillsdale College Press, 2013), 365.

47   **"formed in the war"**: Actually, its roots were in the years before the First World War. Christopher Andrew, *Defend the Realm: The Authorized History of MI5* (New York: Vintage, 2009), introduction.

47   **Lord Randolph Churchill is startled**: Gilbert, *Never Despair*, 370.

48   **"wars like these"**: Gilbert, *Never Despair*, 371–72.

48   **"all the wealth**: Robert Rhodes James, ed., *Chips: The Diaries of Sir Henry Channon* (London: Weidenfeld and Nicolson, 1967), 129 (hereafter cited as Channon, *Chips*).

48   **the senior privy councilor**: The Privy Council is one of the many archaic survivals within the British constitutional system, a body of about six

hundred persons whose job, theoretically, is to advise the sovereign. Anyone who has held ministerial rank in a British administration automatically becomes a privy councilor for life, and so Churchill held this status from 1908 until his death in 1965. Roy Jenkins, *Churchill: A Biography* (New York: Farrar, Straus and Giroux, 2001), xxi.

48   **Churchill gave a nomination speech:** "Changing Over," *The Times*, June 1, 1937.

49   **Churchill paid full tribute:** Martin Gilbert, *Winston S. Churchill*, vol. 5, Companion Part 3, *The Coming of War, 1936–1939* (Boston: Houghton Mifflin Company, 1983), 685n1.

49   **"an able, fiery speech":** Channon, *Chips*, 129–30.

49   **Churchill expanded on the point:** Gilbert, *Churchill*, Companion Volume V(3), 686–87. The article was written May 28, 1937, though not published in *Collier's* until October 16.

49   **"There is too deep a difference":** Robert Self, *Neville Chamberlain: A Biography* (New York: Routledge, 2006), 121.

50   **Their ideas on how to cope:** Chamberlain to Hilda Chamberlain, March 27, 1938, in Robert Self, ed., *The Neville Chamberlain Diary Letters*, vol. 4, *The Downing Street Years, 1934–1940* (Aldershot, UK: Ashgate, 2005) (hereafter cited as Chamberlain, *Diary Letters*), 311.

50   **Chamberlain was under no illusions:** See Chamberlain to Hilda Chamberlain, July 11, 1936, Chamberlain, *Diary Letters*, 201.

50   **The Conservatives overwhelmingly dominated:** *UK Election Statistics, 1918–2017*, House of Commons Library Briefing Paper no. CBP7529, August 23, 2017, 13.

50   **Chamberlain scoffed:** Chamberlain to Ida, March 3, 1935, Chamberlain, *Diary Letters*, 119; Chamberlain to Ida, March 14, 1936, Chamberlain, *Diary Letters*, 179.

51   **"the narrowest, most ignorant":** John Colville, *The Fringes of Power: Downing Street Diaries, 1939–1955* (London: Weidenfeld and Nicolson, 2004), 352.

53   **Even a year before:** Robert Rhodes James, *Churchill: A Study in Failure, 1900–1939* (London: Weidenfeld & Nicolson, 1970), 246.

53   **"If there is going to be war":** Martin Gilbert, *Winston S. Churchill*, vol. 5, *The Prophet of Truth, 1922–1939* (Hillsdale, MI: Hillsdale College Press, 2009), 741, 687.

54   **Churchill had been one of the "economists":** Winston Churchill, *The World Crisis*, Part 1, 1911–1914 (London: Folio Society, 2007), 23–24.

54   **Neville Chamberlain was not yet in formal politics:** Keith Grahame Feiling, *The Life of Neville Chamberlain* (London: Macmillan, 1970), 48.

54   **At the heart of Chamberlain's thinking:** John Charmley, *Chamberlain and the Lost Peace* (Chicago: Ivan R. Dee, 1989), 30–31; Self, *Chamberlain*, 236.

55   **There was nothing new:** Paul Kennedy, "The Tradition of Appeasement in British Foreign Policy 1865–1939," *British Journal of International Studies* 2 no. 3 (October 1976): 195–215.

55   **"how empires think":** Susan Pedersen, *The Guardians: The League of Nations and the Crisis of Empire* (New York: Oxford University Press, 2015), 325–55.

55   **pursuing appeasement meant:** Self, *Chamberlain*, 266–68.

56   **"By careful diplomacy":** Chamberlain to Hilda, November 14, 1936, Chamberlain, *Diary Letters*, 219.

56   **he asked his daughters-in-law:** Andrew Roberts, *The Holy Fox: A Biography of Lord Halifax* (London: Weidenfeld and Nicolson, 1991), 45.

56   **He stood six feet five:** Roberts, *Holy Fox*, 53; Jenkins, *Churchill*, 600.

56   **Born in 1881:** D. J. Dutton, "Wood, Edward Frederick Lindley, first Earl of Halifax," *Dictionary of National Biography*, 82–83.

56   **Shortly before leaving India:** Dutton, "Halifax," 84.

57   **It was the negotiations:** Gilbert, *Prophet of Truth*, 385, 390.

57   **Halifax applied several lessons:** Roberts, *Holy Fox*, 47–48.

57   **Hermann Göring:** Peter Clarke, *Hope and Glory: Britain 1900–2000* (London: Penguin Books, 2004), 110; Nevile Henderson, *Failure of a Mission: Berlin 1937–1939* (London: Hodder and Stoughton, 1940), 50–53; Edward, the Earl of Halifax, *Fullness of Days* (London: Collier Books, 1957), 184.

58   **Halifax duly arrived:** Paul Schmidt, *Hitler's Interpreter* (London: Fronthill Media, 2016), 85; Ivone Kirkpatrick, *The Inner Circle: Memoirs* (London: Macmillan, 1959), 94.

58   **The train arrived at Berchtesgaden:** Halifax, *Fullness of Days*, 185.

58   **"I must candidly confess":** *Hansard*, December 21, 1937, cc. 1831–1833.

59   **"I have brought no new proposals":** Schmidt, *Hitler's Interpreter*, 86.

59   **Hitler began:** Kirkpatrick, *Inner Circle*, 95; Halifax, *Fullness of Days*, 186.

60   **"There were, no doubt, other questions":** Halifax, *Fullness of Days*, 186–87.

60   **Hitler did not hear the message:** Henderson, *Failure of a Mission*, 27–28; Roberts, *Holy Fox*, 68.

61   **Halifax's thoughts:** Halifax, *Fullness of Days*, 189.

61   **The meeting adjourned:** Kirkpatrick, *Inner Circle*, 95–96.

62   **Hitler loved movies:** TBJG, Teil 1, Bd. 5, December 22, 1937, 64.

62   **the Führer had drawn very different lessons:** Kirkpatrick, *Inner Circle*, 97.

62   **Hitler was a bit more civil:** Schmidt, *Hitler's Interpreter*, 87; Kirkpatrick, *Inner Circle*, 98.

63   **the report that Halifax delivered:** Schmidt, *Hitler's Interpreter*, 88; The National Archives (TNA) CAB 23/90a, 43 (37), November 24, 1937, 165–66.

63   **On November 22:** Neurath to German embassies in Italy, Great Britain, France, and the United States, November 22, 1937, doc. 33, DGFP, series D, vol. 1, 68–71.

63   **Hitler soon after saw Joseph Goebbels:** TBJG, Teil 1, Bd. 4, November 21, 1937, 415.

64   **Now the attack on Czechoslovakia:** doc. 506, Noakes and Pridham, *Nazism*, 83–84.

65   **Already in 1901:** *Hansard*, May 13, 1901, vol. 93, cc. 1572.

65   **In 1911:** Jenkins, *Churchill*, 204.

65   **he foresaw the application:** Winston Churchill, *Thoughts and Adventures: Churchill Reflects on Spies, Cartoons, Flying, and the Future* (New York: W. W. Norton, 1991), 289.

65   **He also anticipated:** Churchill, *Thoughts and Adventures*, 290.

66   **"The grand and victorious summits":** Churchill, "Parliamentary Government and the Economic Problem," in *Thoughts and Adventures*, 256.

66   **this enormous electorate:** Churchill, *Thoughts and Adventures*, 246.

66   **his mood grew darker:** Churchill, *Thoughts and Adventures*, 293.

66   **"democracy has shown itself":** Churchill, *Thoughts and Adventures*, 246.

67   **"The British oak":** Winston Churchill, "Introduction," in Otto Forst de Battaglia, *Dictatorship on Trial* (New York: Harcourt Brace and Company, 1931), 8.

67   **He was willing to praise:** Roland Quinalt, "Churchill and Democracy," in David Cannadine and Roland Quinalt, eds., *Churchill in the Twenty-First Century* (New York: Cambridge University Press, 2004), 33; Churchill, in Battaglia, *Dictatorship*, 9.

67   **"We have to consider":** Quinalt, "Churchill and Democracy," 38.

67   **In a 1932 letter:** Jenkins, *Churchill*, 457; Gilbert, *Churchill*, CV V(2).

68   **In the mid-1930s:** Rhodes James, *Churchill*, 284–85.

68   **When Hitler:** William Manchester, *The Last Lion: Winston Spencer Churchill*, vol. 2, *Alone, 1932–1940* (New York: Bantam Books, 2013), 66; Churchill, *Gathering Storm*, 40; Winston Churchill, "Reply to Hitler," November 6, 1938, in Robert Rhodes James, ed., *Winston S. Churchill: His Complete Speeches 1897–1963*, vol. 6, 1935–1942 (New York and London: Chelsea House Publishers, 1974), 6018.

69   **Roosevelt's thoughts and intentions:** Richard Moe, *Roosevelt's Second Act: The Election of 1940 and the Politics of War* (New York: Oxford University Press, 2014), 82.

69   **Louisiana governor (and demagogue):** Kennedy, *Freedom from Fear*, Part 1 (New York: Oxford University Press, 1999), 113.

69   **Roosevelt hated written records:** Francis L. Loewenheim, Harold D. Langley, and Manfred Jonas, eds., *Roosevelt and Churchill: Their Secret Wartime Correspondence* (New York: Da Capo, 1990), xv.

69   **Nor was it:** Kennedy, *Freedom from Fear*, 116–17.

70   **On one occasion:** Blanche Wiesen Cook, *Eleanor Roosevelt: The War Years and After* (New York: Viking, 2016), 3:208.

70   **"Fine, you've convinced me":** There are various versions of this quote, although all sources agree that Roosevelt said it to A. Philip Randolph and it concerned racial integration. Jacob S. Hacker and Paul Pierson, *Winner-Take-All Politics: How Washington Made the Rich Richer and Turned Its Back on the Middle Class* (New York: Simon and Schuster, 2010), 108; Jonathan Rosenberg, *How Far the Promised Land: World Affairs and the American Civil Rights Movement from the First World War to Vietnam* (Princeton, NJ: Princeton University Press, 2006),138; Cook, *Eleanor Roosevelt*, 568.

70   **The British economist:** Ira Katznelson, *Fear Itself: The New Deal and the Origins of Our Time* (New York: Liveright, 2013), 5.

71   **His biographer James MacGregor Burns:** James MacGregor Burns, *Roosevelt: The Lion and the Fox* (New York: Harcourt, Brace and World, 1956), 260, 262.

71   **Roosevelt himself admitted:** Justus D. Doenecke and John E. Wilz, *From Isolation to War, 1931–1941* (Chichester: John Wiley, 2015), 64.

71   **The fight between:** Lynne Olson, *Those Angry Days: Roosevelt, Lindbergh, and America's Fight over World War II* (New York: Random House, 2013), xviii.

71   **On the one side:** David Reynolds, *The Long Shadow: The Legacies of the Great War in the Twentieth Century* (New York: W. W. Norton, 2014), 231–32. See also Wayne S. Cole, *Senator Gerald P. Nye and American Foreign Relations* (Minneapolis: University of Minnesota Press, 1962); Robert A. Divine, *The Illusion of Neutrality* (Chicago: University of Chicago Press, 1962).

72   **The first Neutrality Act:** Katznelson, *Fear Itself*, 291–92; Franklin D. Roosevelt Presidential Library and Museum, Master Speech File no. 807, October 2, 1935.

72   **The main concession:** Katznelson, *Fear Itself*, 292.

72   **No sooner had this extension passed:** Katznelson, *Fear Itself*, 294.

73   **In the wake:** Katznelson, *Fear Itself*, 294–95.

73   **By late July:** Doenecke and Wilz, *From Isolation to War*, 93–95.

74   **Roosevelt came under increasing pressure:** Katznelson, *Fear Itself*, 297; Piers Brendon, *Dark Valley: A Panorama of the 1930s* (New York: Vintage, 2002), 510.

75   **Roosevelt told his audience:** Franklin D. Roosevelt Presidential Library and Museum, Master Speech File no. 1093, October 5, 1937.

75   **a Gallup poll:** Doenecke and Wilz, *From Isolation to War*, 97.

75   **In the wake of these criticisms:** Burns, *The Lion and the Fox*, 318–19; Azar Gat, *Fascist and Liberal Visions of War: Fuller, Liddell Hart, Douhet, and Other Modernists* (Oxford: Clarendon Press, 1998), 236–37.

76   **This was precisely the point:** Reynolds, *The Long Shadow*, 235; Doenecke and Wilz, *From Isolation to War*, 97–98.

5. "HE FEELS IT *HERE*"

77   **a remarkable prophecy:** Piers Brendon, *Edward VIII: The Uncrowned King* (London: Allen Lane, 2016), 3.

77   **Many Britons:** Brendon, *Edward VIII*, 38.

78   **In January 1936:** Ivan Maisky, *The Maisky Diaries: Red Ambassador to the Court of St. James 1932–1943*, ed. Gabriel Gorodetsky (New Haven: Yale University Press, 2015), 64; Brendon, *Edward VIII*, 52; Philip Ziegler, *King Edward VIII: The Official Biography* (London: Collins, 1990), 273–74.

78   **In August 1936:** Brendon, *Edward VIII*, 59.

78   **Churchill explains:** Gilbert, *Prophet of Truth*, 809, 813.

79   **On December 7:** Gilbert, *Prophet of Truth*, 822; John Barnes and David Nicholson, eds., *The Empire at Bay: The Leo Amery Diaries, 1929–1945* (London: Hutchinson, 1988), entry for December 7, 1936, 432.

79   **The hostile reactions:** Gilbert, *Prophet of Truth*, 822–23.

79   **the critical point:** Gilbert, *Prophet of Truth*, 824; Harold Nicolson to Vita Sackville-West, December 9, 1936, in Harold Nicolson, *Diaries and Letters, 1930–1939*, ed. Nigel Nicolson (New York: Atheneum, 1966), 284.

80   **On December 10:** Brendon, *Edward VIII*, 66.

80   **Hitler's immediate response:** Erich Kordt, *Nicht aus den Akten* (Stuttgart: Union Deutsche Verlagsgesellschaft, 1950), 160.

80   **Churchill understands:** Gilbert, *Prophet of Truth*, 830.

80   **"with the certainty of a sleepwalker":** Kershaw, *Nemesis*, 34.

80   **By this time:** Deutsch, *Generals*, 76.

81   **Blomberg believed:** Deutsch, *Generals*, 81.

81   **As war minister:** Schäfer, *Blomberg*, 179.

81   **Blomberg had been a widower:** Deutsch, *Generals*, 82–84; Schäfer, *Blomberg*, 175. Bodenschatz, in a statement on Blomberg in Institut für Zeitgeschichte (IfZ) ZS 10, says he had seen Gruhn's file and noted that she was "mehrfach vorbestraft" (had a substantial criminal record).

81   **There are conflicting stories:** Schäfer, *Blomberg*, 177.

81   **the most plausible account:** Karl Boehm-Tettelbach, *Als Flieger in der Hexenküche* (Mainz: v. Hase und Koehler Verlag, 1981), 54–55.

82   **It is possible:** Deutsch, *Generals*, 80.

82   **Bodenschatz reported:** Karl Bodenschatz, Statement on the Blomberg Case, no date, IfZ ZS 10, 9–13; Hans Bernd Gisevius, *To the Bitter End* (Boston: Houghton Miflin, 1947), 244.

83   **The young man:** This story is attested to independently by Gisevius, Keitel, and Bodenschatz: Deutsch, *Generals*, 87–88.

83   **Within a few weeks:** Deutsch, *Generals*, 87.

83   **He had been locked:** Fritsch, Memo, February 1, 1938, BA-MA N24/29, *Nachlass Hossbach*.

83   **Blomberg informed Hitler:** Hossbach, *Zwischen Wehrmacht und Hitler*, 105.

84   **The ceremony took place:** Meissner and Wiedemann had it that Hitler and Göring volunteered for this right away, but Deutsch says this is wrong. Deutsch, *Generals*, 93–96.

84   **This suited Heydrich:** Deutsch, *Generals*, 95. Deutsch's source for the claim that Fritsch and Raeder were supposed to be the witnesses is two interviews with Schultze in 1969 and 1970, corroborated, as he notes, by numerous other witnesses. This is worth stressing as later authors, notably Janssen and Tobias, have tried to refute Deutsch's careful research. Deutsch, *Generals*, 95–96n52.

84   **At the last minute:** Deutsch seems to have misread Bodenschatz's notes in one minor respect: Bodenschatz clearly refers to Blomberg's children (*Kindern*) being present. Deutsch misread this for "people" (presumably *Leute*). Bodenschatz's statement is handwritten and admittedly difficult to read. Karl Bodenschatz, "Fall Blomberg," n.d., IfZ ZS 10, 9–13; Deutsch, *Generals*, 96–97.

84   **The announcement in the papers:** Gisevius, *Bitter End*, 219.

84   **Gisevius, who had good connections:** Gisevius, *Bitter End*, 233–34.

85   **Eva Gruhn's file:** Deutsch, *Generals*, 103–4; Bodenschatz, "Fall Blomberg." There is a conflict between the accounts of Bodenschatz and Gisevius; according to Gisevius, Helldorff took the file to Göring on the weekend at Göring's country home, Karinhall. Given that Bodenschatz's account is based on personal observation and Gisevius's on hearsay from Helldorff, Bodenschatz's is more likely correct. See also Schäfer, *Blomberg*, 176–81; Hossbach, *Zwischen Wehrmacht und Hitler*, 107.

85   **Fritsch wrote to a friend:** Fritsch to Baroness Schutzbar, January 7, 1938, BA-MA N33/10, *Nachlass Fritsch*, Bl. 5–6.

85   **He remembered later:** Werner von Fritsch, "Eigenhändige Aufzeichung des Generaloberst a.D. von Fritsch: Notiert von Februar bis September 1938, beendet am 27 September 1938 [in Achterberg bei Soltau]," in Horst Muhleisen, "Die Fritsch-Krise im Frühjahr 1938: Neun Dokumente aus dem Nachlass des Generalobersten," *Militärgeschichtliche Mitteilungen* 56, no. 2 (January 1997): 495–96.

85   **On this same day:** Karl Wolff, Aktenvermerk 11.8.1952, IfZ ZS 317, Bd 1. Kershaw, following Janssen and Tobias, says Hitler asked for the file on the 24th, but this is unlikely. Hitler had the "reconstructed" file in his hands at the latest early the following morning. Kershaw, *Nemesis*, 54; Hossbach, *Zwischen Wehrmacht und Hitler*, 107; Deutsch, *Generals*, 109.

86   **When Göring reported the Blomberg case:** Deutsch, *Generals*, 106–9.

86   **It is likely that:** Deutsch, *Generals*, 109; Hossbach, *Zwischen Wehrmacht und Hitler*, 107.

86   **Hossbach arrived at the Chancellery:** Hossbach, *Zwischen Wehrmacht und Hitler*, 108.

87   **Hitler ordered Hossbach:** Hossbach, *Zwischen Wehrmacht und Hitler*, 108–10.

87   **Hossbach warned Fritsch:** Hossbach, *Zwischen Wehrmacht und Hitler*, 110.

87   **On January 26:** Hossbach, *Zwischen Wehrmacht und Hitler*, 110–11.

87   **Hossbach again suspected Himmler:** Wolff, IfZ ZS 317, Bd. 1; Hossbach, *Zwischen Wehrmacht und Hitler*, 112.

88   **not "a man for women":** Hossbach, *Zwischen Wehrmacht und Hitler*, 116.

88   **The reason they were fabricated:** There has been some debate among historians as to whether Hitler himself provoked the crisis over Blomberg and Fritsch, and in particular if he did so because of the opposition to his plans that had arisen at the Hossbach Conference. In the last quarter century, most historians have accepted the view put forward by the intelligence officer Fritz Tobias and the journalist Karl-Heinz Janssen in their 1994 book *Der Sturz der Generäle*: that Hitler did not plan or foresee any actions against the generals and was blindsided by both scandals. But the Tobias-Janssen argument is deeply problematic for a number of reasons. Tobias was also the author of a book making a very similar argument about the Reichstag fire of 1933 (Tobias, *Der Reichstagsbrand: Legende und Wirklichkeit*, 1962), which much

evidence now shows was clearly fraudulent: to support his thesis, Tobias
both fabricated and suppressed evidence, used the power of his office to
threaten and blackmail historians who disagreed with him, and wrote the
book as an assignment from his intelligence agency (the Lower Saxon LfV)
to rehabilitate the reputation of a serious Nazi war criminal employed by the
Lower Saxon government and to create anticommunist propaganda for the
Cold War (see Hett, "This Story Is About Something Fundamental," *Central European History* 48 [2015], 199–224). *Der Sturz der Generäle* is not as
bad a book as *Der Reichstagsbrand* (maybe Janssen kept Tobias a bit more
on the straight and narrow), but it has the same agenda: a sustained effort
to hold Hitler blameless for what happened in his Reich. It also has many
of the same targets, including Hans Bernd Gisevius, one of the few surviving witnesses of the anti-Hitler resistance, for whom Tobias had an almost
pathological hatred. Just how far that hatred went, and just how far Tobias
was willing to warp the results of historical research to pursue it, is shown by
the fact that Tobias thought a vicious Nazi judge named Manfred Roeder—
whose brutal investigations sent many brave and idealistic people, including
Hans von Dohnanyi and Dietrich Bonhoeffer, to their deaths—was a credible witness for the many supposed defects in Gisevius's character. The very
deep and painstaking research by the late Harold C. Deutsch on the subject
of the Blomberg-Fritsch crisis is far more persuasive. I follow it here, along
with the relevant witness accounts like that of Hossbach, who had no doubt
that Hitler was behind the dismissal of Blomberg and Fritsch.

88   **The next morning, January 27:** Schäfer, *Blomberg*, 188.

88   **Hitler asked Blomberg:** Hossbach, *Zwischen Wehrmacht und Hitler*, 115–16.

89   **"There's no question of him":** Walter Warlimont, *In Hauptquartier der deutschen Wehrmacht, 1939–1945* (Frankfurt: Bernard und Graefe, 1962), 29n22.

89   **The parallels:** Schäfer, *Blomberg*, 179n189.

89   **"These old men":** Wilhelm Keitel, *The Memoirs of Wilhelm Keitel* (New York: Stein and Day, 1966), 109.

89   **"What an influence":** Alfred Jodl, diary entry, January 26, 1938, *Trial of the Major War Criminals, Documents*, vol. 28 (New York: AMS Press, 1971), 357.

89   **Hitler seized the opportunity:** Gisevius, *Bitter End*, 241.

90   **The real motive:** *TBJG*, Teil 1, Bd. 5, February 1, 1938, 127.

90   **One of the generals:** Fritsch to Leeb, April 17, 1938, BA-MA N 145/6, *Nachlass Leeb*.

90   **The "whole affair":** *TBJG*, Teil 1, Bd. 5, February 1, 1938, 127.

90   **As Gisevius added:** Gisevius, *Bitter End*, 242.

90   **On February 5:** Ministerbesprechung vom 5. February 1938, Minuth, *Regierung Hitler*, Bd. 5, Nr. 35, 118.

91   **the third of Hitler's major bids:** Kershaw, *Nemesis*, 60.

91   **The bluntly honest Friedrich Hossbach:** Hossbach, *Zwischen Wehrmacht und Hitler*, 108–10.

92   **Enraged by this treatment:** Hossbach, *Zwischen Wehrmacht und Hitler*, 117; Fritsch, "Eigenhändige Aufzeichung," in Muhleisen, "Fritsch-Krise," 496.

92   **"Since I couldn't be gotten around":** Fritsch, Memo, February 1, 1938, BA-MA N24/29, *Nachlass Hossbach*.

92   **His lawyer said:** Rüdiger von der Goltz, Notes on the Fritsch Case, 1945, BA-MA N24/30, *Nachlass Hossbach*.

92   **Soon after Fritsch's dismissal:** Kielmannsegg, "Tragweite," 270; Henderson, *Failure of a Mission*, 108; Engel, *Heeresadjutant*, 20.

92   **Predictably, it was Hossbach:** Hossbach, "Ein Beitrag zur Wahrheit," September 23, 1946, N24/269; Aufzeichnung, July 22, 1963, Betr. SS-General Wolff, BA-MA N24/145, *Nachlass Hossbach*.

93   **The sword:** Hossbach, *Zwischen Wehrmacht und Hitler*, 125.

93   **Senior officers soon learned:** Gisevius, *Bitter End*, 240.

94   **"I would have gone the Führer's way":** Schäfer, *Blomberg*, 170; Blomberg, Haft Tagebücher, December 4, 1945, BA-MA N52/9, *Nachlass Blomberg*.

94   **Even during the Second World War:** Schäfer, *Blomberg*, 156–58.

94   **In late 1937:** Kershaw, *Nemesis*, 84.

94   **Fritsch, too:** Hossbach, *Zwischen Wehrmacht und Hitler*, 86.

94   **Fritsch appeared:** Hossbach, *Zwischen Wehrmacht und Hitler*, 94.

94   **in December 1938:** Ulrich von Hassell, diary entry for December 20, 1938, in Ulrich von Hassell, *The von Hassell Diaries: The Story of the Forces Against Hitler Inside Germany* (London: Hamish Hamilton, 1948), 28; Muhleisen, "Fritsche Krise," 476.

6. "RATHER CONCERNED RE: FUTURE"

95   **bent over his drawing:** J. Smith, "R. J. Mitchell—Aircraft Designer," *Journal of the Royal Aeronautical Society* 58 (May 1954): 312–28, 314.

95   **Mitchell's temper:** Gordon Mitchell, *R. J. Mitchell: Schooldays to Spitfire* (Stroud, Gloucestershire: History Press, 2006), 233; Smith, "R. J. Mitchell—Aircraft Designer," 312–28, 313.

95   **R. J. Mitchell was born:** Mitchell, *Schooldays to Spitfire*, 27–31.

96   **Mitchell finishes his apprenticeship:** Mitchell, *Schooldays to Spitfire*, 32–33, 95.

96   **the brilliant success of the seaplanes:** Mitchell, *Schooldays to Spitfire*, 111–30, 141–42.

97   **Mitchell gives no outward sign:** Mitchell, *Schooldays to Spitfire*, 141.

97   **Mitchell bites back the pain:** Mitchell, *Schooldays to Spitfire*, 145; J. A. D. Ackroyd, "The Spitfire Wing Planform: A Suggestion," *Journal of Aeronautical History* Paper No. 2013/02, 121–35. One of the intriguing debates among experts on the Spitfire is to what extent the wing design was lifted from German sources—probably through Shenstone, who worked in Germany, probably having been placed there by the British military attaché Malcolm Christie. See Lance Cole, *Secrets of the Spitfire: The Story of*

Beverley Shenstone, The Man Who Perfected the Elliptical Wing (Barnsley, Yorkshire: Pen and Sword, 2012).

97   **"Just the kind of bloody silly name"**: Leo McKinstry, *Spitfire: Portrait of a Legend* (London: John Murray, 2007), 55.

97   **"Rather concerned re: future"**: Mitchell, *Schooldays to Spitfire*, 148.

98   **"The new fighter"**: Alfred Price, *The Spitfire Story* (London: Jane's Publishing Company, 1982), 38. Price argues, based on some unclear documentation, that the date of the flight might have been March 6; McKinstry reports that more recently discovered documents point squarely to March 5: McKinstry, *Spitfire*, 60.

98   **After an eight-minute flight:** Jeffrey Quill, *Spitfire: A Test Pilot's Story* (Seattle: University of Washington Press, 1984), 71.

98   **After three more flights:** McKinstry, *Spitfire*, 61.

98   **Lord Balfour of Inchyre:** Quoted in Mitchell, *Schooldays to Spitfire*, 11.

98   **"turned me on":** H. R. "Dizzy" Allen, *Battle for Britain* (London: Barker, 1973), 11.

98   **"Until June":** Mitchell, *Schooldays to Spitfire*, 163.

98   **He can no longer go:** Mitchell, *Schooldays to Spitfire*, 195.

98   **"Mr. R. J. Mitchell—Designer of Racing Seaplanes":** *The Times*, June 12, 1937.

99   **any future war:** David Edgerton, *England and the Aeroplane: Militarism, Modernity, and Machines* (New York: Penguin Books, 2013).

99   **The context for this decision:** CP 316 (37) December 15, 1937, TNA CAB 24/273; CP 24 (38) February 8, 1938, TNA CAB 24/274; Cabinet, December 22, 1937, morning, TNA CAB 23/90a; Joseph Maiolo, *Cry Havoc: How the Arms Race Drove the World to War, 1931–1941* (New York: Basic Books, 2010), 238; N. H. Gibbs, *Grand Strategy*, vol. 1 (London: Her Majesty's Stationery Office, 1976), 279–96; Brian Bond, *British Military Policy Between the Two World Wars* (New York: Oxford University Press, 1980), 252–53; G. C. Peden, *British Rearmament and the Treasury, 1932–1939* (Edinburgh: Scottish University Press, 1979).

100   **The cabinet's acceptance:** Cabinet, December 22, 1937, morning; Cabinet, December 22, 1937, evening, 376–77, TNA CAB 23/90a 346–51, 376–77.

100   **Chamberlain summed up:** Cabinet, December 22, 1937, TNA CAB 23/90A, 373.

101   **"I think it is well":** *Hansard*, November 10, 1932, cc. 525–641. At this time, Baldwin was formally between terms as prime minister and was serving as lord president of the council in the administration of Ramsay MacDonald. But even in this capacity he was the de facto prime minister, an office he in any case officially returned to in 1935.

101   **Their respective nicknames:** Vincent Orange, *Dowding of Fighter Command: Victor of the Battle of Britain* (London: Grub Street, 2011), 11, 31.

101   **Dowding never accepted:** R. J. Overy, *The Air War* (New York: Stein and Day, 1980), 15.

102   **the question of a warning system:** David Zimmerman, *Britain's Shield: Radar and the Defeat of the Luftwaffe* (Stroud, Gloucestershire: Amberley Publishing, 2012), chap. 2.

102   **Early in 1935:** Orange, *Dowding*, 79–80.

102   **Soon, the radar transmitters ... too obvious a target:** Orange, *Dowding*, 82.

103   **"our essentially businesslike tradition":** Basil Liddell Hart, *The British Way in Warfare* (London: Faber and Faber, 1932), 37.

104   **Liddell Hart's "British way":** Hew Strachan, "The British Way in Warfare Revisited," *Historical Journal* 26, no. 2 (June 1983): 447–61, 458.

105   **The First World War confirmed:** This is the argument made by Liddell Hart in *The British Way in Warfare*, chap. 1, "The Historical Strategy of Britain," 13–41.

105   **Liddell Hart thought:** Liddell Hart, *British Way in Warfare*, 39–41.

105   **There was one other key element:** John J. Mearsheimer, *Liddell Hart and the Weight of History* (Ithaca, NY: Cornell University Press, 1988), 115–16, 170.

106   **Liddell Hart's cool-eyed strategy:** Gat, *Fascist and Liberal Visions*, 233–34.

106   **This was a world:** Landesarchiv NRW, Abteilung Rheinland, RW 58/09682/54, Judgment in the Case Against Karl J., December 9, 1941. I am grateful to Dustin Stalnaker for this reference.

106   **Liddell Hart understood:** Liddell Hart, *Europe in Arms* (New York: Random House, 1937), 13–14.

107   **The difficulty lay:** Liddell Hart, *Europe in Arms*, 16.

107   **Young people could not:** Liddell Hart, *Europe in Arms*, 19.

107   **He opposed a draft:** Liddell Hart, *Paris, or the Future of War* (London: Keegan Paul, 1935); Strachan, "British Way," 461; Gat, *Fascist and Liberal Visions*, 234–38.

108   **He drew heavily:** Andrew Lambert, ed., *21st Century Corbett: Maritime Strategy and Naval Policy for the Modern Era* (Annapolis, MD: Naval Institute Press, 2017), 147.

108   **there are many signs of his influence:** Mearsheimer, *Liddell Hart*, 171, although Mearsheimer says Liddell Hart was *not* influential because he expressed an existing consensus.

108   **Shortly before he became prime minister:** Mearsheimer, *Liddell Hart*, 115, 103; Robert Forczyk, *Case Red: The Collapse of France* (London: Osprey, 2017), 94–96; Basil Liddell Hart, *The Liddell Hart Memoirs*, vol. 2, *The Later Years* (New York: Putnams, 1965), 4, 123–24; Williamson Murray and Allan R. Millett, eds., *Military Innovation in the Interwar Period* (New York: Cambridge University Press, 1996), 9–10.

108   **The most important fruit:** Mearsheimer, *Liddell Hart*, 100–101.

108   **Much of Chamberlain's thinking had to do:** Gilbert, *The Prophet of Truth*, 1039, referring to a cabinet meeting of January 1939; Barry Posen, *The Sources of Military Doctrine: France, Britain and Germany Between the World Wars* (Ithaca, NY: Cornell University Press, 1984), 139.

109   **Sir Thomas Inskip:** CP 316 (37) December 15, 1937, TNA CAB 24/273, 267.

109   **As Sir John Simon:** Cabinet, March 14, 1938, TNA CAB 23/92, 371.

109   **The opposite danger:** Quoted in Self, *Chamberlain*, 270.

109   **Neville Chamberlain agreed fully:** McKinstry, *Spitfire*, 11–12.

110   **A few days after:** Mearsheimer, *Liddell Hart*, 148.

110   **If Britain were to prepare:** Posen, *Sources of Military Doctrine*, 149, 159–61.

111   **a remarkable passage:** F. Scott Fitzgerald, *Tender Is the Night* (New York: Scribner, 1934), 72.

111   **After losing her fiancé:** Vera Brittain, *Testament of Youth: An Autobiographical Study of the Years 1900–1925* (London: Weidenfeld and Nicolson, 2009), 450.

111   **"Something new has come to American democracy":** Samuel Strauss, "Things Are in the Saddle," *Atlantic Monthly*, November 1924.

112   **In February 1933:** Tim Bouverie, *Appeasement: Chamberlain, Hitler, Churchill and the Road to War* (New York: Tim Duggan Books, 2019), 24.

112   **In a debate:** *Hansard*, November 12, 1936, cc. 1143–44.

112   **This was the clearest:** *Hansard*, November 12, 1936, cc. 1145–46.

113   **Anthony Eden:** D. R. Thorpe, *Eden: The Life and Times of Anthony Eden, First Earl of Avon, 1897–1977* (London: Chatto and Windus, 2003), 576, 37; Bouverie, *Appeasement*, 41–43.

113   **A dispute:** David Faber, *Munich: Appeasement and World War II* (New York: Simon and Schuster, 2009), 77.

114   **President Franklin Delano Roosevelt:** FO to Lindsay for the PM, January 13, 1938, *Documents on British Foreign Policy* [hereafter cited as *DBFP*], 2nd series, vol. 19, doc. 430 738, and *DBFP*, 2nd series, vol. 19, FO to Lindsay for the PM, January 13, doc. 431 739.

114   **"It is always best":** Chamberlain to Hilda, December 17, 1937, Chamberlain, *Diary Letters*, 294.

114   **"registering disappointment":** Eden to Lindsay, January 16, 1938, *DBFP*, 2nd series, vol. 19, doc. 443, 753.

114   **"douche of cold water":** Sumner Welles, *Seven Decisions That Shaped History* (New York: Harper and Brothers, 1951), 27.

114   **A few days later:** Lindsay to Eden, January 18, 1938, *DBFP*, 2nd series, vol. 19, doc. 445, 754.

114   **The prime minister and the foreign secretary:** Faber, *Munich*, 91–92.

114   **The climax came:** Cabinet, February 19, 1938, TNA CAB 23/92 173 ff.

115   **When Hitler insisted:** Michael Bloch, *Ribbentrop* (London: Bantam Press, 1992), 98.

115   **"He is so stupid":** Chamberlain to Hilda, March 13, 1938, Chamberlain, *Diary Letters*, 304.

115   **Among the many:** *TBJG*, Teil 1, Bd. 5, March 8, 1938, 194; May 6, 1938, 290; May 24, 1938, 416.

115   **"His name he bought":** Rudolf Semmler, *Goebbels—the Man Next to Hitler* (New York: AMS Press, 1981), 18–19.

115   **Even Benito Mussolini:** Galeazzo Ciano, entry for May 6, 1938, *Diary 1937–1943* (London: Phoenix Press, 2002), 88.

116   **Hitler summoned Schuschnigg:** DGFP D/1, no. 294, 513–14, Draft "Protocol of the Conference of February 12, 1938."

116   **Subjected to the full range:** Richard J. Evans, *The Third Reich in Power* (New York: Penguin Books, 2005), 650.

117   **"At first":** Max Domarus, *Hitler: Speeches and Proclamations, 1932–1945,* vol. 2, *1935–1938* (Wauconda, IL: Bolchazy-Carducci Publishers, 1992), 1051–52, translation modified with reference to the German text.

117   **This hasty decision:** Gerhard L. Weinberg, *Hitler's Foreign Policy: The Road to World War II, 1933–1939* (New York: Enigma Books, 2005), 626.

117   **General Wilhelm Keitel:** Keitel, *Memoirs*, 58–59.

117   **After another round:** Evans, *Third Reich in Power*, 651–52.

118   **It was as well:** Faber, *Munich*, 140; Churchill, *Gathering Storm*, 270.

118   **Hitler drove on:** Kershaw, *Nemesis*, 79–80.

118   **Something else died:** Pedersen, *Guardians*, 346.

118   **"Tears in the eyes":** TBJG, Teil 1, Bd. 5, March 13, 1938, 204.

7. SCRAPING AT THE BARS

119   **Even as an old man:** Max Fürst, *Gefilte Fisch und wie es weiterging* (Munich: Deutscher Taschenbuch Verlag, 2004), 512–13. The reading Fürst referred to is from Sallust, *Bellum Iugurthinum*.

119   **When the Nazis came to power:** Benjamin Carter Hett, *Crossing Hitler: The Man Who Put the Nazis on the Witness Stand* (New York: Oxford University Press, 2008), 186–94; Fürst, *Gefilte Fisch*, 727.

119   **In late 1935:** Fürst, *Gefilte Fisch*, 727–28.

120   **After years:** Fürst, *Gefilte Fisch*, 747, 728–29.

120   **Cläre Tisch:** Harold Hagemann, "Cläre Tisch," in Robert W. Dimand et al, *A Biographical Dictionary of Women Economists* (Cheltenham: Edward Elgar, 2000), 426–29.

120   **After Schumpeter:** Tisch to Schumpeter, March 12, 1933, HUG (FP) 4.7.

120   **A few months later:** Tisch to Schumpeter, September 12, 1933, HUG (FP) 4.7.

121   **But there is still the quota:** Tisch to Schumpeter, February 3, 1939, HUG (FP) 4.7.5.

121   **The destruction of the Austrian state:** Snyder, *Black Earth*, 84.

121   **The annexation:** Snyder, *Black Earth*, 86–87.

122   **One of the deported:** Peter Longerich, *Holocaust: The Nazi Persecution and Murder of the Jews* (Oxford: Oxford University Press, 2010), 110.

122   **In the wake:** Longerich, *Holocaust*, 113–20.

122   **In 1933:** Herbert A. Strauss, "Jewish Emigration from Germany: Nazi Policies and Jewish Response," *Leo Baeck Institute Year Book* 25 (1980): 326.

123   **European Jews wryly:** Saul S. Friedman, *No Haven for the Oppressed: United States Policy Toward Jewish Refugees, 1938–1945* (Detroit, MI: Wayne State University Press, 1973), 56. The quote may come from Chaim Weizmann: Irving Abella and Harold Troper, *None Is Too Many: Canada and the Jews of Europe, 1933–1948* (Toronto: University of Toronto Press, 2012), 4.

123 **Franklin Delano Roosevelt:** Richard Breitman and Allan J. Litchtman, *FDR and the Jews* (Cambridge, MA: Harvard University Press, 2013), 8–10.

123 **Early in his administration:** Breitman and Lichtman, *FDR and the Jews*, 60–61.

124 **When Roosevelt appointed:** Arnold A. Offner, *American Appeasement: United States Foreign Policy and Germany, 1933–1938* (Cambridge, MA: Belknap Press, 1969), 68.

124 **Roosevelt knew:** Breitman and Lichtman, *FDR and the Jews*, 63–64.

124 **When it came:** David S. Wyman, *Paper Walls: America and the Refugee Crisis, 1938–1941* (Amherst: University of Massachusetts Press, 1968), 4.

124 **Then there was the tide:** Wyman, *Paper Walls*, 7.

125 **Prohibition had been intended:** See Lisa McGirr, *The War on Alcohol: Prohibition and the Rise of the American State* (New York: W. W. Norton, 2016).

125 **The hugely popular:** Bradley W. Hart, *Hitler's American Friends: The Third Reich's Supporters in the United States* (New York: St. Martin's Press, 2018), 70, 85–86.

125 **But nativism's most direct expression:** Kiran Klaus Patel, *The New Deal: A Global History* (Princeton, NJ: Princeton University Press, 2016), 19; Daniel Okrent, *The Guarded Gate: Bigotry, Eugenics, and the Law That Kept Two Generations of Jews, Italians, and Other European Immigrants Out of America* (New York: Scribner's, 2019), 344, 391–92.

126 **Another critical feature:** Wyman, *Paper Walls*, 1.

126 **There was one loophole:** Patel, *New Deal*, 20.

126 **for most of the 1930s:** Breitman and Lichtman, *FDR and the Jews*, 74–75, 90, 95.

127 **Roosevelt responded with real concern:** Breitman and Lichtman, *FDR and the Jews*, 101–2.

127 **There were conflicts:** Martin Weil, *A Pretty Good Club: The Founding Father of the U.S. Foreign Service* (New York: W. W. Norton, 1978), 90–91.

127 **Roosevelt's administration was heavily penetrated:** Andrew and Mitrokhin, *Sword and Shield*, 106.

128 **"They were all Jewish":** Breckinridge Long, *The War Diary of Breckinridge Long: Selections from the Years 1939–1944* (Lincoln: University of Nebraska Press, 1966), entry for September 18, 1940, 130.

128 **Eleanor Roosevelt:** Cook, *Eleanor Roosevelt*, 3:200, 3:318–82.

128 **in March 1938:** Breitman and Lichtman, *FDR and the Jews*, 104; Michael R. Marrus, *The Unwanted: European Refugees in the Twentieth Century* (New York: Oxford University Press, 1985), 170–71.

128 **Roosevelt's proposal:** Breitman and Lichtman, *FDR and the Jews*, 105.

128 **The nations Roosevelt invited:** Timothy P. Maga, "Closing the Door: The French Government and Refugee Policy, 1933–1939," *French Historical Studies* 12, no. 3 (Spring 1982): 424–42, 436; Breitman and Lichtman, *FDR and the Jews*, 106.

128 **The French delegation:** Maga, "Closing the Door," 436–37; Breitman and Lichtman, *FDR and the Jews*, 110; Marrus, *The Unwanted*, 170–72.

129   **"What a demonstration":** Friedman, *No Haven for the Oppressed*, 65.

129   **Rublee quickly discovered:** Breitman and Lichtman, *FDR and the Jews*, 121; David S. Wyman, *Paper Walls*, 52–53.

130   **By 1938, it was clear:** Breitman and Lichtman, *FDR and the Jews*, 120; Richard Breitman, ed., *Refugees and Rescue: The Diaries and Papers of James G. McDonald* (Bloomington: Indiana University Press, 2009), 332.

130   **Under these difficult circumstances:** Breitman and Lichtman, *FDR and the Jews*, 114–15; Richard Mayers, *FDR's Ambassadors and the Diplomacy of Crisis: From the Rise of Hitler to the End of World War II* (New York: Cambridge University Press, 2013), 57.

130   **The philosopher Hannah Arendt:** Hannah Arendt, *The Origins of Totalitarianism* (New York: Harcourt, 1994), 268–69.

130   **There were many more Jews:** Marrus, *The Unwanted*, 141–43.

131   **The antisemitism behind:** Marrus, *The Unwanted*, 143–45.

132   **In the 1920s:** Marrus, *The Unwanted*, 146.

132   **widespread feeling in France:** Marrus, *The Unwanted*, 147.

132   **In the mid-1930s:** Maga, "Closing the Door," 424–42, 431–32.

132   **The racist writer:** Okrent, *Guarded Gate*, 570.

132   **French refugee policy:** Maga, "Closing the Door," 435; Marrus, *The Unwanted*, 148–49.

132   **Britain's island geography:** Marrus, *The Unwanted*, 149–51.

133   **Under the impact of Hitler:** Pedersen, *Guardians*, 366–67.

133   **The increased Jewish migration:** Marrus, *The Unwanted*, 151–54; Bernard Wasserstein, *Britain and the Jews of Europe, 1939–1945* (Oxford: Clarendon Press, 1979), 19–20; Pedersen, *Guardians*, 368.

133   **"No doubt Jews":** Chamberlain to Hilda, July 30, 1939, Chamberlain, *Diary Letters*, 433.

133   **Chamberlain felt:** Breitman and Lichtman, *FDR and the Jews*, 122.

133   **The same attitude:** Faber, *Munich*, 190.

134   **Rathbone possessed:** Susan Pedersen, *Eleanor Rathbone and the Politics of Conscience* (New Haven, CT: Yale University Press, 2004), 271–77.

134   **Harold Nicolson:** Pedersen, *Rathbone*, 300.

134   **Late in 1938:** Pedersen, *Rathbone*, 296–97.

134   **Rathbone wrote movingly:** Eleanor Rathbone, "A Personal View of the Refugee Problem," *New Statesman and Nation*, April 15, 1939, 568–69.

135   **By the end of 1939:** Marrus, *The Unwanted*, 153–54.

135   **Ships carrying refugees:** Wasserstein, *Britain and the Jews of Europe*, 26–27.

135   **a consistent record of support:** Wasserstein, *Britain and the Jews of Europe*, 33.

135   **Churchill advocated:** Martin Gilbert, *Churchill and the Jews: A Lifelong Friendship* (New York: Henry Holt, 2007), 153, 158.

136   **In the Balfour Declaration:** Pedersen, *Guardians*, 359; Wasserstein, *Britain and the Jews of Europe*, 18.

136   **The fostering of Jewish immigration:** Pedersen, *Guardians*, 392.

136   **"What sort of National Home":** *Hansard*, May 23, 1939, cc. 2172, cc. 2176.

136   **Early one morning:** Fürst, *Gefilte Fisch*, 733.

136   **Safe—but:** Fürst, *Gefilte Fisch*, 733, 736–37, 262–62.

137   **"You probably cannot imagine":** Tisch to Schumpeter, July 10, 1941, Schumpeter Papers, Harvard University Archives.

137   **Cläre wrote:** Tisch to Schumpeter, November 8, 1941, Schumpeter Papers, Harvard University Archives.

137   **They murdered Cläre:** Information from Yad Vashem, https://yvng .yadvashem.org/.

8. "THAT'S WHAT I WANT TO HAVE!"

141   **The chancellor has come:** Heinz Guderian, *Panzer Leader* (New York: Ballantine Books, 1976), 19.

141   **Hitler is primed:** *Mein Kampf 2*, IfZ 1671.

141   **He will soon tell:** Gat, *Fascist and Liberal Visions*, 101–2.

141   **Guderian has found his inspiration:** In his memoir, Guderian also credited Liddell Hart among his early influences, but in fact this was something Liddell Hart, an advocate for many senior German officers through their postwar war crimes and denazification trials, pressured Guderian to add (Mersheimer, *Liddell Hart*, 189–91; Paul Harris, "Introduction," Guderian, *Achtung Panzer*). Azar Gat, however, argues in "British Influence and the Evolution of the Panzer Arm," *War in History* 4, no. 2 (1997): 150–73, that "The fact that [Liddell Hart] was fraudulent" in essentially blackmailing Guderian into including a fulsome tribute to LH's influence in his memoir "does not necessarily mean that he was wholly incorrect." Gat, "British Influence," 153.

141   **the tank offers a way around:** Guderian, *Panzer Leader*, 9–12.

142   **Guderian considers Beck:** Guderian, *Panzer Leader*, 21–22.

142   **things are not quite as Guderian claims:** Murray and Millett, *Military Innovation in the Interwar Period*, 41–42.

142   **Just as in Britain:** Gat, *Fascist and Liberal Visions*, 243–44.

143   **The literary scholar:** Victor Klemperer, *LTI: Notizbuch eines Philologen* (Stuttgart: Reclam, 2015), 12–13. Robert M. Citino correctly insists that the Nazis did not *invent* the idea of fast-moving armored warfare. The point, though, is the *affinity* between Nazi ideas and goals and those of Guderian, et al. See Citino, *The Path to Blitzkrieg: Doctrine and Training in the German Army, 1920–1939* (Boulder, CO: Lynne Rienner Publishers, 1999), 223, as well as Robert M. Citino, *The German Way of War: From the Thirty Years' War to the Third Reich* (Lawrence, KS: University of Kansas Press, 2005).

143   **Guderian claims:** Guderian, *Panzer Leader*, 21–22; Klaus-Jürgen Müller, *Generaloberst Ludwig Beck: Eine Biographie* (Paderborn: Ferdinand Schöningh, 2008), 217.

143   **When a war game:** Citino, *Path to Blitzkrieg*, 240.

143   **Another traditionalist officer:** Guderian, *Panzer Leader*, 13; Murray, *Military Innovation*, 42–43.

143   **By contrast, the most Nazified units:** Forczyk, *Case Red*, 75–76.

144   **Hitler's regime had no time:** Tooze, *Wages of Destruction*, 219–20.

144   **As if he were channeling:** Schwerin von Krosigk, Memo to Hitler, September 1, 1938, in *Nazi Conspiracy and Aggression* (Washington, DC: United States Government Printing Office, 1946), 7:474–78.

145   **Ludendorff published his book:** Erich Ludendorff, *The Nation at War* (London: Hutchinson and Co., 1936), 15.

145   **National politics had to change:** Ludendorff, *Nation at War*, 23–24.

145   **One of those requirements:** Erich Ludendorff, *Kriegführung und Politik* (Berlin: Verlag E. G. Mitler und Sohn, 1922), 336.

145   **The German war veteran:** Abbott Gleason, *Totalitarianism: The Inner History of the Cold War* (New York: Oxford University Press, 1995), 25; Ernst Jünger, "Die totale Mobilmachung," in Jünger, *Sämtliche Werke*, Bd. 7, *Essays 1* (Stuttgart: Klett-Cotta, 1980), 121–42, 126–27.

145   **Hitler and Ludendorff probably first met:** Bruno Thoss, *Der Ludendorff Kreis 1919–1923: München als Zentrum der mitteleuropäischen Gegenrevolution zwischen Revolution und Hitler-Putsch* (Munich: Kommissionsbuchhandlung R. Wölfle, 1978), 253–61.

146   **The scale of the German arms buildup:** Adam Tooze, *The Deluge: The Great War and the Remaking of the Global Order* (New York: Penguin, 2014), 512–13.

146   **But this effort was too much:** Tooze, *Wages of Destruction*, 213.

147   **By the late 1930s:** Tooze, *Wages of Destruction*, 308–11.

147   **"Our economic situation":** Tooze, *Wages of Destruction*, 316. There has long been a debate among historians over whether a domestic economic crisis coupled with popular protest, or at least the threat of it, forced Hitler into war in 1939. In the most deeply researched and persuasive account of this issue, Adam Tooze deliberately avoids calling this a crisis, while fully outlining the economic problems that, given Hitler's plans and assumptions, pressured him into war in 1939. Tooze, *Wages of Destruction*, especially 317–19.

147   **Hitler told Goebbels:** Kershaw, *Nemesis*, 96; *TBJG*, Teil 1, Bd. 5, March 7, 1938, 193; Jodl, entry for March 11, 1938, *Diary*, 372; ADAP D 2, 157n106.

147   **Hitler's full attention:** Kershaw, *Nemesis*, 87.

148   **There was also a crucial difference:** Kershaw, *Nemesis*, 87–88.

148   **Ernst von Weizsäcker:** Weizsäcker, *Erinnerungen*, 165; Weizsäcker, diary entry for October 9, 1938, in Leonidas E. Hill, ed., *Die Weizsäcker-Papiere 1933–1950* (Berlin: Propyläen, 1974), 144.

148   **Hitler drew on tactics:** Weinberg, *Hitler's Foreign Policy*, 648.

149   **He urged Henlein:** Weinberg, *Hitler's Foreign Policy*, 660–61.

149   **Hitler wanted to do:** Weinberg, *Hitler's Foreign Policy*, 663–64.

149   **Keitel remembered:** Weinberg, *Hitler's Foreign Policy*, 735.

149   **The German plan:** Kershaw, *Nemesis*, 97.

149   **At this point:** May, *Strange Victory*, 65.

150   **"the weekend crisis":** There has long been debate about what actually happened in the weekend crisis. Long ago, Gerhard Weinberg argued that the

Czech partial mobilization of the weekend of May 20–22 was an understandable if mistaken response to a generally tense situation. A. J. P. Taylor argued in his usual puckish way that the mobilization was intended by the Czechs as a provocation to derail British appeasement policy. Andreas Krämer, in *Hitlers Kriegskurs, Appeasement und die Maikrise 1938: Entscheidungsstunde im Vorfeld von "Münchener Abkommen" und zweitem Weltkrieg* (Berlin: Walter de Gruyter, 2014), argues that the whole thing was a British Foreign Office plot to push Chamberlain into a tougher policy toward Germany. The most interesting and persuasive answer, presented here, is from work by Igor Lukes, "The Czechoslovak Partial Mobilization in May 1938: A Mystery (Almost) Solved," *Journal of Contemporary History* 31, no. 4 (October 1996): 699–720, drawing on documents received by the Czech military intelligence service, called, like its French model, the Second Bureau. See Gerhard L. Weinberg, "The May Crisis, 1938," *The Journal of Modern History* 29, no. 3 (September 1957): 213–25; A. J. P. Taylor, *The Origins of the Second World War* (Harmondsworth: Penguin, 1984).

150   **On Friday, May 20:** Lukes, "The Czechoslovak Partial Mobilization," 701–3.

150   **What had set this in motion?:** Lukes, "The Czechoslovak Partial Mobilization," 707–9.

150   **on Saturday, May 21:** Lukes, "The Czechoslovak Partial Mobilization," 710–11.

150   **But who was the source:** Lukes, "The Czechoslovak Partial Mobilization," 714–15.

151   **the consequences:** Lukes, "The Czechoslovak Partial Mobilization," 704.

151   **Henderson's smooth and formal manner:** Schmidt, *Hitler's Interpreter*, 96–98.

151   **the British government became convinced:** Chamberlain to Hilda, May 22, and to Ida, May 28, 1938, Chamberlain, *Diary Letters*, 324–25.

151   **"missed the bus":** Chamberlain to Ida, June 18, 1938, Chamberlain, *Diary Letters*, 328.

151   **"Anyone deliberately planning":** Schmidt, *Hitler's Interpreter*, 100.

151   **wiped off the map:** Kershaw, *Nemesis*, 100; Wiedemann, *Der Mann*, 126–28; Müller, *Beck Dokumente*, 512–20 and 290ff.

152   **a "convenient apparent excuse":** May, *Strange Victory*, 66; DGFP D 2, 358–64, here 358n221.

152   **The position held:** Reynolds, *Treason Was No Crime*, 175–76.

152   **Beck believed deeply:** Terry Parssinen, *Die vergessene Verschwörung: Hans Oster und der militärische Widerstand gegen Hitler* (Munich: Siedler, 2008), 67.

152   **Beck responded:** Müller, *Beck Dokumente*, 512–13n1.

152   **heard Hitler say:** Müller, *Beck Dokumente*, 512–13n1.

152   **"three or four years":** Müller, *Beck Dokumente*, 512–13n1; Hitler's words at the meeting come from adjutant Fritz Wiedemann, affidavit in IfZ ZS 191; also Wiedemann, *Der Mann*, 128.

152   **Beck's basic point:** Beck, "Stellungnahme zu den Ausführungen Hitlers am 28.5.1938," dated 29.5.1938, Müller, *Beck Dokumente*, 521–28.

153   **Beck's criticisms:** "Aufzeichnung Becks über die Vertrauenskrise in Wehrmacht und Volk gegenüber der politischen Führung," July 29, 1938, Müller, *Beck Dokumente*, 560–62.

153   **during the Fritsch crisis:** Parssinen, *Vergessene Verschwörung*, 68, citing Peter Bor, *Gespräche mit Halder*, 115.

153   **For his part:** Engel, *Heeresadjutant*, entries for July 18 and August 2, 1938, 27–29.

153   **"What kind of generals":** Parssinen, *Vergessene Verschwörung*, 74–75.

153   **One of his fellow Abwehr officers:** Parssinen, *Vergessene Verschwörung*, 49, citing Höhne, *Canaris*, 252.

154   **as Gisevius remembered:** Hans Bernd Gisevius, *Wo ist Nebe? Erinnerungen an Hitlers Reichskriminaldirektor* (Zürich: Droemer, 1966), 32.

154   **like a number of other officers:** Hans-Adolf Jacobson, ed., *Spiegelbild einer Verschwörung* (Stuttgart: Seewald, 1984), Report of October 2, 1944, 430; Liedig interview with Krausnick, IfZ ZS, 2125, S. 1; Gisevius, *Nebe*, 114.

154   **Lahousen had a strong memory:** Deutsch, *Twilight*, 87–88.

155   **Lahousen later described:** Gisevius, *Bitter End*, 439.

155   **Like most military men:** Michael Mueller, *Nazi Spymaster: The Life and Death of Admiral Wilhelm Canaris* (New York: Skyhorse Publishing, 2017), 112–15.

155   **He liked to imagine:** Weizsäcker, *Memoiren*, 174–76.

156   **"You have no idea":** Gisevius, *Nebe*, 113.

156   **When Ribbentrop asked Weizsäcker:** Diary entry, March 5, 1938, *Weizsäcker-Papiere*, 122.

156   **Just over a month later:** At least this is how the timing seems to be. In *Weizsäcker-Papiere* there is an account of a conversation in a diary entry dated March 5, 1938; in his memoirs, he locates what seems like a very similar conversation with Ribbentrop on Easter Sunday 1938, which was April 17. It is possible that his memory failed when he wrote his memoirs; it is also possible that he did not want to admit to such full knowledge before taking the state secretary position. It is also possible that there really were two separate conversations along these lines.

156   **There would still:** Weizsäcker, *Memoiren*, 154.

156   **Weizsäcker claimed:** Weizsäcker, *Memoiren*, 155.

157   **Early in 1938:** Gisevius, *Bitter End*, 416–17.

157   **"What keeps me going":** Letter, July 3, 1938, *Weizsäcker-Papiere*, 131.

158   **By July:** "Vortragsnotiz Becks über innen- und aussenpolitische Informationen von Hauptmann a.D. Wiedemann und eigene Vorschläge zu Innenpolitischen Maßnahmen der Generalität," July 29, 1938, Müller, *Beck Dokumente*, 557–60.

158   **Beck advocated an active step:** "Vortragsnotiz Becks über mögliche innen- und außenpolitische Entwicklungen, insbesondere über das Verhalten der obersten militärischen Führung angesichts der Gefahr eines Krieges mit der Tschechoslowakei," July 16, 1938, Müller, *Beck Dokumente*, 551–54.

158   **Beck thought:** "Vortragsnotiz Becks über innen- und aussenpolitische Informationen von Hauptmann a.D. Wiedemann und eigene Vorschläge zu Innenpolitischen Maßnahmen der Generalität," July 29, 1938, Müller, *Beck Dokumente*, 557–560.

158   **Beck was now contemplating a coup d'état:** Hoffmann, *German Resistance*, 77.

158   **On August 4:** Hoffmann, *German Resistance*, 79; Parssinen, *Vergessene Verschwörung*, 95.

159   **Other regime skeptics:** Hoffmann, *German Resistance*, 79.

159   **Beck's departure:** Fritsch to Hossbach, November 7, 1938, Beck to Hossbach, November 20, 1938, BA-MA N24/13, *Nachlass Hossbach*.

159   **Beck, Weizsäcker, and Oster:** Weizsäcker, *Memoiren*, 172.

160   **In mid-August:** Ian Colvin, *Master Spy: The Incredible Story of Admiral Wilhelm Canaris* (New York: McGraw-Hill, 1952), 76; Colvin, *Vansittart in Office*, 223; Parssinen, *Vergessene Verschwörung*, 102.

160   **Kleist told Vansittart:** "Note of a Conversation Between Sir. R. Vansittart and Herr von Kleist," *DBFP*, series 3, vol. 2, 686; Hoffmann, *Resistance*, 60–61.

160   **Chamberlain had just received contradictory advice:** *DBFP*, series 3, vol. 2, 686–87.

160   **One of the most determined:** Hoffmann, *Resistance*, 55; Ian Colvin, *Vansittart in Office* (London: Victor Gollancz Ltd., 1965),149–55, 205–6; Peter Hoffmann, *Carl Goerdeler gegen die Verfolgung der Juden* (Cologne: Böhlau Verlag, 2013), 101–4.

161   **Such messages only convinced:** Hoffmann, *German Resistance*, 57, 60–62.

161   **And sometimes:** Colvin, *Vansittart in Office*, 205–6.

161   **many British officials had concluded:** Hoffmann, *German Resistance*, 57–58.

161   **On September 6:** Kordt, *Nicht aus den Akten*, 246–50; Hoffmann, *Resistance*, 66–67n76.

162   **Kordt thought Halifax seemed sympathetic:** Parssinen, *Vergessene Verschwörung*, 145.

162   **Almost everyone:** Bor, *Gespräche*; Gerd R. Ueberschär, *Generaloberst Franz Halder: Generalstabschef, Gegner und Gefangener Hitlers* (Göttingen: Muster-Schmidt Verlag, 1991), 10–25.

163   **Halder had been an anti-Nazi:** Ueberschär, *Halder*, 31; Deutsch, *Twilight*, 31.

163   **When Gisevius met with Halder:** Gisevius, *Bitter End*, 288–89.

163   **probably on September 5:** Hoffmann, *Resistance*, 82 and 557n18.

163   **Gisevius struggled to square:** Gisevius, *Bitter End*, 292–93.

164   **The civilians:** Gisevius, *Bitter End*, 302, 298.

164   **The conspirators were not quite sure:** Hoffmann, *German Resistance*, 90.

164   **Beck and Hans von Dohnanyi:** Hoffmann, *German Resistance*, 90–91.

165   **The conspiracy also had its raiding party:** Hoffmann, *German Resistance*, 91–93.

165   **On September 12:** Domarus, *Hitler*, vol. 2, 1150–51, translation modified with reference to the German text.

9. "OUT OF THIS NETTLE, DANGER"

167   **Grey will admit this:** Viscount Grey of Fallodon, *Twenty-Five Years: 1892–1916* (New York: Frederick A. Stokes Company, 1925), 278–80.

167   **After the May crisis:** John Barnes and David Nicholson, eds., *The Empire at Bay: The Leo Amery Diaries, 1929–1945* (London: Hutchinson, 1988), entry for May 30, 1938, 506.

167   **"I keep racking my brains"** Chamberlain to Ida, September 3, 1938, Chamberlain, *Diary Letters*, 342.

167   **On Wednesday:** Chamberlain, *Diary Letters*, note 104, 344.

167   **That same day:** "Nuremberg and Aussig," *The Times*, September 7, 1938.

168   **Goebbels commented:** *TBJG*, Teil 1, Bd. 6, September 8, 1938, 78.

168   **By September 9:** Chamberlain, *Diary Letters*, note 104, 344.

168   **Chamberlain thought:** Chamberlain to Ida, September 19, 1938, Chamberlain, *Diary Letters*, 345.

168   **Hitler was not happy:** *TBJG*, Teil 1, Bd. 6, September 15, 1938, 91.

169   **Neville Chamberlain was sixty-nine years old:** Self, *Chamberlain*, 311.

169   **I must confess:** Neville Chamberlain to Ida, September 19, 1938, Chamberlain, *Diary Letters*, 345–49. That Hitler had been a house painter was a mistake widely circulated in Britain before the war. Hitler was never a house painter, but rather, for a time, a painter of postcards in Vienna.

169   **Hitler led Chamberlain:** Schmidt, *Hitler's Interpreter*, 106.

169   **"For the most part":** Chamberlain to Ida, September 19, 1938, Chamberlain, *Diary Letters*, 345–49.

170   **Schmidt remembered:** Schmidt, *Hitler's Interpreter*, 106.

170   **Chamberlain responded firmly:** Schmidt, *Hitler's Interpreter*, 106.

170   **Hitler pointed out:** Schmidt, Memorandum, September 15, 1938, DGFP doc. 487, 786–98.

170   **Chamberlain concluded:** Cabinet, September 17, 1938, TNA CAB 23/95, 72, 75.

171   **"Hitler told me":** Self, *Chamberlain*, 314.

171   **The prime minister believed:** Chamberlain to Ida, September 19, 1938, Chamberlain, *Diary Letters*, 345–49.

171   **Hitler described him to Goebbels:** *TBJG*, Teil 1, Bd. 6, September 17, 1938, 94, September 18, 1938, 97; Fest, *Hitler*, 546.

171   **The British cabinet met:** Cabinet, September 17, 1938, TNA CAB 23/95, 110.

172   **The British had to work hard:** Cabinet, September 19, 1938, TNA CAB 23-95, 116.

172   **Ultimately, the French and British:** David Dilks, ed., *The Diaries of Sir Alexander Cadogan, 1938–1945* (New York: G. P. Putnam's Sons, 1972), 100; appendix to cabinet of September 19, 1938, TNA CAB 23/95, 138.

172   **Before he left:** Cabinet, September 21, 1938, TNA CAB 23/95, 136, 163.

172   **Cadogan thought that this point:** Cadogan, *Diaries*, 102.

172   **The destination this time:** Schmidt, *Hitler's Interpreter*, 108. In one of history's little ironies, this hotel would be the headquarters of the Allied High Commission to Germany in the latter stages of the post–World War II occupation, from 1949 to 1955. Ivone Kirkpatrick would return to the Petersberg as the British high commissioner, and André François-Poncet, French ambassador to Germany from 1931 to 1938, would be there on behalf of France.

172   **Business began . . . two o'clock in the morning:** Schmidt, *Hitler's Interpreter*, 110–15.

173   **Chamberlain met his cabinet:** Cabinet, September 24, 1938, TNA CAB 23/95, 168.

173   **Cadogan had been horrified:** Cadogan, *Diaries*, 103; John Julius Norwich, ed., *The Duff Cooper Diaries, 1915–1951* (London: Weidenfeld and Nicolson, 2005), 265.

173   **If he was credulous about Hitler:** Cabinet, September 24, 1938, TNA CAB 23/95, 181.

174   **as his plane returned:** Cabinet, September 24, 1938, TNA CAB 23/95, 180.

174   **A crucial development:** Cadogan, *Diaries*, 103.

174   **Halifax told Cadogan:** Cadogan, *Diaries*, 105.

175   **Quietly but emotionally:** Cabinet, September 25, 1938, TNA CAB 23/95, 199.

175   **After this:** Cadogan, *Diaries*, 105–6; Roberts, *Holy Fox*, 116–18.

175   **The argument in cabinet came down:** Cabinet, September 25, 1938, TNA CAB 23/95, 233.

176   **Chamberlain proposed:** Cabinet, September 25, 1938, TNA CAB 23/95, 240.

176   **Horace Wilson would take the letter:** Cabinet, September 25, 1938, TNA CAB 23/95, 240–45.

176   **Halifax had cabled Chamberlain:** Roberts, *Holy Fox*, 113.

176   **Three days later:** Nicolson, *Diaries 1930–1939*, 367–68.

176   **The Foreign Office:** Telford Taylor, *Munich: The Price of Peace* (Garden City, NY: Doubleday, 1979), 863.

176   **Churchill claimed:** Churchill, *Gathering Storm*, 308–9. Halifax disputed Churchill's claim after the war, and Halifax's memory seems more plausible in this case: Roberts, *Holy Fox*, 119.

176   **The government began:** Taylor, *Munich*, 862–63.

177   **Horace Wilson was sent:** Cabinet, September 26, 1938, TNA CAB 23/95, 248.

177   **Horace Wilson visited Hitler:** Cabinet, September 27, 1938, TNA CAB 23/95, 263ff; Domarus, *Hitler*, 2:1196.

177   **On Monday evening . . . "will always back me":** Domarus, *Hitler*, 2:1182–94, translation modified with reference to the German text.

178   **The American radio reporter:** William Shirer, *Berlin Diary: The Journal of a Foreign Correspondent, 1934–1941* (Baltimore, MD: Johns Hopkins University Press, 2002), 141.

178   **Shirer thought:** Shirer, *Berlin Diary*, 142.

178   **Shirer and others who heard:** *TBJG*, Teil 1, Bd. 6, September 27, 1938, 115.

179   **When Hitler was finished:** Domarus, *Hitler*, 2:1194.

179   **A "curious audience":** Shirer, *Berlin Diary*, 141.

179   **That became clear:** Shirer, *Berlin Diary*, 142–43.

179   **On Tuesday morning:** Paul Schmidt, Memorandum, DGFP, series D, vol. 2, no. 634, 963–65; Cabinet, September 27, 1938, TNA CAB 23/95, 263–68.

180   **That evening, Chamberlain spoke:** Neville Chamberlain, *The Struggle for Peace* (London: Hutchinson, 1939), 274–75.

180   **Then came Chamberlain's ideas:** Chamberlain, *Struggle for Peace*, 276.

181   **Duff Cooper was irritated:** Duff Cooper, *Diaries*, 268.

181   **Chamberlain's tone probably reflected:** Quoted in Cadogan, *Diaries*, 108.

181   **When Hans Bernd Gisevius:** Gisevius, *Bitter End*, 322.

182   **Yet, when the news:** Gisevius, *Bitter End*, 323.

182   **The resisters kept doggedly:** Gisevius, *Bitter End*, 323–24.

182   **"For the first and the last time":** Gisevius, *Bitter End*, 324.

182   **That night Heinz met:** Hoffmann, *German Resistance*, 96.

182   **Canaris had told the Abwehr officer:** Parssinen, *Vergessene Verschwörung*, 216–17.

182   **Despite the rising tension:** Hoffmann, *German Resistance*, 96.

183   **"While Brauchitsch":** Gisevius, *Bitter End*, 325.

183   **a day that Jodl:** Jodl, entry for September 28, *Diary*, 388; Wiedemann, *Der Mann*, 177.

183   **"a kind of standing colloquium":** Weizsäcker, *Erinnerungen*, 187.

183   **That morning in Rome:** Schmidt, *Hitler's Interpreter*, 118; Kordt, *Nicht aus den Akten*, 270–71.

184   **One source was a telegram from President Roosevelt:** Roosevelt to Hitler, DGFP, series D, vol. 2, doc. 632, 958–59.

184   **Hitler told Göring:** Weizsäcker, *Erinnerungen*, 188; Wiedemann, *Der Mann*, 176.

184   **"We could not understand":** Gisevius, *Bitter End*, 326.

185   **Walking to the House of Commons:** Nicolson, *Diaries 1930–1939*, 369.

185   **A little after three:** Nicolson, *Diaries 1930–1939*, 368–69.

185   **as The Times reported:** *The Times*, "Dramatic Climax to Prime Minister's Speech," September 29, 1938.

185   **"we were all conscious":** Nicolson, *Diaries 1930–1939*, 370.

186   **What had happened:** Cadogan, *Diaries*, 109; *The Times*, "Dramatic Climax to Prime Minister's Speech," September 29, 1938.

186   **Members of the House of Lords:** *The Times*, "Dramatic Climax to Prime Minister's Speech," September 29, 1938.

186   **Virtually all members:** Faber, *Munich, 1938*, 397–98.

186   **Harold Nicolson did not rise:** Nicolson, *Diaries 1930–1939*, 371.

186   **Lord Dunglass heard Annie Chamberlain:** Faber, *Munich*, 399. The source is from Dunglass (later Prime Minister Sir Alec Douglas-Home), and Faber was the first to quote it.

187   **"Out of this nettle, danger":** Faber, *Munich*, 401.

187   **French ambassador André François-Poncet:** André François-Poncet, *The Fateful Years: Memoirs of a French Ambassador in Berlin* (New York: Harcourt, 1949), 269.

187   **Things got under way at 12:45:** François-Poncet, *Fateful Years*, 271.

187   **Weizsäcker recalled:** Weizsäcker, *Erinnerungen*, 189.

187   **Hitler thanked everyone:** DGFP doc. 670, 1003–5; Ciano, *Diary*, 135.

188   **For the last time:** Weizsäcker, *Erinnerungen*, 190; François-Poncet, *Fateful Years*, 269–71.

188   **In the early afternoon:** François-Poncet, *Fateful Years*, 270.

189   **The conference broke for lunch:** François-Poncet, *Fateful Years*, 271–72.

189   **The settlement provided:** Agreement, September 29, 1938, DGFP doc. 675, 1014–15.

190   **"Everyone is satisfied":** Ciano, *Diary*, 136.

190   **"I asked Hitler":** Chamberlain to Hilda, October 2, 1938, Chamberlain, *Diary Letters*, 349–51.

190   **Chamberlain explained his strategy:** Alec Douglas-Home, *The Way the Wind Blows: An Autobiography* (London: Collins, 1976), 83.

190   **"had a very friendly & pleasant talk":** Chamberlain to Hilda, October 2, 1938, Chamberlain, *Diary Letters*, 349–51.

190   **Ciano wrote:** Ciano, *Diary*, 136.

190   **Daladier had expected:** May, *Strange Victory*, 186–87.

190   **"The people are crazy":** Hugh Ragsdale, *The Soviets, the Munich Crisis, and the Coming of World War II* (Cambridge, UK: Cambridge University Press, 2004), 169.

190   **"Even the descriptions of the papers":** Chamberlain to Hilda, October 2, 1938, Chamberlain, *Diary Letters*, 349–51.

10. "LIVING AT THE POINT OF A GUN"

192   **Radio listeners hear:** Howard Koch, *The Panic Broadcast: Portrait of an Event* (Boston: Little, Brown and Company, 1970), 36–37, 40.

192   **The bulletins keep coming:** Koch, *Panic Broadcast*, 41–42.

193   **The world is a nervous place:** Hadley Cantril, *The Invasion from Mars: A Study in the Psychology of Panic* (Princeton, NJ: Princeton University Press, 1940), 159–61.

194   **Koch himself is skilled:** Aljean Harmetz, *Round Up the Usual Suspects: The Making of Casablanca: Bogart, Bergman, and World War II* (New York: Hyperion, 2002), 52.

194   **Orson Welles thinks a lot:** Cantril, *Mars*, xi–xii; Robert J. Brown, *Manipulating the Ether: The Power of Broadcast Radio in Thirties America* (Jefferson, NC: McFarland and Co., 1998), 199, 226; A. Brad Schwartz, *Broadcast Hysteria: Orson Welles's War of the Worlds and the Art of Fake News* (New York: Hill and Wang, 2015).

194   **A few days after the broadcast:** Dorothy Thompson, "Mr. Welles and Mass Delusion," *New York Herald Tribune*, November 2, 1938. A. Brad Schwartz has

argued recently, on the basis of an extensive survey of listeners' letters, that the real panic was over the terrible influence new media such as radio could have on gullible citizens: Schwartz, *Broadcast Hysteria*. I am grateful to Henry Hemming for drawing this book to my attention. On Cantril's activities, see British Security Coordination, *The Secret History of British Intelligence in the Americas, 1940–1945* (New York: Fromm International, 1999), 222–26; Henry Hemming, *Agents of Influence: A British Campaign, a Canadian Spy, and the Secret Plot to Bring America into World War II* (New York: Public Affairs, 2019), 245. Again, I am grateful to Henry Hemming for this information.

195   **Daladier told his aides:** May, *Strange Victory*, 168.

195   **Ciano recorded:** Ciano, *Diary*, 136.

195   **Much like Daladier:** Parker, *Chamberlain*, 181; Feiling, *Chamberlain*, 382; Halifax letter to *The Times*, October 28, 1948. In his letter, Halifax argued that Chamberlain had meant the adulation of the crowds, not the settlement with Hitler.

195   **He was exhausted:** Chamberlain to Hilda, October 2, 1938, Chamberlain, *Diary Letters*, 349–51.

196   **considerable bitterness in eastern Europe:** Ragsdale, *Soviets and Munich*, 169.

196   **On the evening of September 29:** Duff Cooper, *Diaries*, 270.

196   **Churchill directed his anger:** Duff Cooper, *Diaries*, 270; Faber, *Munich*, 417–18.

197   **As they passed an open door:** Gilbert, *Prophet of Truth*, 990.

197   **The day began:** *Hansard*, October 3, 1938, cc. 29–40.

197   **He was a core member:** Gerard J. De Groot, *Liberal Crusader: The Life of Sir Archibald Sinclair* (New York: New York University Press, 1993), 120; Jenkins, *Churchill*, especially 481–504.

198   **Under the cover . . . in the olden time:** *Hansard*, October 5, 1938, cc. 360–73.

201   **Much of the press:** Gilbert, *Prophet of Truth*, 1002.

201   **Only two dozen Conservative members:** Faber, *Munich*, 425.

201   **Hans Bernd Gisevius still hoped:** Gisevius, *Bitter End*, 326.

201   **Ambassador Nevile Henderson:** Hoffmann, *German Resistance*, 96.

201   **His anger poured out:** Domarus, *Hitler*, 2:1221–24.

202   **Chamberlain's efforts:** Domarus, *Hitler*, 2:1221–24.

202   **At the end of the year:** Pedersen, *Rathbone*, 293–94.

202   **Roosevelt had suffered from ambivalence:** Dallek, *Franklin D. Roosevelt and American Foreign Policy*, 164.

203   **I guess my best bet:** John Morton Blum, *From the Morgenthau Diaries: Years of Crisis, 1928–1938* (Boston: Houghton Miflin Company, 1959), 519.

203   **On September 19 . . . "hopelessly prejudiced":** Lindsay to Halifax, September 20, 1938, DBFP, 3rd series, vol. 7, Appendix 4 (v), 627–29.

204   **"Good man":** Burns, *The Lion and the Fox*, 387.

205   **"There can be no peace":** Radio message to the *Herald Tribune* Forum, October 26, 1938, FDR Master Speech File no. 1177. The idea of Munich as a turning point for FDR is thoroughly canvassed in Barbara Farnham,

Roosevelt and the Munich Crisis: A Study of Political Decision Making (Princeton, NJ: Princeton University Press, 1997).

205   **"It would not hurt us":** Entry for December 24, 1938, Harold L. Ickes, *The Secret Diary of Harold L. Ickes*, vol. 2, *The Inside Struggle 1936–1939* (New York: Simon and Schuster, 1954), 533.

205   **One of Roosevelt's worries:** Robert Edwin Herzstein, *Roosevelt and Hitler: Prelude to War* (New York: Paragon House, 1989), 220, 240, 243, 294.

205   **Over the Christmas season:** Burns, *The Lion and the Fox*, 388–89.

206   **"In reporting on the state of the nation":** FDR State of the Union address, January 4, 1939, Master Speech File no. 1191-B.

206   **It was coined in 1937:** Harold D. Lasswell, "Sino-Japanese Crisis: The Garrison State Versus the Civilian State," *The China Quarterly* 11 (Fall 1937): 643–49, reprinted in Harold D. Lasswell, *Essays on the Garrison State* (New York: Routledge, 2017), 43–54; Harold D. Lasswell, "The Garrison State," *American Journal of Sociology* 46, no. 4 (January 1941), 455–68, 455–56, 458.

207   **Ludendorff had seen:** Lasswell, "Garrison State," 467.

207   **Lasswell was not alone:** Lippmann, *Phantom Public*, 182–83.

207   **Former president Herbert Hoover:** Herzstein, *Roosevelt and Hitler*, 224; Doris Kearns Goodwin, *No Ordinary Time: Franklin and Eleanor Roosevelt: The Home Front in World War II* (New York: Simon and Schuster, 1994), 54; David Nasaw, *The Patriarch: The Remarkable Life and Turbulent Times of Joseph P. Kennedy* (New York: Penguin Press, 2012), 373.

207   **But liberal-minded anti-Nazis:** Walter Lippmann, "The Atlantic . . . and America," *Life*, April 7, 1941, 84–92, here 86–87, 92; Reynolds, *Long Shadow*, 263.

208   **In a 1936 message:** Patel, *New Deal*, 1.

208   **On the eve:** FDR, Radio Address, November 4, 1938, FDR Master Speech File no. 1179-A.

208   **The second element:** J. Garry Clifford and Samuel R. Spencer Jr., *The First Peacetime Draft* (Lawrence: Kansas University Press, 1986), 41.

208   **Tukhachevsky had poured scorn:** N. Iu. Berezovskii, "Na bor'bu s 'limitrofami,'" *Voenno-istoricheskii Zhurnal*, no. 4, 1993, 53–62.

209   **Britain and America were alike:** Tami Davis Biddle, *Rhetoric and Reality in Air Warfare: The Evolution of British and American Ideas About Strategic Bombing, 1914–1945* (Princeton, NJ: Princeton University Press, 2002), 174–75; Michael S. Sherry, *The Rise of American Air Power: The Creation of Armageddon* (New Haven, CT: Yale University Press, 1987), 53.

209   **This point was critical for democracies:** Richard Overy, *The Bombing War: Europe, 1939–1945* (London: Allen Lane, 2013), 52.

209   **the United States led the world:** Biddle, *Rhetoric and Reality*, 146–47.

210   **One of Roosevelt's first actions:** Doenecke and Wilz, *From Isolation to War*, 92–93.

210   **the air corps budget nearly tripled:** Biddle, *Rhetoric and Reality*, 145–46.

210   **Roosevelt, much like Chamberlain:** Meeting at the White House, November 14, 1938, *Morgenthau Diary*, 150:338.

210   **In the run-up to Munich:** Harold Ickes, entry for September 18, 1938, *Diary*, 2:469.

210   **United States made critical contributions:** Biddle, *Rhetoric and Reality*, 156–57; Ickes, entry of September 18, 1938, *Diary*, 2:469.

211   **The defeat of the Confederacy:** Biddle, *Rhetoric and Reality*, 157.

211   **Frances Perkins:** Frances Perkins, *The Roosevelt I Knew* (New York: Penguin Books, 2011), 316.

212   **historian Ky Woltering:** Ky Woltering, *"A Christian World Order": Protestants, Democracy, and Christian Aid to Germany, 1945 to 1961*, PhD diss., City University of New York, 2018. Recent historical research has stressed the influence of a Christian outlook on American foreign policy: See, for instance, Jason Stevens, *God Fearing and Free: A Spiritual History of America's Cold War* (Cambridge, MA: Harvard University Press, 2010); Jonathan Herzog, *The Spiritual Industrial Complex: America's Religious Battle Against Communism in the Early Cold War* (New York: Oxford University Press, 2011).

212   **in his 1939:** FDR, State of the Union address, January 4, 1939, Master Speech File no. 1191-B.

213   **Ickes never worried:** Jeanne Nienaber Clarke, *Roosevelt's Warrior: Harold L. Ickes and the New Deal* (Baltimore, MD, and London: Johns Hopkins University Press, 1996), 3–23; Olson, *Those Angry Days*, 21–22.

213   **On December 18:** *New York Times*, December 19, 1938, "Ickes Hits Takers of Hitler Medals."

214   **But what followed . . . "of any country":** "What Ickes Said That the Nazis Now Protest," *New York Herald Tribune*, December 23, 1938.

215   **It had been clear:** Saul Friedländer, *Prelude to Downfall: Hitler and the United States, 1939–1941* (New York: Alfred A. Knopf, 1967), 5–6; Farnham, *Roosevelt and the Munich Crisis*, 5–6, 137–72; Brendon, *Dark Valley*, 545.

215   **This was the context:** Ickes, *Diary*, December 24, 1938, 533.

215   **Hitler was highly attentive:** May, *Strange Victory*, 103.

216   **Ickes surmised:** Ickes, entry for December 24, 1938, *Secret Diary*, vol. 2, 533.

216   **But the Nazis found:** "Amerika und Deutschland," *Völkischer Beobachter*, January 1, 1939; Kennedy, *Freedom from Fear*, 391.

216   **The reaction to Roosevelt's speech:** "Selbstentlarvung der Heuchler von Washington," *Völkischer Beobachter*, January 6, 1939.

217   **The Nazi press:** "Roosevelts Kriegshetze," *Völkischer Beobachter*, January 8, 1939.

217   **laced with antisemitism:** "USA unter jüdischer Diktatur: Um Roosevelt und Ickes wimmelt es von Juden," *Völkischer Beobachter*, January 8, 1939.

217   **The week before the speech:** TBJG, Teil 1, Bd. 6, January 24, 1939, 237.

217   **"hard polemic":** TBJG, Teil 1, Bd. 6, January 31, 1939, 244–45.

217   **Hitler poured scorn:** Max Domarus, *Hitler: Speeches and Proclamations, 1932–1945*, vol. 3, *1939–1940* (Wauconda, IL: Bolchazy-Carducci Publishers, 1997), 1436–59, translation modified with reference to the German text.

218   **Ickes was delighted:** Ickes, *Diary*, February 4, 1939, 572–73.

219   **he told the Soviet ambassador:** Maisky, *Diaries*, 107, 110, 122.

219   **a much more jaundiced view:** Chamberlain to Ida, March 20, 1938, Chamberlain, *Diary Letters*, 307.

219   **The Soviet Union did not border:** Kotkin, *Stalin: Waiting for Hitler*, 562–63.

220   **Nonetheless, Stalin mobilized:** Kotkin, *Stalin: Waiting for Hitler*, 564–69.

220   **During the Munich crisis:** Andrew and Mitrokhin, *The Sword and the Shield*, 81.

220   **A few years later:** Milovan Djilas, *Conversations with Stalin* (New York: Harcourt, Brace and World, 1962), 114.

220   **"By attacking Poland":** Ragsdale, *The Soviets*, 167.

221   **As the Czech crisis blew up:** Kotkin, *Stalin: Waiting for Hitler*, 562.

221   **On September 15:** Snyder, *Black Earth*, 91.

221   **The fifth partially mobilized Soviet Army group:** Ragsdale, *The Soviets*, 144.

221   **As a route to Czechoslovakia:** Ragsdale, *The Soviets*, 157–58.

222   **only a few days after:** Kotkin, *Stalin: Waiting for Hitler*, 568–69, 573–76.

222   **Another fundamental change:** Kotkin, *Stalin: Waiting for Hitler*, 495–96, 578.

223   **The brilliant and courtly general:** Rodric Braithwaite, *Moscow 1941: A City and Its People at War* (New York: Alfred A. Knopf, 2006), 38–41; Snyder, *Bloodlands*, 97–99.

11. "A DISSEMINATION OF DISCORD"

224   **The event is controversial:** "1,300 Police to Guard Bund Rally Tonight," *New York Herald Tribune*, February 20, 1939.

224   **Outside the Garden:** "Miss Thompson Issues Protest on Bund Rally," *New York Herald Tribune*, February 21, 1939; *A Night at the Garden*, dir. Marshall Curry, documentary film, 2017.

225   **Thompson hears speakers:** Dorothy Thompson, "To the Intolerant," *New York Herald Tribune*, February 22, 1939.

225   **The crowd boos:** "Many Injured in Bund Riots," *Los Angeles Times*, February 21, 1939.

225   **One man goes further:** "Many Injured in Bund Riots," *Los Angeles Times*, February 21, 1939; *A Night at the Garden*.

226   **Yet the Bundists:** "Many Injured in Bund Riots," *Los Angeles Times*, February 21, 1939; "22,000 Nazis Hold Rally in Garden," *New York Times*, February 21, 1939; *A Night at the Garden*.

226   **"If . . . this democracy allows a movement":** "Miss Thompson Issues Protest on Bund Rally," *New York Herald Tribune*, February 21, 1939.

226   **The Great Depression:** Bureau of Labor Statistics, *Historical Statistics of the United States Colonial Times to 1970*, Part I (Washington, DC: U.S. Government Printing Office, 1975), series D, 85–86 Unemployment: 1890–1970, 135; National Income and Wealth, 232; Manufactures, 666.

227	**Two days after:** Ronald Steel, *Walter Lippmann and the American Century* (New York: Routledge, 2017), 300.
227	**Roosevelt's New Deal:** Katznelson, *Fear Itself*, introduction, 3–26.
227	**The Republican senator William Borah:** Patel, *New Deal*, 18.
227	**Madison Grant:** Okrent, *Guarded Gate*, 380.
227	**During the 1920s:** Frank Costigliola, *Awkward Dominion: American Political, Economic and Cultural Relations with Europe, 1919–1933* (Ithaca, NY: Cornell University Press, 1988), 15–24; Patel, *New Deal*, 2.
228	**This had been brewing:** See generally Okrent, *The Guarded Gate*.
228	**The war gave a dramatic boost:** Patel, *New Deal*, 18–19.
228	**In this atmosphere:** See generally Linda Gordon, *The Second Coming of the KKK: The Ku Klux Klan of the 1920s and the American Political Tradition* (New York: Liveright, 2017); on the German parallel, see Hett, *Death of Democracy*.
228	**Of course, this effort:** Katznelson, *Fear Itself*, 15, 140, 150–51, 167.
229	**the German American Bund:** Hart, *Hitler's American Friends*, 8, 40, 93, 16.
229	**even to the New Deal:** Patel, *New Deal*, 50.
229	**He was a great admirer:** Hitler, *Mein Kampf*, IfZ 2:1111, 2:1117.
229	**When the Nazis took power:** James Q. Whitman, *Hitler's American Model: The United States and the Making of Nazi Race Law* (Princeton, NJ: Princeton University Press, 2017), 5–8, 137–40.
229	**"classic example":** Whitman, *Hitler's American Model*, 3–4.
230	**the First World War:** *Evening News*, September 29, 1914; *The Times*, May 10, 1915; Catriona Pennell, "Believing the Unbelievable: The Myth of the Russians with 'Snow on Their Boots' in the United Kingdom, 1914," *Cultural and Social History* 11, no. 1 (2014): 69–88.
230	**a short book:** Steel, *Lippmann*, 148, 171–72.
230	**The number of Americans:** Lippmann, *Phantom Public*, 26–27.
230	**"We do not first see":** Lippmann, *Public Opinion*, 39; Steel, *Lippmann*, 181.
230	**"Public men":** Lippmann, *Phantom Public*, 149–51.
230	**The new breed:** Lippmann in the *New York World*, October 27, 1927, quoted in Steel, *Lippmann*, 218.
231	**One of the pioneers:** Ray Eldon Hiebert, *Courtier to the Crowd: The Story of Ivy Lee and the Development of Public Relations* (Ames: Iowa State University Press, 1966), 284–92; Michael Schudson, *Discovering the News: A Social History of American Newspapers* (New York: Basic Books, 1978), 134–44; Jill Lepore, *These Truths: A History of the United States* (New York: W. W. Norton, 2018), 412; Daly, *Covering America*, 148–49.
231	**Here the pioneers:** Lepore, *These Truths*, 446–49, 452.
231	**a simple theme:** Lepore, *These Truths*, 449–51.
232	**For his part:** Hitler, *Mein Kampf*, IfZ 2:1191–93, 2:1195, 2:1477.
232	**Hitler had the same low opinion:** Hitler, *Mein Kampf*, 1:505–9.
232	**Just as Ivy Lee:** Hitler, *Mein Kampf*, 1:617.
233	**"When I look":** Domarus, *Hitler*, 2:1251–52.
233	**Goebbels expressed the same contempt:** Evans, *Third Reich in Power*, 136.

233   **Goebbels drew an important:** Joseph Goebbels, "Was will eigentlich Amerika?" *Völkischer Beobachter,* January 21, 1939.

234   **It remained for Hitler:** Domarus, *Hitler,* 2:1244–55, translation modified with reference to the German text; "Rede Hitlers vor der deutschen Presse," *Vierteljahrshefte für Zeitgeschichte* 2 (1958): 174–91.

235   **Nazi police and intelligence forces:** Charmian Brinson, *The Strange Case of Dora Fabian and Mathilde Worm* (Berne: Peter Lang, 1996), 13, 53–61.

235   **Also in 1935:** Brinson, *Dora Fabian,* 14, 44–61, 132; material on the investigations and witness statements in TNA MEPO 3/871. There is also a powerful and beautifully written novel about this story and Fabian's connection to the exiled writer Ernst Toller: Anna Funder, *All That I Am* (New York: HarperCollins, 2012). I am grateful for having had the chance to discuss the case with Anna Funder.

236   **There was institutional organization:** Brinson, *Dora Fabian,* 35–40.

236   **"We have learned":** FDR State of the Union address, January 4, 1939, Master Speech File no. 1191-B.

236   **"a dissemination of discord":** Fireside Chat, May 26, 1940, Master Speech File no. 1283-A.

236   **A few months later:** Quoted in Cook, *Eleanor Roosevelt,* 3:376.

236   **In the late 1930s:** Hart, *Hitler's American Friends,* 97–98, 100, 103–4, 107; Hemming, *Agents of Influence,* 36–42.

237   **Shortly before Lundeen:** Hart, *Hitler's American Friends,* 111–14.

237   **The German government:** Hart, *Hitler's American Friends,* 116–35; Olson, *Those Angry Days,* 182–83.

238   **The agent:** Wolfgang Gans Edler Herr zu Putlitz, *The Putlitz Dossier* (London: Wingate, 1957), chap. 5, 91, 96.

238   **He communicated with MI5:** Peter Wright, *Spycatcher: The Candid Autobiography of a Senior Intelligence Officer* (New York: Viking, 1987), 68; Peter Day, *Klop: Britain's Most Ingenious Agent* (London: Biteback Publishing, 2014), chap. 8.

238   **The team of Putlitz and Klop:** Andrew, *Defend the Realm,* 196–204.

239   **SIS and MI5:** Andrew, *Defend the Realm,* 201–4.

239   **But the response:** M. H. Jay to Mr. Jenkins, February 21, 1985; Cadogan note, December 1, 1938, TNA FO 1093. I am very grateful to Professor John Ferris, one of the leading experts on British intelligence, who brought this file to my attention.

239   **MI5 also secured:** Hesse to Ribbentrop, November 25, 1938, BNA FO 1093. The file contains a modified version dated November 26, apparently after edits from Dirksen; it omits the line about agitators having a spoke put in their wheel, but this presumably doesn't change the fact that Steward said this to Hesse.

241   **On the night of February 6:** May, *Strange Victory,* 116.

241   **Blum came into office:** Julian Jackson, *The Popular Front in France: Defending Democracy, 1934–1938* (New York: Cambridge University Press, 1988), 149, 151, 189, 251.

242   **Blum's government managed:** May, *Strange Victory,* 123–24.

242   **The political polarization:** Jackson, *Popular Front*, 250.

242   **François de La Roque:** Robert O. Paxton, *The Anatomy of Fascism* (New York: Vintage, 2004), 68–73.

243   **Not only was there no election:** May, *Strange Victory*, 155–56.

244   **"Neville, you must remember":** Self, *Chamberlain*, 235.

244   **"vividly demonstrated":** James D. Margach, *Abuse of Power: The War Between Downing Street and the Media from Lloyd George to Callaghan* (London: W. H. Allen, 1978), 51.

244   **George Orwell wrote:** Samuel Hynes, *The Auden Generation: Literature and Politics in England in the 1930s* (Princeton, NJ: Princeton University Press, 1982), 373.

244   **In his 1939 novel:** George Orwell, *Coming Up for Air* (New York: Harcourt, 1999), 445.

245   **a senior Conservative official worried:** Self, *Chamberlain*, 261–62.

245   **John Colville:** May, *Strange Victory*, 172; Colville, *Fringes of Power*, February 2, 1940, 57–58.

245   **Chamberlain's loyal supporters:** Self, *Chamberlain*, 350.

245   **Margach called him:** Margach, *Abuse of Power*, 50–53.

246   **Margach remembered:** Margach, *Abuse of Power*, 59.

246   **The reason:** Margach, *Abuse of Power*, 62.

246   **"black is white":** Richard Cockett, *Twilight of Truth: Chamberlain, Appeasement, and the Manipulation of the Press* (London: Weidenfeld and Nicolson, 1989), 7.

247   **By this time:** Hansard, August 2, 1939, cc. 2438, cc. 2441–45.

247   **After Churchill spoke:** Hansard, August 2, 1939, cc. 2469, 2484–85.

248   **"I am profoundly disturbed":** Hansard, August 2, 1939, cc. 2493–95.

248   **Cartland had spoken:** Lynne Olson, *Troublesome Young Men: The Rebels Who Brought Churchill to Power and Helped Save England* (New York: Farrar, Straus and Giroux, 2007), 17; Nicolson, *Diaries 1930–1939*, August 2, 1939, 407.

248   **But Chamberlain easily won:** Olson, *Troublesome Young Men*, 19.

249   **With his impenetrable self-righteousness:** Chamberlain to Ida, Chamberlain, *Diary Letters*, 436–38.

249   **On May 30:** Olson, *Troublesome Young Men*, 318.

12. "I HAVE TO TELL YOU NOW . . ."

253   **On February 1:** Weizsäcker, diary entry, February 1, 1939, *Weizsäcker-Papiere*, 149.

253   **Hitler's armed forces adjutant:** Hermann Teske, *Die Silbernen Spiegel: Generalstabsdienst unter der Lupe* (Heidelberg: K. Vowinckel, 1952), 59–60. Teske writes that he made these notes of what Schmundt had said right after the conversation.

254   **Hitler hardly keeps it:** Weizsäcker, diary entry, date unclear (mid-September 1938), *Weizsäcker-Papiere*, 143; Erich Kordt, *Wahn und Wirklichkeit* (Stuttgart: Union Deutsche Verlagsgesellschaft, 1948), 779.

254   **After Munich:** May, *Strange Victory*, 85.

254   **At the end of January:** *TBJG*, Teil 1, Bd. 6, January 31, 1939, 244.

254   **By early 1939:** Hjalmar Horace Greeley Schacht, *My First Seventy-Six Years: Autobiography* (London: Wingate, 1955), 386.

254   **On January 7:** Hjalmar Horace Greeley Schacht, *Account Settled* (London: Weidenfeld and Nicolson, 1949), 134–35.

254   **One official:** Schacht, *My First Seventy-Six Years*, 392.

254   **Joseph Goebbels:** *TBJG*, Teil 1, Bd. 6, January 20, 1939, 233.

254   **Late on the evening:** Schacht, *Account Settled*, 136.

255   **The next morning:** Schacht, *Account Settled*, 136–37. Schacht's account is certainly self-serving. But that the conversation really did go something like this finds substantial conformation in the diary entry of Joseph Goebbels for January 21, 1939: "[Hitler] told me about Schacht's dismissal. The conversation was very short. The Führer just gave it to Schacht straight. He was as if struck by lightning." This is exactly how, in an effort to maintain his dignity, Hitler would convey the kind of conversation that Schacht related. *TBJG*, Teil 1, Bd. 6, January 21, 1939, 234.

255   **"a nasty regime":** Kotkin, *Stalin: Waiting for Hitler*, 596.

256   **Hitler wanted Poland:** Snyder, *Black Earth*, 95–96; Memorandum, January 5, 1939, DGFP, series D, vol. 5, doc. 119, 152–58. Although Danzig was a free city, the Treaty of Versailles and other international agreements gave control of its defense and foreign relations to Poland. See E. P., "The Free City of Danzig: Some Questions Regarding Its Status," *Bulletin of International News* 16, no. 14 (July 15, 1939): 3–8.

256   **Beck met with Ribbentrop:** Memorandum by the Foreign Minister, January 6, 1939, DGFP, series F, vol. 5, doc. 120, 159–61.

256   **Ribbentrop traveled to Warsaw:** Memorandum by the Foreign Minister, February 1, 1939, DGFP, series D, vol. 5, Document 126, 167–68.

256   **the Poles were so stubborn:** Józef Beck, *Final Report* (New York: R. Speller, 1957), 173–74.

256   **Ribbentrop meant:** Rolf-Dieter Müller, *Der Feind steht im Osten: Hitlers geheime Plan für einen Krieg gegen die Sowjet Union im Jahr 1939* (Berlin: Ch. Links, 2011), 108; Snyder, *Black Earth*, 96.

257   **the Nazis used Slovakia:** Kershaw, *Nemesis*, 168–69; May, *Strange Victory*, 86; Kordt, *Wahn und Wirklichkeit*, 144.

258   **In the House:** May, *Strange Victory*, 192.

258   **French foreign minister:** Cabinet, March 15, 1939, TNA CAB 23/98, 6–8.

258   **On March 31:** *Hansard*, March 31, 1939, cc. 2415.

258   **A week later:** May, *Strange Victory*, 193; Cadogan, *Diaries*, 173.

258   **The Chamberlain government:** David French, "British Military Strategy," in John Ferris and Evan Mawdsley, eds., *The Cambridge History of the Second World War*, vol. 1, *Fighting the War* (Cambridge, UK: Cambridge University Press, 2015), 55–57.

259   **On March 21:** Memorandum by the Foreign Minister, March 21, 1939, DGFP, series D, vol. 6, 70–72.

259   **Lipski did not:** Müller, *Feind steht im Osten*, 120.

259   **Hitler emphasized:** Józef Lipski, *Diplomat in Berlin, 1933–1939: Papers and Memoirs of Józef Lipski, Ambassador of Poland* (New York: Columbia University Press, 1968), 522–23.

259   **The Germans saw:** Lipski, *Diplomat in Berlin*, 522–23.

259   **Gisevius recorded:** Gisevius, *Bitter End*, 363.

259   **Poland was militarily weaker:** May, *Strange Victory*, 192–93.

259   **When Neville Chamberlain:** A. J. P. Taylor, *Origins of the Second World War*, 277.

259   **He did not think:** Chamberlain to Ida, March 26, 1939, Chamberlain, *Diary Letters*, 396.

260   **In 1943, Sir William Strang:** Strang cited in Lothar Kettenacker, "The Anglo-Soviet Alliance and the Problem of Germany, 1941–1945," *Journal of Contemporary History*, 17, no. 3 (July 1982): 435–58, here 449; Mark Mazower, *Hitler's Empire: How the Nazis Ruled Europe* (New York: Penguin Press, 2008), 565.

260   **Its intelligence services:** Andrew and Mitrokhin, *Sword and Shield*, especially 73–75.

261   **historian Timothy Snyder:** Snyder, *Bloodlands*, 111.

261   **To make matters worse:** Kotkin, *Stalin: Waiting for Hitler*, 616–17.

261   **Even in April 1938:** Ragsdale, *Soviets*, xvi–xvii.

261   **His intelligence agencies:** Andrew and Mitrokhin, *Sword and Shield*, 81.

262   **"I cannot rid myself":** Chamberlain to Ida, May 21, 1939, Chamberlain, *Diary Letters*, 417.

262   **At the beginning of May:** Kotkin, *Stalin: Waiting for Hitler*, 623. It is also possible that the timing of Litvinov's sacking was coincidental and had nothing to do with Germany: Geoffrey K. Roberts, *The Soviet Union and the Origins of the Second World War* (London: Macmillan, 1995), 72.

262   **More information:** Coulondre to Bonnet, May 7, 1939, *Documents Diplomatiques Français*, 2. Serie, Tome 16, 221–27.

262   **On May 10:** Potemkin to Molotov, May 10, 1939, *God Krizisa 1938–1939: Dokumenty i Materialy*, Tom 1, Doc. 336, 444.

262   **spoken out of turn:** Molotov, Note, May 11, 1939, *God Krizisa, 1938–1939: Dokumenty i Materialy*, Tom 1, Doc. 332, 448–49.

263   **After a meeting with Halifax:** Maisky, *Diaries*, 192.

263   **But as the Soviet ambassador reported:** Kotkin, *Stalin: Waiting for Hitler*, 647.

263   **Cadogan noted:** Cadogan, *Diaries*, May 12, 1939, 179.

263   **The British tried:** R. A. C. Parker, *Chamberlain and Appeasement: British Policy and the Coming of the Second World War* (London: Macmillan, 1993), 231–32.

263   **In June, Molotov insisted:** Parker, *Chamberlain*, 236–38.

264   **Looking back:** Roberts, *Holy Fox*, 178.

264   **"We are only spinning":** Chamberlain to Ida, July 23, 1939, Chamberlain, *Diary Letters*, 432; Roberts, *Holy Fox*, 156–59.

264   **On July 23:** Parker, *Chamberlain*, 241.

264   **"There is no basis":** Astakhov, Note, August 2, 1939, *Dokumenty Vneshnei Politiki 1939 God*, Tom 22 (1), Doc. 445, 566–69.

264   **Astakhov reported to Molotov:** Astakhov to Molotov, August 8, 1939, Doc. 455, *Dokumenty Vneshnei Politiki 1939 God*, Tom 22 (1), 585–87.

264   **Later in August:** Note of a Conversation between Molotov and Schulenburg, August 19, 1939, Doc. 474, *Dokumenty Vneshnei Politiki 1939 God*, Tom 22 (1), 615–17.

265   **By this time:** Kotkin, *Stalin: Waiting for Hitler*, 656–57.

265   **The head of the French:** Parker, *Chamberlain*, 241–43.

265   **Voroshilov asked repeatedly:** "Procès-Verbaux Détaillés de Séances," *Documents Diplomatiques Français*, 2. Série, Tome 18, Addenda, 549–83.

266   **The Western delegations:** Parker, *Chamberlain*, 244.

266   **Weizsäcker complained:** Weizsäcker, diary entries for July 30 and August 6, 1939, *Weizsäcker-Papiere*, 157–58.

266   **Stalin told Voroshilov:** "Instruktsia," Doc. 453, *Dokumenty Vneshnei Politiki 1939 God*, Tom 22 (1), 584.

267   **The day before:** Ambassador in Moscow to Foreign Ministry, August 20, 1939, DGFP, series D, vol. 7, Doc. 132, 140–41.

267   **On August 20:** Foreign Minister to the Embassy in the Soviet Union, August 20, 1939, DGFP, series D, vol. 7, doc. 142, 156–57.

267   **Stalin ordered:** Kotkin, *Stalin: Waiting for Hitler*, 660–61.

267   **"The people of our countries":** Ambassador in the Soviet Union to Foreign Minister, DGFP, series D, vol. 7, doc. 159, 168.

267   **The war had to come now:** Speech by the Führer, August 22, 1939, DGFP, series D, vol. 7, doc. 192, 200–204; Second Speech by the Führer, August 22, 1939, DGFP, series D, vol. 7, doc. no. 193, 205–6.

267   **At his meeting with Stalin:** Record of Conversation between Ribbentrop and Stalin, August 24, 1939, DGFP, series D, vol. 7, doc. no. 213, 225–29.

267   **The pact:** Treaty of Non-Aggression Between Germany and the USSR, DGFP, series D, vol. 7, doc. no. 228, 245–46; Secret Additional Protocol, DGFP, series D, vol. 7, doc. no. 229, 246–47.

268   **Ribbentrop had wanted:** Roger Moorhouse, *The Devils' Alliance* (New York: Basic Books, 2014), 27.

268   **"time for action":** *Hansard*, September 1, 1939, cc. 127.

268   **Bafflement, discontent:** See Olson, *Troublesome Young Men*, 204–7.

269   **Chamberlain told the House:** *Hansard*, September 2, 1939, 281.

269   **The next speaker:** Olson, *Troublesome Young Men*, 208–10; *Hansard*, September 2, 1939, 282. Harold Nicolson thought another politician, the Churchill protégé Bob Boothby, made this interjection, which Boothby was happy to claim in 1965. This is a case of misidentification and faulty memory, respectively. Boothby was responsible for the other interjection about honor. Nicolson, *Diaries 1930–1939*, September 2, 1939, 419; *Hansard*, September 2, 1939, 282–83.

269   **Now the prime minister:** Olson, *Troublesome Young Men*, 209; Amery, entry for September 2, 1939, *Diaries*, 570.

269   **"I wonder how long":** *Hansard*, September 2, 1939, cc. 282–83.

269   **It was clear:** Amery, entries for September 2 and September 3, 1939, *Diaries*, 570–71.

270   **"This morning":** Neville Chamberlain, September 3, 1939, BBC transcript, http://www.bbc.co.uk/archive/ww2outbreak/7957.shtml?page=txt.

270   **The comedian:** Spike Milligan, quoted in R. J. B. Bosworth, *Explaining Auschwitz and Hiroshima: History Writing and the Second World War, 1945–1990* (London: Routledge, 1993), 31.

270   **"Your courage":** A. J. P. Taylor, quoted in Bosworth, *Explaining Auschwitz*, 36.

270   **The Poles . . . were in a hopeless position:** Evans, *Third Reich at War*, 7; Snyder, *Bloodlands*, 122; Robert Forczyk, *Case White: The Invasion of Poland, 1939* (New York: Osprey, 2019), 325, 333.

271   **WINSTON IS BACK:** Gilbert, *The Prophet of Truth*, 1113.

271   **"It is because":** Roosevelt to Churchill, September 11, 1939, in Loewenheim et al., *Secret Wartime Correspondence*, 89.

272   **In the early part of the war:** Cadogan, *Diary*, entry for September 23, 1939, 219; Chamberlain to Ida, September 10, 1940, Chamberlain, *Diary Letters*, 445.

272   **a ringing statement of the war's meaning:** Roberts, *Churchill*, 616.

272   **The indomitable Eleanor Rathbone:** Pedersen, *Rathbone*, 293, 308; Roberts, *Churchill*, 635.

13. "THESE ARE PRUSSIAN OFFICERS!"

275   **The obvious role model:** May, *Strange Victory*, 24–27. May has some of this wrong, however, writing for instance that Seydlitz was killed at Kunersdorf; he was not. See also Dennis Showalter, *Frederick the Great: A Military History* (London: Frontline Books, 2012), 236–50.

276   **King Frederick William:** Christopher Clark, *Iron Kingdom: The Rise and Downfall of Prussia, 1600–1947* (Cambridge, MA: Harvard University Press, 2006), 357–60.

276   **Prussia's superpatriotic historians:** Heinrich von Treitschke, *German History in the Nineteenth Century* (New York: Nast, Bride and Company, 1915), 1:491–92.

277   **On October 6:** Domarus, *Hitler*, 3:1828–48.

277   **On October 9:** Office of the U.S. Chief of Counsel for Prosecution of Axis Criminality, *Nazi Conspiracy and Aggression* (Washington, DC: U.S. Government Printing Office, 1946), 6:880–81.

277   **Even Walther von Reichenau:** Helmuth Groscurth, *Tagebücher eines Abwehroffiziers*, ed. Helmut Krausnick, Harold C. Deutsch, and Hildegard von Kotze (Stuttgart: Deutsche Verlags-Anstalt, 1970), introduction, 51.

277   **Ludwig Beck played a role:** Beck, "Zur Kriegslage nach Abschluss des polnischen Feldzuges," Groscurth, *Tagebücher*, Appendix 64, 474–78.

278   **Beck thought:** Beck, "Zur Kriegslage," 476–78.

278   **A few days later:** Beck, "Das Deutsche Friedensangebot vom 6.10.39 und der mögliche weitere Kriegsverlauf," Groscurth, *Tagebücher*, Anhang 2, doc. 65, 479–85.

278   **the moral foundations of political action:** Gisevius, *Bitter End*, 430, 422–443.

278   **He had never made much effort:** Wilhelm Ritter von Leeb, *Generalfeldmarschall Wilhelm Ritter von Leeb: Tagebuchaufzeichnungen und Lagebeurteilungen aus zwei Weltkriegen*, ed. Georg Meyer (Stuttgart: Deutsche Verlags-Anstalt, 1976), 40.

279   **Leeb had been:** Leeb, *Tagebuchaufzeichnungen*, 42–49; Fritsch to Leeb, April 17, 1938, BA-MA N 145/6, *Nachlass Leeb*.

279   **Like many senior officers:** Leeb, *Tagebuchaufzeichnungen*, 50–51.

279   **Shortly after the defeat:** Leeb, *Tagebuchaufzeichnungen*, 52.

279   **Leeb began:** Leeb, *Tagebuchaufzeichnungen*, Appendix 5, 468–69.

279   **In a passage:** Leeb, *Tagebuchaufzeichnungen*, 469–70.

280   **Brauchitsch thought:** Franz Halder, entry for October 14, 1939, *Kriegstagebuch*, Bd. 1, ed. Hans-Adolf Jacobsen (Stuttgart: W. Kohlhammer, 1962), 105.

280   **The full barbarity:** Evans, *Third Reich at War*, 15.

281   **"What conditions":** Groscurth, entry for October 16, 1939, *Tagebücher*, 218.

281   **It says a lot:** I owe this insight to my colleague and friend Christoph Kimmich.

281   **The same stern principles:** Groscurth, entry from November 1938 [undated], *Tagebücher* 157; Groscurth, *Tagebücher*, 49; Groscurth, entry for September 8, 1939, *Tagebücher*, 201; Groscurth, *Tagebücher*, 50.

281   **Groscurth launched:** Deutsch, *Twilight*, 184.

282   **it was to Engel:** Engel, *Heeresadjutant*, entry for November 18, 1939, 67–68.

282   **Blaskowitz was undeterred:** Blaskowitz, Report, February 6, 1940, in Léon Poliakov, ed., *Das Dritte Reich und seine Diener: Dokumente* (Berlin: Arani, 1956), 516–18.

282   **This memo forced:** Deutsch, *Twilight*, 187–88; Helmut Krausnick, "Hitler und die Morde in Polen," *Vierteljahrshefte für Zeitgeschichte* 11 (1963): 196–209.

282   **For the handful:** Deutsch, *Twilight*, 188.

283   **Through October and November:** Groscurth, entry for October 25, 1939, *Tagebücher*, 220; entry for November 2, 1939, 223; entry for October 16, 1939, 218; entry for November 1, 1939, 222–23; introduction, 54–55.

283   **In the first days:** Gisevius, *Bitter End*, 386.

283   **Hitler had ordered:** Gisevius, *Bitter End*, 387.

283   **Replacements had not yet been integrated:** Halder, entry for November 3, 1939, *Kriegstagebücher*, vol. 1, 117–18.

284   **It got worse:** Groscurth, entry for November 5, 1939, *Tagebücher*, 234–35.

284   **"Please do not":** Deutsch, *Twilight*, 34, citing Halder interview June 1958. See also Walter Warlimont, *Inside Hitler's Headquarters, 1939–1945* (New York: Praeger, 1964).

284   **"A discussion with Hitler":** Halder, entry for November 5, 1939, *Kriegstagebücher*, 1:120.

284   **"At Zossen":** Gisevius, *Bitter End*, 387.

284   **Halder ordered:** Groscurth, entry for November 5, 1939, *Tagebücher*, 225.

284   **A few years later:** Hossbach to Halder, February 11, 1948, BA-MA N24/233, *Nachlass Hossbach*.

284   **Kurt von Tippelskirch:** Groscurth, entry for November 6, 1939, *Tagebücher*, 225; entry for November 16, 1939, *Tagebücher*, 232.

285   **On November 23:** Domarus, *Hitler*, 3:1894.

285   **Leeb tried:** Leeb, *Tagebuchaufzeichnungen*, 53.

285   **Leeb took one more step:** Groscurth, *Tagebücher*, 238; Leeb, *Tagebuchaufzeichnungen*, Appendix 7, 473.

285   **The Gestapo started:** Leeb, *Tagebuchaufzeichnungen*, 54.

285   **The first plans:** Fedor von Bock, *Generalfeldmarschall Fedor von Bock: Zwischen Pflicht und Verweigerung: Das Kriegstagebuch* (Munich: Herbig, 1995), 65.

286   **They were probably right:** May, *Strange Victory*, 233–35.

286   **The attack in the west:** May, *Strange Victory*, 224–26.

286   **More dramatically:** Erich von Manstein, *Verlorene Siege* (Bonn: Athenäum, 1955), 116.

286   **When Halder and Brauchitsh:** Bock, entry for October 25, 1939, *Tagebuch*, 69; Halder, entry for October 25, 1939, *Kriegstagebücher*, Bd. 1, 113; Hans-Adolf Jacobsen, *Fall Gelb: Der Kampf um den deutschen Operationsplan zur Westoffensive 1940* (Wiesbaden: F. Steiner, 1957), 40, 51, 102, 147.

286   **After the generals had left:** Keitel, *Memoirs*, 102–3.

287   **General Erich von Manstein:** Manstein, *Verlorene Siege*, 76–77; Mungo Melvin, *Manstein: Hitler's Greatest General* (New York: St. Martin's Press, 2010), 124; Engel, entry for February 19, 1940, *Heeresadjutant*, 75.

287   **Manstein and Heinz Guderian:** Guderian, *Panzer Leader*, 67–68; Manstein, *Verlorene Siege*.

287   **the High Command punished:** Manstein, *Verlorene Siege*, 118.

288   **And they objected:** Melvin, *Manstein*, 132.

288   **In the fall of 1939:** Melvin, *Manstein*, 132.

288   **His army adjutant:** Engel, *Heeresadjutant*, December 10, 1939, 68–69. Ernest May writes that as Manstein and Rundstedt continued to press for a massive tank attack through the Ardennes, Hitler began to suspect that this was just another way of delaying the offensive. May cites Jacobson, *Dokumente zur Vorgeschichte*, doc. 4, and Engel, *Heeresadjutant*, 69. But May mistranslated Engel, who in fact made the *opposite* point. Engel wrote that Hitler "[s]ieht keine Bedenken, Panzer durch die Berge zu führen," or Hitler "has no doubts about sending tanks through the mountains." May renders this as Hitler "saw no reason for sending tanks through mountains." May, *Strange Victory*, 236.

289   **On February 4:** Engel, *Heeresadjutant*, entries for February 4 and 5, 1940, 73–74.

289   **Manstein was duly summoned:** Melvin, *Manstein*, 126; Manstein, *Verlorene Siege*, 119–20; Engel, *Heeresadjutant*, entry for February 19, 1940, 75.

289   **They followed:** Manstein, *Verlorene Siege*, 119–20.

14. "LET US GO FORWARD TOGETHER"

290   **First Lord of the Admiralty:** Andrew Roberts, *Churchill: Walking with Destiny* (New York: Viking, 2018), 262–63.

290   **He believes:** Roberts, *Churchill*, 263–64.

291   **No one thinks:** Roberts, *Churchill*, 263–66.

291   **It all goes badly:** Roberts, *Churchill*, 282.

292   **"die of grief":** Jenkins, *Churchill*, 276.

292   **The ever-loyal Clementine:** Jenkins, *Churchill*, 275.

292   **When the Germans:** Max Hastings, *Inferno: The World at War, 1939–1945* (New York: Alfred A. Knopf, 2011), 43.

292   **Through the autumn:** Gerhard L. Weinberg, *A World at Arms: A Global History of World War II*, 2nd ed. (New York: Cambridge University Press, 2005), 72–73, 113–14; Martin Gilbert, *Winston S. Churchill*, vol. 6, *Finest Hour* (Boston: Houghton Mifflin, 1983), 174–82.

293   **The day before:** Roberts, *Churchill*, 655; Gilbert, *Finest Hour*, 223–26.

293   **The British should:** Roberts, *Churchill*, 656.

294   **The perceptive Clementine:** Gilbert, *Finest Hour*, 286–87.

294   **But Labour always refused:** Jonathan Schneer, *Ministers at War: Winston Churchill and His War Cabinet* (New York: Basic Books, 2014), 8.

294   **By the beginning of May:** Channon, *Chips*, entries for April 30 and May 1, 1940, 243–44.

294   **When Harold Macmillan:** Harold Macmillan, *The Blast of War, 1939–1945* (London: Macmillan, 1967), 74.

294   **The members of the House:** Harold Nicolson, *Diaries 1939–1945: The War Years*, ed. Nigel Nicolson (New York: Atheneum, 1967), entry for May 4, 1940, 75.

295   **"The House is crowded":** Nicolson, *Diaries 1939–1945*, entry for May 7, 1940, 76–77; *Hansard*, May 7, 1940, cc. 1129.

296   **the stakes of . . . the war:** *Hansard*, May 7, 1940, cc. 1140, 1146.

296   **"too strong meat":** Amery, *Diaries*, May 7, 1940, 592.

296   **"We are fighting":** *Hansard*, May 7, 1940, cc. 1150.

296   **"I may or may not have made":** Amery, *Diaries*, May 7, 1940, 592–93.

297   **"Our chief anxiety":** Macmillan, *Blast of War*, 72.

297   **"It is not a question":** *Hansard*, May 8, 1940, cc. 1283; Nicholas Shakespeare, *Six Minutes in May: How Churchill Unexpectedly Became Prime Minister* (London: Harvill Secker, 2017), 251.

297   **"must not allow himself":** *Hansard*, May 8, 1940, cc. 1283.

297   **"One saw at once":** Channon, *Chips*, entry for May 8, 1940, 246.

298   **"He thought he had some friends":** *Hansard*, May 8, 1940, cc. 1362.

298   **"the weakness of the Margesson system":** Nicolson, *Diaries 1939–1945*, May 7, 1940, 76–77.

298   **when the vote came:** Gilbert, *Finest Hour*, 299. There are surprisingly many ways to count the vote totals. See Jorgen.S. Rasmussen, "Party Discipline in War-Time: The Downfall of the Chamberlain Government," *Journal of Politics*

32, no. 2 (May 1970): 379–406. Rasmussen gives the total number of government supporters opposing Chamberlain as 42, while 88 more "did not vote," which presumably includes both those abstaining and those who were absent.

299   **In a private meeting:** Cadogan, *Diary*, May 9, 1940, 280; Churchill, *Gathering Storm*, 662–63. Churchill mistakenly dated the meeting to May 10.

299   **"Usually I talk a great deal":** Churchill, *Gathering Storm*, 663.

299   **according to new information:** Shakespeare, *Six Minutes in May*, 363; Cadogan, *Diary*, May 9, 1940, 280.

299   **"By the time [Halifax]":** Churchill, *Gathering Storm*, 663.

300   **"The sun is shining":** Erich Kuby, *Mein Krieg: Aufzeichnungen aus 2129 Tagen* (Munich: Nymphenburger Verlagshandlung, 1975), 34–35.

300   **A little before dawn:** Hastings, *Inferno*, 51.

300   **No one woke up:** Hastings, *Inferno*, 52–53.

301   **These dramatic events:** Churchill, *Gathering Storm*, 662.

301   **At a war cabinet meeting:** Gilbert, *Finest Hour*, 310–12.

301   **When Chamberlain went to see King George VI:** Gilbert, *Finest Hour*, 313.

301   **In his memoirs:** Churchill, *Gathering Storm*, 665.

301   **Churchill promised:** Churchill, *Gathering Storm*, 665.

302   **"nothing to offer":** Speech of May 13, 1940, National Churchill Museum, https://www.nationalchurchillmuseum.org/blood-toil-tears-and-sweat.html.

302   **Something else had arrived:** Maurice Cowling, *The Impact of Hitler: British Politics and British Policy 1933–1940* (Cambridge, UK: Cambridge University Press, 1975), 1–12; Paul Addison, *The Road to 1945: British Politics and the Second World War* (London: Pimlico, 1994), 9. The scale of the change was hidden for a time by personal continuities, such as Chamberlain and Halifax remaining in Churchill's government. In the early days, Churchill's government was often criticized for being just another edition of the old gang. See Olson, *Troublesome Young Men*, chap. 19, "A Question of Loyalty." But the most important of these continuities proved to be of short duration.

303   **As the historian Jonathan Schneer writes:** Schneer, *Ministers at War*, 23.

303   **"As I went to bed":** Churchill, *Gathering Storm*, 667.

304   **"We have been defeated":** Winston Churchill, *Their Finest Hour* (Boston: Houghton Mifflin, 1949), 42.

304   **Case Red:** Forczyk, *Case Red*.

304   **In just a few weeks:** Tony Judt, "The Catastrophe: The Fall of France," in *Reappraisals: Reflections on the Forgotten Twentieth Century* (New York: Penguin Books, 2008), 183; May, *Strange Victory*, 7.

305   **For Churchill:** Max Hastings, *Winston's War: Churchill 1940–1945* (New York: Alfred A. Knopf, 2010), 25.

305   **As early as May 15:** Churchill to Roosevelt, May 15, 1940, Loewenheim et al., *Secret Wartime Correspondence*, 94.

306   **A few days later:** Churchill to Roosevelt, May 20, 1940, Loewenheim et al., *Secret Wartime Correspondence*, 97.

306   **On June 10:** FDR Master Speech File no. 1295.

306   **The historian Paul Kennedy:** Paul Kennedy, *Engineers of Victory: The Problem Solvers Who Turned the Tide in the Second World War* (London: Allen
Lane, 2013), 157.

307   **It seemed:** "Augenzeugenbericht lt. d Reserve Rosenhagen über den Tod
des GenObersten Frhr. von Fritsch," BA-MA N 33/23, *Nachlass Fritsch*.

307   **Fritsch had visited:** Reynolds, *Treason Was No Crime*, 185–86.

307   **"All my world" and "There is no pleasure":** Chamberlain to Hilda, May 17,
1940, Chamberlain, *Diary Letters*, 531; Chamberlain to Hilda, June 15,
1941, Chamberlain, *Diary Letters*, 541.

307   **"considerable trouble":** Chamberlain to Ida, July 21, 1940, Chamberlain,
Diary Letters, 553.

307   **The doctors informed him:** Self, *Chamberlain*, 442–43.

308   **Still unaware:** Self, *Chamberlain*, 443–47; Feiling, *Chamberlain*, 453.

308   **In mid-October:** Kennedy, diary entry for October 19, 1940, in Amanda
Smith, ed., *Hostage to Fortune: The Letters of Joseph P. Kennedy* (New York:
Viking, 2001), 476–77.

308   **Churchill's eulogy:** *Hansard*, November 12, 1940, cc. 1617–18.

308   **We see it this way because:** David Edgerton, *Britain's War Machine: Weapons, Resources, and Experts in the Second World War* (New York: Oxford
University Press, 2011), 46.

309   **He explained his actions:** Kennedy, diary entry for October 19, 1940, in
Hostage to Fortune, 476–77.

309   **"That consciousness of moral right":** Chamberlain to Ida, September 10,
1939, Chamberlain, *Diary Letters*, 445.

310   **It was well into 1943:** This is the general argument of Kennedy, *Engineers of
Victory*.

311   **"all Europe may be free":** Churchill, speech of June 18, 1940, https://www
.nationalchurchillmuseum.org/their-finest-hour.html.

311   **"fight by armaments alone":** FDR Master Speech File no. 1335a.

EPILOGUE: "THE END OF THE BEGINNING"

312   **The hard-bitten German immigrant:** Karl May, *Winnetou: Der Rote Gentleman* (Freiburg: Verlag von Friedrich Ernst Fehlenfeld, 1893), 9, 1–2.

312   **But in his years in America:** May, *Winnetou*, 3.

313   **one of the best-selling:** W. Raymond Wood, "The Role of the Romantic West in Shaping the Third Reich," *Plains Anthropologist* 35, no. 132
(November 1990): 313–19.

313   **When the news:** Timothy W. Ryback, *Hitler's Private Library: The Books
That Shaped His Life* (New York: Alfred A. Knopf, 2008), 13, 179–80.

313   **he can echo:** Brendan Simms, *Hitler: A Global Biography* (New York: Basic
Books, 2019), 91.

313   **Hitler doesn't see just:** Simms, *Hitler*, 258, 336; Mary Nolan, *Visions of
Modernity: American Business and the Modernization of Germany* (New
York: Oxford University Press, 1994), 34, 232–33.

314   **he ordered a reduction:** Halder, entry for June 15, 1940, *Kriegstagebuch*, Bd. 1, 357; Müller, *Der Feind steht im Osten*, 191.

314   **gave a narrative:** Domarus, *Hitler*, 3:2042–63.

315   **"The fact which dominates our world":** FDR, Radio Message Accepting Third Term Nomination, July 19, 1940, Master Speech File no. 1291.

316   **"fanatical hatred":** Ambassador Dieckhoff, Memorandum, July 21, 1940, DGFP, series D, vol. 10, 259–60.

316   **"English ideological":** Dieckhoff, Memorandum, July 29, 1940, DGFP, series D, vol. 10, doc. 252, 350–62.

316   **"hoping and praying":** Ciano, *Diary*, July 19, 1940, 371.

316   **Halifax referred:** Lord Halifax, "Great Britain shall go forward," July 22, 1940, http://www.ibiblio.org/pha/policy/1940/1940-07-22a.html.

316   **"take up the Russian problem":** Halder, entry for July 22, 1940, *Generaloberst Halder: Kriegstagebuch*, Bd. 2, ed. Hans-Adolf Jacobsen (Stuttgart: W. Kohlhammer, 1963), 32–33.

317   **Halder had briefed Hitler:** Halder, entry for July 13, 1940, *Kriegstagebuch*, Bd. 2, 21.

317   **A week later:** Halder, entry for July 22, 1940, *Kriegstagebuch*, Bd. 2, 30–32; Horst Boog et al., eds., *Das Deutsche Reich und der Zweite Weltkrieg*, Bd. 4, *Der Angriff auf die Sowjetunion* (Stuttgart: Deutsche Verlags-Anstalt, 1983), 150–51, 159; Gerhard L. Weinberg, *World in the Balance: Behind the Scenes of World War II* (Hanover, NH: University Press of New England, 1981), 84.

317   **On July 31:** Halder, entry for July 31, 1940, *Kriegstagebuch*, Bd. 2, 40.

317   **The invasion:** Among many excellent books on the criminality of Barbarossa, see Götz Aly and Susanne Heim, *Architects of Annihilation: Auschwitz and the Logic of Destruction* (Princeton, NJ: Princeton University Press, 2002); Snyder, *Bloodlands*; Dieter Pohl, *Die Herrschaft der Wehrmacht: Deutsche Militärbesatzung und einheimische Bevölkerung in der Sowjetunion, 1941–1944* (Munich: Oldenbourg, 2008); Christian Gerlach, *Kalkulierte Mord: Die deutsche Wirtschafts- und Vernichtungspolitik in Weissrussland 1941 bis 1944* (Hamburg: Hamburger Edition, 1999).

318   **As with so much:** Lloyd C. Gardner, "The Atlantic Charter: Idea and Reality, 1942–1945," in Douglas Brinkley and David R. Facey-Crowther, eds., *The Atlantic Charter* (New York: St. Martin's Press, 1994), 45–82, 51.

318   **it would be tactically wise:** Theodore A. Wilson, "The First Summit: FDR and the Riddle of Personal Diplomacy," in Brinkley and Facey-Crowther, eds., *Atlantic Charter*, 1–32, 13.

318   **And yet the Charter:** Gardner, "The Atlantic Charter," 46–48; Wilson, "The First Summit," 17.

318   **The main product:** Text of the Atlantic Charter at https://avalon.law.yale.edu/wwii/atlantic.asp.

319   **Early in 1942:** Mark Mazower, *Governing the World: The History of an Idea* (New York: Penguin Press, 2012), 194–98.

319   **He accepted the Charter:** Mazower, *Governing the World*, 194–98.

319   **The Atlantic Charter was like this:** David Reynolds, "The Atlantic 'Flop': British Foreign Policy and the Churchill-Roosevelt Meeting of August 1941," in Brinkley and Facey-Crowther, eds., *Atlantic Charter*, 129–50, 130.

319   **Nelson Mandela wrote:** Dan Plesch, *America, Hitler and the UN: How the Allies Won World War II and Forged a Peace* (London: I. B. Tauris, 2011), 24–27.

320   **"We shall no doubt pay dearly":** Amery, entry for August 14, 1941, *Diaries*, 710.

320   **Stalin replied angrily:** Gardner, "The Atlantic Charter," 54.

320   **"flew into a passion of rage":** Nicolaus von Below, *At Hitler's Side: The Memoirs of Hitler's Luftwaffe Adjutant* (London: Greenhill Books, 2001), 110.

320   **"dangerous dynamite":** *TBJG*, Teil 2, Bd. 1, August 19, 1941, 269.

320   **In mid-August:** Tobias Jersak, "Die Interaktion von Kriegsverlauf und Judenvernichtung: Ein Blick auf Hitlers Strategie im Spätsommer 1941," *Historische Zeitschrift* 268 (1999): 311–74, 333–37.

321   **in the wake of the Atlantic Charter:** There is a rich and controversial literature on the timing of the decision for genocide and the factors leading up to it. See Christopher Browning, "The Nazi Decision to Commit Mass Murder: Three Interpretations: The Euphoria of Victory and the Final Solution: Summer–Fall 1941," *German Studies Review* 17, no. 3 (October 1994): 473–81; Saul Friedländer, *Nazi Germany and the Jews*, vol. 2, *The Years of Extermination, 1939–1945* (New York: HarperCollins, 2007), especially 263–65; Longerich, *Holocaust*, especially 267–71.

321   **"every trace of Hitler's footsteps":** Churchill, "Our Solid, Stubborn Strength," Speech to the Dominion High Commissioners and Allied Countries' Ministers Conference, June 12, 1941, in Rhodes James, *Complete Speeches*, vol. 6, 6424.

322   **"the end of the beginning":** Churchill, "A New Experience—Victory," Speech at the Mansion House, November 10, 1942, in Rhodes James, *Complete Speeches*, vol. 6, 6693.

ACKNOWLEDGMENTS

This book has been an adventure into areas in some ways very different from those of my previous books. It is a pleasure to thank the people who have made this adventure both easier and more enjoyable than it might have been.

At Germany's Federal Military Archives (*Bundesarchiv Militärabteilung* Freiburg), I am grateful for the assistance of Christiane Botzet and Ralf Schneider, who among other things allowed me to examine a huge swath of uncatalogued material from the papers of Friedrich Hossbach. This book has benefited greatly from that opportunity. I must also thank the owners of the papers of Werner von Blomberg, who kindly gave me permission to read the unpublished memoir in volumes 1–6 of Blomberg's *Nachlass*. At the Koblenz branch of Germany's Federal Archives, Alexandra Kosubek helped me navigate the copious papers left by Fritz Tobias.

For advice on literature and sources, I must thank Professor John Robert Ferris, who was particularly generous in telling me about the Foreign Office documents recording MI5's concerns about Neville Chamberlain. I thank KC Johnson, Susan Pedersen, and Danny Orbach as well. Idan Liav provided very able research assistance. I owe a particular debt to my former graduate student, Dr. Ky Woltering, who helped me with research on the American material and to whom I owe the concept of the Christian-totalitarian dichotomy.

Although this book rests on a good deal of archival and published primary sources, a project of this nature must also necessarily draw on a wide range of published scholarship. Many brilliant historians have dedicated themselves to the issues discussed here. It has been a pleasure to read and learn from their work, the influence of which is readily apparent from the end notes.

As always, I owe huge thanks to my agent, Scott Mendel, for his unfailing encouragement, enthusiasm and support. The professionalism and good humor of everyone at Henry Holt makes it a delightful publishing house for a writer to work with. My editor, Paul Golob, has continued to amaze me with his erudition and the skill with which he can nurse a rambling manuscript into something much better. Production editor Hannah Campbell has been a model of efficiency while Jenna Dolan's painstaking copyediting and fact-checking has made this a much more accurate book in all respects. Natalia Ruiz has helped with a myriad of matters large and small. Finally, I am grateful to be able to work with Marian Brown on publicity. Many thanks to all.

Several friends and colleagues read various drafts of the manuscript, providing essential feedback and saving me from many errors: Sam Casper, KC Johnson, Christoph Kimmich, Philip Klinkner, Eric Lane, Elidor Mehili, and Steve Remy. These friends could not talk me out of all my wayward interpretations, and for those, as well as all remaining errors, I am solely responsible.

Some years ago, over a beer in Berlin, Steve Remy and I swapped rueful stories about the things that spouses or partners of historians like us must endure—distraction, extended research trips, the renunciation of normal life as deadlines approach. "And after all that," said Steve, "they get books about Nazis dedicated to them." This book actually owes its inspiration to a comment my wife, Corinna, made after reading my last one, *The Death of Democracy*: she said she wanted to read about what happened next. Through the writing of this book, and some personal ups and downs that went along with it, Corinna has been a constant source of love and support. Here is your book about Nazis, Corinna! Despite the subject matter, all my love goes with the dedication.

INDEX

ABOUT THE AUTHOR

BENJAMIN CARTER HETT is the author of *The Death of Democracy, Burning the Reichstag, Crossing Hitler,* and *Death in the Tiergarten.* He is a professor of history at Hunter College and the Graduate Center of the City University of New York and holds a PhD in history from Harvard University and a law degree from the University of Toronto. Born in Rochester, New York, he grew up in Edmonton, Alberta, and now lives in New York City.